Music and Theatre

Essays in honour of Winton Dean

Music and Theatre

Essays in honour of Winton Dean

Edited by
NIGEL FORTUNE

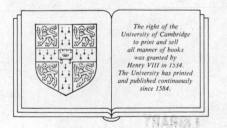

The right of the
University of Cambridge
to print and sell
all manner of books
was granted by
Henry VIII in 1534.
The University has printed
and published continuously
since 1584.

CAMBRIDGE UNIVERSITY PRESS

Cambridge
London   New York   New Rochelle
Melbourne   Sydney

Published by the Press Syndicate of the University of Cambridge
The Pitt Building, Trumpington Street, Cambridge CB2 1RP
32 East 57th Street, New York, NY 10022, USA
10 Stamford Road, Oakleigh, Melbourne 3166, Australia

First published 1987

Printed in Great Britain at the
University Press, Cambridge

British Library cataloguing in publication data

Music and theatre: essays in honour of
Winton Dean.
1. Opera
I. Fortune, Nigel II. Dean, Winton
782.1   ML1700

Library of Congress cataloguing in publication data

Music and theatre.
Bibliography.
1. Opera. 2. Dean, Winton. I. Dean, Winton.
II. Fortune, Nigel.
ML55.D36   1987   782.1   86-11781

ISBN 0 521 32348-7

SE

Contents

v

Illustrations

Preface

Winton Dean celebrated his seventieth birthday on 18 March 1986. Three years ago – a little late, perhaps, for us to hope to achieve publication by the actual birthday   an editorial committee was set up to plan and guide a volume of essays to salute the occasion. It consisted of Anthony Hicks, Curtis A. Price, John Warrack and myself, together with Rosemary Dooley of Cambridge University Press (succeeded, when she left the firm, by Penny Souster). I was invited to be editor; I gratefully acknowledge the advice and support of my colleagues, as well as assistance from John H. Roberts.

Winton's devotion to opera and other dramatic music ensured that the broad theme of the book virtually chose itself. From the start we aimed at a relatively small number of substantial essays rather than a larger number of short ones, even though this meant that we had, with regret, to disappoint several scholars who would doubtless have graced the volume no less than those whose contributions appear in it. We felt it appropriate that about half the essays should concern Handel, or matters from his lifetime, the remainder being devoted to the work of later opera composers, including those, such as Janáček and Britten, with whom, as with Handel, Winton has shown particular sympathy. We decided to round out the book with two further contributions: Stephen Dean agreed to compile a list of his father's writings; and for an appreciation of Winton as man and scholar we turned to Philip Radcliffe, who knew Winton longer than any other scholar – in fact from the time he greeted the eighteen-year-old Cambridge freshman until his deeply regretted death in a car accident while this book was in proof.

The members of the editorial committee join with the other contributors in paying tribute to Winton for his outstanding scholarly achievements and in sending him our warmest good wishes for happy and productive years to come.

Except in a few cases explained as they occur, bibliographical sources are spelt out throughout the book; the one general exception is *The New Grove*

Dictionary of Music and Musicians, ed. S. Sadie (London, 1980), which is referred to simply as *The New Grove*. Musical pitches are referred to by the Helmholtz system, in which c′ is middle C.

NIGEL FORTUNE

Birmingham

Winton Dean

PHILIP RADCLIFFE

Winton Dean went from Harrow to King's College, Cambridge, in 1934, as a classical scholar. His father, Basil Dean, was an eminent theatrical producer, and his mother, Esther van Gruisen, came from a distinguished family, being the niece of Rufus Isaacs, the first Marquis of Reading. Winton read Classics and English and achieved good results, but his interests moved increasingly towards music and drama. He appeared twice on the stage, in 1936 as Demeter in Aristophanes' *The Frogs* and a year later in Handel's *Saul*, in which he was cast as Jesse, with a white beard and followed by a long procession of descendants. He also showed skill in the difficult art of translating words from a foreign language to fit music. This he did for the choruses in Walter Leigh's music for *The Frogs* and again for Weber's *Abu Hassan*; the latter was very effective on the stage, especially the words 'Cash, cash, cash' sung by the chorus of creditors. At about this time he met Thalia Shaw; they were married in 1939, and she has been the most devoted of wives.

Winton's intelligence and vitality, which have remained undiminished, were widely noticed and appreciated, but it seemed uncertain in what direction they would lead him. A dissertation on Walter Savage Landor did not bring him the Fellowship at King's for which he had hoped, and during the next few years he was torn between the writing of fiction, drama and poetry (not always serious). During the 1939–45 war he worked for Naval Intelligence. Shortly afterwards he embarked on an intensive study of the music of Bizet, to which he has always been devoted. This resulted in the volume on the composer in the Master Musicians series (1948), and its notable success showed that Winton had found his true métier. He had not studied music academically at Cambridge, but he was a keen attender of concerts and operas, with a remarkable memory and strongly developed critical instincts. His sympathies inclined more to the Latin than to the Teutonic, and he was ideally equipped to write about a composer whose music, because it is immediately attractive, has sometimes been patronized by the over-solemn.

The book contains much valuable material on Bizet's lesser-known works, especially the important *La Coupe du roi de Thulé*, but also succeeds in the harder task of making original and perceptive comments on works as familiar as *Carmen* and the *L'Arlésienne* music. The depiction and development of character in opera have always been of vital interest to Winton, and here he is particularly happy in his observations on Don José. The various elements in Bizet's style and their gradual integration are traced with clarity and sympathy, and the complicated and frequently contentious background of French opera is vividly portrayed. In 1965 a revised edition appeared, incorporating much new material resulting from the researches of Mina Curtiss. Winton also wrote the articles on Bizet in the fifth edition of *Grove's Dictionary* and in *The New Grove*, as well as a short study of Carmen published by the Folio Society in which the opera is considered side by side with Mérimée's novel. His writings have led to a far more balanced estimate of Bizet and an enhanced understanding of his achievements.

Although in later years Winton has been increasingly concerned with Handel, he has continued to write on other composers. In 1971 he contributed to *The Beethoven Companion* (ed. D. Arnold and N. Fortune) the admirable chapter 'Beethoven and Opera', comparing the versions of *Fidelio* and demonstrating how that of 1814 shows at the same time an increased musical maturity and a lessening of dramatic power. In 1974 he read to the Royal Musical Association an interesting paper on Donizetti, stressing his influence on Verdi. More comprehensive is the chapter 'Shakespeare and Opera' in *Shakespeare and Music* (ed. P. Hartnoll, 1964). This essay, which is both erudite and entertaining, examines innumerable operas, from the masterly to the preposterous; the descriptions of the plots of some of the more bizarre and obscure ones are often hilarious, while the discussions of *Otello* and *Falstaff* are so perceptive and sympathetic that one wishes that one day Winton might write a book on Verdi. Equally valuable are his chapters on French, Italian and German opera in vol. 8 of the New Oxford History of Music (*The Age of Beethoven 1790–1830*, ed. G. Abraham, 1982). His inherited love of the theatre, allied to sensitive musicianship – and no doubt reinforced since his Cambridge days by the strong influence of Edward Dent, whose passion for opera was equalled only by his dislike and suspicion of all things ecclesiastical – has ensured that Winton is particularly at home writing about dramatic music.

Somewhat apart from Winton's other writings is the long article on criticism that he originally produced for *Grove 5* and which has reappeared in revised form in *The New Grove*. An exhaustive history of criticism through the ages is followed by a section on the nature of criticism. Winton has long been an admirable reviewer of books and performances, and he is fully aware of the problems involved. The article ends with an impressive summing-up of the necessary qualifications for a critic. In many ways this is one of the most remarkable of Winton's writings. Towards the end of it he observes: 'With very few exceptions active composers and performers make bad critics'; the fact that he himself is neither a composer nor a performer has probably been an asset. Though he has decided musical tastes, these are barely perceptible in the article, which contains this memorable sentence: 'One of the critic's roles is that of watchdog, and he must bark as appropriate.'

In his own criticism Winton has followed his precepts admirably. The critic must approach opera with care: it is only too easy to stress some of its many elements at the expense of others, but Winton has always maintained a fine balance between them. An article in the *Musical Times* (cxix (1978), pp. 854–8), 'Opera and the Literary Approach', is an excellent demonstration of his approach; it is a detailed review of three books on opera, obviously of unequal value, which are assessed with masterly clarity and scrupulous fairness. This same balance of judgement can be found throughout Winton's many critical writings, both substantial and occasional; for instance, he recognizes Donizetti's influence on Verdi without exalting the older composer at the expense of the younger, and he has always shown a healthy independence in his attitude towards fashions. The fascination with characterization so apparent in his book on Bizet indeed pervades all his work.

Probably the most celebrated element in Winton's output is his work on Handel, the product of an enthusiasm dating back to his years at Cambridge. The estimation of Handel's music in England has fluctuated widely. A hundred years ago it was he who drew the large audiences (though for rather a narrow range of works), while Bach was the scholars' composer. But now the position, if not completely reversed, is very different. The popularity of Bach has steadily increased during the present century, and the fact that Handel's music is now the object of detailed study by distinguished scholars has resulted in a broader and deeper knowledge of his enormous output and has shown that his range is far wider than was realized by those who knew him simply from hearing inflated performances of *Messiah*. Cambridge played an important part in the new attitude to Handel. In 1925 *Semele* was very successfully performed there on the stage, and it was gradually realized that many of the more dramatic oratorios are more effective in a theatre than when performed in evening dress in a church or concert-hall. Some of the directions in the early editions of the librettos, such as 'exit David through the window' in *Saul*, suggest that Handel himself would have enjoyed seeing the works performed in this way. Mention has already been made of Winton's appearance in *Saul*; it is appropriate that one of Handel's greatest works should have been the starting-point of his career as a Handel scholar. The rediscovery of Bach in England undoubtedly affected the attitude of many scholars towards Handel, and this applied especially to the oratorios. Ernest Walker, for example, is frequently castigated by Winton for his rather ambivalent view of them. But it is only fair to add that Walker wrote enthusiastically about certain things in them and also about secular works such as *Semele* and *Acis and Galatea*; he was certainly not wholly anti-Handel but felt most sympathy for the works that could not challenge comparison with Bach. When two composers of equal stature are born in the same year it is hard to take a completely balanced view of them, and it is typical of Winton's fair-mindedness that, although he surely finds Handel the more congenial, he never makes the mistake of belittling Bach.

Handel's Dramatic Oratorios and Masques (1959) is planned on a spacious, almost Wagnerian scale. After a first part containing chapters on the nature and background of the oratorio, the far longer second part consists mainly of admirable detailed analyses of all the individual works; much work also went into the twelve appendices. The book was quickly acclaimed as a first-rate piece of scholarship, and, if anything, it has grown in stature with the passing years. It shows deep knowledge not only of Handel's music but also of that of his contemporaries; it is very well informed about the complicated interactions between the various genres of music at the time; and, with all its learning, it is always thoroughly readable. Winton never fails to discriminate between the greatest and the less great moments. An enthusiast for music in the theatre, he is alive to potential absurdities, as a remark such as the following shows: 'Alexander, even slower off the mark than most operatic heroes, sings three recitatives and two airs and rushes to war.'

The idea of Handel as first and foremost a musical dramatist may have seemed shocking to many traditional Handelians, but Winton presented it with great conviction in what is so far his largest single work. But it was not, of course, to be his last word on Handel. In 1965 he went for a year to Berkeley as Ernest Bloch Professor and delivered a course of lectures on Handel's operas as well as undertaking other teaching. John H. Roberts has kindly provided this impression of the impact that Winton made:

For those of us lucky enough to participate in one of Winton's seminars it was an unforgettable year. He charmed us all, of course, and awed us with his prodigious knowledge of Handel and opera. But what above all made the experience so extraordinary for a group of American graduate students was his refusal to separate the scholarly and the social. Our class meetings, though rich in intellectual content, were a little like parties, with each of us vying to provide the most sumptuous refreshments, and our frequent extramural gatherings, usually to hear some choice tape, were hardly less educational. The high point of the year was perhaps the party for Winton's birthday – his fiftieth – when he was presented with a large basket of avocados and serenaded with a Mozart canon retexted by Sally Fuller as 'Felicitas tibi Wintonius et jocunda nativitas'.

The lectures were eventually published in book form as *Handel and the Opera Seria* (1969). In the preface Winton explains how, having said comparatively little about the operas in his book on the oratorios, he has become increasingly aware of their merits. He divides the operas into various categories and examines them in some detail with his characteristic blend of erudition and humour. With John Merrill Knapp he embarked in the 1960s on a more monumental study of the operas rivalling his book on the oratorios, and, as I write, the first volume, covering the operas up to 1726, is in proof.

Looking back for a moment at Winton's work as a whole, it impresses not only by its erudition but also by the elegance and clarity with which it is presented. However abstruse the matter, the style is never pontifical or dry: his study of English and the Classics, and his natural feeling for the language, have ensured the total absence from his writings of the peculiar language that Eric Blom once called 'musicologese'.

When Winton arrived in Cambridge it was soon realized that he was someone in whose company nobody could feel dull, and his resilience has always been a strength to him. His life has had its sadnesses; his undergraduate years were clouded by family troubles, and in 1945 his two-year-old daughter died tragically. Against this must be set the unfailing sympathy and devotion of Thalia as wife, typist and chauffeuse and in many other capacities, and also his very happy relationships with his son Stephen and his adopted daughter Diana and her family. Three times a year the Deans go to Fairnilee in the Scottish borders, where Winton is liable to undergo a surprising transformation from musical scholar to sporting country squire. Since 1957 they have lived near Witley, Surrey, in Hambledon Hurst, a house that formerly belonged to Winton's grandparents and has always had happy associations for him; no one who has been there will forget its warm, friendly and stimulating atmosphere and the lively conversation ranging not only over music and the theatre but quite possibly over such matters as current politics or cricket (another of Winton's enthusiasms). For one who has known Winton for over half a century it is a real pleasure to send him affectionate greetings on his seventieth birthday.

Political allegory in late-seventeenth-century English opera

CURTIS A. PRICE

Many French and Italian Baroque operas were occasional. In the early days, premières were planned to coincide with celebrations of political events – coronations, royal weddings, battlefield victories, the ratifying of peace treaties, and so forth; later, when opera became a regular feature of the theatrical season, librettos often made direct or oblique references to such events.[1] In France during the reign of Louis XIV this practice was carried to extremes, as each of Lully's *tragédies en musique* included a topical prologue to flatter the king and to glorify the state. Some of these operas seem to comment metaphorically on court intrigues. Whether such interpretations were intended by the librettist or were simply construed by cynics and courtiers with guilty consciences is debatable, but Philippe Quinault, Lully's main librettist, was in fact banned from court for two years after the production of *Isis* in 1677, because Juno had been seen as a caricature of Mme de Montespan, while the title role was taken to represent the king's new mistress, Mme de Ludres.[2]

Late-seventeenth-century English opera was also occasional. Like Stuart masques, some were produced to commemorate specific events or to honour the monarch or an important aristocrat. The prime example is John Dryden's *Albion and Albanius* of 1685, which is an allegory of the Restoration and reign of Charles II. But not all English operas were so royalist, and in this essay I argue that, beginning with the Commonwealth, some operatic works adopted an anti-establishment stance which later in the century developed into veiled satires on the monarch, especially during the reign of William and Mary. Such hidden designs, which have been hitherto unnoticed or flatly denied by scholars, were not the sort of good-humoured references to the king's peccadilloes that got Quinault into trouble, but cleverly encoded comments on heady and potentially

[1]   See L. Bianconi and T. Walker, 'Production, Consumption and Political Function of Seventeenth-Century Italian Opera', *Early Music History*, iv (1985), pp. 209–96.
[2]   See R. M. Isherwood, *Music in the Service of the King: France in the Seventeenth Century* (Ithaca, 1973), pp. 219–21.

1

dangerous issues such as Elective Kingship and Loyalty to the Pretender. English dramatists had long used the stage to air their political views, and, if openly treasonable, their plays were censored, actors banned, or the offending theatre ordered to close. But for operas to have defiled the very institution that had in other countries inspired and nurtured them is striking testimony to the audacity of certain English librettists and to their underlying distrust of an exotic (that is, foreign) form of entertainment.

Albion and Albanius is a transparent political allegory. It is also the first full-length, all-sung English opera for which the complete music survives, and though the first production was cut short when the theatres closed at the outbreak of Monmouth's Rebellion in June 1685, there is no evidence that the work was regarded as an artistic failure. Louis Grabu's full score was published two years later and the libretto reprinted in 1691. The music, which has generally been derided by modern scholars, is beginning to be reappraised and its virtues acknowledged.[3] But the real significance of *Albion and Albanius* is political. It was composed at the express wish of the king to help commemorate his delivery from the Rye House assassination plot and the resolution of the Exclusion Crisis. Charles wanted to bring over the Paris Opéra to mark the occasion but had to settle instead for this home-grown work, which was nevertheless set by a French-trained composer and is a *tragédie en musique* in all but language. Dryden, the Poet Laureate, who had never before attempted a true opera, produced a polished libretto without resorting to spoken dialogue, which was a characteristic of English music drama at the time.

Albion represents Charles II, Albanius his brother James Duke of York. As the editors of the new Dryden edition have remarked, to give Albanius so prominent a role was itself a political statement – a public affirmation of the Catholic succession.[4] Act 1 ends with the restoration of Albion, assisted by Archon, who is clearly General George Monck, later the Duke of Albemarle. Other correspondences are equally plain: Acacia (or Innocence) is Catherine of Braganza; Pluto and Zelota are the perpetrators of the Popish Plot. Most of the action of Acts 2 and 3 centres on various attempts to undermine Albion's reign, and the reasons for Albanius's being sent into exile are explored in painful detail. While Dryden may have stopped short of drawing 'warts-and-all' portraits of the royal brothers, the libretto shows an allegorical frankness that would have astonished Quinault. The only major figure in the struggles of Charles's final years who is not represented is the Duke of Monmouth, his illegitimate son and the darling of the Exclusionists. As is explained below, Dryden chose to dramatize

3   See *The Works of John Dryden* (Berkeley and Los Angeles, 1956–), xv, ed. E. Miner, F. B. Zimmerman *et al.*, pp. 323–55; and C. A. Price, *Henry Purcell and the London Stage* (Cambridge, 1984), pp. 265–70.

4   Op. cit., xv, p. 329.

Monmouth's activities elsewhere. The king attended several rehearsals of *Albion and Albanius* in early 1685 but died before the première. Dryden states in the preface to the libretto that this calamity might well have wrecked the opera, 'but the design of it Originally, was so happy, that it needed no alteration . . . for the addition of twenty or thirty lines, in the Apotheosis of Albion, has made it entirely of a Piece'. Would that the allegorical designs of other late-seventeenth-century English operas had been so clearly chalked out.

With the example of *Albion and Albanius* to work from, John Buttrey has interpreted most operas of the period as grand compliments to the monarch, which were supposedly first performed as near to the royal birthday as possible. Yet his attempts to locate the kind of political metaphor that is the essence of Dryden's opera are often unsettling. For instance, he views Purcell's *Dido and Aeneas* (1689), with its several allusions to sharing the throne and (in the prologue) the clear identification of Phoebus and Venus with William and Mary, as an offering to the newly installed monarchs. But in the light of Aeneas's abandonment of Dido and its tragic consequences, Buttrey is forced to conclude that the opera is a cautionary tale: Nahum Tate, the librettist, dramatizes 'the possible fate of the British nation should Dutch William fail in his responsibilities to his English Queen'.[5] In moving beyond the obvious symbolism, Buttrey has encountered what John M. Wallace calls the allegorical conundrum: are political meanings 'in' the work, or have we put them there?[6] Wallace cuts the Gordian knot: 'they are there if we see them, and if we can establish a contemporary background that makes them likely'. Seventeenth-century literati were accustomed to looking for various layers of meaning in poetry; and dramatists in particular were skilled at inventing emblematic characters and symbolic actions. During the turbulent years between the Popish Plot and the Exclusion Crisis (1678–82), when direct reference to the usurpation of a crown or satires on Roman Catholicism were nearly taboo in drama, Dryden and Nathaniel Lee (among others) wrote plays that seem to refer obliquely though unmistakably to contemporary politics. And after 1688, when James II fled abroad, plays in which exiled kings are treated sympathetically, even though they might have been written years before, could provoke scandal.[7]

In spite of the existence of a sizeable number of plays that seem to offer specific advice on contemporary politics, there is a danger that almost any drama of the period can be interpreted allegorically simply by digging

5   'Dating Purcell's Dido and Aeneas', *Proceedings of the Royal Musical Association*, xciv (1967–8), p. 60.

6   'Dryden and History: a Problem in Allegorical Reading', *English Literary History*, xxxvi (1969), p. 272.

7   See Price, op. cit., p. 293.

deeply enough into historical detail; one can always find persons and events that seem to have inspired plots. As Wallace succinctly puts it, 'commentary turns all works into allegories'.[8] I would add that the more contrived and more detailed the metaphor seems to us, the less likely the poet intended it – or, at least, the more vehemently he would deny it. Therefore, in this study I have tried to avoid constructing elaborate metaphors that involve minor political figures or events that were not common knowledge at the time, even though English opera, with its rich spoken dialogue, offers more fertile ground for speculation than, say, a *tragédie en musique*. As we shall see in the case of Dryden – the greatest master of the weaving of political allusions into dramas – treasonable double meanings are most effective when drawn with broad strokes; even then, they are unlikely to be noticed by blockheads.

THE COMMONWEALTH

With Charles II in exile abroad and most of the politically minded gentry dispersed to the country, masques and lavish theatrical spectacles were impossible and the public playhouses closed during the Protectorate years. Sensing the winds of change, Sir William Davenant, who hoped to secure a theatre monopoly upon the restoration of the king, outflanked other would-be producers by finding a way round the ban on public entertainments, which did not apparently cover dramas 'sung in Recitative Musick'. He thus created the first English opera, *The Siege of Rhodes* (1656).[9] This was already too delicate a venture to be put at even greater risk by introducing blatant political comment or royalist sentiments, but the curiously inconclusive plot does, I think, take notice of the unstable and complex political situation prevailing in England in the mid-1650s. The opera is based on a historical event – the 1522 siege and easy conquest of the Knights of St John by the Ottomans. In Davenant's libretto the Admiral and Grand Master of Rhodes, along with knights from various countries, chief among them Duke Alphonso of Sicily, face annihilation at the hands of the Turks under the sultan Solyman. Alphonso expects reinforcements from France, Italy and England. But no rescue is attempted, because in spite of their good intentions the allies are preoccupied with the Crusades. Disaster is averted when Alphonso's wife Ianthe sails valiantly from Sicily; captured by the Turks *en route*, she is released because Solyman admires her courage and determination. Alphonso is humiliated by his wife's bold initiatives and dishonoured by his own inaction. Yet nothing is settled and there is no grand finale. Davenant was too good a

8   Op. cit., p. 265.
9   The music, composed by Matthew Locke, Henry Lawes, Henry Cooke, Charles Coleman and George Hudson, is lost.

dramatist to have allowed the plot to trail off for lack of invention. The non-resolution of the drama – a probing study of a prince who is stranded, let down by his allies amid promises of help and forced to stand by powerlessly as incompetents work to realize his goal – was surely an allusion to the exiled King Charles, frustrated by hollow French promises to raise an army against Cromwell.

The one other important music drama mounted during the Cromwellian era, *Cupid and Death* by Christopher Gibbons and Matthew Locke, is more emblematic (the dramatis personae include Cupid, Folly, Nature, Death, Despair and Mercury) and also more topical. Based on Aesop, the masque tells the story of a chamberlain at an inn where Cupid and Death are lodging who, for a mindless prank, exchanges their arrows. Cupid leaves the ground strewn with the bodies of young lovers, while Death rejuvenates the old and infirm and causes soldiers to embrace their enemies. To appease Mother Nature, who is horrified at the disruption, Mercury descends in a cloud and returns the arrows to their rightful owners; Cupid is banished from court and Death forbidden to visit any mortals 'in whose breast divine Marks of Art or honour shine'. The libretto is by James Shirley, who was, ironically, the author of the most extravagant of all the Stuart masques, *The Triumph of Peace* (1633), and was now called upon to produce a bauble for the Portuguese ambassador, who was in London in 1653–4 to conclude a peace treaty between John IV and Cromwell. The allegory seems absurdly plain: the chamberlain's prank represents the overturning of the natural political order by the Commonwealth, while Mercury's grand entrance symbolizes a desired restoration. The producer–director of a recent revival of the masque, to justify a decision to dress Mercury as Charles II, proposed a more detailed interpretation.

Cupid represents the indulgence of the earlier court life – the pleasure-seeking of the world of the court . . . Self-interest is embodied in the *Chamberlain* who would shift sides and loyalties as it served him . . . *Death* symbolises himself for he was to be seen everywhere, but perhaps too the opposition with Cupid in this drama suggests an identification with the steely, roundhead forces at present in power. Dangerous thoughts, these, but hardly to be missed by anyone at that time with royalist tendencies . . . *Nature* is the nation – the whole of England mourned for lost loved ones, and all was dis-eased by tragedy. Truly the natural order of things seems to have been reversed . . . But *Mercury* puts all to rights, and he is an anticipation of the return of kingship.[10]

First performed in public on 26 March 1653, the masque was revised in 1659 by Locke, who converted much of the spoken dialogue in the Fifth Entry into recitative. The text of the libretto itself was unchanged, except

10   Anthony Rooley, in the programme note for a performance at the Queen Elizabeth Hall, London, 17 August 1984.

for two minor deletions which nevertheless reveal that the 1659 producers were aware of its political overtones. In the First Entry the following remark about Folly and Madness – a half-hearted gibe at the *ancien régime* – was prudently cut:

> CHAMBERLAIN: A pair of precious instruments, and fit
>   To be o'th' privy counsell.
> HOST: We may see
>   What most of our Nobility are come to.
> CHAMBERLAIN: Sure they are well descended sir.[11]

The seditious allegorical design of *Cupid and Death*, which seems a particularly daring gesture considering the occasion of its 1653 première, anticipates the even more subversive operas of the 1690s, in which patriotism is used to disguise attacks on an unpopular king.

CHARLES II, JAMES II

The operatic activities of Davenant and Locke during the waning years of the Commonwealth proved a flash in the pan, because after the Restoration, when new companies were formed and theatres reopened, the spoken play reigned supreme for more than a decade. But by the mid-1670s, when English music drama seemed to be moving in a line of development parallel with the French, several operatic works were produced under royal protection and encouragement which were certainly occasional and in at least one case plainly political. *Ariane, ou Le Mariage de Bacchus* was performed at the Theatre Royal in late March 1674. The libretto is by Pierre Perrin, one of the founders of the Académie Royale de Musique; the score, which does not survive, was evidently a revision by Grabu, then Master of the King's Music, of the original by Robert Cambert, who was exiled to London after Lully took over the Académie. Sung in French by members of the short-lived Royal Academy of Musick,[12] the opera was occasioned by the marriage of the Duke of York to his second wife, Mary of Modena, the ceremony being concluded by proxy on 30 September 1673 over the strong objections of the Earl of Shaftesbury and others who feared further Roman Catholic incursion into the royal family.

---

[11]   A few lines earlier the following obscure reference was also deleted:
>   CHAMBERLAIN: He [Death] is kin to the devouring Gentleman
>   Of the long robe –
>   HOST: That has bespoke a Chamber
>   In'th' College among the Bears, and means to be
>   In commons with them.
These variants between the 1653 and 1659 versions are not mentioned in the notes to the score in Musica Britannica, ii, ed. E. J. Dent, rev. B. Harris *et al.* (London, 1965).

[12]   See P. Danchin, 'The Foundation of the Royal Academy of Music in 1674 and Pierre Perrin's *Ariane*', *Theatre Survey*, xxv (1984), pp. 55–66.

The princess landed at Dover two months later, but Charles II did not publicly acknowledge the intensely unpopular marriage until September 1674. Nevertheless, there are clear references to it in *Ariane*, which, according to the dedication, received the king's approbation.

In the prologue (presumably the work of Perrin and Grabu, though this part of the libretto is unascribed) three nymphs representing the Thames, the Tiber and the Seine pay their respects to Albion and his brother. They are identifiable as Charles and James in the English version of the text (it is more than a translation), which was published as a separate quarto in early 1674. The Seine sings of the recent war:

J'ai veû l un de tes Fils,	[I have seen the] Warlike Duke of thine,
Soûs l'Enseigne des Lyz,	Whose Lofty Meen speaks him of Royal Line
Du superbe Mastricq, forcer la Resistance:	In *Lewis*'s sight, his valliant hand imbrues
Dans sa Noble fierté, dans ses Trais, dans ses Yeuz,	In *Belgian*-blood, and *Maestrickt*-Wals subdues.
Je reconnais le Sang des Grand Rois ses Ayeulz.	

The French libretto has no equivalent of the following lines found in the English version: '*Vallor* and *Justice* both may act their parts, / But Love makes *Charles* to Rule his Peoples hearts.' (The lifting of the allegorical veil is most curious. Dryden also dispenses with the metaphorical pretence at a few places in *Albion and Albanius*.) Near the end of the prologue, a fourth nymph, representing the River Po, enters to cap the occasion. At this point the French is the more unguarded:

Reine des Flots, belle Thamise;	
Qui dans l'Eclat où ton Grand Roi t'a mise,	
N'as point d'êgale soûs les Cieux:	Suffer this happy Day, that I
Soufre qui je vienne en ces Lieux,	May through thy Chrystal Waves
Malgré les Destins & l'Envie,	draw nigh,
Joindre ma Divine Marie	And my Princess divine,
Au plus Grand de tes Demidieux.	To thy great Heroe joine.

In her song of welcome, Thamesis acknowledges the initial lack of enthusiasm for the duke's marriage: while the people both love and honour the new Duchess of York,

This Bliss, thou ow'st to her alone, whose Charm,
In 'spight of Fate, all resistance disarm:
    And makes Envy it self t'adore
    Her now, whom it oppos'd before.

In spite of the royal connections (or perhaps because of them), *Ariane* sank without a trace. Less than a year later a far more important work in the history of English music drama had its première: Thomas Shadwell and Matthew Locke's *Psyche* (February 1675), the archetypal semi-opera. It too may have been planned to mark the Duke of York's second marriage (see below), because Shadwell says in the preface that he had written the bulk of the libretto sixteen months before, that is, in October 1673, just before Mary of Modena arrived at Dover. The king may have helped the Duke's Company to obtain dancers and singers for the production, and both the libretto and Locke's printed score are dedicated to Monmouth, who also danced in the belated première. The duke's support of *Psyche* has led one modern scholar to view the opera as a Protestant, anti-Gallic reply to *Ariane*.[13] Such factionalism was certainly rife at both court and theatre in the mid-1670s, but *Psyche* owes a great debt to the *tragédie–ballet* of the same name; furthermore, Shadwell's version also seems to allude to the Duke of York's wedding, though the allegory is more obscure than in the prologue to *Ariane*.

Because it is so closely related to *Psyché* (1671) – a collaboration of Molière (who wrote the lion's share), Corneille, Quinault and Lully – one must wonder whether the English semi-opera on the subject of the marriage of a god and a mortal princess was anything more than a *pièce d'occasion*, like Perrin's recycled opera on a similar theme. Shadwell, however, chose a story with closer parallels to the more controversial ramifications of the royal marriage of 1673: a princess more beautiful than Venus herself is betrothed to what she believes is a dreadful monster but which turns out to be the god of love. Shadwell defended himself against charges of plagiarism by claiming rightly that his version was 'more of a play' than Molière's. The significant differences are: the main events in the drama happen on stage rather than being reported by messengers; the musical episodes are woven into the action rather than being confined to a prologue and entr'actes as are Lully's; and Shadwell altered the story to make it reflect the circumstances surrounding the Duke of York's marriage.

Mary was a reluctant bride. One of at least three princesses proposed at various times by Louis XIV as suitable wives for the widower James, she was minded to enter the nunnery of the Visitation near the ducal palace at Modena and was persuaded to forsake the veil only by Pope Clement X himself. The other serious contender for the duke's hand was Princess Eleanora of Modena, Mary's aunt, who was at the time twice her age. The first scene of Shadwell's semi-opera, which has no counterpart to Molière's, finds Psyche in a deep wood in retreat from the strife of court

[13]   M. Lefkowitz, 'Shadwell and Locke's *Psyche*: the French Connection', *Proceedings of the Royal Musical Association*, cvi (1979–80), pp. 42–55.

and city, sheltered from factions that 'undermine each other, all mean ways they take / Each strives who shall his Monarch lead, / Though at the price of his own Father's Head: / Nor care they how much they their Prince misguide . . .' Shadwell's play is always more political than Molière's.

In the *tragédie–ballet* the heroine is courted by a pair of insipid princes, Cleomenes and Agenor, who, because of her extreme beauty and innocence, 'go with one accord' to declare their passion to her. Psyche's jealous elder sisters, Aglaura and Cidippe, are unable to stir up any divisive rivalry between the suitors. Shadwell exaggerates the age difference between Psyche and her sisters (perhaps to allude to Princess Eleanora) and makes the princes (whom he calls Nicander and Polynices) spirited rivals who agree to bury the hatchet only at Psyche's request; they later become the symbiotic champions of her liaison with Cupid. This added twist may refer to the proxy marriage at Modena in September 1673, when Henry Mordaunt, second Earl of Peterborough, stood as substitute for the Duke of York. Seconding him as emissary for Louis XIV was Philippe de Courcillon, Marquis of Dangeau. Having been on opposite sides in the Second Dutch War, the two men now shared the honour of escorting Mary to London. Nicander and Polynices perform a similar duty for Psyche in the first scene of Act 5.[14]

Shadwell also politicizes the central event of the drama, the union of Cupid and Psyche, by giving it contemporary overtones. The first scene of Act 2, which has no equivalent in Molière, takes place in the Temple of Apollo, where the oracle announces that the princess is to be sacrificed:

> You must conduct her to that fatal place . . .
> On *Venus* Rock upon the Sea,
> She must by you deserted be;
> A poys'nous Serpent there she'l find
> By Heav'n he *Psyche*'s Husband is design'd.

In the political mythology of seventeenth-century Britain, Venus had supposedly changed her dwelling, forsaking the Cyprian grove for the Fairest Isle ('*Venus* Rock upon the Sea'); the implication that the 'poys'nous serpent' represents the Duke of York is thus rendered felicitous when Cupid later tells a bemused Psyche that he is the monster she had feared. One could continue to embroider this design – to see the vengeful Venus as Catherine of Braganza and the reconciling Jupiter as Charles II. But, as these characters behave much as they do in Molière, the links are only a happy coincidence. The new scenes do, however, seem to underscore Shadwell's covert message: the royal marriage of 1673 was not the dreaded monster that Shaftesbury was claiming it to be.

[14] For this and other insights into the possible political content of *Psyche*, I am indebted to John Wagstaff.

The climax of King Charles's infatuation with Frenchified music drama was John Crowne's lavish pastoral–ballet *Calisto*, which had its 'première' in February 1675 after numerous public rehearsals.[15] A court production in which all the speaking parts were taken by princesses or maids of honour and the songs and dances performed mostly by professionals,[16] it was called a masque. *Calisto* is, however, much more like a play than *Psyche*: it is as long as most heroic dramas of the period, and its musical scenes are confined to the prologue and entr'actes. As Crowne reports in the preface to the playbook, he was initially flattered by the royal command to devise a brisk allegorical drama with Princesses Mary and Anne, future queens of England, and Sarah Jennings, later Duchess of Marlborough, in the leading roles. But, being allowed only a few hours in which to choose a subject, he hit upon the worst imaginable in the circumstances. Crowne then faced the difficult task of writing 'a clean, decent, and inoffensive Play, on the Story of Rape'. The first draft, which was rejected because Jupiter's assault on Calisto's virtue was thought to be too brutal, must have been exceptionally bold, because the published version is lewd and suggestive enough, especially in the mouths of little princesses. Yet the casting itself rendered harmless what in the professional theatre would have been a wicked satire on the king's promiscuity and abuse of sexual prerogative. For Princess Mary, already the personification of the purity of the state, to act Calisto prevented all misapplication, and the pastoral edged towards reality: Mary was Calisto; Calisto was Mary.

WILLIAM AND MARY

In the preface to *Calisto* Crowne humbly apologizes for being unable to satisfy both the understanding and the senses: 'had it been written by him, to whom by the double right of place and merit, the honour of the employment belonged, the pleasure had been in all kinds complete'. This clearly refers to Dryden, the Poet Laureate, whose success in fulfilling both requirements came not in the court opera *Albion and Albanius*, whose allegory certainly did not challenge the understanding, but in the semi-opera *King Arthur*. I have written elsewhere about the political aspects of the two works;[17] the present study summarizes their joint gestation, adds further evidence to support my claim that a cynical vein flows beneath the patriotic skin of *King Arthur*, and attempts to show that *Albion and*

---

[15]   The work is discussed in detail in E. Boswell, *The Restoration Court Stage* (London, 1932), *passim*.

[16]   The ubiquitous dancer Monmouth was a notable exception.

[17]   *Henry Purcell and the London Stage*, pp. 290–5.

Fig. 1 *Chronology of* Albion and Albanius *and* King Arthur

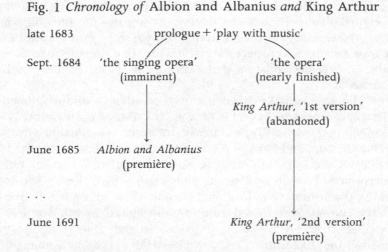

late 1683   prologue + 'play with music'

Sept. 1684   'the singing opera'   'the opera'
                 (imminent)   (nearly finished)

                                      King Arthur, '1st version'
                                          (abandoned)

June 1685   *Albion and Albanius*
                 (première)

. . .

June 1691   *King Arthur*, '2nd version'
                                          (première)

Albanius, an isolated example of a true-blue royalist opera, was itself dragged through the political mud of the late 1690s.

Dryden conceived *Albion and Albanius* as a one-act prologue to a blank-verse tragicomedy 'adorn'd with scenes, Machines, Songs and Dances', that is, a semi-opera. But because of 'some intervening accidents' the play had to be abandoned, and the prologue was then expanded into the three-act libretto set by Grabu in 1684–5. The former was of course *King Arthur*, which Dryden separated from its prologue as early as summer 1684. The semi-opera lay unperformed until 1691, when it was revised for Purcell, this being their only major collaboration. (The chronology is outlined in Fig. 1.) The reasons why *King Arthur* was shelved will never be known for certain because the original version does not survive, but the 'intervening accidents' are easily deduced.

In the preface to the 1691 playbook, Dryden all but admits that the original draft was a political allegory, and in order 'not to offend the present Times, nor a Government which has hitherto protected me, I have been oblig'd so much to alter the first Design . . .'. That some changes might have been necessary should come as no surprise: in the interval between the two versions had occurred the death of Charles II, the accession of James II, the Glorious Revolution and the coronation of William and Mary; Dryden had been stripped of his offices and ridiculed for an ill-timed conversion to Roman Catholicism. Almost all modern authorities have echoed Sir Walter Scott's opinion that the playwright was forced 'to convert an ingenious, and probably highly poetical political drama, into a mere fairy tale, as totally divested as possible of any meaning beyond extravagant adventure'.[18] (But how could Scott have known that the original play was 'ingenious'?) Dryden compares the alterations made to *King Arthur* in 1691 to the refitting of a royal ship, with the implication that drastic changes were necessary; but, when one attempts to recover the parable, it becomes apparent that beneath the waterline the vessel was untouched.

The plot is essentially Dryden's own creation, a disappointment to modern audiences who expect to encounter Guinevere, Sir Launcelot and the knights of the Round Table. Instead, the argument is Arthur's quest for a unified Britain, and most of the action centres on Emmeline, the blind daughter of the Duke of Cornwall. She is betrothed to Arthur but has formerly been courted by Oswald, the Saxon King of Kent. Defeated in battle by the Britons, Oswald abducts Emmeline, who is at length freed by Arthur. The coarsest thread running through this thin story is the reconciliation of princes, and, if placed in the context of the years following the Exclusion Crisis, *King Arthur* is a metaphor of the reconciliation of Charles II and the Duke of Monmouth that Dryden had prophesied at the end of the preface to *Absalom and Achitophel*. Arthur could then represent either King Charles or James Duke of York, Oswald the belligerent Monmouth, Emmeline the National Conscience, and the other dramatis personae the advisers of the two dukes. By dissociating Oswald from the plots of his evil magician Osmond, Dryden exonerates the Saxon king and thereby alludes to Shaftesbury's using Monmouth as a pawn in his stratagems to block the succession of the Duke of York. But the rapprochement that the original semi-opera was evidently meant to herald and ultimately to consecrate never happened: Charles died without forgiving Monmouth, who led a rebellion in June 1685 and was executed the following month. *Albion and Albanius*, whose allegory was insipid, retrospective and uncontroversial, was put into production, while *King Arthur*, which treated much more volatile current affairs, was pushed into the wings.

How would this drama have translated into the political climate of the early 1690s, assuming for the purposes of argument that the vessel had only been refitted, not refounded? While there is a consensus among Dryden scholars that several of his pre-1688 plays are strongly royalist, the stage works produced after the Glorious Revolution are politically less transparent. Most authorities argue that Dryden was effectively emascu-

---

[18]   *The Works of John Dryden*, ed. Scott (Edinburgh, 1821), viii, p. 111. The *Dictionary of National Biography* says simply that *King Arthur* was adapted to the times 'by omitting the politics'; Roberta Florence Brinkley (*Arthurian Legend in the Seventeenth Century* (Baltimore, 1932), p. 144) suggests that 'all the real substance of the story had been removed, and what remained was only a fantastic account of Arthur's battle with the Saxons'; Joanne Altieri ('Baroque Hieroglyphics: Dryden's *King Arthur*', *Philological Quarterly*, lxi (1982), p. 450) states categorically that attempts to decipher topical allusions in the work are 'doomed to failure'.

lated as apologist for the Jacobite cause, since his later plays were heavily censored before production or publication. In the commentary to *Don Sebastian*, Earl Miner states that in 1689, when prominent Catholics 'were being arrested for high treason only on the suspicion of adhering to that religion', 'Dryden could not possibly attack the government of a prince he considered a usurper [that is, William III] nor express his allegiance to his true king', James II.[19] A small minority of scholars believe that Dryden, in opposition for the first time in his career as 'shadow' poet laureate, was no less political in his post-1688 writings but, rather, was forced to find more ingenious ways of hiding political allusions.[20] But even this second camp dismiss *King Arthur* from serious consideration, apparently in the belief that Dryden would not have bothered to construct a satirical design for a work whose chief purpose was musical and scenic diversion.

The final, 1691 version of the semi-opera is on the surface a paean to the British monarchy, an epic reaffirmation of the royal lineage from Aeneas, through Brutus and Arthur, down to William III, to whom direct reference is made in the final masque.[21] Queen Mary gave Dryden her approbation, and none of her subjects is known to have expressed the slightest doubt about Dryden's sincerity, in spite of the poet's private loathing of the Dutch king and continued loyalty to the Pretender. Nevertheless, I believe a strong case can be made for viewing *King Arthur* as an elaborate, backhanded compliment to the monarch, a technique that Dryden later perfected in his translation of Virgil.

The verse translation of the *Aeneid*, published in 1697 – though it had occupied Dryden for several years – is a universally admired achievement. Yet scholars have regarded its dedication (or introduction) as an embarrassment. Parts of the rambling discourse are taken without adequate acknowledgement from various French authors, and some aspects of Dryden's interpretation, particularly of Book IV, are distinctly odd in their flagrant manipulation of Roman history. The *Aeneid*, he claims, is an allegory, as useful to the Romans of Virgil's age as the *Iliad* was to the Greeks of Homer's time. Aeneas was meant to be a direct reflection of Augustus Caesar, at one level simply to show the lineage of the Roman people descending from the Trojans, but more furtively to curry favour with the emperor by constructing parallels which would show recent dubious events in a favourable light: namely, to justify Augustus's subversion of the old form of government by showing Aeneas's sovereignty as a paragon of Elective Kingship. The only firm evidence that Dryden offers to support this novel interpretation is that Virgil asked for

---

19   *The Works of John Dryden*, xv, p. 406.
20   See J. R. Moore, 'Political Allusions in Dryden's Later Plays', *Publications of the Modern Language Association*, lxxiii (1958), pp. 36–42.
21   Just before the climactic single combat in Act 5, Arthur evokes his 'Fam'd Ancestor' Aeneas when he 'Fought for a Crown, and bright *Lavinia*'s Bed'.

all copies of the *Aeneid* to be destroyed after his death because he regarded the poem as imperfect, but that Augustus commanded its preservation because he was aware of the honour it brought him.

Whether or not Dryden actually believed that he had discovered the underlying allegory of the *Aeneid* is beside the point; his chief aim was to encourage his readers to draw parallels between Virgil's supposed design and events and figures of Williamite England. Of course no British monarch would have objected to being linked with the great-grandfather of Brutus of Albion; quite the contrary, such obeisance would have been *pro forma*. But the longest and most cogent section of the dedication, a discussion of the means by which Aeneas gained his crown, seems to have another purpose. The crux of Dryden's argument is a passage which contrasts Aeneas's and Latinus's kingships. Latinus was a hereditary monarch, lawfully descended from Saturn, a just and gracious prince, 'always Consulting with his Senate to promote the common Good'. Aeneas, in contrast, was at best an elected king, at worst an invader and usurper. This is the crucial sentence: '*Aeneas*, tho' he Married the Heiress of the Crown, yet claim'd no Title to it during the Life of his Father-in-law.'[22] Who could have missed the analogy between Latinus and James II, between Aeneas and William of Orange and between Creusa and Queen Mary? This whole attitude spills over into the translation itself, especially Book VII (Aeneas's entry into Latium). As Steven Zwicker has recently shown, 'the steady shading of the language, the consistent impulse to render entry as conquest, can only be the translator brooding over the injustice and perhaps the inevitability of such conquest of Latium by Aeneas and of England by William III'.[23]

The proof of Dryden's intention can be found in the engravings illustrating the 1697 edition of the *Works of Virgil*, which the publisher Jacob Tonson simply reprinted with slight modifications from those in John Ogilby's 1654 translation. Each plate is dedicated to one of Dryden's subscribers, and a line of the *Aeneid* is referred to by numbers at the bottom.[24] Furthermore, every depiction of Aeneas has been retouched, as can be seen by comparing the details of the engravings given in Plate 1,

---

22   See 'The Dedication of the Aeneid', *The Poems of John Dryden*, ed. J. Kinsley (Oxford, 1958), iii, p. 1017, ll. 569–71.

23   *Politics and Language in Dryden's Poetry: the Arts of Disguise* (Princeton, 1984), p. 186.

24   Zwicker shows that the careful matching of subscriber and engraving reflects 'ties of patronage, friendship, and politics' (op. cit., p. 191). Some are complimentary, others perfunctory; engravings depicting altars, sacrifices and divining scenes are dedicated to prominent Roman Catholics. And a few of the ascriptions are veiled insults, such as the one to Dryden's brother-in-law Sir Robert Howard. It illustrates the battle of Aeneas with Cydon's seven brothers in Book X and refers to line 450, in which Aeneas threatens to cure Cydon's pederasty by the sword. Dryden must have been pleased that his erstwhile enemy had paid five guineas for the privilege of having his name thus immortalized.

Plate 1 Engravings depicting the first meeting of Dido and Aeneas
(a) from *The Works of Publius Virgilius Maro*, trans. J. Ogilby (London, 1654)
(b) from *The Works of Virgil*, trans. J. Dryden (London, 1697)

which shows Dido and Aeneas's first meeting. That the figure with the hooked nose (b) was meant to resemble William III is confirmed by Dryden himself in a letter of 3 September 1697. More astonishing is that the same letter reveals that Tonson was completely unaware of the hidden derogatory message of the introduction to the *Aeneid*: the publisher 'has missd of his design in the Dedication: though He had prepard the Book for it: for in every figure of Eneas, he has causd him to be drawn like K. William, with a hookd Nose'.[25] Dryden's stroke of genius is that, under the guise of scholarly discourse and through only the subtlest shading of meaning in the translation, he made Aeneas reflect King William, while at the same time launching a bitter attack on Elective Kingship. That this doubly concealed allegory should have escaped Tonson, a noted man of letters, in a book that he himself was publishing will help put the problem of interpreting *King Arthur* in perspective.

A further analogy can be drawn between the translation of the *Aeneid* and *King Arthur*. Both were pre-existing texts that embraced fundamental issues of how kingships are acquired, and both had several built-in parallels with the politics of the reign of William and Mary. Through editing, Dryden could either obscure the connections or enhance them to reflect his own cynical view of current affairs. In a sense *King Arthur* should have been less problematic than the translation of Virgil: since the first version of the semi-opera was probably guyed to the events of 1681–4, why should Dryden have been obliged to alter it at all, given the completely different circumstances of 1691 – a foreign prince sharing the throne with the daughter of the king he had deposed? As with the subtle shifts of meaning in the translation of the *Aeneid*, perhaps the alterations were intended to make *King Arthur* more rather than less topical.

Arthur could now be read as William III and Oswald as the discredited James II, to whom Dryden, one should recall, remained loyal to the end. Perhaps this explains the soft treatment the antagonist receives: for all his treachery, Oswald is unbowed. Emmeline in her innocence can still represent the national conscience, but her placement directly between the Saxons and the Britons was uncomfortably similar to Queen Mary's extraordinarily awkward position between her husband and her exiled father. Merlin is the one member of the dramatis personae whose allegorical identity need not have changed from 1684 to 1691; in both versions the wizard can represent the Earl of Halifax, the work's dedicatee and adviser to Charles II, James II and William III.

This interpretation of *King Arthur* has a major weakness: it runs exactly counter to Dryden's post-revolution politics. Superficially, the drama seems to advocate the reconciliation of William and James for the greater

---

25   *The Letters of John Dryden*, ed. C. E. Ward (Durham, North Carolina, 1942), p. 93.

good of the kingdom; but Saxon Oswald, an invader from the continent, is in all ways a better reflection of William than of James. And the clear reference to the Dutch king in the Grand Chorus of the final masque ('. . . Foreign Kings, Adopted here, / Their Crowns at Home despise') is at best a dubious compliment. In this light certain speeches take on an amazing irony, none more than Arthur's gloating over his defeat of Oswald in Act 5: 'I wou'd Restore thee fruitful *Kent* . . . But that my *Britains* brook no foreign Power, / To Lord it in a Land, Sacred to Freedom.' *King Arthur* had to be ambiguous in tone, because Dryden chose to interweave a laudatory allegory with a seditious one. In both the semi-opera and in the later translation of the *Aeneid*, the satire is aimed obliquely at the figure the works supposedly honour: William III.

Dryden's perverse reading of Virgil bears indirectly on *Dido and Aeneas*. In *Henry Purcell and the London Stage* I maintained that the opera was not professionally produced during the composer's lifetime because Tate's libretto, while probably not a deliberate allegory (even though it alludes to the new monarchs), nevertheless became increasingly embarrassing in its political implications as William's absences from England grew longer and more frequent. And, after Queen Mary's death in December 1694, a public performance 'would have been unthinkable, since the tragic ending would have implied that William's neglect was in some way responsible for his wife's passing'.[26] Dryden's dedication to the *Aeneid* lends weight to my hypothesis. He claims that Virgil showed Aeneas's abandonment of Dido as a parable to justify Augustus's divorce from Scribonia, at the same time 'to espouse the Cause and Quarrel of his Country against Carthage' by sullying the reputation of the foundress of that city (ll. 1142ff). While few if any of Dryden's contemporaries would have been as callous, even as ruthless, in their reading of Book IV, the reign of William and Mary was obviously not the right time for an opera based on this part of the *Aeneid*. There were simply too many uncomfortable coincidences.

A few operas and musical entertainments mounted in the middle years of William's reign, after Mary's death, also pay him equivocal obeisance. The most curious by far is *A New Opera; called, Brutus of Alba: or, Augusta's Triumph* (October 1696), the first new semi-opera produced after Purcell. His brother Daniel wrote or arranged much of the music for this anonymous play. Though the fact has gone unnoticed until recently, the protagonist, King Locrinus of Britain, who is also called Brutus and occasionally Albion, represents William III.[27] Borrowing the plot outline from *Measure for Measure*, the opera revolves round Brutus's hypocritical deputy Asaracus, who is left to govern Britain while the king is away

---

26   Op. cit., p. 262.
27   This work is not, as has been frequently stated, an adaptation of Tate's 1678 heroic play of the same name. See ibid., pp. 235–6.

fighting in Gaul.[28] The climax is reached at the king's return, when he is welcomed at Dover by Augusta (London), Thamesis, Apollo, Neptune and others, who perform a masque in his honour. In 1696 William was also abroad fighting the French, and the libretto is rife with allusions to his military exploits, modest though they were during that year. The music embellishes not only the king's triumphs but his griefs as well; in the opening masque Augusta sings of the late Queen Mary:

> O *Hermes*, pity take
> Of her, who *Europe*'s Pride was seen,
> And this fair Isle's Imperial Queen.
> *Albion*'s Darling Bride adorn'd,
> Till my Absent Lord I mourn'd.

Brutus of Alba is at once so openly laudatory of the king and so badly written that one would scarcely expect to find the sort of ingenious subtext that was posited for *King Arthur*. Yet close inspection reveals any number of anomalies, not the least of which is that the verses of nearly all the musical scenes are paraphased from Dryden's *Albion and Albanius*, including the lament for Queen Mary quoted above, which is based on Augusta's opening air (Act 1 scene 1, ll. 12ff):[29]

> O *Hermes*! pity me!
> I was, while Heav'n did smile,
> The Queen of all this Isle,
> *Europes* Pride,
> And *Albions* Bride;
> But gone my Plighted Lord! ah, gone is Hee!

It is typical of the anonymous adapter's method that the reworked verses are fitted into radically different contexts or their meaning inverted. Three of Daniel Purcell's songs are settings of paraphased lyrics, and though he did not indulge in musical parody to any appreciable degree, there is, for example, enough similarity between his 'Great Queen of Hymen's hallowed fires' and Grabu's 'Great Queen of Nuptial Rites' to suggest that Purcell knew the earlier score.[30]

The scene of *Brutus of Alba* closest to its model in content and spirit is 4.2, in which the king is welcomed at Dover. Most of the lyrics are based on

---

28   Asaracus may represent Charles Talbot, Duke of Shrewsbury, who became Secretary of State and effectively head of the administration from 1694; two years later he was charged with complicity in a plot against William III, having long been suspected of correspondence with James II.

29   As Peter Holland points out, several sets used in *Brutus of Alba* were also borrowed from *Albion and Albanius*: see *The Ornament of Action: Text and Performance in Restoration Comedy* (Cambridge, 1979), p. 45.

30   Compare *Albion and Albanius* (London, 1687), pp. 68–9, with *The Single Songs, With the Dialogue, Sung in the New Opera, Call'd Brutus of Alba* (London, 1696), p. 5.

Albion and Albanius 2.2, lines 128ff, in which Albanius (James Duke of York) is conducted dejectedly into exile by Apollo, Thamesis and a chorus of nymphs and tritons. Whether or not this transformation was an implied insult to William III, one must at least appreciate the irony that a Jacobean opera had insinuated itself into a work that outwardly bade him every good wish. With this knowledge, the paean of 1696 begins to crumble. Even Brutus's resolution at the end of Act 5 ('And then to War I will again return') is rendered an ill omen, as it recalls Spenser's account of Albion's death in Gaul in the eleventh canto of the fourth book of *The Faerie Queene*:

> For Albion the soone of Neptune was,
>   Who for the proofe of his great puissance,
>   Out of his Albion did on dry-foot pas
> Into old Gall, that now is cleeped France,
> To fight with Hercules, that did advance
> To vanquish all the world with matchlesse might,
> And there his mortall part by great mischance
> Was slain . . .

While blunt in its execution, *Brutus of Alba* is subtle in its underhand-edness. It is also untypical of the many semi-operas mounted in the last years of the century, which show a marked trend away from the robustly political works of Dryden. I can find, for instance, little evidence of allegorical designs in Thomas Durfey's *Cinthia and Endimion* (December 1696),[31] Elkanah Settle's *The World in the Moon* (June 1697), John Dennis's *Rinaldo and Armida* (December 1698) or Peter Motteux's *The Island Princess* (February 1699). All contain an occasional allusion to King William, but no hidden disobedience on the scale of *Brutus of Alba*. Motteux even dashed off a masque and a musical interlude about the time of the signing of the Peace of Ryswick that amount to little more than glorified battle reports: *The Taking of Namur and His Majesty's Safe Return* and *Europe's Revels for the Peace* (November 1697).[32] But no musical drama of the period went quite so far politically as did Nicholas Rowe's tragedy

---

[31]   But see C. Kephart, 'Thomas Durfey's *Cinthia and Endimion*: a Reconsideration', *Theatre Notebook*, xxxix (1985), pp. 134–9, which argues that Durfey's masque, which may have been written in the mid-1680s, parallels the patriotic theme of *Albion and Albanius*. Yet Durfey's masque seems to hint at politics only in the sub-plot of the rustics, who react to the raping and harassing satyrs by planning a revolution against the government of Pan. In Act 3 scene 1 Collin says, 'I declare I'm for a Common-Wealth'. And, as Kephart suggests, this sub-plot may have been introduced when Durfey revised the work for a public performance in the mid-1690s.

[32]   Motteux's masque *The Rape of Europa by Jupiter* (1694), whose title promises so much, would appear not to have political application. Lucyle Hook argues on slim evidence that John Eccles's setting was inserted into the rape scene of a 1694 revival of Rochester's alteration of John Fletcher's *Valentinian*, 'to represent in classic story on stage what was happening off-stage': see The Augustan Reprint Society, Publication No. 208 (Los Angeles, 1981), p. vi.

Tamerlane (December 1701). In the dedication the playwright refuses to deny what 'Some People . . . have fancy'd, that in the Person of *Tamerlane* I have alluded to the greatest Character of the present Age', namely, William III. He does admit, however, that drawing parallels to powerful figures in public entertainments is a risky business, and he suggests modestly that 'It may be a Task indeed worthy the greatest Genius, which this, or any other Time has produc'd', apparently a reference to Dryden (who had died in the previous year). (Had Rowe, like Tonson, missed the point of the introduction to the *Aeneid* and other anti-Williamite works?) *Tamerlane* was so glowing a representation of William (and the antagonist Bajazet so unflattering a picture of Louis XIV) that later in the century the custom was established of reviving the play on the king's birthday, 4 November.[33]

In spite of these strong royalist tendencies in turn-of-the-century drama, even so rabid a jingo as Motteux (a Huguenot immigrant) was capable of taking a good-humoured swipe at the king. The moral of his masque *The Loves of Mars & Venus* (1696), set by Daniel Purcell and Godfrey Finger and originally designed to be inserted into Edward Ravenscroft's three-act farce *The Anatomist* (November 1696), is to expose 'the Frailty of a Warrior', though nothing suggests that the over-sexed Mars was meant to represent the king. The spoken prologue explains that 'what we call a Masque some will allow / To be an Op'ra, as the World goes now'; but Motteux need not have apologized, because *Mars & Venus* is a true comic opera with no spoken dialogue, bustling with wit and charm, the antithesis and equal of *Dido and Aeneas*. (Unfortunately, the recitatives do not survive.[34]) Venus is a vain, ageing beauty, almost a pantomime dame. Vulcan, who chides his wife for patching and painting, seems to deserve cuckolding, but in Act 3 a genuine display of remorse, intensified by Jealousy, who sings Monteverdian echoes, deepens his character. When Vulcan discovers the adulterers *in flagrante delicto* in Act 2, the pimp Gallus improvises an explanation for his master: Venus was not embracing Mars, rather she was measuring him for armour. Taking his cue, Mars commands Vulcan to make him an impenetrable shield and to enrich it with various figures:

> Let future Heroes there appear:
> Place *Greece's*, *Rome's*, and brave *Britain's* there.
>   Let *Alexander*, *Caesar*, *Arthur* meet,
> And all their *Lawrels* lay at greater *William's* Feet.

[33]   For an attempt to identify other members of the dramatis personae, see W. Thorp, 'A Key to Rowe's *Tamerlane*', *Journal of English and Germanic Philology*, xxxix (1940), pp. 124–7.

[34]   For locations of the songs and dialogues, see C. L. Day and E. B. Murrie, *English Song-Books 1651–1702* (London, 1940).

This hasty invention, the product of deception and cuckoldry, is followed by two further verses, more hyperbolical than the first, which were cut in performance:

> *William*, more God-like, and as brave,
> Shall only fight th'endanger'd World to save:
>   *William*, my other self shall be;
>   Inspir'd by *Themis*, and by me.

> Immur'd in Steel now Warriors safely fight;
>   But Balls unseen with rapid Flight
> One day shall deal Destruction through the Field:
> *William*, with Brest unarm'd, shall face those fiery Foes;
>   And *Mars* must kindly interpose,
>   His Representative to shield.

The bawdy *double entendre* of the third verse aside, the last two lines, while perhaps the fruit of the purist intention, are especially liable to be misconstrued. Yet the implied ridicule of King William derives more generally from the context: his visage is to be 'immur'd in Steel' by the world's first cuckold.

ANNE

At the end of the reign of William III and during the early years of Queen Anne's, operas were either unpolitical or studiedly patriotic and staunchly anti-Gallic, paying perspicuous obeisance to the monarch.[35] What political subversion there may have been centres mainly on sub-royals, notably the Duke and Duchess of Marlborough, whose fluctuating fortunes gave the librettist more to work with than the dull affairs of the queen. Yet two semi-operas, *The Grove* and *The Virgin Prophetess*, gingerly allude to the circumstances surrounding the accession of the last Stuart, and the former glances wistfully back on the ageing exile, James II, for one last time.

John Oldmixon's *The Grove, or, Love's Paradice* (February 1700, music by Daniel Purcell), conceived as a pastoral but with the dignity of its characters elevating it 'into the form of a Tragedy' (preface), includes no obvious allusions to major figures, and the details of the plot seem to fit no template of contemporary affairs; yet it still makes a strong political point.

[35]   See, for example, Motteux's all-sung 'interlude' *Britain's Happiness* (1704), which was designed as an allegorical prologue addressed to Queen Anne for an unperformed opera called *The Loves of Europe*. The prologue was originally set by Richard Leveridge and was later given to John Weldon by some aristocratic subscribers to provide the backbone of a musical entertainment offered on the eve of Marlborough's campaign which was to have its climax at Blenheim. Weldon's version was performed at Drury Lane on 22 February and Leveridge's followed at Lincoln's Inn Fields on 7 March.

While on a state visit to Italy, Emperor Arcadius of Greece grows envious of the wealth and tranquillity of the petty fief of Lord Amintor, who is actually Eudosius, Prince of Thrace, in disguise. Arcadius later discovers that his long-lost daughter Aurelia is Eudosius's wife. Standing back from the overwrought plot, one will see that the essence of the story is the reconciliation on foreign soil of an embittered old king and his estranged daughter, who is a queen in her own country. The possible metaphorical meaning of the drama, a work which Oldmixon stresses is his own invention and not a translation or adaptation of another play, comes into focus when viewed in the light of the persistent rumours at the time of a reconciliation arranged by the Duke of Marlborough between the exiled James II and Princess Anne. But the Pretender died (on 16 September 1701) without re-establishing relations with his daughter.

In a similar vein, the prominence given the little prince Astianax in Settle's otherwise conventional semi-operatic dramatization of the fall of Troy, *The Virgin Prophetess* (May 1701, music by Godfrey Finger), may have been inspired by the sad death of Princess Anne's last surviving child, the Duke of Gloucester, on 30 July 1700. With him rested the only hope for the continuation of the Protestant Stuart line. In the opera Astianax, Paris's nephew, is also the last of a line, the only member of the royal family with a moral right of succession. Buffeted by the opposed influences of Cassandra and Helen, he bravely condemns his uncle's excesses. It is tempting to see the opera as a metaphor of the demise of the House of Stuart itself, with Paris representing King William, Helen of Troy Princess Anne, and Cassandra (perhaps) the Duchess of Marlborough; but the unembellished plot does not entirely support such a cynical reading.

The two operas in which the Duke of Marlborough is symbolically enshrined could not be more different in structure and tone, though the one is in several key ways derivative of the other: George Granville's *The British Enchanters* (February 1706), the last successful semi-opera; and Joseph Addison's *Rosamond* (March 1707), the first thoroughly English full-length, all-sung opera. *Rosamond* is discussed first, because it inspired Granville's revision of *The British Enchanters* in 1707.

Addison's only libretto was set by Thomas Clayton, at whose door the opera's spectacular failure is usually laid.[36] It is nonetheless a splendid rendition of the Fair Rosamond myth, which centres not on Henry II's ill-fated mistress but on Queen Eleanor (a role created by Catherine Tofts, England's first great operatic soprano), who wins back her husband's loyalty and affection by appealing to his sense of destiny. Far subtler than

[36]   This may be an unfair judgement based, admittedly, on the execrable arias published in *Songs in the New Opera Called Rosamond Compos'd by M*^{r}*. Tho: Clayton* (London, [c1707]). The recitative, which comprises much the greater share of the libretto, does not survive.

any of the contemporaneous pastiche librettos of Motteux and others to which the previously composed music of Bononcini, Alessandro Scarlatti and Albinoni was carelessly affixed, *Rosamond* is provided with a comic sub-plot for Sir Trusty (keeper of the Bower at Woodstock) and his wife Grideline, which is a parody of the serious story, an intricate intellectual design similar to those of Dryden's so-called 'split-plot' plays of the early 1690s. And, unlike what passed for Italian opera in London at the time, *Rosamond* places its arias squarely in the thick of the action rather than introducing them only to punctuate static emotions. The composer, flushed with the success of his thoroughly Italianate setting of *Arsinoe*, was clearly out of his depth.

With Marlborough back in England briefly between campaigns and planning his palace–monument in Woodstock Park, no one should be surprised to discover that Addison alludes generally to foreign British victories and particularly to the duke himself. (Little significance should, I feel, be attached to the dedication of the libretto to the Duchess of Marlborough, who was then a keen supporter of opera, especially the Italian.) At the beginning of the drama, Henry's return from abroad is eagerly awaited by both wife and mistress. In Act 1 scene 1 a page suggests that, once he is safely within the Bower, the king 'will soon forget the Toils of War', while in the next scene a messenger announces his return 'from purple Fields with Slaughter spread, / From Rivers choak'd with Heaps of Dead'. During the lovers' reunion in Act 2 scene 1, Henry exclaims that

> Not the loud *British* Shout that warms
> The Warrior's Heart, nor clashing Arms,
> Nor Fields with hostile Banners strow'd,
> Nor Life on prostrate *Gauls* bestow'd,
> Give half the Joys that fill my Breast,
> While with my *Rosamond* I'm blest.

Such 'Gaul'-bashing would seem no more than routine topicality in those post-Blenheim years, but Addison's bending of history (Henry II already controlled Anjou, Normandy, Aquitaine and Brittany) encouraged the audience to draw closer parallels between the opera and Marlborough's military career. Incidentally, the librettist completely ignores the one other near-contemporary dramatization of the Fair Rosamond story: John Bancroft's tragedy *Henry the Second, King of England* (November 1692), in which the protagonist would travel into Normandy only to confront a rebellious son.[37]

---

[37]   In *English Theatre Music in the Eighteenth Century* (London, 1973), Roger Fiske guesses that Addison drew on Thomas May's poem 'The Death of Rosamond', presumably the fifth book of *The Reigne Of King Henry The Second* (1633). But, unlike Addison's, May's account is entirely traditional, with no attempt to soften Eleanor's action:

The parallel between Addison's Henry and the Duke of Marlborough is narrowed considerably in the first scene of Act 3, a dream sequence in which two angels, representing War and Peace respectively, persuade Henry to give up Rosamond.[38] Owning that they are effective guardians against the dangers of battle and treasonous plots yet powerless against the rage of love, they show him a vision of future glories:

> FIRST ANGEL: To calm thy Grief and lull thy Cares,
>   Look up and see
> What, after long revolving Years,
>   Thy Bow'r shall be!
> When Time its Beauties shall deface,
> And only with its Ruins grace
> The future Prospect of the Place.
> [*Scene changes to the Plan of* Blenheim *Castle.*]
>   Behold the glorious Pile ascending!
>   Columns swelling, Arches bending,
>   Domes in awful Pomp arising,
>   Art in curious strokes surprizing,
>   Foes in figur'd Fights contending,
>   Behold the glorious Pile ascending!
> SECOND ANGEL: He sees, he sees the great Reward
> For *Anna*'s mighty Chief prepar'd:
> His growing Joys no Measure keep,
> Too vehement and fierce for Sleep.

But this striking scene is in fact redundant to the plot, since in scene 3 of the preceding act Eleanor, to give the king time to return to the straight and narrow of his own volition, offers Rosamond a sleeping draught instead of the traditional deadly choice of a bowl of poison (or a dagger). Wittily combining the climaxes of *Romeo and Juliet* with 'Pyramus and Thisbe', Sir Trusty, upon discovering the king's unconscious mistress, writes his master an operatically blunt note ('Your Rosamond is Dead') and drinks from the same cup. When Henry comes upon the mock havoc, he tells his wife in a deeply ironic exchange that he was about to renounce his mistress in favour of glory.

Although Henry surely represents the Duke, and Queen Eleanor the Duchess of Marlborough, which is at all events a bitingly Whiggish

> Nought did the Queene by this dire slaughter gaine;
> But more her Lords displeasure aggravate;
> And now, when he return'd in prosperous state [from bloodless victories
>   in France],
> This act was cause, together with that crime
> Of raising his unnaturall sonnes 'gainst him,
> That she so long in prison was detain'd,
> And, whilest he liv'd, her freedome never gain'd.

[38]   Samuel Johnson admired this scene: see Fiske, op. cit., p. 47. The angels' names are found only in Clayton's published songs.

commentary on their positions *vis-à-vis* Queen Anne, I would not complete the love triangle by proposing so definitive a counterpart for Rosamond. In the light of the highly moralistic–chauvinistic tone of the entire opera, it is more likely that she was meant simply as the personification of Worldly Diversion or even Sloth and not as a direct reflection of, say, Abigail Hill, whose star in 1707 was rising as quickly in royal favour as Sarah's was falling. The opera was thus a compliment to the duchess and a cautionary tale for her husband.

Granville's purpose in revising *The British Enchanters* in 1707 to include a 'Woodstock scene' was not so straightforward. The performance history of the semi-opera is a good illustration of the idea that political allegory need not be purposely built into a libretto but simply pointed out or sharpened up when subsequent events come to imitate art – the process to which Thomas Betterton seems to have subjected Massinger and Fletcher's *The Prophetess* when transforming it into *Dioclesian*.[39] Granville's semi-opera is based firmly on Quinault and Lully's *Amadis* of 1684. The most conspicuous alteration of the source – shifting the action from Gaul to Britain and creating the characters Celius (King of Britain, a Betterton role) and Constantius (Emperor of Rome) – do not appear to have been motivated by politics, rather by the English genre itself; the preponderance of spoken dialogue in semi-opera demanded a more developed plot and a larger dramatis personae than did through-composed opera. True, Granville's *Amadis* shares many of the attributes and circumstances of the Duke of Marlborough in 1706: he is a great warrior recently returned from foreign victories. But the date of composition of *The British Enchanters* is too uncertain for these to be interpreted as intentional links. Stoddard Lincoln suggests that it was written between 1701 and 1703 (the Battle of Blenheim was fought in summer 1704).[40] But in the preface to the opera as published in Granville's collected works (F1732), the author explains that *The British Enchanters* was 'the first Essay of a very infant Muse'; thus it precedes his comedy *The She-Gallants*, which was written in the mid-1680s and first performed in December 1695.[41] Betterton, 'having had a casual Sight of [the opera] many Years after it was written, begg'd it for the Stage, where it found so favourable a Reception, as to have an uninterrupted Run of at least Forty Days'.[42] Its success surprised the librettist, who says that he allowed the opera to be mounted in its uncorrected state.

What prompted him to revise the work soon after its première was not

39 See Price, *Henry Purcell and the London Stage*, pp. 270–2.
40 'The Anglicization of *Amadis de Gaul*', *On Stage and Off: Eight Essays in English Literature*, ed. J. W. Ehrstine *et al.* (n.p., 1968), p. 48.
41 *The Genuine Works in Verse and Prose, Of the Right Honourable George Granville, Lord Lansdowne* (London, 1732), i, after p. 191.
42 Granville is exaggerating: see R. D. Hume, 'Opera in London, 1695–1706', *British Theatre and the Other Arts, 1660–1800*, ed. S. S. Kenny (Washington, 1984), p. 91 n. 64.

only an awareness of its flaws but also the Lord Chamberlain's reorganization of the London theatres in early autumn 1706, an act which stripped the Queen's Theatre in the Haymarket, where the opera was in repertory, of all its singers. At first mortified that this 'Child of my Brain' would have to be mounted henceforth without its music and dances,[43] Granville quickly made the alterations and additions 'to fill up the Spaces occasion'd by the Necessity of leaving out the Mixture of Musical Entertainment'.[44] Furthermore, he took the opportunity to make the political implications, which are vague in the 1706 version, absolutely clear.

In the first edition (Q1706), Act 5 is set in Urganda's 'Bower of Bliss', where Amadis, having just defeated the evil enchanter Arcalaus in a wild battle that rages in the air and on the stage, finally wins Oriana's heart. In the revised play (Q1710), the Bower of Bliss was more precisely described as '*a Representation of* Woodstock-Park', which, as Urganda later tells the hero,

> . . . Mortals shall hereafter *Blenheim* name,
> Delicious Seat, ordain'd a sweet Recess
> For thee, and for a future *Amadis*.

Having followed Addison's lead by taking this giant leap towards the present, Q1710 appends a patriotic epilogue spoken by Urganda in front of a scene which represents '*the Queen, and all the Triumphs of her Majesty's Reign*'. The closing couplets sweep aside the allegorical device:

> If curious to inspect the Book of Fate,
> You'd farther learn the destin'd Time and Date
> Of *Britain*'s Glory, know, this Royal Dame
> From *Stuart*'s Race shall rise, ANNA shall be Her Name.

If the new setting at Woodstock has not already confirmed the allegorical identity of Amadis, two couplets found only in the epilogue as published in F1732 remove all doubt:

> Next to her side, victorious MARLBRO' stands,
> Waiting, observant of her dread Commands;
> The Queen ordains, and like ALCIDES, He
> Obeys, and executes her high Decree.

---

[43]   See Price, 'The Critical Decade for English Music Drama, 1700–1710', *Harvard Library Bulletin*, xxvi (1978), p. 60.

[44]   The second edition was printed in 1710 and issued later with Granville's *Poems upon Several Occasions* (London, 1712). The instrumental music, composed by William Corbett, was published by Walsh in *Harmonia Anglicana* (c1706). The vocal music was supplied by various hands, including John Eccles, Bartholomew Isaac and perhaps even Nicola Haym, who may have set the 'Ode of Discord' in Act 3.

Many years later when Granville revised *The British Enchanters* for the collected edition of his works, he suppressed all these topical allusions.[45] Yet other subtle changes elsewhere in Q1710 (and retained in F1732) also seem to point indirectly at Marlborough. The most significant of these occur in a new scene in which Oriana is made to doubt Amadis's fidelity and is reluctant to marry him. Of course this is not really new, as Granville is recalling the central element of Quinault's original: Amadis's dalliance with Briolanie. But in the opera-turned-play, Oriana's jealousy is given full vent in an extraordinary scene added to Act 2 – her first encounter with the hero.

Unlike their ecstatic meeting in Q1706, Oriana rebukes Amadis in the new episode as a traitor and curses him for leaving her and breaking her heart. In the first of several allusions to the *Aeneid*, he says that his absence from Britain was ordained by the gods and prolonged by tempests and shipwrecks ("Twas Infamy to stay, 'twas Death to part'). Finally, Oriana's anger at him erupts into an anti-Gallic frenzy:

> The *Briton* to the *Gaul* henceforth shall bear
> Immortal Hatred, and Eternal War;
> Nor League, nor Commerce, let the Nations know,
> But Seeds of everlasting Discord grow;
> With Fire and Sword the faithless Race pursue,
> This Vengeance to my injur'd Love is due.

And then, paraphrasing Dido's curse near the end of Book IV, she continues,

> Rise from our Ashes some avenging Hand,
> To curb their Tyrants, and invade their Land.[46]

Oriana will not be consoled by Amadis, comparing herself directly to the abandoned Dido: 'Lead me, O lead me, where the bleeding Queen, / With just Reproaches, loads perfidious Men . . .'

Granville's outward purpose is striking: to allegorize the origins of British Gallophobia through the story of Dido and Aeneas, as Virgil had supposedly done in justifying the illegal reign of Augustus Caesar. And, if

---

45 The epilogue from Q1710 was, however, included as a separate poem (i, pp. 163–5) headed '*Urganda*'s Prophecy. *Spoken by way of* Epilogue *at the first Representation* [*sic*] *of the* British Enchanters.'

46 'Exoriare aliquis ex nostris ossibus altor', which Dryden rendered as 'Rise some Avenger of our *Lybian* Blood, / With Fire and Sword pursue the perjur'd Brood' (Book IV, ll. 901–2). Granville obviously knew Dryden's translation. Cf. the lines quoted above ('Nor League, nor Commerce, let the Nations know . . .') with lines 898–900: 'Nor League, nor Love, the Hostile Nations know: / Now, and from hence in ev'ry future Age, / When Rage excites your Arms, and Strength supplies the Rage.'

Dryden had misapplied Book IV to contemporary politics, then Granville completely inverted its implications. Oriana (Dido), the virgin British princess, has been abandoned by Amadis (Aeneas), who now returns to Britain (Carthage) from Gaul (Rome) after conquering it. If this parable fails to satisfy either its local function in the drama or its panegyrical purpose of welcoming the Duke of Marlborough home from foreign battles, perhaps that is because the aims of the added scene were less grand: it may allude to one of the Marlboroughs' famous marital rows, which grew more frequent when the duchess's influence on Anne began to wane in late 1707. In the light of the queen's conciliatory appearance in the epilogue – itself an extension of the celebration of the union (and reunion) of Amadis and Oriana – the latter interpretation is the more satisfactory.

The practice of embedding political allusions in English opera did not, I suspect, die with *The British Enchanters* and *Rosamond*. Granted, the polyglot, cannibalized librettos of the Italianate pasticcio operas mounted in London in the first decade of the eighteenth century probably do not carry sophisticated sub-texts, but I should be surprised if Congreve, Hill, Hughes and the other English writers who turned their hands to through-composed opera at the time did not continue the tradition outlined above.[47] Brian Trowell has recently attached contemporary politics to Handel's first London opera, *Rinaldo* (1711), the libretto of which (by Giacomo Rossi) was sketched out by Aaron Hill. In its reworked form the climactic story of Tasso's *Gerusalemme liberata* seems to have acquired a new symbolism: Goffredo, Eustazio and the other crusaders represent the northern Protestant alliance, while Argante, Armida and the other 'alluring but insidious pagans' can be seen as their Catholic opponents.[48] To go beyond this – to interpret Goffredo, for instance, as the Elector of Hanover – would be to stretch the point, but one should not ignore the political implications of this and other Handel librettos.

This essay has been concerned with two distinct levels of allegory in English music drama. The first is inherent in almost all Baroque operas based on classical subjects: the singers are perforce emblematic and thus represent things besides the gods, shepherds and heroes they portray. It is

---

[47]   The spoken prologue to Motteux's *Thomyris, Queen of Scythia* (April 1707) is an extended paean to the reign of Queen Anne. But in a postscript the librettist denies that the opera itself is political:
>   Yet, when this Day we show a Scythian Queen
>   Think not we dare attempt a Modern Scene.
>   As Britain's Beauties all the World's excel,
>   Great ANNA's Reign disdains a Parallel.
This disclaimer surely confirms the practice.

[48]   See Trowell's programme note for the première of the Metropolitan Opera production of *Rinaldo* in New York, 19 January 1984.

surely no accident that the earliest operas are centred on Orpheus, the perfect musician, who, by singing his own story, was able to surmount the irrationality of *dramma per musica*, while at the same time representing an abstraction such as the Power of Music. The very existence of the second allegorical level – the political substratum discussed above – depends ultimately on authorial intention, the critic's unicorn. One can be absolutely certain of the secondary meaning of *Albion and Albanius*, thinly veiled though it may be, only because Dryden has explained it. With *King Arthur* and other seditious operas, one must tease out their underlying designs by reading between the lines or moving backwards from works such as the dedication to the *Aeneid*, whose subversive political stance is undeniable, though carefully concealed. Other music dramas, especially revivals or adaptations, must be interpreted against the background of ever shifting political loyalties. The last category suggests that the construction of a topical allegory was no great intellectual feat; indeed, librettists seem to have regarded this as a common procedure which could be accomplished with a few broad hints. Only in Dryden did the mixture of genius and bitterness produce a work, *King Arthur*, in which a stock metaphorical device (legendary king/protagonist as reigning monarch) is perfectly fused with the political message (an attack on William III). In this venture there was little danger that the poetical revenge would be detected by those whose vanity was fanned by the outward obeisance. As is shown by Tonson's failure to grasp the design of the translation of the *Aeneid*, even men of wit and intelligence are liable to miss the moral when the tale is told by a master.

Acis, Galatea and Polyphemus: a 'serenata a tre voci'?

BRIAN TROWELL

INTRODUCTORY

Twenty-eight years have passed since Winton Dean published the long and fundamental study of *Acis and Galatea* that opens Part II of *Handel's Dramatic Oratorios and Masques* (1959).[1] In many ways it was the most remarkable chapter in that remarkable book. Dean made us realize how important *Acis and Galatea* had been to the composer's development and to the process of naturalizing himself in his adoptive country. It was Handel's first extended setting of English verse, and his first encounter with an English libretto in dramatic form. However strangely altered, its revival as a concert piece in 1732, soon after a similar revival of *Esther*, played a vital part in familiarizing the London public with the new convention of performing dramatic works without stage action in the manner that Handel was to employ for his dramatic oratorios, for *Semele* and *Hercules*, and indeed for his revivals of the all-English *Acis and Galatea* of 1739–42. Others besides himself performed the work, though neither he · nor they ever revived it in its original shape, and during his lifetime it became the most popular of his dramatic oratorios and masques and his first dramatic piece of any kind to achieve publication in full score: Dean made sense for the first time of the confusing complexities of its later history.[2] Undoubtedly the most spectacular of Dean's revelations – certainly for performers – was his demonstration of the unique chamber-music qualities of the original Cannons version of *Acis and Galatea*, qualities which Handel himself had disguised and which had lain buried and unrecognized beneath the surface of Walsh's score of 1743 for over two centuries. Many performances, especially those given in intimate

---

[1] W. Dean, *Handel's Dramatic Oratorios and Masques* (London, 1959), pp. 153–90. Henceforth 'Dean'.

[2] For the performance history, see ibid., Appendix C, pp. 629–31. See also W. C. Smith, '*Acis and Galatea* in the Eighteenth Century', *Concerning Handel, his Life and Works* (London, 1948), pp. 197–265, which is of high bibliographical value. Henceforth 'Smith'.

31

surroundings, have since confirmed how aptly and vividly the colours and proportions of the work spring into life when it is given by the miniature forces that Dean recommended. Finally, his valuable and original investigation of the London theatre masques of 1715–18, small-scale Italianate operas with English words which offer a context and models for certain aspects of *Acis and Galatea*, has stimulated a doctoral dissertation on Pepusch's theatre music[3] and performances of two of the works in question.[4]

All this amounts to an impressive achievement for a chapter that is only thirty-eight pages long. It is the more impressive, perhaps, when one comes to realize that in certain areas where hard facts were lacking, Dean had to carry forward the argument by intelligent speculation, imaginative empathy and persuasive logic, rather than by conclusive proof. One such area surrounds the mystery of the first performance or performances of the Cannons *Acis and Galatea*. We still do not know the exact date or precise location of the première at Cannons, though Dean's dating of 1718 has now been proved correct. We still have no external evidence to prove or disprove Dean's contention that the work is a practicable masque designed for stage performance. We have no idea who the singers were. No libretto has survived, if indeed one was thought necessary, and we cannot tell how Gay, its principal author, would have set out the words on the printed page, since he died seven years before the first printing of an authentic Handelian libretto in 1739. The all-important conducting score prepared for the Cannons performance of 1718 remains lost; it was presumably the copy that appears in an inventory of the Duke of Chandos's music drawn up by one Noland and signed by Pepusch on 23 August 1720, where it is listed as '"O the pleasure of the plain", a *masque* for five voices and instruments, in score'.[5]

NEW SOURCES; OTHER RECENT WORK

In recent years, however, several early manuscript copies of *Acis and Galatea* have come to light which were unknown or unavailable in 1959 or

3   D. F. Cook, *The Life and Works of Johann Christoph Pepusch (1667–1752), with Special Reference to his Dramatic Works and Cantatas* (unpublished dissertation, University of London, 1983).

4   By Holme Pierrepont Opera, directed by Peter Holman, at Holme Pierrepont Hall, Nottingham: *Venus and Adonis* in 1980 and *The Death of Dido* in 1981, the latter revived at the 1985 Edinburgh Festival.

5   C. H. C. and M. I. Baker, *The Life and Circumstances of James Brydges, First Duke of Chandos* (Oxford, 1949); the list of eighty-nine items is given on pp. 134ff. Brydges was still only Earl of Carnarvon in 1718, but it is convenient to call him Duke of Chandos throughout, and to use the accepted spelling 'Cannons', rather than 'Canons', which was also known.

were not believed to be relevant to the discussion. Six of them form a group with a number of significant variants in common, and four of these were copied in whole or in part by the known Handelian scribes J. C. Smith and RM1. The text which this group transmits does not derive directly from the autograph and evidently must stem from the lost conducting score, so that we now have the exciting possibility of reconstructing it.[6] While I have not seen all these manuscripts myself, and one, the earliest, was not available for me to inspect, enough is known about them for the purpose of the present investigation. Three of the copies mentioned are described in Wolfram Windszus's critical commentary to his forthcoming editions of *Acis and Galatea*, the Italian *Aci, Galatea e Polifemo* and the bilingual *Acis and Galatea* of 1732–41. He published the commentary separately in 1979, in advance of the music text, which is still in the press.[7] The fortunate decision of the *Hallische Händel-Ausgabe* to publish music and commentary together in future volumes has afforded him the opportunity to revise his preface and commentary in order to take account of the remaining three new sources, and I was privileged to examine his splendid new edition before it was sent to the printers. In all cases where I have been able to check, his useful lists of variants, observations on the manuscripts and prints, and elaborate stemma of all known sources have proved extremely accurate. The six manuscripts referred to above are listed in Table 1.[8]

There will be much more to say later on about these sources, the variants that link them and other new evidence that they contain; they tell us a good deal more about the manner of performance and intended genre of *Acis and Galatea* than it was possible to know in 1959. For the moment, the place-name 'London' or 'Londres' in Nos. 1 and 4 deserves comment. Was it the place of copying or composition, or of performance? If the latter, could 'London' include Edgware in Middlesex, where Cannons was

---

[6] At the time of writing, the students in my postgraduate seminar at King's College, London, are about to begin on it.

[7] W. Windszus, *Georg Friedrich Händel: Aci, Galatea e Polifemo, Cantata von 1708; Acis and Galatea, Masque von 1718; Acis and Galatea, italienisch-englische Serenata von 1732: Kritischer Bericht im Rahmen der Hallischen Händel-Ausgabe* (Hamburg, 1979). Henceforth 'Windszus'.

[8] My numbering in Table 1, 1–6, corresponds to Windszus's sources C2, C, C1, D, D1 and F respectively; sources C1, C2 and D1 are not in his published *Bericht* of 1979, but all are in his revised commentary, as yet unpublished; he suggests that my No. 3 may be the conducting score itself, but the date of gift, 1719, suggests that it was copied from the score kept by Pepusch and catalogued by Noland. Windszus describes copyists Kp4, Kp6 and Kp7 on pp. 143f, Kp14 only in the unpublished revised commentary. The date of No. 2 has been tentatively advanced a year or two by Dean, who also points out that No. 1 may be as late as March 1719 if the date 1718 is Old Style: see his essay 'Handel's Early London Copyists', *Bach, Handel, Scarlatti: Tercentenary Essays*, ed. P. Williams (Cambridge, 1985), p. 95; he also (ibid., p. 89) identifies Windszus's Kp4 as RM1.

Table 1 *Six early sources for Acis and Galatea deriving from the conducting score of 1718*

No.	Location	Title	Date	Copyist(s)	Other comments
1	The Earl of Malmesbury's private collection	Acis and Galatea. An English Opera.	Anno 1718. London	RM1, Smith	Autograph *ex-libris*: 'Elizabeth Legh her book 1718'
2	The Gerald Coke Handel Collection	(Acis and Galatea)	[c1719]	Smith	Title not in Smith's hand
3	Washington, Library of Congress M.2.1.H 22.A.3.	(Acis and Galatea)	(1719)	Smith	'Set by Mr Hendel'; 'Ex dono nobilissimi Ducis Chandos 1719'; neither this nor title in Smith's hand
4	Berlin, Staatsbibliothek, Mus. ms. 9042	Opera call'd Acis and Galatea	[c1722?]	RM1, Smith	'Mr Hendel' (Kp4). Front cover label: 'Opera. / Acis et Galatea. / Dell' Sig^r Hendel. / à Londres. 1720.' On spine: 'Hendel / Acis and / Galatea 1721.'
5	Durham Cathedral Library, MS. E.17	——	[after 1722]	Kp14	MS embedding Walsh's print of the songs (1722 or 1725)
6	Manchester Central Library, Henry Watson Music Library, MS 130 Hd4, v. 2	The Pastorall Opera call'd Acis and Galatea	[before 1730]	Kp6, Kp7	'by Mr Hendel'; belonged to Charles Jennens; Aylesford Collection

situated, eleven miles out of the city? To Elizabeth Legh, whose family home was in Cheshire, it may have done. Or could *Acis and Galatea* have been performed at the Duke of Chandos's town house in Albemarle Street, perhaps repeated there after a première at Cannons? One notes, too, the phonetic spelling 'Hendel' repeated in Nos. 3, 4 and 6. Finally, there is the curious diversity in titling, or absence of titling, by the original scribes: this strongly suggests that the exemplar, presumably the conducting score, was a working-copy which, like the autograph, had no title or title-page; and this in turn increases the likelihood that the copy listed by Noland in 1720 (see above, p. 32) was indeed the conducting score and the exemplar for this group of manuscripts. It is worthy of note that, in order to identify the work, Noland used the first words of the first chorus: he must have had to turn over several leaves of the volume, past the opening Sinfonia, in order to find them. The first page evidently did not bear the title *Acis and Galatea*, or he would have used it. It therefore follows that he almost certainly did not find the designation 'masque' written there either, and that we owe the choice of it to him and not to the manuscript he was describing.

The date 1718 on the Malmesbury title-page, confirmed by its owner, was originally reported by Terence Best;[9] it leads us quite naturally into a recapitulation of the new archival and literary evidence, for it tallies perfectly with the date of composition suggested by a letter of 27 May 1718, first published by its finder, Henry T. Dickinson,[10] and communicated to the world of musical scholarship by Patrick Rogers.[11] The letter is addressed to Hugh Campbell, 3rd Earl of Loudoun, by Sir David Dalrymple and follows a visit he paid to Cannons between 24 and 27 May; he speaks of 'a little opera now a makeing', which can only be *Acis and Galatea*,[12] with words by Pope and Gay and music by Handel and some contribution coming also from the poets' great friend Dr John Arbuthnot, 'who is one of the club of composers'; the opera is intended for the Duke of Chandos's private diversion and its music will not be made public; the work is 'as good as finished'. A further development on the literary front is the inclusion of *Acis and Galatea* in the new edition of Gay's dramatic works by John Fuller.[13] This contains valuable introductory comments and notes, together with the interesting observation that the 'Argument' prefacing the 1732 version of the libretto by Thomas Arne, father of the composer (printed by John Watts), was lifted from Motteux's libretto for

9   Letter in *The Musical Times*, cxiii (1972), p. 43.
10 In *The Scriblerian*, v (Spring 1973), p. 118.
11 'Dating "Acis and Galatea"', *The Musical Times*, cxiv (1973), p. 792.
12 This point is to be discussed in a further article. See below, p. 93.
13 *John Gay: Dramatic Works*, ed. J. Fuller (Oxford, 1983), pp. 265–76; cf. Introduction, pp. 32–5.

John Eccles's *Acis and Galatea*, first performed in 1701 (this had been reprinted by James Roberts in 1723). Unfortunately, however, the editor has used the unauthentic Arne libretto for his basic text, relegating most of the readings of Handel's 1739 libretto, along with variants from the autograph, to footnotes. If Arne's stage directions had made better dramatic sense, one would not have minded Fuller's choice so much.

ACIS AND GALATEA AS ORIGINALLY PERFORMED

It is not yet possible to say whether all of the scores listed in Table 1 were copied individually from the conducting score or whether certain of them depend upon an intermediary. Five of their common variants are nevertheless worth recording here. They are noted in Windszus's revised commentary, except for some from the Malmesbury manuscript, which neither he nor I have been able to consult directly; I am most grateful to Terence Best and Winton Dean for information about the copy, and to Anthony Hicks for kindly checking many details for me. The numbering of items in the score of *Acis and Galatea*, which corresponds with that of the arias in Windszus's forthcoming edition, is as follows:

1	Sinfonia	12a	Whither, Fairest
2	O the Pleasure of the Plains	13	Cease to Beauty
3	Ye verdant Plains	14	Would you gain
4	Hush, ye pretty warb'ling Choir	14a	His hideous Love
5	Where shall I find	15	Love sounds the Alarm
5a	Stay, Shepherd	16	Consider, fond Shepherd
6	Shepherd, what art thou pursuing?	16a	Cease, O cease
6a	Lo! here, my Love	17	The Flocks shall leave
7	Love in her Eyes sits playing	18	Help, Galatea
7a	O didst thou know	19	Mourn all ye Muses
8	As when the Dove	20	Must I my Acis still bemoan?
9	Happy, happy, happy we	20a	'Tis done
10	Wretched Lovers	21	Heart, the Seat of soft Delight
11	I rage, I melt	22	Galatea, dry thy Tears
12	O ruddier than the Cherry		

1.   In arias Nos. 4 and 12, 'Flauto picc(i)olo octavo' or 'Flauto octavo' is specified, confirming Dean's opinion that the upper octave was intended.[14]

2.   In the dialogue No. 20 for Galatea and male voice ensemble, the Basso line at the beginning is marked 'Fagotto e violoncello', providing as one might expect a woodwind bass for the oboe solo.

3.   In the accompanied recitative No. 11 – except in the Malmesbury manuscript – the phrases 'feeble god' and 'god-like steps' are replaced by 'feeble boy' and 'portly steps'. Dean had been inclined to attribute this bowdlerization to

---

[14]   Dean, pp. 77, 163.

the Rochetti benefit of 1731;[15] but it was already present in Walsh's print of the songs in 1722. Its absence from the Malmesbury copy may suggest that the alteration was entered into the conducting score after the first performances, for some later revival mounted by Chandos.

4.   The aria No. 14 is ascribed to 'Coridon. Ten: 3' (in the Malmesbury manuscript to 'Coridon. 3. Tenor'), a baptism hitherto known only from non-Handelian sources and therefore believed to be unauthentic, deriving from the Rochetti benefit.[16]

5.   In the chorus No. 19 and the dialogue No. 20, the usual part-designations Canto, Tenor 1–3 and Basso are omitted; in their place appear the names of the five dramatis personae in the order Galatea, Acis, Damon, Coridon, Polyphemus. In the other choruses, Nos. 2, 10 and 22, the usual part-designations are given. In the Malmesbury copy, however, the scribe RM1 has added all the characters' names except Coridon's to the appropriate lines of the first chorus; Miss Legh, the owner, who may conceivably have seen a performance or questioned those who had, has inserted Coridon's and went on to add all five names in the remaining choruses, Nos. 10 and 20.

These last two sets of variants are of great interest. Winton Dean had persuasively argued 'that at Cannons Handel had only one voice to a part' in the choruses, and thought it possible that Galatea sang the choral canto part throughout (it employs the same compass and is in the same clef); but he also believed that 'the high first tenor part seems to have been intended for a countertenor'.[17] Of course, had he known that the aria No. 14 was sung by a third tenor named Coridon, the coincidence that the five soloists' vocal ranges were identical with those of the five choristers would not have escaped him. Even without that, he began his discussion of the chamber-music *Acis and Galatea* by observing that the work 'could be given in full – though hardly on the stage – with a grand total of a dozen performers, five singers and seven instrumentalists'.[18] Before looking into the implications of his no doubt regretful parenthesis, we ought to examine points 4 and 5 above a little more closely.

First, it is curious that Coridon is called 'Tenor 3' in his aria No. 14. It can refer only to the third tenor part in the choral line-up. Presumably the aria had been written for the third tenor chorister – a soloist, as evidently the others must also have been – before a name had been invented for him. (The aria is missing from the autograph, though Handel added the cue 'NB aria' at the end of No. 13.) Second, we need to consider whether RM1 and Miss Legh were entitled to add the characters' names to the vocal lines in choruses Nos. 2, 10 and 22 or whether it was only Nos. 19 and 20 that Handel had intended to be sung by the named characters. The process of

15   Ibid., p. 186.
16   Loc. cit.; Smith, pp. 210f.
17   Dean, p. 169.
18   Ibid., p. 169.

extending the principle seems logical enough. There is no greater dramatic implausibility involved in the five characters' singing Nos. 2, 10 and 22 than is already involved in their singing Nos. 19 and 20, where Acis must mourn his own death and advise Galatea about his own apotheosis, seconded by his rival and murderer, Polyphemus. The autograph bears only the usual part-designations in the choruses (though Handel entered, but deleted, the names of three tenor soloists in the first chorus): if the name 'Coridon' was invented only at the last moment, the scribe of the lost conducting score may well have started by copying the normal part-designations in the opening chorus, come to realize after copying aria No. 14 that he now had a full complement of named dramatis personae, substituted all their five names for the part-designations in the next two choruses that he copied, Nos. 19 and 20, but may have forgotten to do the same in the final chorus. In the Malmesbury score, RM1 started to complete the process (but did not know or could not remember Coridon's name when he copied the first chorus), and Miss Legh finished the job.

The possibility remains that the soloists may have been reinforced by further choristers, but in view of Dean's observations on vocal/instrumental balance, that seems unlikely. We know from surviving performance material prepared for the oratorios that the chorus parts were copied into the soloists' scores, presumably so that they could if necessary lead the chorus voices.[19] I know of no case, however, where lines allotted in the score to soloists were also taken up by choristers without the addition of further performance-directions.

What would a fully staged production of *Acis and Galatea* have been like, if the intentions apparently expressed in the conducting score were strictly followed? With the choruses sung by the five dramatis personae (and I shall later adduce other arguments that this was Handel's original purpose), Galatea, Acis and Polyphemus would have had to switch between their roles as characters and their roles as choral commentators in a manner that would sometimes have conflicted with the normal standards of verisimilitude expected in contemporary opera and masque. Since the earliest descriptions of the Cannons version ascribe the work to both of these genres, we have a problem here. It was no normal opera or masque. We may approach the problem in five stages. We need first of all to review the dramatic implausibilities and see what possible compromise solutions might obviate them; secondly, to investigate a non-Handelian manuscript score which solves the problems; thirdly, to look again at what is known of the Rochetti and Arne productions, both of which were given in a theatre; fourthly, to reconsider Handel's reaction to these and to the revivals of *Esther* in 1732, relating his methods of presentation to the terminology that

[19]   Cf. ibid., p. 430.

he employed in introducing his own performances; and finally, to return to the Cannons *Acis and Galatea* with a clearer notion of the genre to which it seems to have belonged and the conventions which seem to have governed its original performance.

DRAMATIC VERISIMILITUDE; COMPROMISE SOLUTIONS

Before discussing the acting, it is worth mentioning the scenic difficulties of staging *Acis and Galatea*. They are of an order that only an experienced operatic scene-designer, working with the resources of a professional theatre, could have been expected to solve. One of the characters is a giant, who throws a massive rock at Acis and completely crushes him; Acis's blood flows out from beneath the rock but changes to clear fresh water; the rock then splits to reveal the source of a stream, out of which climbs the metamorphosed Acis as a river-god, with horns on his brow from which reedy wreaths depend, and holding an urn from which the new river's waters flow. All this might have been managed at Cannons, especially if the performance took place out of doors among the elaborate basins and water-works that adorned the gardens. But the really important point about the scenic requirements is that they have to be deduced entirely from the words of the dialogue. They are not present in the scores, nor is any reference to the actors' movements. It is very strange, if *Acis and Galatea* was intended to be staged at Cannons, that no Handelian source appears to be known which contains either scene descriptions or stage directions; even the basic numbering of rehearsal scenes giving the characters' entrances, and the usual indication 'exit', are missing. Yet we find them in abundance in the dramatic oratorios and in *Semele* and *Hercules*, often in greater detail in Handel's autographs than in the librettos. We do find stage directions in the Arne libretto of 1732. They are at times extremely inept and can hardly have come from Gay or Handel: Galatea, for example, remains off-stage when Acis sings 'See, at thy Feet the longing *Acis* lies', and for the whole of the ensuing aria, 'Love in her Eyes sits playing'.

Ineptitude, however, is not necessarily the same thing as implausibility. In attempting to stage *Acis and Galatea* with only five solo singers and with a plausible degree of verisimilitude, one can solve most of the problems only by various hair-raisingly quick changes of costume. It is simple enough, using a modern convention, to present Galatea as a happy but anonymous pastoral nymph in the opening chorus – she must not yet see Acis, nor he her – and to robe her in a wave-coloured mantle before she sings the first recitative in her own character; it is no great problem that she sings about herself in the third person in the final chorus. Polyphemus has greater difficulties: he can start and finish as a binocular shepherd, but must dash off-stage in the few seconds between the end of 'Wretched

Lovers' and the following recitative to don a shaggy cloak, wig, single eye-piece and 'lifts' and to snatch up his pine staff and panpipe, shedding them all later while Acis dies. Acis himself faces us with the greatest problem. Provided that a statue or an extra is used to personate his apotheosis as river-god, Acis has to leave the stage – with no black-out possible – either before his dying recitative No. 18 (singing it from the wings) or after it, and thereafter must either sing Tenor 1 from off-stage during three choruses or re-emerge differently costumed as an unexplained supernumerary shep-herd who looks suspiciously like the river-god. Alternatively, he may become the river-god (there is ample time to change), and an extra (and still unexplained) singer must then take Tenor 1 in the last three choruses. All this is possible, as I know from direct experience,[20] and a modern audience, with a little goodwill, has no insuperable difficulty in swallowing such expedients; but they lack the dignity and stylishness of a consistent stage convention, and run the risk of evoking unwanted laughter – and would have in 1718. This can of course all be avoided, either by the use of a separate body of singers for the chorus or by replacing at least Polyphemus and Acis with two further solo choristers, a bass and a high tenor.

A STAGEABLE ADAPTATION OF *ACIS AND GALATEA*

This is exactly what has been provided for in the curious arrangement of *Acis and Galatea* that we find in British Library Add. MS 36710. It is a non-Handelian manuscript, copied in an unknown and rather amateurish hand, and is at present impossible to date, though it seems fairly early. The original cover bears the legend 'The Score of Mr. Handle's Pastoral' ['An Original Copy', deleted] 'The First Compleat Score that ever was wrote out' – untrue, for, as Windszus points out, it descends from the lost conducting score, though altering the words and even the instrumentation in places.[21] It ascribes the verses to Pope. After an elaborate explanation of the mythological background and a full transcript of Ovid's tale in Dryden's version, there is a description on folio 8 of the 'Persons consarn^d in the vocal performance of the ffollowing musick', which indeed matches what appears in the score itself. Galatea is to sing the treble throughout, in the choruses too. 'The first Tennor is appropriated to Acis till he is kill^d, & then, the ffollowing part is suppos^d to be perform^d by young Pallemon, an intimate friend & Shepherd of their Sociaty.' Damon sings second Tenor, 'a shepherd also & particular ffriend & associate, who is very free of, (& louder in) his advice to Acis & Gallatea'. 'Corridon' sings Tenor 3, 'another shepherd also & jntimate friend & aquaintance, he not only Gives Good

20   Directing performances at the Athens Festival in 1979 and the English Bach Festival (London) in 1980.
21   Windszus's source H, pp. 102–4.

Advice to Acis & Gallatea but also even to Pollyphemus himself for their sakes'. Polyphemus sings only where he appears in his own character; otherwise 'The Basse . . . is perform^d by Strephon, another of the same class & particular ffriend . . . and after the Death (or rather transformation) of Acis, Strephon resumes the Basse part again.'

The manuscript introduces a certain number of stage directions;[22] but even if it had not, the creation of two new characters by dividing up the roles of Acis and Polyphemus would have been undertaken only by somebody wishing to make possible a full theatrical performance with seven solo singers. This is emphasized by the fact that the opening chorus may retain a wording that was once in the lost conducting score, with a singular 'plain', as noted by Noland (though Noland's 'pleasure' was also singular): 'O the pleasures of the plain', it reads, which of course continues 'Happy nymph and happy swain', denoting the single hero and heroine, Acis and Galatea. This adaptation demonstrates how an anonymous contemporary of Handel's faced and solved the problems posed by applying normal standards of theatrical verisimilitude to a production of *Acis and Galatea* which was to employ only solo voices throughout in the most economical way possible. For whom was it designed? Neither text nor distribution of roles matches the libretto for the Arne production of 1732; Arne divided the work rather unsuitably into three acts, whereas it is here presented as one continuous whole. No other early theatrical performance of *Acis and Galatea* is recorded, except perhaps the Rochetti benefit of 1731, for which we have no libretto or other direct evidence that it was actually staged. William C. Smith associated Add. MS 36710 with Rochetti's performance, though probably for the wrong reason, the mention in both of 'Coridon', whom we now recognize as an authentically Handelian character.[23] But his suggestion fits the known facts for another reason.

The Rochetti benefit performance

It is a tempting coincidence that Rochetti's first advertisement in *The Daily Journal* for 13 March 1731 should have announced a performance by seven singers: 'Acis by Mr. Rochetti; Galatea, Mrs. Wright; Polypheme, Mr. Leveridge; and the other Parts by Mr. Legar, Mr. Salway, Mrs. Carter, and

---

22 'The order & method of the performance' tells us that 'Pollyphemus appears at a distance' in No. 10, that in No. 16 'Damon endeavers to diswaide Acis from his resolution of engaging in Battle with Pollyphemus', and that in No. 20 Galatea 'is Join^d by her four friends, perswading her to cease to Grieve'; in the musical text of the trio No. 15, we read: 'here Polyphemus begins his song interrupting them but they keep on as not seeing or not minding him'.

23 Smith, 'Verzeichnis der Werke Georg Friedrich Händels', *Händel-Jahrbuch*, 2nd ser., ii (1956), p. 148.

Mr. Papillion'.[24] The performance was, however, delayed from 17 to 26 March, as the same notice allows us to conclude; and two days later Rochetti advertised a cast from which the otherwise unknown Mrs Carter and Mr Papillion have vanished. Singers, then as now, were no doubt inclined to make a fuss about their publicity (or lack of it), and the omission looks very like the consequence of a change of plan associated with the nine-day postponement, rather than a mere oversight. The new advertisement names only five characters, exactly those required in the lost Cannons conducting score in place of the seven specified by Add. MS 36710; to the first three principals are added 'Coridon, Mr. Legar; Damon, Mr. Salway'. There is no mention of any Chorus in the advertisement. Since Arne's later publicity in 1732, as we shall see, makes a particular feature out of the 'Grand Chorus's' and equally out of the fact that his own production of Acis and Galatea was 'the first Time it ever was performed in a Theatrical way', it is a reasonable deduction that he was trying to over-trump Rochetti's efforts in both respects. Rochetti's advertisements do not promise a full staging of the 'Pastoral', though they do not deny one either: they simply say that it 'will be presented'. It seems likely that he had originally hoped to act it with full theatrical verisimilitude, without chorus but with seven solo singers, but that he gave up this plan, perhaps because the formidable scenic difficulties were too much for his budget; at least, he seems to have reverted to a performance without full illusion, and with the choruses sung as solo ensembles, using only five singers instead of the seven that he would otherwise have needed. My hypothesis would make sense of the evidence independently of the possible association of Add. 36710 with Rochetti's performance. The solution that the score offers could have occurred to any competent man of the theatre and we may note in passing that it must surely be significant that Handel himself seems never to have felt the need for it. In either case, Mr Papillion would have needed to be a bass in order to take over Strephon's functions; and Mrs Carter would have been a contralto, taking 'young Pallemon's' high tenor part in the last three choruses and leaving the singer of Acis free to change costume and appear as the river-god. A contralto Pallemon is not far-fetched: in the published score, Handel himself altered the clef of the first tenor part of the last chorus to contralto, without changing any of the notes; in No. 19 the part also lies in a high tessitura; in No. 20 Mrs Carter might conceivably have taken the second tenor, which for much of the time keeps higher than the first.

---

[24]   The advertisements are given in Smith, pp. 209f. A Mrs Carter was in charge of the women dressers at the Lincoln's Inn Fields theatre in 1724–5: see E. L. Avery, *The London Stage 1660–1800*, Part 2: *1700–1729* (Carbondale, 1960), i, p. lxvii.

THE ARNE PERFORMANCES

The sequence of advertisements for the Arne performances of 1732, interestingly enough, offers a similar picture of disorganization.[25] Again we have a postponement, which again may be connected with a significant alteration in the wording. The preliminary puff in *The Daily Post* for 2 May says 'that the Proprietors of the English Opera will very shortly perform a celebrated Pastoral Opera call'd Acis and Galatea . . . with all the Grand Chorus's and other Decorations, as it was perform'd before his Grace the Duke of Chandos, at Cannons; and that it is now in Rehearsal'. The exact nature of the presentation of the 'opera' is not spelt out. The 'Grand Chorus's' receive special mention, since they have not yet been published or heard in public except as solo ensembles, if I am right, in the Rochetti performance.[26] The choruses seem also to be considered as one of the visual attractions of the piece as presented at Cannons, since the phrase runs 'with all the Grand Chorus's *and other Decorations*'. Handel's advertisement for his own concert performance of 24 March 1732 was also careful to say that the chorus of nymphs and shepherds would be 'dispos'd amongst a Rural Prospect of Rocks, Grotto's, &c.'.

Arne's first performance, at the New Theatre in the Haymarket, was advertised for 11 May in the newspapers on 6 and 8 May and on the 10th, the very eve of the première. But on 11 and 12 May the advertisements announced a postponement of six days to 17 May, 'it being impossible to get ready the Decorations before that time'. On 6 May, however, five days before the original date fixed for the first night, the terms of the advertisement had already changed. The work is to be given 'in English', presumably to obviate misunderstandings arising from that fact that Handel's Italian operas were advertised with English titles, e.g. *Julius Caesar* for *Giulio Cesare*. More significant, however, are (*a*) the addition of scenes (in the plural) and theatrical machines to the wording, (*b*) the claim that this is to be the first theatrical production, and (*c*) the simultaneous banishment of the phrase 'as it was perform'd before his Grace the Duke of Chandos'. The passage now reads: 'With all the Grand Chorus's, Scenes, Machines, and other Decorations; being the first time it ever was performed in a Theatrical Way'. It is possible, as Dean thought, that the words 'Scenes, Machines' had been inadvertently omitted from the notices of 2 and 3 May and that 'in a Theatrical Way' means 'in a regular opera season';[27] but it is perhaps more likely that the wording means what it

---

25 For the advertisements, see Smith, pp. 212ff.
26 The Grand Choruses were taken by more than one voice to a part in the Arne production, since a stage direction speaks of 'Shepherds and Shepherdesses' and there is only one part for female voice; but the term need not imply this, since it is also used for all the choruses in Add. MS 36710, which are solo ensembles.
27 Dean, p. 172.

appears to say, and that the changes reflect a change of plan.

The printed libretto was advertised for sale on the day of the original première, 11 May, and contains a bookseller's advertisement of the same date; it must have been set up in type a few days beforehand. If there were a late change of plan – causing the alterations in the wording of the notices from 6 May and the postponement announced at the last moment on 11 May, the very day of the first performance – then there would quite possibly have been no time to alter the libretto to incorporate any consequential amendments. This in fact seems to be the case. The libretto contains no scene descriptions or changes of scene, though it divides the work into three acts, and the very features which would have required elaborate machines appear to have been deliberately removed. Acis goes off-stage before the end of the trio No. 17, and Polyphemus kills him, therefore, by hurling his 'massy ruin' off-stage after him. '*Polyphemus* kills *Acis* with a great Stone, which he gathers from a Rock'; this done, 'Enter ACIS, supported by SHEPHERDS', to sing his dying words, after which he apparently remains on-stage as a defiantly un-crushed corpse. When we come to Galatea's aria No. 21, the words which describe the splitting of the rock and the gushing of the new river's spring have been omitted ('Rock, thy hollow Womb disclose; the bubling Fountain, lo, it flows!').[28]

[28]   Ibid., p. 183. Handel himself cut this passage in 1734, because the aria, which now followed the opening chorus (!), had an Italian text which necessarily omitted the recitative section. Windszus has retrieved the basso continuo part from British Library Egerton MS 2953, which agrees with a note in the autograph showing that bars 25–30 were to be replaced. It is possible to reconstruct a soprano line, which like the new bass seems to have derived from the original. The Italian text in the example is Handel's; the English shows how Arne might have dealt with the same passage.

Is this another error, or is it a deliberate simplification? It seems more likely that Arne *père* had originally planned the very bare and artificial kind of staging that the libretto suggests, falling short of complete theatrical illusion in certain respects, and that he may quite possibly have believed that he was reproducing the work more or less 'as it was perform'd before his Grace the Duke of Chandos, at Cannons'. He would have had a pastoral backcloth and no doubt costumes, such as Handel himself was to employ for his own concert performances of the bilingual *Acis and Galatea* less than a month later at the King's Theatre; unlike Handel though, he intended to use realistic acting, with the characters making the sometimes rather oddly timed exits and entrances indicated in the libretto. He used a chorus, though Handel had not, to make the piece theatrically viable. Coridon therefore became superfluous, so he allotted his air No. 14, 'Would you gain the tender Creature', to Damon (a lady, in this version); while this saved a soloist's fee, it turned Damon into something of a hypocrite, since he twice urges Acis to give up his immoderate passion for Galatea, but now, taking over Coridon's aria, he has to tell Polyphemus merely to adopt different tactics in pursuit of even more reprehensible desires. (Handel, nevertheless, eventually decided to effect the same economy and the same upward transposition.) As rehearsals proceeded – the work was 'now in rehearsal' on 2 May – Arne realized that something more was possible, indeed desirable, if he were to eclipse Rochetti's evidently sub-theatrical performance; and so he decided to attempt full theatrical illusion, with 'Scenes and Machines'. The resulting complications would have tested his knowledge of carpentry; upholsterer though he was, he was new to the theatre. Hence the delay; but he had achieved, if I am right, and at the cost of only six days' postponement, a remarkable theatrical 'first'. Would he really have dared to advertise the occasion as 'the first Time [*Acis and Galatea*] ever was performed in a Theatrical Way' if the work had in fact been so performed at Cannons, when there were so many persons living, including Handel and the Duke of Chandos himself, who could have given him the lie?

HANDEL'S PERFORMANCES

Neither Handel nor anyone else gave him the lie, which suggests, in that age of theatrical wars and Grub Street tittle-tattle, that Arne was telling the truth. Instead, as is well known, Handel used his Italian opera company to mount a rather large-scale concert performance of a composite work which mingled music from *Acis and Galatea*, much of it translated into Italian, with music from his Neapolitan *Aci, Galatea e Polifemo* of 1708, together with pieces from yet other sources and a little new composition. He performed it on the stage of a theatre, but expressly warned his public, almost as if he were reproaching Arne, that there would be 'no Action on the Stage'. This was almost exactly how, just over a month earlier, he had mounted his revival of *Esther*, which is also thought to have been a response to a pirate performance. The presentation of *Esther* had been received with some astonishment, at least by the author of the anonymous pamphlet *See and Seem Blind*: 'a mere Consort, no Scenary, Dress or Action, so necessary to a Drama . . .'[29] Perhaps that is why the concert *Acis and Galatea* paid more attention to the visual appearance of the proceedings. With the revival of *Esther*, Handel had introduced the London public to the static manner of presenting sacred musical drama familiar in the Italian tradition, for which he employed the appropriate term, 'oratorio'. In the case of his polyglot *Acis and Galatea* he introduced them to the Italian manner of presenting secular dramatic music in the same way, and again employed the correct and even more unfamiliar genre-title, 'serenata'.

It has been thought, because so much of the music came from what appears to have been an Italian serenata, and many of the items from *Acis and Galatea* were sung in Italian, that what had been a 'masque' or 'opera' was now extinguished in a serenata.[30] As with many Baroque terms, however, it is the manner (and originally place and time) of performance that helps to define a serenata: if Handel's performance in the King's Theatre on 10 June 1732 had consisted solely of the Cannons *Acis and Galatea*, given in costume and in front of a painted scene (as it was), but without entrances, exits or any action beyond what was possible with the characters holding books in their hands (as they no doubt did), then an Italian visitor would still have called it a serenata.[31] Handel's concert-fashion revivals of the English *Acis and Galatea* from 1739–42 were of a very similar nature; the singers were probably not costumed, but at least the theatre performances would have had some kind of decorative

29   For passages from the pamphlet, see O. E. Deutsch, *Handel, a Documentary Biography* (London, 1955/R1974), pp. 300f.
30   Dean simply says that the title serenata was 'transferred' from the Italian one of 1708: p. 159.
31   See below, pp. 49f.

backdrop behind them; and he was essentially correct in calling them serenatas. Walsh translated the term into English for his fourth edition of the songs (1739), which was advertised on 13 December as 'a Serenade (as it is now perform'd)'. Walsh had called the work an opera or masque ('mask') in his earlier editions, but the only instance where Handel is likely to have directly sanctioned the public use of one of these titles, 'masque', was for the concert performances in 1742 in provincial Dublin, where the term 'serenata' was probably still unfamiliar; in any case, many elements in the libretto in question seem to have been derived from a non-Handelian exemplar of 1741, so that the title 'masque' may also have been taken from it.[32] The full score of *Acis and Galatea* that Walsh issued in 1743 was, it is true, advertised as a 'Masque' and published as a 'Mask'; Windszus has demonstrated, however, that Walsh's copy-text was British Library Add. MS 5321, which lacks a contemporary title;[33] this leaves open the possibility that the publisher may have invented his own title and reverted to the more familiar designation that had been preferred in the 1720s.

No other work of Handel's ever attracted such a bewildering number of different designations as *Acis and Galatea*, as Dean's discussion shows.[34] Besides 'opera' (variously qualified), 'masque' or 'mask', and 'serenata', or 'serenade', it crops up as 'pastoral', 'pastoral entertainment', 'bucolic poem', 'musical entertainment', simply as 'music', 'entertainment', or 'story', or even as 'oratorio', which last we can certainly agree that it was not. A satisfactory explanation of its correct genre would not only have to 'place' it convincingly but also to explain why so many people, many of them no doubt musically literate, clearly did not know what to call it. (Very few, of course, had been privileged to attend a private performance of the Cannons version.) If its genre was not self-evident, that could only have been because that genre's characteristics and name were not widely known. We must therefore consider seriously the claims of 'serenata' as the correct designation for the original version. The term and its Italian traditions were known to few in England before Handel himself popularized them. The earliest reference to the Italianate usage of the word in the *Oxford English Dictionary* is dated as late as 1743 (Boyce's *Solomon*); I have, however, found it in the preface that the poet John Hughes contributed for Pepusch's *Six English Cantatas*, published in 1710.[35]

32 Dean, p. 187; Windszus, p. 138.
33 Windszus, p. 106.
34 Dean, pp. 159f.
35 The anonymous author of *A Critical Discourse Upon Operas in England and a Means Proposed for Their Improvement* in F. Raguenet, *A Comparison Between the French and Italian Musick and Opera's, Translated from the French, with Some Remarks* (London, 1709/*R*1968 with Introduction by C. Cudworth), p. 74, complains that an Italian pastoral drama, originally given as a concert-cum-puppet-show, was adapted for the stage 'without considering it was Originally Design'd to be Sung in a Room, with the

Hughes (who has a verse in *Acis and Galatea*) was a well-informed musician, anxious to naturalize Italianate music in England by providing good English texts for it; and the cantata is very close to the serenata.

CANNONS REVISITED

The time has come to return to the question of the original manner of performance at Cannons. If Handel had staged *Acis and Galatea* with a separate body of choristers, or with two extra soloists after the model of Add. MS 36710, then it could have been performed with full observance of the prevailing norms of theatrical verisimilitude, and its proper title would have been 'opera' or 'masque'. These, together with the neutral 'pastoral', are indeed the earliest designations known. 'Serenata' does not appear before 1732; though it alone unquestionably enjoys the direct authority of Handel, he applied it to two later recensions of the music, the earlier very different indeed from the Cannons version, in circumstances where the static nature of the performance would in itself have justified the use of the term. There is no evidence, beyond the early descriptions 'opera' and 'masque', that he staged the work at Cannons with full theatrical illusion; and the placing of the five characters' names in the six early manuscripts deriving from the conducting score suggests a performance with the dramatis personae themselves singing the choruses, which would in fact mean that he employed the sub-theatrical convention of the serenata. We now know a great deal more about the serenata than it was possible to know in 1959, and it will be worth setting out its conventions more fully.

THE SERENATA CONVENTION

Thomas Edward Griffin's article 'Serenata' in *The New Grove* provides a convenient but very short summary of the state of our knowledge on the subject in the late 1970s.[36] More recent and much more detailed information is now available in Michael Talbot's magnificent pioneering analysis of a great number of Venetian serenatas of the seventeenth and eighteenth centuries; though he keeps to the repertory of one area, his findings appear to tally with the developments noted in brief by Griffin.[37] The present short account borrows gratefully from both publications. It

parts in the Singers Hands, and not to be Perform'd off hand on a Theatre; and since the Styles proper for the Chamber and the Stage are perfectly different, it was impossible it cou'd have any good Effect'. This was in 1708 and shows understanding of the characteristics of the smaller serenata, though the author does not name the genre. See also Deutsch, *Handel*, p. 125, for a Scarlatti serenata advertised in 1721.

[36]   *The New Grove*, xvii, pp. 160ff.

[37]   M. Talbot, 'The Serenata in Eighteenth-Century Venice', *R.M.A. Research Chronicle*, xviii (1982), pp. 1–50.

will be seen that *Acis and Galatea*, performed as the lost conducting score seems to have prescribed, corresponds well with many of the features listed below.

Nomenclature. Burney describes serenatas as 'cantatas of considerable length' for 'several singers'. The commonest designations are 'cantata' and 'serenata', the latter preferred in Venice until c1720; a great variety of other names were also used, mostly of literary derivation, such as 'festa teatrale', 'festeggio armonico', 'componimento di camera', 'componimento musicale', 'poemetto dramatico', 'favoletta drammatica' and 'applauso genetliaco' (a birthday tribute); 'pastorale' also occurs, though rarely, since in Venice it normally signified an opera.

Characters. There were normally at least two characters and most commonly three or four; more were possible. They are nearly always gods, mythological herocs, allegorical figures, or pastoral Arcadians such as we find in cantatas and pastoral operas; there are also personifications of places, rivers or natural objects. Historical characters are extremely rare.

Length. The serenata was longer than a solo cantata but shorter than an opera; its duration varied from a single 'round' of arias for each character, followed by an ensemble, to the equivalent of two acts of an opera, with twenty or even twenty-five arias. Many serenatas are continuous, but there is often a division into two and occasionally into three parts; the commonest is the two-part division also characteristic of the oratorio.

Words. These were in verse, using the same techniques as in opera, cantata and oratorio, sometimes with greater sophistication than in opera; there were shorter recitatives and more da capo arias than was normal in opera. Often written hurriedly for special occasions by local poets, librettos were nevertheless often printed, no doubt as a keepsake commemorating an occasion or honouring a guest.

Occasion. Usually serenatas were occasional pieces, often prepared at short notice, designed to honour or entertain a noble personage or visiting dignitary, or to grace a state occasion. Crescimbeni, describing the Roman scene around 1700, had heard many 'given with great magnificence and splendour by ambassadors and other princes and personages of this great court'. Very few serenatas did not form part of some larger festivity: they were frequently performed during or after a banquet, often followed by a ball at which the same musicians played the dances.

Time and place of performing. Normally they were given at night and often in the open air, as the name suggests, with artificial lighting. Very few were performed in theatres. A stage or 'theatre for a day' might be constructed in a garden, courtyard or public square, often over a canal or river, both drama and music exploiting the surroundings; indoor performances were usually in banqueting-halls and ballrooms.

Presentation. 'They are performed, like oratorios, without change of scene, or action' (Burney). Only the very few given in theatres were sometimes acted. The librettos lack scene changes, scene divisions indicating entrances, and exit markings. Scenery was employed, usually as a decorative backing, and sometimes moving machines (as in oratorio), though in Venice these were less common by the eighteenth century. The singers wore quasi-theatrical costume but normally held their music-books in their hands and did not move about or make entrances and exits. This convention may in part owe its origin to the frequent lack of notice in preparing a serenata, which left little time for memorizing or rehearsal by singers who would often have been hired specially for the occasion; but it was also the normal procedure in an oratorio, of which the serenata was in some ways a kind of secular equivalent. Since the music was occasional (and the occasion often private), it was ephemeral and rarely published, and the songs did not normally find their way into general circulation.

Chorus and orchestra. Only the grandest serenatas used a chorus; the orchestra was sometimes very large, with spectacular effects.

ACIS AND GALATEA AS A SERENATA

From the above, we can easily perceive why Handel called his 1732 *Acis and Galatea* a serenata, quite apart from the fact that *Aci, Galatea e Polifemo* seems also to have been a serenata, composed for a wedding. What of the Cannons version? The lack of total realism characteristic of the serenata convention, which allowed limited acting but also permitted the soloists to combine more artificially into an ensemble, would have favoured a performance on the lines set out in the lost conducting score. There would probably have been a pastoral back-scene, as in 1732, perhaps recalling Claude Lorrain's famous painting of Acis, Galatea and Polyphemus, now in Dresden.[38] There could have been machinery, in a different plane from the actors, to depict the flying rock and the apotheosis, particularly if the performance were out of doors: the basins and fountains must surely have boasted a river-god or two among their statuary. The puzzle over the varied nomenclature may in part be explained by English unfamiliarity with the genre, in part by the variety characteristic of the genre itself. *Acis and Galatea* has five characters (though originally only three were planned, as I hope to demonstrate) and, as was normal in the serenata, no chorus. The cast are shepherds, divinities and demigods, and Acis is a personification of a river. The work as eventually completed lasts about as long as two acts of an opera. Originally planned as a continuous whole of about two-thirds the present length, a division was introduced (even in the Cannons version, though it is not marked as such) between the duet No. 9

[38]   'Coastal View with Acis and Galatea' (1657), Gemäldegalerie, Dresden.

and the chorus 'Wretched Lovers', No. 10.[39] The verse resembles that of the London theatre masques of 1715–18 or, at its best, that of Addison's *Rosamond* and Congreve's *The Judgement of Paris* or *Semele*; it evinces remarkable variety (as we shall see) but also betrays signs of haste. The recitatives are exceptionally short; nearly all are rhymed, unlike the *versi sciolti* of Italian recitative.[40]

Of the occasion for *Acis and Galatea* we know nothing; the conferral of Chandos's dukedom would have provided a suitable occasion; but in spite of massive bribes it was long delayed, and he did not receive it until April 1719, when the work might appropriately have been repeated. A performance of *Acis and Galatea* would very likely have formed part of a larger festivity such as the 'Masquerade' for which the Duchess of Chandos sent Lady Buck two tickets in 1720, at which the work might well have been revived. (The masquerades at the opera-house regularly began with a serious concert of opera music by the Academy singers and orchestra, after which the orchestra played for the dancing.)[41] The lack of a surviving libretto (perhaps lost by chance) and the printing of the songs in 1722 reverse the usual situation; but the libretto pays no overt compliments to a distinguished person, and the music is of quite exceptional quality and by London's leading composer. The autograph and other scores of *Acis and Galatea* and the later Handelian librettos lack scene descriptions, scene changes, scene numberings and stage directions; Handel's 1732 libretto for the composite *Acis and Galatea* does, however, start, like many an oratorio libretto, with a scene description. The singers on that occasion wore 'Habits . . . suited to the Subject', and the singers at Cannons may have done so too. An untypical note, though not without parallels, is the smallness of the orchestra compared with the serenatas of both 1708 and 1732; this may partly be explained by the size of the duke's band of musicians before he expanded it in 1719 but probably owes much, as I shall explain, to Pope's view of what was fitting in a pastoral.

It would seem that from many points of view *Acis and Galatea* would pass muster as a serenata, though in English, in its first form as in its later recensions.

'MASQUE' AND 'OPERA'

One may readily imagine that anyone seeing such a 'semi-staged' serenata, evidently in dramatic form, and not knowing the correct term or its

---

39   See below, pp. 56f.
40   This was the native English tradition and also facilitated borrowings from Dryden's translation; the use of blank verse for Polyphemus's first recitative effectively interrupts the ordered flow.
41   For Lady Buck, see Deutsch, *Handel*, p. 112; for the concert element in masquerades, *ridotti*, assemblies and the *passo tempo*, see ibid., pp. 133f, 137, 148f.

conventional implications, would naturally approximate it to a more familiar experience such as a masque or opera. This would equally be true of a German copyist who had not been to Italy, like Smith, who would probably call it an opera, or of an English publisher like Walsh, inspecting the score and wondering what title would most readily be understood by its prospective purchasers. That Handel set out to naturalize the serenata in English is not to deny in any way that he would have learnt a good deal about English taste, word-setting and dramatic conventions by studying the London theatre masques of 1715–18; he would have been foolish not to have done so, and the easy tunefulness, graceful proportions and delicate scale of his work do indeed recall (though they far excel) those of the masques. It remains perfectly legitimate to see *Acis and Galatea*, staged with full theatrical verisimilitude in one of the ways outlined earlier, as the climax of the long tradition of the English masque.[42] It is, however, quite distinct from the masques, and unlike Handel's earlier operas, in one very important respect: the number, size and dramatic weight of its choruses. One of the most original and extraordinary pieces in the work is in fact a chorus, 'Wretched Lovers', and the management of the vocal ensemble in general looks forward to the world of oratorio, not backwards to the homophony of the short choruses in masque and opera.

It is perhaps worth noting at this point that 'masque' need not necessarily mean a practicable theatre masque, though it usually did. The Earl of Egmont (a friend of Pope) three times referred in his diary to the 1732 serenata version of *Acis and Galatea* – presented concert-fashion and containing a great deal of music that had never been intended for the theatre – as a masque.[43] Walsh's full score of 1743 uses the title 'masque', as we have seen; but it transmits (with the restoration of some cuts) the concert version of the English *Acis and Galatea*, more or less as performed by Handel from 1739 to 1742.

The designation is also found in ten librettos printed during Handel's lifetime; but they too were intended to accompany concert performances.[44] The term may quite possibly have been understood as referring in these cases to the dramatic form of the words rather than to any practical dramatic intention or to the continuing memory of a performance that had actually been staged with full theatrical verisimilitude.

The designation 'opera', used before the event by Dalrymple and after it by the copyists of at least three early scores and by Walsh on the title-page of the first edition of the songs,[45] cannot quite so easily be explained in this

---

42   Cf. Dean, p. 155.

43   Ibid., p. 160; Deutsch, *Handel*, pp. 295, 402, 513; the earl's last visit was in 1741, not 1736.

44   See Windszus, pp. 136–9; Dean, pp. 185–9.

45   Smith, p. 204; the work is called a mask in the 'Table of the Songs', and the title-page has been adapted from one used for *Muzio Scevola* and other works; but it could have been further adapted to remove the word 'Opera' if that had been thought desirable.

way. Handel had come to England, though, as a composer of operas, and it was in this capacity that his name was more widely known in fashionable circles. We know nothing of Dalrymple's musical qualifications. As Lord Advocate in Scotland for Queen Anne and George I, he may not have spent much time in London, though he was also a member of parliament for a time; but even a musically well-qualified person, informed that Handel the opera composer was writing an English entertainment whose words were in dramatic form, might well have described it as a 'little opera'. And an audience watching a serenata-style performance, partly acted in front of a scenic background, might equally have called it an opera, particularly since the style of acting would necessarily have been more static and artificial than playhouse acting: it would have had to match the slower pace of the music and the constant repetitions of the words, in exactly the manner familiar from Italian opera.

SERENATA INTO MASQUE, OR MASQUE INTO SERENATA?

I have assumed hitherto that the directions in the lost conducting score represent Handel's original intentions in composing *Acis and Galatea* and that they would have needed altering in order to permit a fully staged performance. It might be argued that the reverse was the case, that he set out to write a practicable little English opera with a small chorus, found that the duke's chapel singers did not possess the necessary stage experience or deportment to carry off the acting of the choruses, and therefore decided that the work had better be converted into a serenata, performed entirely by five singers from the professional stage.[46] The autograph, after all, does not allot the choruses to the named characters, and one might even argue, as Windszus does, that Handel's deletion of three solo singers' names from the first chorus could imply that he had decided not to perform the choruses with one voice to a part.[47] It is happily possible to demonstrate with a fair degree of certainty that the original plan of Handel and his librettists was to write a piece for only three principals: Galatea, Acis and Polyphemus (the only three in Ovid's story), for whom he planned three-part ensembles. By the time he came to write out the autograph, Damon had been invented and Coridon was in prospect,

[46]   Dalrymple's phrase 'sung by his own servants' (talking of the chapel music) probably meant exactly that: at least one of the Cannons singers is known to have served as a domestic, and at least two of the instrumentalists; 'in order to make room for visiting gentlemen's servants, staying the night, the musicians had to be drawn "into a narrower compass", and bedded in empty rooms over the stables' (Baker, *The Life and Circumstances of James Brydges*, p. 134). Such singers would probably have lacked the deportment and stage experience necessary for a staged or semi-staged performance, particularly if professionals, who would have shown them up, were also involved.

[47]   Dean, p. 169. Windszus, p. 39; see also p. 16, which reminds us that Blackley and Row are named in the Chandos Te Deum in B flat and were therefore presumably chapel singers.

and the number of voices in the choruses had been increased to five. If an independent chorus had been expected from the first, this expansion from STB to STTTB would not have been necessary; it was the increase in the number of soloists that led to the expansion of the choruses. This conclusion, which I first proposed at a colloquium at King's College, London, in 1980, was arrived at independently of the evidence from the conducting score; it casts light on yet other aspects of *Acis and Galatea*.

DISCONTINUITIES IN THE LIBRETTO

The musical style of *Acis and Galatea* is so perfect that its charm has prevented commentators from noticing a number of odd features and poor dovetailings in the continuity of the action. While no single one of them may be thought important or conclusive in itself, the pattern of the whole sequence is extraordinarily suggestive.

(*i*) The very opening passage after the first chorus is strangely repetitive and unwittingly almost comic. Enter Galatea, looking for Acis (Nos. 3 and 4); exit Galatea. Enter Acis, looking for Galatea ('Where shall I seek the charming Fair?', No. 5); if this aria had been introduced by a bald recitative to the same effect, any audience would probably have laughed at the two lovers so narrowly missing each other. At the beginning of the recitative 'Lo! here my love!' (No. 6a), Galatea has to return to the stage with no words to sing; her only motive is to look for Acis, yet she must elaborately avoid noticing him, so that he has to add, 'Turn, Galatea, hither turn thy Eyes'. In an intimate performance on a small stage, this would be decidedly inept. It would work much better if she were already on-stage, and he entering. Noting how aptly Acis's words 'hither turn thy Eyes' pick up Galatea's 'Bring back my *Acis* to my Sight' in No. 4, one might reasonably conclude that No. 6a and the aria No. 7, whose opening line again refers to her eyes, were meant to follow No. 4.

(*ii*) The words and music of Coridon's charming aria No. 14, 'Would you gain the tender Creature', a late addition with words by Hughes, plainly interrupt the dramatic impetus which requires Acis to begin his ensuing recitative on a furious top G (g′): 'His hideous Love provokes my Rage'. 'His' means Polypheme's, and Acis's anger has evidently been excited by, and should follow, the giant's brutal aria 'Cease to Beauty to be suing', No. 13. This is all the more obvious when one reads the lewd text that this aria at first carried, which ends 'Force her if she's worth enjoying, / She'll forgive you when 'tis over.' To match this, Acis's recitative originally began 'His saucy Love'. (Handel himself entered the alterations in the autograph.)

(*iii*) In the recitative that follows Damon's aria 'Consider, fond Shepherd' (No. 16), Galatea has to say, with every appearance of rudeness,

'Cease, oh cease, thou gentle Youth': these words are of course addressed to Acis and should follow on from his martial aria 'Love sounds th'Alarm', No. 15.

In a serenata-style performance, such inconsistencies would be less noticeable; but they are matched by similar puzzles in the music.

DISCONTINUITIES IN THE MUSIC

Anyone familiar with Handel's operas will be puzzled, and any singers attempting to act *Acis and Galatea* will be hampered, by the absence of recitative before certain items. It was Handel's habit in his operas to write short introductory arias without recitative at the beginning of an act or following a scene change, where the situation and words were clear; these 'cavatinas', as they came to be called, are usually slowish and lyrical, and establish a change of mood better than recitative could; nearly always they have no middle section or da capo, and not infrequently they are mere ariosos that never really end but melt into recitative. Otherwise, an aria is normally prefaced by a recitative, however short, which sets the situation and mood and allows one to interpret the orchestral ritornello with which an aria usually begins, before the singer confirms its affective message by adding the words. In *Acis and Galatea* there are three arias and a duet, all full-length pieces with middle section and da capo, which lack introductory recitatives:

No. 5, 'Where shall I seek the charming Fair?', is sung as Acis enters an empty (or recently vacated) stage, and might perhaps be classified as one of Handel's usual entrance arias were it not for the fact that it is a full-length piece and uncharacteristically agitated and impetuous in mood.

No. 9, the duet 'Happy we!', for two characters already on-stage, would unquestionably have been prefaced in an opera by a phrase or two of recitative to explain and prepare the change of mood to fizzing exuberance, after the gentle reproaches of the preceding aria, Galatea's 'As when the Dove' (No. 8).

No. 14, 'Would you gain the tender Creature', as we now know, is sung by Coridon, a minor shepherd whose identity we have not been told and cannot guess. Whether or not it was intended to replace No. 13 (as Watkins Shaw has suggested, noting that Handel always cut the latter in his later performances[48]), it would in an opera almost certainly have had an introductory recitative.

No. 16, Damon's 'Consider, fond Shepherd', like all the above items, carries a clear message in its words but has an exceptionally long opening ritornello whose affective intention is by no means clear from the music alone; a recitative would have explained it.

[48]   Preface to his revision of Barnby's vocal score in the Novello edition; but, in spite of the librettos, no manuscript or printed score is known that omits the aria, for all that Handel may have disliked the bowdlerized text.

In No. 13, where Galatea has sung the last speech of the preceding recitative, Polyphemus's anger needs no further explanation: his outburst answers her rejection of him, just as it might in an opera. Nor is recitative needed before No. 20, Galatea's 'Must I my Acis still bemoan', which is part of a sequence moving from the F minor of Acis's death and the ensuing chorus (Nos. 18 and 19) by a magical change of mode and texture to the F major of Galatea's expected lament: no recitative must intrude on this holy ground.

CONSISTENT INCONSISTENCIES

The pattern that emerges from all these discontinuities clearly suggests that it was not only Coridon's aria No. 14 that was inserted into the scheme at a late stage (as the autograph shows): Damon's second aria, No. 16, is also to be seen as an interruption. This makes one look more closely at his other aria, No. 6, which has so far received only indirect comment. Although it has a recitative, it directly follows another aria which has come under suspicion, Acis's entrance aria, No. 5; we have also observed that Acis's recitative No. 6a ('Lo! here my Love!') would follow on very naturally from Galatea's aria No. 4. Damon's recitative and aria No. 6 form the second element in the intervening sequence and must be considered a possible intrusion on that account also. The other item that seems uncomfortably placed in a continuous performance in one act is the duet No. 9. This creates a tonal discontinuity precisely at the point where Handel divided the work into two acts from 1739 onwards, when he substituted a choral da capo (at first with carillon) for that of the duet and emphasized the break still further by inserting an organ concerto. Previous commentators have not been disturbed by the unusual progression from C major to B♭ major between Nos. 9 and 10; but B♭ is not a natural relation of C major in eighteenth-century theory,[49] and the strangeness of the jump is here made all the more bewildering by the change of texture from the brilliance of the full band to the sad voice of a lonely solo cello. There may be those who are prepared to argue that the effect is deliberate, but I have not found a similar case in other works by Handel except where he once or twice upset an original normal key-scheme by hasty revision.[50] One suspects that he

---

49   See Cook, *The Life and Works of Johann Christoph Pepusch*, i, pp. 37ff, citing Pepusch and Alexander Malcolm; the natural relations of, for instance, C major are the keys whose tonic triads may be erected on the notes of the hexachord, their thirds 'naturally' major or minor according to the key-signature of C major, i.e. C, d, e, F, G, a.

50   Cf. the remarkable move from F minor to G minor between Lichas's 'No longer, fate, relentless frown' and Dejanira's 'Oh Hercules' in *Hercules*, Georg Friedrich Händel's Werke: Ausgabe der Deutschen Händelgesellschaft [HG] (Leipzig and Bergedorf, 1858–1902, reprinted Farnborough, 1965), ed. F. Chrysander, iv, p. 15, caused by a later interpolation.

inserted the duet at this point not merely to join the lovers in ensemble in the usual way, or to make an ironic contrast with the coming change in their fortunes expressed in 'Wretched Lovers', but principally because the addition of four extra arias and a recitative, as outlined above, had so increased the length of the work that it now required a brief interval. We have also noted the common division of the serenata into two parts: a short break at this point would not completely destroy the effect of the intended contrast but would at the same time palliate the shock of the tonal progression.

We are now, though, in danger of constructing hypotheses on the backs of hypotheses. What other tests might be applied, in order to prove or disprove what has so far been suggested? First, are there any features in the technique of the verse which distinguish the suspect material from the rest of the piece? Second, if all the arias (and the one recitative) of Damon and Coridon had been an afterthought, what about their roles in the choruses? Were the choruses conceived in five parts, and were Damon and Coridon favoured with arias because they would otherwise have appeared only in ensemble, in the anomalous and slightly demeaning capacity of unidentified shepherds? Or were the choruses, too, originally conceived as three-part ensembles for Galatea, Acis and Polyphemus, and expanded to include Damon and Coridon for the sake of stylistic consistency? Finally, is there any clue in the autograph to support these speculations?

THE VERSE TECHNIQUE

An analysis of the metrical schemes and the use of rhyme in the verses of the arias and duet confirms in almost every detail that the suspect material, like the text of Coridon's aria (which we know to be Hughes's work), is quite distinct from what we must now begin to call the 'original layer'. Since all the verses of the later layer except the recitative No. 5a take the form of da capo arias, we may confine the detail of our comparison to the da capo forms of the original layer.

Original layer. The aim in the aria verses is constant variety of rhyme and metrics. Their rhyme schemes set them apart from the recitatives, which are all, except for five blank lines in No. 11, in rhymed couplets (as also is Damon's No. 5a, 'Stay, Shepherd, stay!': no difference here). All the choruses, too, are in rhymed couplets, apart from the middle section of the first. The only aria to share this characteristic is Galatea's last, No. 21, which has no middle section or da capo; it includes a couplet of recitative, and its final couplet is to be repeated, slightly modified, in the final chorus, so that these four lines dictate the pattern of the preceding quatrain. This aria and the trio No. 17, which likewise has no middle section or da capo, need not concern us further at this point. All the other items are in da capo form and are tabulated below. Table 2 gives for each line of the verse a letter showing the rhyme (w, x, y and z for unrhymed lines here and in Table 3), and a figure indicating the syllable-count. The first and the middle sections of the da capo form are placed in separate columns. No. 2 has two couplets of trochees in the first section, strongly contrasted with two matching quatrains of iambics in the second. No. 4 is equally varied but mixes iambs and trochees within each section. Both differ from No. 7, whose two mellifluous quatrains have the same alternately rhymed iambics (with some reversed initial feet). Different again is No. 8, whose two sections again contrast iambics with trochees: the first has two tercets linked by terminal rhyme; the second, two couplets of contrasting length, the second of which happens to repeat the rhyme of the opening couplet of the first section. No. 12, like No. 7, has a matching scheme for each section; but its quintets are made from long-lined triplets framing short couplets, with a quite different, comic effect. No. 13 (which preserves exactly the same scheme that we find in the two sets of verses that Handel deleted) has the only routine arrangement in this group, an alternately rhymed quatrain in trochees, divided at the mid-point. No. 15 contrasts two long dactylic or trochaic couplets (also analysable as four shorter lines, the first of each pair unrhymed) with a dactylic quatrain, alternately rhymed. Common to all except No. 13 is the striking absence of the almost universal device of Italian opera lyrics, a shared terminal rhyme at the end of each section, linking the two halves of the aria verse (a very frequent example of the latter would be the pattern axab cycb). In No. 13, the effect is produced almost accidentally, simply because it is the only quatrain in the group and happens to be alternately rhymed; it is not really long enough for the music it sustains, and Handel had great trouble in devising repeats of the words, so as to accommodate them to the scale of the aria from *Agrippina* from which he borrowed so many phrases.[51]

Second layer. The very varied structures of the original layer, and their lack of linked terminal rhyme between sections, stand in strong contrast to the verses of the second layer, which are analysed in Table 3 as before. In this group, no fewer than four of the five items display the linked terminal rhyme characteristic of Italian opera verses. The fifth, No. 9, which has a very odd structure indeed, at least has a linked initial rhyme. It is also the only aria to attempt a minimal contrast between its two sections; even that, I suspect, may be due to Handel, not to the poet, who seems to have intended two matching tercets, as in Nos. 6 and 16, but in this case in *terza rima*. Handel may have transferred a line intended for the first part into the second (cf. the aria 'O Jordan, sacred Tide' in *Esther*); the result is that the first section of the duet as commonly heard has only two words, 'Happy we', to which I have added 'Happy, happy, happy Pair', restoring the

---

[51]   The aria reworks a good deal more than merely the ritornello of Claudio's 'Io di Roma il Giove sono' (*Agrippina*, Act 3 scene 8).

Table 2 *Analysis of rhyme and metre in da capo forms of original layer*

No.			
2	'O the Pleasure of the Plains' (Chorus) [originally, but deleted]	$a^7a^7b^7b^7$	$c^6d^6c^6d^6e^6f^6e^6f^6$ $c^6e^6c^6e^6$]
4	'Hush, ye pretty warb'ling Choir!' (Galatea)	$a^7b^4b^4a^6$	d^7d^8
7	'Love in her Eyes sits playing' (Acis)	$a^7b^6a^7b^6$	$c^7d^6c^7d^6$
8	'As when the Dove' (Galatea)	$a^4a^4b^6c^4c^4b^6$	$d^4d^4a^7a^7$
12	'O ruddier than the Cherry' (Polyphemus)	$a^7a^7b^4b^4a^7$	$c^7c^7d^4d^4c^7$
13	'Cease to Beauty to be suing' (Polyphemus)	a^8b^8	a^8b^8
15	'Love sounds the Alarm' (Acis) [or	$a^{10} \quad a^{11}$ $x^4a^6 \quad y^5a^6$]	$b^7c^5b^6c^5$

Table 3 *Analysis of rhyme and metre in da capo forms of second layer*

No.			
5	'Where shall I seek the charming Fair' (Acis)	a^8b^{11}	a^8b^{11}
6	'Shepherd, what art thou pursuing?' (Damon)	$a^8a^8b^7$	$c^8c^8b^7$
9	'Happy, happy, happy we' (Acis, Galatea)	a^7b^7	$a^8c^7b^7c^8$
14	'Would you gain the tender Creature' (Coridon)	a^8b^8	a^8b^8
16	'Consider, fond Shepherd' (Damon) [or	$a^{12} \quad b^{11}$ $w^6a^6x^5b^6$	$a^{12} \quad b^{11}$ $y^6a^6z^6b^5$]

rhyme scheme from a variant in the manuscripts copied from the conducting score. In Nos. 5, 14 and 16 the matching terminal rhymes result, as in No. 13, from the division of a common form, the alternately rhymed quatrain. There is some attempt at metrical variety between the iambics of No. 5, the trochees of Nos. 6, 9 and 14 and the amphibrachs of No. 16. But there is no contrast between sections, and almost everywhere the four-footed line reigns supreme; its monotony is broken only by the ponderous Italianate hendecasyllabics introduced into No. 5.

One might perhaps imagine that the monotony of the verse forms (which is fortunately banished in performance by the inexhaustible variety of the music) was intended to depict the comparative ordinariness of the thoughts purveyed by Damon and Coridon; but no, it extends also to Acis's aria and the duet and is matched by other features not apparent in the rest of the work. There are several poor rhymes: 'Fair'/'Dear' (No. 4), matched in Damon's ensuing recitative by 'Air'/'hear'; in No. 6 'pursuing'/'Ruin'; in No. 14, 'Creature'/'treat her'. These are in a different class from the usual licences, such as 'Love'/'Grove' and 'Gods'/'Abodes', taken by all poets of the period except the fastidious Swift, who complained of Pope's use of the second in the *Iliad* translation.[52] The verses of the later layer are also quite lacking in the poetic quality and concrete imagery of the earlier. They are not pastoral so much as vaguely rural. They employ routine expressions ('the charming Fair'), rejoice in unsingable clumps of consonants ('youths thou', 'nymphs thou'), and clumsily repeat rhymes which were already present in surrounding material such as 'Mountains'/'Fountains' in No. 5 (cf. Nos. 3 and 17) or 'Pleasure'/'Measure' in No. 16 (cf. 'Treasure'/'Pleasure' in the preceding aria, No. 15). This suggests that whoever added them had not been conscientious enough to study what had already been written or had simply not had time or opportunity to do so. The worst cacophony of all is the two-vowelled line that begins No. 13, whose revised text (but not the deleted original) must surely belong among the second-layer additions: 'Cease to Beauty to be suing' (ee-oo-oo-ee-oo-ee-oo-i). There are, as we shall later see, one or two odd features and hasty and careless lines in the early layer, such as we find from time to time in Gay (though almost never in Pope); but nothing as bad as that. We shall return later to the 'club of composers' and the question of authorship.

THE CHORUSES

Three of the choruses, Nos. 2, 10 and 22, offer abundant evidence in their part-writing that they were first planned for only three voices. Where there are sets of thematic imitations, they have in nearly every case been designed as strettos of three vocal entries (see Exx. 1 and 2). In Ex. 3 the

[52]   See *The Correspondence of Alexander Pope*, ed. G. Sherburn (Oxford, 1956), i. p. 301.

Ex. 1 No. 2, bars 30ff

Ex. 2 No. 10, bars 65ff

tramping of the Cyclops is depicted in a double imitation between Tenor and Basso, while the Canto takes towering strides in the opposite direction. Tenors 1 and 2 have to combine; Tenor 3 plays no part in the above-mentioned imagery, though he naturally has to share in the amazed intake of breath suggested by the rests; except for that, his part is merely a filler, as two significant *pentimenti* (shown in brackets) demonstrate. The matrix of themes in No. 10, when the sad exclamation 'Wretched Lovers' is combined with the terrified shouts of 'Behold the Monster *Polypheme*', is in triple invertible counterpoint. Ex. 4 shows how Handel can keep all five voices in simultaneous action only by a great deal of doubling and the addition of free material; it is true that this technical defect is in the end a dramatic gain, since the very unpredictability increases the sense of panic.

In some places a tune destined for three-voice harmonization and doubled by instruments has been distributed between the five voices of the choral ensemble in a way that almost recalls the use of migrant cantus firmus in English music of the fifteenth century. In Ex. 5 a change of ink confirms that the voice parts were composed last; in Ex. 6 the *pentimenti* tell the same story. The middle section of the first chorus contains two solos, marked as such, which one would imagine are intended for Galatea and Acis respectively. It is odd that the tenor solo is copied on the line for Tenor 2, which is designated as Damon's part in the Malmesbury manuscript, as in choruses Nos. 19 and 20: did Handel at first intend Acis to sing Tenor 2? There is another little duet for Canto and Tenor towards the end of the first section, to which Handel started to add a part for Basso in the autograph, as shown in Ex. 7, but deleted it; the doubled tenor line quite spoils the effect, and Tenor 3 adds nothing at all. Such doublings and triplings of the lines at the unison (once at the octave), always involving the tenors, are found in no fewer than thirty-two places in Choruses Nos. 2, 10 and 22.[53] In *Esther*, composed for a similar combination of five voices, the tenors unite only once. We find precisely the same sort of doublings in two of the later rearrangements of Chandos anthems where the number of parts has been increased.[54] The conclusion is inescapable that the choruses from

[53]   No. 2, bars 16–17, 27–8, 30–2, 31–2, 34–5, 36–8, 37–8, 42–3, 46–51, 60–4, 68–72; No. 14, bars 18–19, 33–46, 34–6, 52–60, 65, 65–8; No. 22, bars 1–8, 22–37, 42, 44, 54–7, 68–9, 76–7, 77–9, 89–92, 95–104, 108–10, 112–15, 120–2.

[54]   See, for example, Anthem No. 11, 'Let God Arise', where a four-voice original has been rearranged and partly recomposed for six voices: see HG, xxxv, pp. 259 and 294f respectively. This is probably a very close analogy with the expansion and partial recomposition of choruses in *Acis and Galatea* by the addition of two voices to the original three. (See also such passages as Anthem No. 8, ibid., pp. 51ff, and Anthem No. 10, ibid., pp. 159ff). The Chandos anthems also contain reminiscences of passages in *Acis and Galatea*: see Nos. 5A, HG, xxiv, p. 158 ('Happy we'); 6A, ibid., p. 228 ('Say what comfort' in No. 20); and 7, HG, xxxv, pp. 8 ('Wretched Lovers') and 26 ('Die, die', bars 66ff of No. 20); and there are others.

Ex. 3   No. 10, bars 57ff

Ex. 4   No. 10, bars 33ff

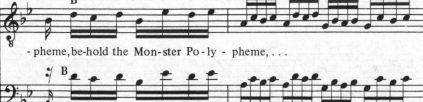

Dream! . . .

be - hold, be - hold!

be - hold, be - hold! be -

the

quit ____

- hold!

Mon - ster Po - ly-pheme!

your   Dream,

Ex. 5   No. 2, bars 68ff

Ob 1

Vln 1

Canto

Tenor 1

Tenor 2

Tenor 3   For us   the Win - ters   rain,   For   us   the Sum - mers

Basso

shine, Spring swells for us the Grain, And Au-tumn bleeds the Vine.

Ex. 6   No. 22, bars 42ff

Ob 1

Canto

Tenor 1
Tenor 2

Hail!   thou   gen - tle   murm' - ring   Stream,

Tenor 3

Basso

Ex. 7   No. 2, bars 46ff

mer - ry, free and gay,

Acis and Galatea discussed above, like the earlier of the Chandos Anthems, were originally designed for three voices.

What of the remaining two choruses, Nos. 19 and 20, from which these features are absent? They are the two items specifically marked, in all scores deriving from the conducting score, for the solo characters to sing. Should one therefore argue from the relative purity of their part-writing that they alone were specifically intended as more personal and intimate items for the dramatis personae to sing in solo ensemble, and that a larger chorus should dignify No. 2, which opens the work, No. 10, which introduces Part 2, and No. 22, the finale? (It is hard for two soloists to blend their voices in unison, as they are so often required to do in these choruses, but the problem would vanish with more voices taking each line.)

Such a deduction seems unwarranted. A simple explanation might be that Nos. 19 and 20 were conceived after the decision had been taken to employ five voices, so that Handel did not here have to adapt his thinking with the drastic results detectable elsewhere. That may have been so, but other explanations are still more likely. Nos. 19 and 20 are entirely homorhythmic, so that the problem of adapting preconceived triple counterpoint for five voices would simply not have arisen. The homorhythmic passages in the first section of the opening chorus also contain no doublings (except the octaves of 'Free and Gay', plainly a

Ex. 8   No. 22, bars 1–4

Ex. 9   *Agrippina*, final Coro, bars 1–4

deliberate effect); its middle section does introduce unison doublings and triplings in homophony (see Ex. 5 above), but that is because Handel is adapting from the three-voice accompaniment of a pre-existing melody (and the bass lies high, allowing no room for manoeuvre); a similar explanation accounts for Ex. 6 above, from the final chorus, and also for the opening of the chorus (Ex. 8). Here again the bass lies high, and we are fortunately able to show that both Ex. 6 and the opening melody, in which all three tenors unite, derive from a pre-existing idea, the first phrase of the final chorus of *Agrippina* (see Ex. 9). It is worth noting that the original here was a three-part ensemble for soloists (three sopranos, two altos and three basses); Handel may also have turned to it because, like No. 22, it is an apostrophe to a river ('May the Tiber happily ripple his waves').

The likely significance of Handel's turning to a three-voice passage as his model in No. 22 is increased when we note that the two other choruses are similarly based. No. 10, as is well known, borrows the two semiquaver themes shown in Ex. 4 above, and the idea of the accompanying suspensions, from the duet cantata 'Caro autor di mia doglia'. The chorus No. 19 incorporates almost the whole of the Trio of Believers ('O Donnerwort! O schrecklich Schreien') from the *Brockes Passion*, probably composed in 1716. Like the ensemble from *Agrippina*, the latter was composed as a three-part piece for solo singers. In *Acis and Galatea* its opening has been altered, though the basic harmonic progression is retained; thereafter only the two violin parts and the bass line are strictly preserved (the viola disappears); the upper four vocal parts of No. 19 take only a phrase or two from the original soprano and alto, which have quite lost their former identity in the new five-part writing (see Ex. 10).

If Nos. 10, 19 and 22 had their origins in a three-part piece, what of No. 20? Here we are on less firm ground. Its colouring is extraordinary, recalling the ensemble between Pamina, Tamino and the two Armed Men in the Act 2 finale of *The Magic Flute* (STTB); it seems perfectly possible that this dialogue between Galatea and the male voices is an original conception, arrived at after the decision to add Damon and Coridon to the cast – or at least Damon, for a male voice trio would preserve much of the movement's essential character. Certain features lead one to suspect that some adaptation may have taken place. The two pairs of consecutive fifths in bars 39–42, later corrected in the autograph (but not, apparently, in the conducting score)[55] are unlikely to have resulted from the direct process of composition; they look more like the consequence of some rearrangement of the parts, as indeed is demonstrable in the case of the second (bar 41). Ex. 11 gives the passage as it originally stood (and incidentally as Walsh printed it in 1743), with Handel's corrections above (or below) the notes. In bar 41, the pair of fifths in the instrumental parts results from the transposition and inversion of the innocuous fourths between Tenor 1 and Tenors 2/3. Could the same sort of explanation hold for bar 39? If the original had been a trio as in Ex. 12 (or even a duet, with Polyphemus taking the line I have marked for Damon and leaving the bass to the continuo instruments), we could understand how the consecutives, which are of a very elementary kind, came into being. Although the final version of the male-voice ensemble produces a convincing and even compelling effect, the part-writing is at times very awkward. There are avoidable and probably inadvertent consecutive unisons in bar 47 and consecutive octaves by contrary motion in bars 49–50, each time between Tenors 2 and 3, and consecutive fifths between Tenor 2 and Bass in bar 78. The instrumental accompaniment to the male voices is written in three mostly

---

[55]   Windszus, p. 175, and revised commentary to No. 20.

Ex. 10

(a) *Brockes Passion*, Trio of Believers, bars 1–9

(b) *Acis and Galatea*, No. 19, bars 1–8

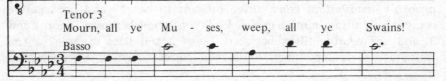

Ex. 11   No. 20, bars 39–42 (omitting Galatea and Oboe 1)

Ex. 12   No. 20, bars 39–42 (hypothetical vocal trio or duet)

Ex. 13 No. 20, bars 55–8 (strings and male voices)

Be-wail not whom thou canst relieve, whom thou canst re - lieve.

admirable parts, but its simple and logical lines have been divided up very strangely between the three tenors, as Exx. 13 and 14 show (the consecutive fifths between the third and fourth quavers of the violins in Ex. 13, however, must here too have originated from inversion of the fourths in Tenors 1 and 2). This ungrateful fragmentation of perfectly singable lines between the three tenors suggests very strongly that an orchestral texture derived from a trio of male voices has been used as the basis of a rearrangement for quartet, a proceeding paralleled in No. 19. But while it is easy enough to rewrite the lower parts as a trio, one must confess that the gain in clarity and ease of line is balanced by a loss of the oracular thickness of utterance that gives the dialogue its peculiar colour.

Ex. 14   No. 20, bars 71–5 (strings and male voices)

Table 4 *Autograph* pentimenti *in the choruses*

No.	A Instrumental corrections	B Vocal corrections	A:B(%)
2	37 (only 5 in violins)	60	62
10	116	137	85
19	2 (in Oboe 1)	79	2.5
20	5 (in Oboe 1 and Bass)	40	12.5
22	6	45	13
Total	166	361	46
Total without No. 10	50	224	22

Other corrections in the autograph show that Handel experienced unusual and general difficulty with the vocal lines in choruses. A count of altered notes (omitting altered words) gives the figures shown in Table 4, which reveals a surprising imbalance between the number of corrections in the five instrumental parts and those in the five vocal parts, beyond what the various doublings of the instruments might account for. Only in No. 10 are the proportions anything like equal, and we may conclude in this case (where the contrapuntal nature of the instrumental parts poses unusual difficulties) that Handel worked simultaneously on both voices and orchestra. In No. 19 he was working directly from a model. In Nos. 20 and 22 he seems to have been working from a sketch and rearranging the vocal parts. The alternative explanation – that he worked out the vocal parts first, solving the problems by frequent correction, so that it was then easy to derive the instrumental parts from them – seems (from all that I have said above) to hold good only for the violin parts of No. 2.

A count of the *pentimenti* in the arias, duet and trio reveals a strikingly different picture. The number of corrections in their instrumental parts is 104, in the vocal, 110, yielding a proportion between the former and the latter of 94.5%.

Statistics so used, however, and the mere listing of borrowings, are no very precise tools of investigation. A closer study of Handel's first thoughts in the choruses of *Acis and Galatea*, though fascinating, cannot do more than provide indirect support in favour of the hypothesis that Handel made late additions and alterations to the scheme. He may in some instances have worked from well-developed three-voice sketches, but he seems not to have done so in No. 10; and in No. 19, where he incorporated almost the whole of an earlier piece, he so imaginatively altered and extended its ideas to fit the new context that the 'borrowing' became a new act of composition.

Even in No. 2 there are *pentimenti* in the vocal and instrumental bass lines in bars 11 and 14 which suggest that, if a three-part sketch existed, he was exercising his composer's prerogative to alter it as he went along.

DISCONTINUITIES IN THE AUTOGRAPH

The ordering of the autograph does, however, show that Handel did not sit down with a complete libretto and compose it straight through. We know that it lacks Coridon's aria No. 14. There are other places where a blank page or a cue affords evidence of a plan that developed even in the course of the work's composition. I need not repeat here Windszus's excellent analysis of the make-up of the manuscript, whose paper, rastration and handwriting betray no significant differences.[56] We need only to look at the points where material suspected to be 'late' joins on to its surroundings, and at one or two other curious features. Table 5 gives a foreshortened view of the two sequences in question.

The first clump of suspect items is the scene for Acis and Damon, Nos. 5–6. It occupies the fourth gathering. There is no room for a recitative at the join with gathering 3, whose last side is completely filled by the end of Galatea's aria No. 4. The recitative 'Lo! here my Love' (No. 6a) is copied quite normally on the lower part of the leaf after the end of Damon's aria on folio 16v, so that it looks at first as if Handel had all the words of this scene in his possession before he started composing. The bifolium containing Acis's aria No. 5 (ff. 13r–14v) is, however, an insertion – a very early one, since there is no difference of paper and rastration (though Handel used the leaves upside-down, relative to the rest of the manuscript). The original conjugates of folios 15 and 16 were once present in the form of two unfoliated stubs with some remains in Handel's writing visible on them; these, the former folios 13–14, have been removed in the process of 'restoring' the volume (which seems a strange concept of conservation). It was once possible to discern the part-designations, clefs and key-signature of an aria for Acis at the head of stub 13, and the words 'Da Capo' at the bottom of stub 14v. From the instrumentation, key-signature and length, this was an aria in C minor or E♭ major which might have been a version either of No. 5, a suspected interpolation, or of No. 7, 'Love in her Eyes', which may have followed No. 4 in the original plan. There would in the latter case have been no room for its introductory recitative, 'Lo! here my Love', so that the excised aria was more likely an alternative to No. 5. It may not perhaps have been an earlier and rejected draft of it, however, since I was also able to make out the tail of a descending beamed

[56]   Windszus, pp. 82–9. Donald Burrows tells me, however, that folios 1–5 and 8 have the watermark Be, not Bc; and the stubs mentioned as folios 12a and b on page 87 in Windszus do not figure in the table on page 83.

Table 5 *The placing of second-layer items in the autograph* 79

Gathering	Folios	No.	Title; comments
3 (ff. 9–12)	12v	4	'Hush, ye pretty warb'ling Choir' (Galatea): ends
4 (ff. 13–16)	[13–14(old)]		[Two stubs with remains of da capo aria for Acis]
	13r–14v	5	'Where shall I find' (Acis). Inset bifolium
	15r	5a	'Stay, Shepherd, stay' (Damon, recit.)
	16r–16v	6	'Shepherd, what art thou pursuing' (Damon)
	16v	6a	'Lo! here my Love' (Acis, recit.)
5 (ff. 17–20)	17r–18v	7	'Love in her Eyes' (Acis)
	18v	7a	'O didst thou know' (Galatea, recit.)
	19r		Top: 'Segue l'Aria. As when the Dove'. Bottom: cancelled first version of bar 54 of No. 10, 'Wretched Lovers' (Chorus)
	19v	8	'As when the Dove' (Galatea): begins
6 (ff. 21–4)	22r	8	Ends
	22v–24v	9	'Happy we' (Galatea and Acis); folio 24 once lost, now replaced; folio 25 is modern
7 (ff. 26–9)	26r	10	'Wretched Lovers' (Chorus): begins
9 (ff. 34–7)	35v–36r	12a	'Whither, fairest' (Galatea, Polyphemus, recit.) ends on top two lines of folio 36
	36r	13	'Cease to Beauty' (Polyphemus): begins
10 (ff. 38–41)	38r	13	Ends, followed by note: 'NB aria'
		[14]	['Would you gain the tender Creature' (Coridon): never entered in autograph]
	38v	14a	'His hideous Love' (Acis, recit.); top two lines
	38v–40v	15	'Love sounds the Alarm' (Acis)
	41r		Note, 'Segue l'aria di Damon'; ruled staves
	41v		Blank; ruled staves
11 (ff. 42–5)	42r–44r	16	'Consider, fond Shepherd' (Damon)
	44v	16a	'Cease, O cease' (Galatea, recit.)
	[45r (lost)]		[Missing; blank; ruled staves]
	[45v (lost)]	17	[Missing; must have contained first six bars of 'The Flocks shall leave' (Galatea, Acis, Polyphemus); present folio 45 is modern]

demisemiquaver at the end of stub 13 which cannot now be matched in either aria No. 5 or aria No. 7. All that we are entitled to conclude from this disturbance is that it is evidence of revision, though the point at which it occurs is certainly suggestive.

The next interruption comes in the middle of gathering 5 (ff. 17–20). No. 7, 'Love in her Eyes', ends on folio 18v; since it takes up only the top six lines, Handel copied Galatea's recitative No. 7a, 'O didst thou know', on the bottom four. There is no reason to doubt that he followed his usual practice of writing out the words of the recitative in their proper place as soon as he had completed the preceding aria, returning to compose the music for them at a later stage. Galatea's ensuing aria No. 8, 'As when the Dove', does not, however, follow on immediately. Before we come to it, there is at the foot of folio 19r a cancelled version of the vocal and continuo parts of bar 54 of No. 10, 'Wretched Lovers'; it is a sketch in the sense that it contains four corrections that are incorporated, together with a fifth, into the version of the bar as copied in its proper place in the chorus (ff. 26–32). This later version of bar 54 on folio 30r, however, begins a new gathering (8); and since on folio 19r the parts are copied at the bottom of the page in their proper place, leaving the top four lines free for the entering of the violin and oboe parts, it would appear that at this point Handel was not sketching but had just completed bar 53 – the last bar in gathering 7 – and had simply picked up a blank quaternion in order to continue the work he was engaged on. Bar 54 gave him rather more trouble than the other frequent and heavy corrections in 'Wretched Lovers', because he started with the slow theme in Tenors 1 and 2 and did not allow enough space for the semiquavers of the other parts; it looks a muddle, so he abandoned it, deleted the bar and reached for a second blank quaternion, the present gathering 8. He re-used the spoilt quarternion, for its present contents, turning it inside-out so that the spoilt side became folio 19r, half-way through gathering 5, knowing that he would be able to fit two arias and a recitative on either side of it. The cancelled passage must already have been there, or else he would have started copying 'As when the Dove' on folio 19r, straight after its recitative on folio 18v; instead of this he worked round it, adding at the head of folio 19r the note 'Segue l'Aria. As when the Dove'. This at first sight over-detailed and fussy reconstruction of the sequence of events enables us to conclude (a) that Handel did not waste paper and (b) that he did not compose even the basic layer of *Acis and Galatea* straight through in order but began writing its most difficult and challenging chorus, 'Wretched Lovers', before composing Nos. 6a–8 in gatherings 5–6. This, of course, would weaken any other arguments that one might draw from the discontinuities in the copying of the autograph; but the facts must be honestly stated.

There is no disturbance or gap between the end of No. 8 and the beginning of the duet No. 9, 'Happy we', which ends gathering 6,[57] nor between No. 13, 'Cease to Beauty', and the preceding recitative, though the aria's ending on folio 38r is followed, as we have noted, by the cue for the missing No. 14, 'Would you gain the tender Creature'. Acis's recitative No. 14a follows in the normal way on folio 38v.

After Acis's aria No. 15, 'Love sounds the Alarm', though, the rest of gathering 10 is empty: there are two sides ruled with staves (ff. 41r–41v), the first of which has the note 'Segue l'aria di Damon'. This long aria, 'Consider, fond Shepherd' (No. 16), begins gathering 11 and occupies five sides, folios 42r–44r; Galatea's ensuing recitative No. 15a, 'Cease, O cease', for which there is no room on folio 44r, is copied on folio 44v. Then came a leaf now missing, folio 45, the last in gathering 11; the recto must have been blank, save perhaps for a note such as 'Segue il trio', since the missing first six bars of the trio No. 17, 'The Flocks shall leave the Mountains', would have fitted easily on to folio 45v. Handel must presumably have had some reason for wasting paper at this point: why should Damon's aria and the following recitative be preceded by a gap of two sides and followed by a further blank side? There seem to be three possibilities:

(*i*) Handel did not have the words of the aria and stopped work; when he received them, he did not have gathering 10 to hand and therefore began a new gathering. Why, then, should there be a blank side between the recitative No. 16a and the trio No. 17?

(*ii*) Handel had already composed the aria before finishing the previous one and had started a new gathering with it. To this there is the same objection as in (*i*) above.

(*iii*) Handel did not have the words of the aria and could see from the words of Galatea's ensuing recitative, 'Cease, O cease, thou gentle Youth', which were intended to follow Acis's aria No. 15, that they might need altering to follow on from the additional aria proposed for Damon. He therefore left a longer gap than usual, both because he had envisaged a long, slow aria ('As when the Dove', the longest in *Acis and Galatea*, occupies six sides) and because the recitative might need changing; he therefore left a gap of either ten or eight sides and continued composing with the trio No. 17 on folio 45v, the last leaf of a new gathering (11), omitting its introductory recitative for the moment. Since a gap of eight

---

[57] Gathering 6 at one point lost its final leaf, which has since been restored; so – alas, permanently – did gatherings 11 and 16. This suggests that the work was kept in three bundles of six, five and five gatherings (1–6, 7–11, 12–16), whose last leaves were vulnerable and became detached. Gathering 6 ends what was probably Part I, but there was no structural division coinciding with the end of gathering 11. Windszus (p. 82) speaks of a further division, determined by thread-holes, between gatherings 1–4 and 5–16; it seems to me, after what had to be a very hasty inspection, that the holes between gatherings 3 and 4 do not in fact match, but they are extremely hard to distinguish, since they have been filled up during restoration.

sides seems sufficient, it is likely that gathering 10 had meanwhile been sent off to the copyist of the conducting score and parts. In the event, no altered words were provided for the recitative.

In possibilities (*i*) and (*ii*) above, Handel would have had the text of aria No. 19 to hand and would presumably have known before starting on gathering 11 that the recitative was to remain unaltered. Whether or not explanation (*iii*) seems acceptable – and who can prove such a hypothesis at this distance of time? – the arguments all serve to demonstrate that there was an interruption in the normal flow of Handel's process of composition at this point, and that it was caused by an aria which appears on other grounds to have been a late interpolation. All in all, there seems to be enough evidence in the sequence of the autograph to allow our theory of a late change of plan some support in the cases of Nos. 5–6, 14 and 16; but from the undisturbed joins between Nos. 6 and 6a, 8 and 9, and 12a and 13, it is evident that most of the hypothetical changes had been agreed, and text provided, before the process of writing the autograph began.

The 'club of composers' and John Hughes

Who provided the additional text, and why? Its verse technique and literary tone, as I have already suggested and will shortly confirm, do not seem characteristic of Pope and Gay. Dalrymple's letter of 27 May 1718 (see p. 35 above) added a third literary figure to the 'club of composers', Dr John Arbuthnot, a fellow member of the Scriblerus Club who had frequently collaborated with Pope and Gay in prose, most recently in another dramatic piece, the short-lived farce *Three Hours Before Marriage*, staged and published in January 1717. Samuel Arnold's preface to *Omnipotence* (1774), admittedly a very late and in other respects inaccurate source, gives the credit for both *Acis and Galatea* and *Esther* (also 1718) to the triumvirate. Arbuthnot was in fact named as sole author of *Esther* in a Dublin libretto for a non-Handelian performance of 1741, and the attribution was repeated in another libretto prepared for Handel's own performances there in the following year;[58] but we knew of no contemporary witness to connect him with *Acis and Galatea* before the discovery of Dalrymple's letter. Arbuthnot was a wealthy man, court doctor to Queen Anne, and rich enough in 1719 to promise a bond of £200 and become one of the first directors of the Royal Academy of Music, which was even then in process of foundation.[59] His learning in the ancient classical theory of music may not have been much use to his co-directors, but his connoisseurship in the matter of voices and his knowledge of the

[58]   Dean, pp. 197, 220.
[59]   Deutsch, *Handel*, p. 96; J. Milhous and R. D. Hume, 'The Charter for the Royal Academy of Music', *Music & Letters*, lxvii (1986), p. 51.

technique of musical composition must have been.[60] He was an intimate of Chandos, whose archives contain between forty and fifty letters written to Arbuthnot and his immediate family between 1712 and 1735.[61] The wording of Dalrymple's letter suggests that his knowledge of the 'little opera' comes via Arbuthnot, a fellow Scot, who has promised to procure him copies of 'some of the Songs'. Very likely Arbuthnot had been the intermediary who had brought Chandos into contact with Pope and Gay over the idea of an English pastoral with music by Handel, and who was arranging everything on his behalf. One of the chief duties of the Scriblerians at this time was trying to help Gay, who was feckless and improvident and had held no paid employment since 1714; he seems, indeed, to have written nothing except his contribution to *Acis and Galatea* between 1717 and 1720.[62]

POPE AND GAY: PASTORAL THEORY

Pope, on the other hand, was at that time extraordinarily busy with his translation of Homer's *Iliad* and is unlikely to have contributed more than a few lines of verse; but he also brought with him his important ideas on pastoral theory, in which he was widely read, and long experience of its practice. He had first made his name, as Virgil himself was supposed to have done, with a series of pastoral poems, republished in his *Works* of 1717 and there prefaced with 'A Discourse on Pastoral Poetry'.[63] The following points that he there sets out are highly relevant to *Acis and Galatea*, though it of course belongs to the modern genre of the dramatic pastoral, developed by Tasso and others from the dialogue form of many ancient bucolic poems. Pope's discussion blends ideas from many sources, especially seeking to reconcile the recent controversy between two French writers, Rapin, who in 1659 had advocated the neo-classical pastoral of older theory and practice, and Fontenelle, who in 1688 had suggested a more up-to-date approach depending more on reason than on received authority. Rapin had been translated into English in 1684, Fontenelle in

---

60 See G. A. Aitken, *The Life and Works of John Arbuthnot* (Oxford, 1892). For ancient theory, see pp. 327, 329ff, 420f, 474; on singers, including Cannons singers controlled by Pepusch, see pp. 112f, 114, 126f, 154f, 184, and *The Correspondence of Jonathan Swift*, ed. F. E. Ball (London, 1910–14), iii, pp. 22f (on the Roseingraves); for his anthem, see Aitken, op. cit., p. 113; in his message to Dean Aldrich of Christ Church, Oxford of 25 January 1698 that 'Mr Pate has brought from Italy all Chaussune's musick' (p. 24) we may surely read 'Charissimi's'.

61 Sherburn, '"Timon's Villa" and Cannons', *Huntington Library Bulletin*, viii (October 1935), p. 148.

62 L. Melville, *Life and Letters of John Gay (1685–1732)* (London, 1921), p. 45.

63 *The Twickenham Edition of the Poems of Alexander Pope*, ed. J. Butt, i: *Pastoral Poetry and An Essay on Criticism*, ed. A. Audra and A. Williams (London and New Haven, 1961), pp. 23–33; there is an excellent short introduction on pages 13–20, from which I gratefully borrow.

1695 (by Motteux, as it happens, whose *Acis and Galatea* had made a mockery of the legend, with a flirtatious Galatea and a coarse sub-plot from modern village life).

The pastoral, says Pope, should imitate the action of a shepherd, or one considered so (as Acis and Polyphemus are). The story should be simple, the manners of the characters neither too polite nor too realistically rustic, the thoughts plain, yet with a little quickness and passion, though that too must be short and flowing. The language must be humble, but as pure as possible, neat without floridity, easy yet lively. Simplicity and brevity should make the poem natural, and delicacy delightful. The poet should remember that the shepherds of the Golden Age were not humble peasants; some were 'the best of men'. The pastoral is an illusion, concealing the real hardships of a rural existence. While some flavour of the antique is desirable in the language, it is good also to reveal some actual knowledge of pastoral life, especially in the imagery. Variety is essential, and the language should also include 'elegant turns on the words'; but the versification (and Pope is here thinking in terms of the heroic couplet) should be smooth and flowing, not grand as in the epic. Of modern pastoral writers he especially admires Tasso and Spenser; in certain respects critical of the latter, he nevertheless praises him particularly for the idea of a monthly calendar of pastorals, though he himself (as his four *Pastorals* show) would prefer the more readily distinguishable cycle of the four seasons.

His footnotes reveal that by 'elegant turns on the words' he is referring to Rapin's '*repetitions*, and *doublings* of some words: which, if they are luckily placed, have an unexpressible quaintness, and make the Numbers extream sweet, and the turns ravishing and delightful'. The original layer of *Acis and Galatea* affords many instances of such repetitions and doublings, and in two passages at least we may detect the hand of Pope. The middle section of the first chorus employs iteration:

> For us the Zephyr blows,
> > For us distils the Dew,
> For us unfolds the Rose,
> > And flow'rs display their Hue,

> For us the Winters rain,
> > For us the Summers shine,
> Spring swells for us the Grain,
> > And Autumn bleeds the Vine.

The last quatrain originally read (but was altered in the autograph):

> for us unfolds the Rose
> > and sweet[s] the Air perfume
> for us the apple glows,
> > for us the peaches bloom.

It is fairly plain that Pope, disliking Gay's repetition of a whole line from the first quatrain and the resulting monotony of rhyme, and the two specimens of 'hiatus' (see below), seized the chance to replace it with a quatrain encapsulating his pet idea of the cycle of the seasons; it is a pity that 'Spring swells for us the grain' (in which the brief line, like the swelling ear of corn, is packed to bursting-point) should accommodate itself so badly to Handel's already composed semiquaver up-beat. Pope seems to have recalled this passage, perhaps deliberately, in a letter to the painter Jervas: its prose suddenly starts to dance with the words 'For you my Structures rise; for you my Colonades extend their wings; for you my Groves aspire, and Roses bloom.'[64]

The repetitions in 'Love in her Eyes sits playing' (No. 7) also read like Pope, who had imitated Cowley before, and here, as Fuller notes,[65] pays a graceful compliment to 'The Change':

> LOVE in her Sunny Eyes does basking play;
> *Love* walks the pleasant Mazes of her Hair;
> *Love* does on both her lips for ever stray,
> And *sows* and *reaps* a thousand *kisses* there . . .

Pope's imitation of Waller, 'On a Fan' (1712), has also contributed to No. 7, and to the preceding recitative:

> . . . While at her feet her swain expiring lies,
> Lo the glad gales o'er all her beauties stray,
> Breathe on her lips, and in her bosom play! (ll. 4–6)

Galatea's native element is well caught in the 'doublings' of her recitative No. 16a, whose phrases advance wave-like to break over into the oath-taking of the ensuing trio:

> Trust my Constancy and Truth;
> Trust my Truth and Pow'rs above,
> The Pow'rs propitious still to Love.

Other features besides the verbal text of *Acis and Galatea* may owe their character to Pope's views on pastoral. Though its apparently miniature scoring may have been restricted by the size of Chandos's musical resources or by cramped indoor performance in a not very big house (Cannons was no Blenheim or Holkham), it is just as likely that Pope's insistence on the modesty, humility, purity, simplicity, brevity and above

---

64   *The Correspondence of Alexander Pope*, ii, p. 24.
65   *John Gay: Dramatic Works*, p. 452. We may also note parallels with Pope's *Eloisa to Abelard* (1717), lines 121–3: 'Still on that breast enamour'd let me lie,/Still drink delicious poison from thy eye,/Pant on thy lip, and to thy heart be press'd'; and many passages in his translation of the *Iliad* (1715–20) – cf. Books III, lines 79, 489f, 559; XIV, 332–6, 386; XXI, 591f.

all plainness necessary to the pastoral may have influenced Handel, especially in the almost unbroken colouring of oboe(s) with strings; only pastoral flutes (recorders) three times vary the equally pastoral oboe tone. It is possible, too, that the device of beginning with a recorder in a bird-song aria owes less to Pepusch's flageolet air 'Chirping warblers' in *Venus and Adonis* (1715) than to the idea, familiar to Pope from Rapin, that the first shepherds discovered the vocal art by imitating bird-song.[66] Galatea's opening complaint, an image of intolerable heat filled with the amatory sounds of nature, is in fact imitated from line 13 of Virgil's second *Eclogue*, 'sole sub ardenti resonant arbusta cicadis', via Dryden's translation: 'The creaking Locusts with my Voice conspire, / They fried with Heat, and I with fierce Desire.' Pope had replaced the cicadas with sheep in his 'Summer' (ll. 19–20): 'The bleating Sheep with my Complaints agree, / They parch'd with Heat, and I inflam'd by thee'; neither Sicilian cicadas nor English sheep, however, suggested a suitable obbligato, so Pope and Gay substituted the 'trilling strains', as Handel's 1732 libretto describes them, of the Duke of Chandos's own instrument, a flute. In an outdoor performance at Cannons, of course, set in the 83-acre walled area of pleasure-gardens, Galatea and her octave flageolet would have had to contend with a further obbligato of 'storks and whistling ducks, mock-birds and macaws, . . . flamingos, eagles and other birds'.[67]

What about more direct borrowings? There are dozens of echoes of lines from Pope's earlier works in the old layer, but none that Gay, his bosom companion, could not have read and remembered; there are rather more echoes of Gay, but his own verse was frequently submitted to Pope for correction. There is no space here to set them all out; stylistic analysis is in any case fraught with hazard when so much of the diction is in fact an inheritance from Dryden's greatly admired translations of Ovid and Virgil. The dangers are well illustrated by a quatrain in No. 17, attributed to Pope[68] because it compresses lines 44–6 from 'Autumn' in his *Pastorals*, which read:

> Not balmy Sleep to Lab'rers faint with Pain,
> Not Show'rs to Larks, nor Sunshine to the Bee,
> Are half so charming as thy Sight to me!

---

66   '*Sheapards* . . . were the first that either invited by their leisure, or . . . in imitation of Birds, began a tune': *The Twickenham Edition*, i, p. 23 n. 14. John Lockman also asserts that 'Birdsong first suggested singing to men' on page xi of 'Some Reflexions concerning *Operas, Lyric Poetry, Music,* &c.' prefixed to his libretto *Rosalinda, a Musical Drama . . . Set to music by Mr. John Christopher Smith* (London, 1740).

67   Baker, *The Life and Circumstances of James Brydges*, p. xvi.

68   The lovers' quatrains in the trio and the chorus 'Wretched Lovers' are admitted to the canon of authentic poems, though with a cautionary note, in *The Twickenham Edition*, vi: *Minor Poems* (1954), pp. 215–17.

In *Acis and Galatea* Gay has rearranged this into a stanza which, though it sings well, contains unpleasant and pointlessly accelerating repetitions of the vowel sound 'ee': 'pleasing' . . . 'Bee' . . . 'Sleep' . . . 'easing' . . . 'these dear' . . . 'me':

> Not Showers to Larks so pleasing,
>   Nor Sunshine to the Bee;
> Not Sleep to Toil so easing,
>   As these dear Smiles to me.

Pope was a master of varied vowels, and disliked similarities of rhyme. His choruses for *Brutus* do not contain such lapses, for all that they were intended for singing (they were set by Bononcini).[69] There is, however, a reasonably objective technical test by which we may measure the extent of Pope's likely contribution. Strictly applied, it would limit his authorship of first-layer pieces to Nos. 7, 7a, 8, 10, 12, 15, 18 (but this is straight Dryden) and 19. Apart from No. 16 in the later additions, all the other items offer examples of a fault that Pope much disliked. He called it the 'hiatus', which he defined as a 'Gap between two words which is caus'd by two Vowels opening on each other',[70] one at the end of a word and the other at the beginning of the next. There is an example in the quatrain just cited, at 'so easing'. (If such a pair of vowels can be elided to count as one syllable in the metre, which is often shown by suppressing the first, as in 'Love sounds th'Alarm', there is no problem; but if they are to be counted as two separate syllables, both necessary to the metre, the flow of the prosody suffers an unpleasant disturbance, since the reader must emphasize the second vowel where in ordinary speech he would glide smoothly from one to the other.) 'The *Hiatus* which has the worst effect, is when one word begins with the same Vowel that begins the following: and next to this, those Vowels whose sounds come nearest to each other are most to be avoided. O, A, or U, will bear a more full and graceful Sound than E, I, or Y.' Pope avoided the hiatus wherever possible, as a sin against 'correctness', and would doubtless have agreed with his admired Dryden that 'wheresoever I have not, 'tis a fault in sound'.[71] He gives a triple example of it as a warning in a passage illustrating various poetic sins, at line 345 of *An*

---

69   *Correspondence*, ii. pp. 220ff.

70   Ibid., i. p. 24 (22 October 1706, but thought to have been fabricated and extended in 1735 from Pope's letter to Cromwell of 25 November 1710, ibid., pp. 105ff, also highly relevant here).

71   Dryden's discussion of the necessary observance of the *synalepha* or elision is in the dedicatory letter prefixed to his *Examen Poeticum* (London, 1693), in which his translation of 'The Fable of Acis, Polyphemus, and Galatea' first appeared: see lines 249–81, *The Poems of John Dryden*, ed. J. Kinsley (Oxford, 1958), ii, pp. 796f. Pope told Cromwell on 7 May 1709 that 'The Hiatus in particular I would avoid as much as possible', having observed after reading the whole of Malherbe that 'there is but one throughout all his poems' (*Correspondence*, i, p. 57).

Essay on Criticism (published in 1711): 'Tho' oft the Ear the *open Vowels* tire . . .' One might imagine that in verse intended for singing he would have relaxed his vigilance, since the addition of music makes it easier to distinguish the open vowels by quantity and pitch; but in four 'Pieces for Music'[72] dating from before *Acis and Galatea* (though also in their later revisions), he used the hiatus only eight times in 248 lines, an average of once every thirty-one lines; two of these instances are a repetition of the hardly avoidable 'To arms', and if they are subtracted the average falls to once in forty-two lines. In *Acis and Galatea* there are seventeen examples of the hiatus in the 156 lines of the first layer, and six in the thirty-eight of the second layer, an average of one to every nine lines in the former, and to every six in the latter.[73] Though none takes the form of two identical vowels, which Pope particularly disliked, some are distinctly unpleasant, such as 'ye yield' and 'Hither turn thy Eyes'; the latter could have been avoided by using the normal form 'thine Eyes'. The presence of so many examples of hiatus suggests that Pope did not extensively revise the first layer (though he probably removed two from the middle section of the first chorus); this tends to confirm my belief that the text passed out of his and Gay's hands before it was completed by another.

HUGHES AND ARBUTHNOT

My quest for phrases and rhythms echoed in earlier works by Pope and Gay drew an almost total blank in relation to the pieces which seem to be later additions. A quick glance at Arbuthnot's three known poems, none of which is exactly lyrical (though one is in a bawdy strain which might have engendered the original version of No. 13), yielded only two insignificant echoes, both of pieces from the early layer and both from his serious poem *Gnothi Seauton: Know Yourself*, published posthumously in 1734.[74] It is not known when he wrote it. The first echo, which recalls No. 21, is Drydenesque (ll. 11–12, 1734 version):

> The purple stream that through my vessels glides,
> Dull and unconscious flows like common tides . . .

---

[72] The 'Ode for Music on St Cecilia's Day', 'Two Chorus's to the Tragedy of Brutus', the 'Ode on Solitude' and 'The dying Christian to his Soul'.

[73] First layer: in Nos. 2 'free and'; 'the air', 'the apple' (original middle section); 3 'ye yield' (Pope regards 'y' as a vowel); 4 'my *Acis*'; 6a 'thy Eyes'; 11 'me a', 'Beauty and'; 12a 'to Empire'; 13 'be a' (first text); 14a 'I am'; 16a 'Constancy and'; 17 'so easing'; 20 'my *Acis*', 'Constancy and'; 20a 'I exert', 'thou immortal', 'thou art'; 21 'lo! it'. Second layer: in Nos. 5 'me, if'; 5a 'melancholy Air'; 6 'Joy, our'; 9 'thou all' (twice); 14 'You enjoy'.

[74] Aitken, *The Life and Works of John Arbuthnot*, pp. 436ff, 439ff. His poems 'The Quidnunckis' and the 'Ballad' on Nelly are in *The Works of Jonathan Swift*, ed. Sir W. Scott (London, 1883), xiii, pp. 333f, 311ff; for the former, see also *John Gay: Poetry and Prose*, ed V. A. Dearing, with C. E. Beckwith (Oxford, 1934), i. pp. 285–7.

The second (l. 119) is a mere intonation: 'Too faint to mount, yet restless to aspire' (cf. Galatea's 'Too faint the Gales' in No. 3).

Dean has drawn attention to parallels with John Hughes's verse, and instances might be multiplied. Hughes's 'How happy are we', cited by Dean from *Apollo and Daphne*, becomes *ter felix*, as in 'Happy, happy, happy we' (No. 9) in Hughes's *A Pastoral Masque*:[75]

> How happy, how happy, how happy are we
> Where Cupid and Hymen in Consort agree.

The bad rhyme 'pursuing'/'Ruin' in No. 6, already mentioned, may be paralleled in a stanza that Hughes provided for Galliard's fifth cantata (1716), which employs exactly the same verse form:[76]

> When again I ask, pursuing,
> If you'll stay and see my Ruin?
> Fly — but let me with you go.

No. 5 appears to borrow from the impatient King Henry in *Rosamond* (1707), by Hughes's friend and mentor Joseph Addison, in 1718 no friend to Pope:

> Where is the tender, charming fair? . . .
> Where is my love, O tell me where? . . .
> Where is my love, O tell me where? (Act 1 scene 6)

A much stronger case for Hughes's authorship, however, would rely on his favourite verse forms and his propensity for linking the two sections of a da capo aria with a common terminal rhyme in the Italian manner. To take the latter point first, an analysis of all the thirty-eight da capo pieces in his texts for *Calypso and Telemachus*, *Apollo and Daphne* and Pepusch's and Galliard's cantatas shows thirty-three instances (87%) with terminal rhyme and only five without, a mere 13%. While I have not made a syllable-count, the pattern of rhyme schemes in the thirty-eight da capo pieces shows an overwhelming preference for two of the three schemes used in the additions to *Acis and Galatea*; Table 6 demonstrates this. One of Hughes's schemes without terminal link-rhyme also happens to match 'Love in her Eyes sits playing', which must surely be Pope's.

It would require much more work than I can at present undertake to sort out all the metrical schemes as well, and still wider research to determine whether the forms with link-rhyme are peculiar to Hughes, who showed an individual and missionary zeal in attempting to naturalize Italianate

---

[75] Dean, p. 157, J. Hughes, *Poems on Several Occasions* (London, 1735), i, p. 155; probably set in 1710. The tune to Daphne's air, ironically enough, was later filched by Gay and fitted out with the new text 'When you censure the Age' as Air XXX of *The Beggar's Opera* (Act 2 scene 10).

[76] Quoted from *Poems*, i, p. 177.

Table 6 *Rhyme schemes in Hughes's da capo verse forms and in Acis and Galatea*

Scheme	No. of items	% of total	Use in *Acis and Galatea*
(a) with link-rhyme			
aab ccb	10	26.3	Nos. 6, 14
ab ab	8	21.1	Nos. 5, 13 (all three versions), 16
aa bba	2	5.3	——
aab ab	2	5.3	——
others (all different)	11	28.9	——
(b) without link-rhyme			
aa bb	2	5.3	——
abab cdcd	1	2.6	No. 7 (first layer)
others (both different)	2	5.3	——

music to English forms. Even so, that would still not enable us to rule out Arbuthnot, who also knew a good deal about Italian opera: we have no lyrical verse that is certainly his for the purpose of comparison.

If, however, Arbuthnot were the poet of the additions, and if he also had a hand in *Esther*, written at the same time for the same patron, then we might expect to find him using the same rhyme schemes. Nine of the thirteen airs in *Esther* are in da capo form, and four of them employ terminal link-rhyme between sections: a lower proportion than with Hughes, but certainly not conclusive. The rhyme schemes for non-da capo airs are also included in Table 7, since they match the others and may have been intended for setting as da capo airs; in some cases, the decision not to set them as such could well have been Handel's, not the poet's.

The picture presented in Table 7 is not substantially different from that seen in Table 6. Among the five airs without link-rhyme, however, is the scheme of the trio No. 19 (where the lovers share the quatrain and Polyphemus has the couplet), which is not a da capo form, and that for Galatea's aria No. 4. This might be thought to favour the cause of Arbuthnot, but the sample is very small, and the possibility would still remain that Hughes, who was asked to contribute an aria to *Acis and Galatea*, might also have been called in for *Esther*, since Arbuthnot (as my second article will show) spent the summer of 1718 in France.

Table 7 *Rhyme schemes in airs from* Esther *and* Acis and Galatea

Scheme	Da capo airs		Non-da capo airs		All airs		Use in *Acis and Galatea*
	No. of items	% of total	No. of items	% of total	No. of items	% of total	
a) with link-rhyme							
aab ccb	3	23.1	1	7.7	4	30.8	Nos. 6, 14
ab ab	1	7.7	—	—	1	7.7	Nos. 5, 13 (all 3 versions), 16
b) without link-rhyme							
aa bb	1	7.7	2	15.4	3	23.1	——
abab cc	3	23.1	1	7.7	4	30.8	No. 17, repeated (trio, first layer)
abba cc	1	7.7	—	—	1	7.7	No. 4 (first layer)

The name of Damon is taken from 'Spring', the first of Pope's *Pastorals*, in which Damon is the evidently senior and respected shepherd who judges between the songs of the younger Daphnis and Strephon; the 'Epistle to Mr. Pope' by Thomas Parnell (d. 1717), a fellow Scriblerian, refers to the pastoral and employs the latter names for Virgil and Pope respectively; Parnell imagines them vying for the poetic palm, 'While some old Damon, o'er the vulgar wise,/Thinks he deserves, and thou deserv'st the prize.'[77] Pope himself refers to Damon in a letter to Matthew Prior of February 1720, in which he mentions a tiny fault in one of Prior's poems in order, as he says, 'to have the vanity of pretending, like Damon himself, to have advised you'.[78] In 'Spring' Damon does not in fact give his young friends any advice, nor in Virgil's eighth *Eclogue* – from which his name ultimately derives – where he is simply a shepherd singer: this phrase would hardly have made sense to Prior unless he had seen or read *Acis and Galatea*, in which Damon is certainly, in the words of British Library Add. MS 36710, 'very free of, (and louder in) his advice to Acis and Gallatea'.

If the provision of verses for Damon had to be farmed out, there would have been a touch of typically Scriblerian humour in entrusting them to Hughes. He was himself a Damon by nature and inheritance, a sober-sided dissenter who had withdrawn most of his pieces from Steele's *Poetical*

[77]   T. Parnell, *Poems on Several Occasions* (London, 1722 [really December 1721]); the volume was edited by Pope. For 'deserves', read 'deserved'?

[78]   *Correspondence*, ii, p. 30.

Miscellany (1714) when he learnt that Pope's contribution was to include 'The Wife of Bath, from Chaucer' and other pieces that he judged improper.[79] Steele tells us, however, that 'His Incapacity for more frolick Diversions never made him peevish or sour to those he saw in them'.[80] In spite of his authorship of 'Would you gain the tender Creature', his collaborations with Pepusch and his theatrical experience, he was nevertheless a Whig and a member of the group around Addison who frequented Buttons coffee-house, and would not have been a natural person for Pope and Gay to turn to.[81] He had also published an anonymous epigram in 1714, 'Advice to Mr. Pope, On his intended Translation of Homer's Iliads', following the expensive subscription scheme that Pope had launched; he contrasts blind Homer's lot, who 'sung and begged', with the handsome income that Pope would receive.[82] 'Be early wise', he tells Pope,

> First take the gold – then charm the list'ning ear;
> So shall thy father Homer smile to see
> His pension paid – tho' late, and paid to Thee.

Pope knew Hughes but kept him at a respectful distance. He sent him the volumes of his *Iliad* translation as they appeared, perhaps as a generous reproach, in view of the first sentence of his letter to Hughes of 7 October 1715;[83] but he refused him a prologue for *The Siege of Damascus*.[84] He may not have known who wrote the epigram until it was printed in Hughes's posthumous *Poems on Several Occasions* in 1735. In answer to an enquiry

---

[79]   See *Dictionary of National Biography*.

[80]   Preface to *Poems*, p. xliii, citing R. Steele, *The Theatre*, xv, 16–20 February 1719/20.

[81]   Ellen T. Harris is quite wrong in asserting that Hughes was 'a prominent member' of the Scriblerus Club, to which he never belonged; nor did Congreve, though he was certainly a good friend of Pope's (*Handel and the Pastoral Tradition* (London, 1980), p. 198). Pope and Gay were also at odds with all four of the authors involved in the London theatre masques of 1715–18, however close Handel may have been to the composers and singers and to Hughes (see Dean, p. 155). Barton Booth and Colley Cibber were two of the three joint managers of the Drury Lane theatre who had withdrawn *Three Hours after Marriage* in January 1717 'after a rather uproarious but far from unsuccessful week', which seems, 'when all reports have been considered, to have been an invidious, if not unwarrantable decision' (N. Ault, *New Light on Pope* (London, 1949), pp. 308f); Cibber had satirized Pope in *The Non-Juror* later that year, but the poet's hatred of the actor–manager must date from an episode that took place during the winter of 1714/15 (ibid., pp. 309ff, 301f). Pope's dislike of Lewis Theobald dates from 1715 'if, as Pope thought and maintained years later, he was in part responsible for *A Complete Key to . . . The What D'ye Call it*, which attacked the farce that Pope had helped Gay to produce' (ibid., p. 164).

[82]   Quoted from *Poems*; see also Ault, *New Light on Pope*, p. 104.

[83]   'Ever since I had the pleasure to know you, I have believed you one of that uncommon rank of authors, who are undesigning men and sincere friends . . .': *Correspondence*, i, p. 316.

[84]   Ibid., ii, pp. 28f.

from Swift, who had been presented with a copy and noted Pope's name among the subscribers, but had never heard of Hughes and found him mediocre, Pope replied: 'I did just know him. What he wanted as to genius he made up as an honest man: but he was of the class you think him.' There is no bitterness here; Hughes's other virtues evidently outweighed his epigram. Pope had also been grateful for Hughes's edition (the first cver) of his favourite Spenser,[85] and no doubt 'Eloisa to Abelard' (1717) owed something to Hughes's popular translation of their letters. Like Pope, he was a chronic invalid.[86] Like Pope, he had been called upon by Steele to provide verses for music in connection with his 'Censorium', and also by Rowe (for Eccles to set).[87] He published at least one translation of an episode in the *Metamorphoses*,[88] and his *Apollo and Daphne* was also, of course, based on Ovid. By 1718 he had become the most prolific writer of English lyrics and librettos. On balance, he seems a good candidate as third librettist, and one would be happy to subscribe to Dean's shrewd conjecture that Hughes may have contributed more to *Acis and Galatea* than is commonly supposed.[89]

Envoi

The notion that *Acis and Galatea* was originally planned as a three-voiced serenata for the principal characters alone raises further questions which there is no space to explore here. In this shape the work would have been far closer in spirit to such pieces as *Clori, Tirsi e Fileno* (1707) or indeed *Aci, Galatea e Polifemo*; it seems reasonable to presume that Handel's English librettists, anxious to form some idea of the serenata convention, would have asked Handel to play through to them his earlier treatment of the subject proposed and would have studied its text. A comparison of the Italian serenata with the three-voiced *Acis and Galatea* turns out to be almost as interesting as a comparison of the latter with the five-voiced version. There is more to say, too, on the literary side, and on the way in which the work fits into the biographies and intellectual preoccupations of Pope and Gay. These matters are to be discussed in a later study.

85   Ibid., i, p. 316.
86   Ibid., ii, pp. 28, 33.
87   Ibid., i, pp. 131f, 152, 165, 174; *The Correspondence of John Hughes*, ed. W. Duncombe (London, 1774), i. pp. 36–43, 74, 84. A letter of 22 May 1712 (ibid., pp. 45f) asserts that a Mr Bridges, 'Surveyor-general of the ordnance at Wallington', was 'very pleased' when David Mercator read Hughes's *Calypso and Telemachus* to him: was this a relative of Chandos, or possibly a mistaken reference to the man himself, then plain James Brydges? In 1705 he had been very near to taking the above post, but opted instead for the paymaster-generalship (Baker, *The Life and Circumstances of James Brydges*, pp. 23, 30). Hughes was appointed to a position in the Ordnance office.
88   The tale of Pyramus and Thisbe, from Book IV: see *Poems*, i, p. 123.
89   Dean, p. 157.

George I's Venetian palace and theatre boxes in the 1720s

COLIN TIMMS

It may surprise some readers to learn that George I rented a palace and a number of theatre boxes in Venice. He did not go there after his accession to the English throne in 1714, and he is generally thought to have been rather thrifty and not very interested in the arts. At the beginning of his reign as Elector of Hanover in 1698 he had cut back on court expenditure and closed the opera-house which his father, Ernst August, had built. As Ragnhild Hatton explains, however, his failure to reopen it after the customary year of discontinuation on his father's death was due above all to external factors – the outbreak of the War of the Spanish Succession, his later preoccupation with the Great Northern War, and 'the fact that from 1698 the Osnabrück income which Ernst August had enjoyed, and from which he had defrayed the expenses of the Hanover opera, ceased'.[1] In the 1720s, moreover, George gave £1,000 per annum to the Royal Academy of Music in London and attended performances of opera there – though, when he did, he evidently preferred to avoid the royal box.[2]

Whether or not his retention of a palace and of theatre boxes in Venice was a sign of personal interest in opera or the city, it certainly represents the continuation of a long Hanoverian relationship with the Serenissima. For decades the dukes and princes of Brunswick had been going to Venice to savour the delights of the carnival season. They had bought the Palazzo Non nobis Domine from the Loredan family for 60,000 ducats in 1581,[3] but it was in the second half of the seventeenth century, when Venetian opera was in the ascendant, that their visits became particularly frequent, almost regular.[4] The principal visitors were George's father and his uncles Georg

[1]   R. Hatton, *George I, Elector and King* (London, 1978), p. 364 n. 53. I am grateful to Donald Burrows for drawing this note to my attention.
[2]   J. H. Plumb, *The First Four Georges* (London, 1956), pp. 39, 41.
[3]   P. Paoletti, *L'architettura e la scultura del Rinascimento in Venezia* (Venice, 1893–7), part II, p. 187. Two years later they sold it to the Duke of Mantua for 91,000 ducats.
[4]   The principal secondary sources for the following account are: G. Fischer, *Musik in Hannover* (Hanover, 1903); R. E. Wallbrecht, *Das Theater des Barockzeitalters an den welfischen Höfen Hannover und Celle* (Hildesheim, 1974); Hatton, op. cit.; and L.

Wilhelm and Johann Friedrich. Between 1654 and 1694 nearly thirty librettos were dedicated to them and other members of the family.[5] Johann Friedrich went to Venice on five occasions; during his third visit, in 1667–8, the house of Brunswick was admitted to the nobility in recognition of the military support that he gave to the Republic in its continual battles against the Turks.[6] Ernst August supplied further military assistance and visited Venice at least seven times. His last two visits were marked by entertainments on a particularly spectacular scale. In August 1685 he was treated at Piazzola sul Brenta, the country seat of Marco Contarini, to 'a series of tournaments, mock naval battles and mini-operas, all of which enacted the imminent fall of the Ottoman empire at the hands of the Duke and his son [Maximilian Wilhelm]';[7] and in 1686, when he was accompanied by Georg Ludwig, later George I, he brought his visit to a splendid conclusion by giving an elaborate regatta on the Grand Canal.[8]

Ernst August stopped going to Venice as he approached the age of sixty, and started to develop the carnival at Hanover. The high point of the season was, of course, the Italian opera. Antonio Sartorio had been appointed Kapellmeister in 1666, but it was only with the opening of the magnificent new theatre in 1689, to the strains of Steffani's *Henrico Leone*, that opera at Hanover was established on a more permanent basis. Like the composer, the librettist (Ortensio Mauro), stage-designer (Tommaso Giusti) and many of the other artists involved came from the Veneto. The carnival of 1693, which celebrated the recent elevation of Hanover to the status of an electorate, was particularly lavish and is reported to have cost 34,511 thalers.[9] Although the opera was closed by Georg Ludwig on the

Bianconi and T. Walker, 'Production, Consumption and Political Function of 17th-Century Opera', *International Musicological Society: Report of the Twelfth Congress, Berkeley 1977*, ed. D. Heartz and B. Wade (Kassel, 1981), pp. 680–5. The full version of Bianconi and Walker's paper is in *Early Music History*, iv (1984), pp. 209–96.

5   In addition, at least four books of instrumental music were dedicated to members of family (see C. Sartori, *Bibliografia della musica strumentale italiana stampata in Italia fino al 1700*, ii (Florence, 1968), 1656d, 1667h, 1685s and p. 175); Barbara Strozzi's *Arie* (Venice, 1664) was dedicated to Sophie, Ernst August's consort, during her one visit to Venice, but G. A. Rusconi had already dedicated to her the Venice, 1660, reprint of his *Dieci libri d'architettura . . . secondo i precetti di Vetruvio.*

6   An account of the family appeared in C. Freschot, *La nobiltà veneta* (Venice, 2/1707), pp. 165f.

7   Bianconi and Walker, op. cit., p. 684. The timetable of events (*L'orologio del piacere*) and the librettos, all by Francesco Maria Piccioli, were printed at Piazzola in 1685. Cf. also P. Camerini, *Piazzola* (Milan, 1925).

8   See G. M. Alberti, *Giuochi festivi, e militari, danze, serenate, machine, boscareccia artificiosa, regatta solenne . . . esposti alla sodisfattione universale dalla generosità dell'A. S. D'Ernesto Augusto . . .* (Venice, 1686).

9   A detailed account of the carnival appears in C. E. von Malortie, *Der Hannoversche Hof unter dem Kurfürsten Ernst August und der Kurfürstin Sophie* (Hanover, 1847), pp. 152–5. The cost is given in E. Schuster, *Kunst und Künstler in den Fürstenthümern Calenberg und Lüneburg in der Zeit von 1636 bis 1727* (Hanover, 1905), p. 44.

death of his father, Carnival continued to be celebrated at Hanover, without opera, until 1733;[10] and the Venetian atmosphere was intensified at Herrenhausen, the summer palace which was built by a number of architects and artists from the Republic (including a Count Giacomo Querini),[11] by the construction of a special gondola lake and the employment of a Venetian gondolier.[12]

There is no thorough study of the tenure and running of the Hanoverians' Venetian palace and theatre boxes, but a fragmentary account can be pieced together from a number of secondary sources.[13] It was soon after his accession as Duke of Hanover in 1648 that Georg Wilhelm took out a long lease on a palace and seven boxes at a cost of 208 thalers per annum. In 1672 the boxes were administered for Johann Friedrich by Pietro Dolfin, the librettist of Sartorio's *Adelaide*, which was given that year at the Teatro S. Salvatore and dedicated to the duke.[14] The palace used from at least 1679 was the Palazzo Foscari on the Grand Canal; it was managed by Giovanni Matteo Alberti, Ernst August's doctor in Venice, who was to publish an account of his regatta. Alberti's book reveals that the Palazzo Foscari was still used by the duke in 1686.[15] By 1683–4 the number of theatre boxes had risen to nine and the cost of them and the palace to 270 thalers per annum. According to Fischer, boxes were taken in 1685 in such theatres as S. Moisè, S. Salvatore, SS. Giovanni e Paolo, S. Samuele and S. Giovanni Grisostomo – but not, apparently, in S. Angelo.

Although Ernst August's visit of 1686 was his last, a palace, the boxes and private gondolas were retained so that he or his successors could return to Venice if they wished. In fact, no member of the Brunswick–Lüneburg family appears to have held court in the palace after that date, though Prince Ernst August the younger stayed there in the autumn of 1707 and Steffani did the same in April 1709, when the palace was not fully furnished. Georg Ludwig also put the theatre boxes at the disposal of friendly visitors, among them King Frederik IV of Denmark in the winter of 1708–9.

The administration of the palace and boxes from 1690 was in the hands

[10] See J. Lampe, *Aristokratie, Hofadel und Staatspatriziat in Kurhannover* (Göttingen, 1963), i, p. 137.
[11] See U. von Alversleben, *Herrenhausen: die Sommerresidenz der Welfen* (Berlin, 1929), p. 73; R. Tardito-Amerio, *Italienische Architekten, Stukkatoren und Bauhandwerker der Barockzeit in den welfischen Ländern und im Bistum Hildesheim* (Göttingen, 1968), pp. [3], 160–6, 187–90.
[12] See Wallbrecht, op. cit., p. 76, and G. Schnath, *Geschichte Hannovers im Zeitalter der neunten Kur und der englischen Sukzession 1674–1714*, iii (Hildesheim, 1978), p. 512.
[13] Principally Fischer, Wallbrecht and Schnath, op. cit.
[14] Cf. *Kataloge der Herzog August Bibliothek Wolfenbüttel*, xiv: *Libretti*, ed. E. Thiel and G. Rohr (Frankfurt am Main, 1970), p. 5.
[15] Alberti, *Giuochi festivi*, pp. 14f. Fischer refers throughout to the Palazzo Foscarini.

of Pandolfo Mendlein, a merchant who had been appointed as Ernst August's agent in Venice the previous year. Following his death in 1700 they were managed by his successors as agent – Gian Battista Zanovello (d. 1713), Giovanni Battista Farinelli (the violinist and former Hanover 'maître des concerts' Jean-Baptiste Farinel, who was recalled in 1720) and Giuseppe Sorosina (dismissed 19 February 1726).[16] The cost of maintaining the palace and boxes does not appear in the Hanover chamber accounts ('Kammerrechnungen'), so Schnath concluded that it must have been met out of George I's private funds – the 'Schatullkasse' – for which no accounts have survived.[17] According to Fischer, the agents' instructions reveal that the palace and boxes were given up between 1720 and 1726, but Worsthorne mentions a document, dated 1728, in the Venetian State Archives, in which George II instructed the Resident in Venice to allow Field-Marshal von Schulenburg to have unrestricted use of his boxes.[18] The field-marshal in question was Count Johann Matthias von der Schulenburg (1661–1747), the eldest brother of George I's mistress Melusine and, from 1715, commander of all Venetian land forces, who had settled in Venice after his brilliant defence of Corfu against the Turks in 1715–16; he lived in splendid style in the Palazzo Loredan and amassed one of the greatest collections of paintings in eighteenth-century Venice.[19]

AGENTS' INSTRUCTIONS

The running of George I's palace and theatre boxes in the 1720s is greatly illuminated by the agents' instructions, which are preserved in the Niedersächsisches Hauptstaatsarchiv in Hanover, and by a fascinating series of documents among the Steffani papers in the archives of the Sacra Congregatio pro Gentium Evangelizatione seu de Propaganda Fide in Rome (the Fondo Spiga). These instructions and documents are presented in the Appendix below (pp. 115–30); the purpose of this essay is to explore some of their implications.

The instructions issued to Giuseppe Sorosina in March 1720 on his

---

16   See *Repertorium der diplomatischen Vertreter aller Ländern seit dem Westfälischen Frieden (1648)*, ii, ed. F. Hausmann, (Zürich, 1950), p. 179.

17   Receipts for sums paid out of the Schatullkasse are preserved in Hanover, Niedersächsisches Hauptstaatsarchiv, Dep. 84, Cal. Br. 22, XIII, Anhang 3. According to J. M. Beattie, *The English Court in the Reign of George I* (Cambridge, 1967), p. 260, some of them relate to the king's theatre subscriptions. Sorosina claimed to have sent receipts to Hanover, as we shall see, but these do not appear to be in the archives today. For information on these archives I am indebted to Ragnhild Hatton and Christoph Gieschen.

18   S. T. Worsthorne, 'Venetian Theatres: 1637–1700', *Music & Letters*, xxix (1948), p. 268.

19   See F. Haskell, *Patrons and Painters* (New Haven, rev. 2/1980), pp. 310ff. Cf. also J. M. von der Schulenburg, *Leben und Denkwürdigkeiten* (Leipzig, 1834).

appointment as George I's agent in Venice resemble those that had been given to Zanovello and Farinelli before him: they make clear that he was to be responsible for the king's furniture in Venice; his theatre boxes and the keys to them; his palace, where Sorosina would be allowed to live; and the king's mail (cf. Appendix, sect. I). Sorosina's successor, Ferdinando Crivelli, was also made responsible for the palace, furniture and mail, but not for the theatre boxes. His instructions, which are dated 8/19 February 1726, are identical to Sorosina's except that they lack the paragraph about the boxes (para. 2). The writer of the document started to copy it, but when he had finished the words 'Theatri di Venezia' he stopped, crossed it out and went on to the third paragraph, to which he gave the number 2 (see Pl. 2). One's first reaction on seeing Crivelli's instructions is to conclude, along with Fischer, that the boxes were given up at the time of Sorosina's dismissal; but, since George II appears to have had boxes in Venetian theatres in 1728, it seems more likely that responsibility for them was taken away from the king's agent and given to somebody else.

SOROSINA'S LETTER TO GÖRTZ AND HIS 'RELAZIONE' AND AFFIDAVITS

Sorosina clearly felt that his dismissal in 1726 was unfair and did everything he could to justify his conduct during his term of office. He wrote a passionate letter to Baron Friedrich Wilhelm von Görtz, the *Kammerpräsident* and chief minister at Hanover, who, it transpires, had appointed him; drafted a more detached account of his actions during his years in service; collected a number of sworn affidavits from contacts in Venice bearing witness to his loyalty, honesty and conscientiousness; and made a fair copy of the list of people to whom he had allocated the theatre boxes in 1725. These are the documents that are in the Fondo Spiga. They all speak favourably of Sorosina, but they also provide reasons why he might have been dismissed and shed light on the difficulties of administering the palace and boxes in the 1720s.

His letter to Görtz (Appendix, sect. II), which is dated 5 April 1726, reveals that his dismissal had not been an honourable discharge – far from it. He had apparently been found guilty of unpunctuality (or incompetence) as George I's agent, and in his defence he was sending Görtz his account of his conduct ('relazione giustificativa') and seven affidavits marked A–F and [G]. It is clear that this was not the first occasion on which he had written to Görtz for protection and that he felt that he had for some time been the victim of a determined campaign to discredit him. He admitted that he had delayed paying the rental on the boxes at the Teatro S. Cassiano, explained why he thought he had been right to do so and said that he had paid the rental for 1722 and 1723 on the instructions of a

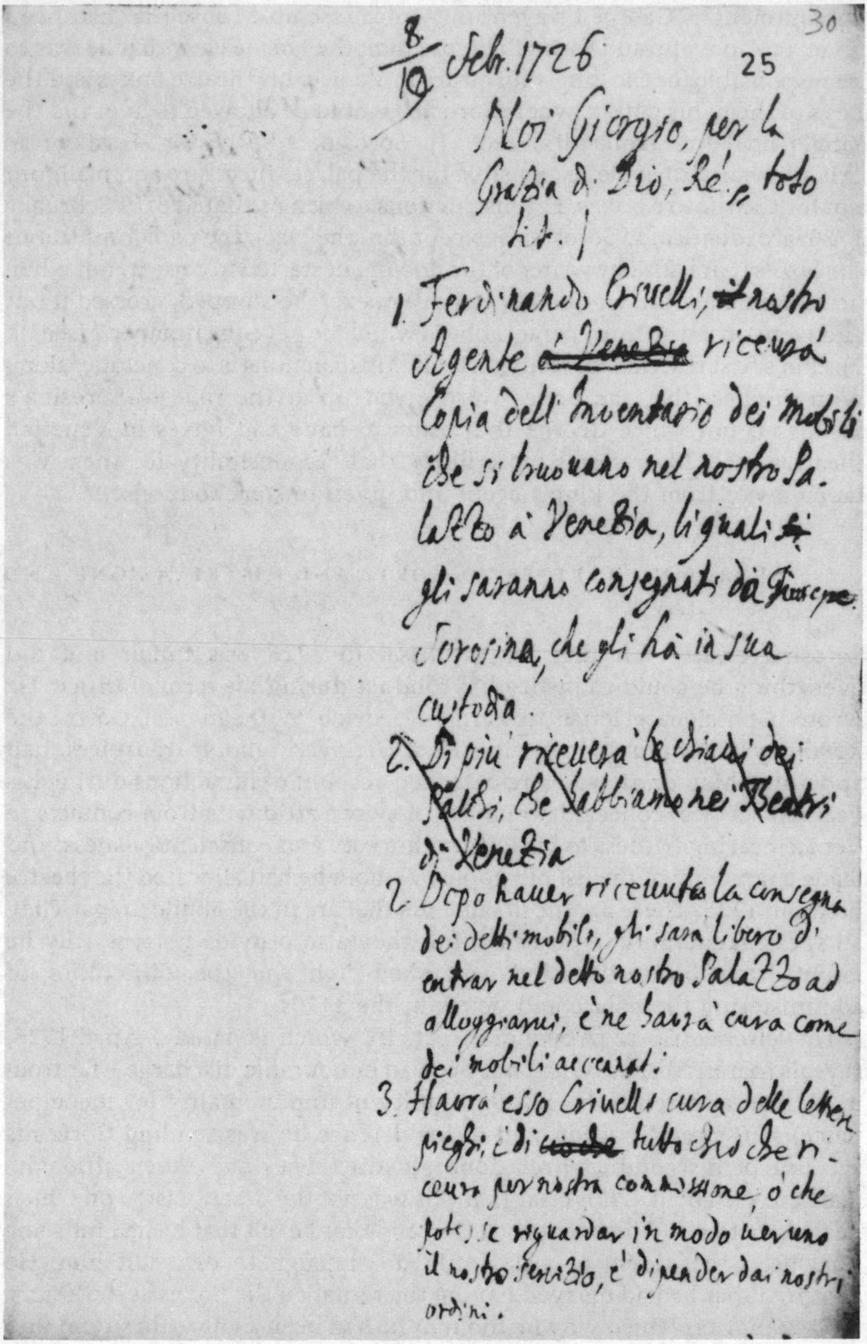

8/19 Feb. 1726 25 30

Noi Giorgio, per la Grazia di Dio, Rè, e tutto Tit.]

1. Ferdinando Crivelli, ~~il~~ nostro Agente ~~à Venezia~~ riceverà Copia dell'Inventario dei Mobili che si trovano nel nostro Palazzo à Venezia, li quali ~~gli~~ gli saranno consegnati da ~~Giuseppe~~ Torosina, che gli hà in sua custodia.

~~2. Di più riceverà le chiavi dei Palchi, che habbiamo nei Teatri di Venezia~~

2. Dopo haver ricevuta la consegna dei detti mobili, gli sarà libero di entrar nel detto nostro Palazzo ad alloggiarvi, è ne haverà cura come dei mobili accennati.

3. Havrà esso Crivelli cura delle lettere pieghi, è di ~~tutto~~ tutto ciò che riceverà per nostra commissione, ò che potesse riguardar in modo veruno il nostro servizio, è dipender dai nostri ordini.

Plate 2 Instructions to Ferdinando Crivelli on his appointment in 1726 as George I's agent in Venice 'cavagliere consaputo' (whose identity will emerge in due course). He had made a record of his disposition of the boxes day by day because he had foreseen the possibility of trouble from a superior ('da chi invigilava sopra di me'). Similar delays had occurred under his predecessors, who had also profited from the boxes at their disposal. He asked for the restitution of his honour and for the pension enjoyed by Farinelli, who appears to have died fairly recently;[20] and in an addendum he sought to explain some confusion over payment for the box at S. Moisè.

Further information on these and related matters is provided by Sorosina's 'relazione' (Appendix, sect. III), which, though undated, must have been written at around the same time as the letter. It emerges that Sorosina had been accused of deferring payment of the rental on the palace as well as the boxes. He admitted that he had done so on the palace, but only in order to try to force the proprietors to carry out necessary repairs – which, he said, was normal practice in Venice. He cited the case of Field-Marshal von Schulenburg, who had been forced to pay out of his own pocket for repairs to George I's palace, where he was living, and to a house belonging to it in which part of his retinue was accommodated; the field-marshal would certainly vouch for Sorosina, if approached.

Although no affidavit from Schulenburg appears to survive in the Fondo Spiga, there is in the collection one unmarked attestation of 4 May 1726 to which Sorosina never refers but which supports his statements about the palace (Appendix, sect. IV, [H]). If this item is read in conjunction with Sorosina's 'relazione', it emerges that the palace rented by George I, in which Schulenburg lived, was the Palazzo Loredan in the vicinity of S. Trovaso. This was not the Palazzo Non nobis Domine, which is near S. Marcuola, belonged in this period to the Grimani family and later became known as the Palazzo Vendramin-Calergi,[21] but the Palazzo Loredan 'dell'Ambasciatore' in the *contrada* of S. Barnaba, which had belonged to Antonio Loredan, *provveditor* of Corfu at the time of the siege in 1715–16 (cf. Pl. 3). Its sobriquet derives from Francesco Loredan, who, having been elected doge in 1752, let the palace to the Imperial ambassadors as the seat of their embassy and residence. He stipulated that they should hire the building for a minimum of twenty-nine years, pay the rent for that period in advance, and bear the cost of any repairs. The first ambassador to live in the palace, Count Philipp Orsini-Rosenberg, took up residence in 1754; ten years later he was succeeded by Count Giacomo Durazzo, the former impresario and patron of Gluck.[22]

20   The date of Farinelli's death is given as 'c1720' in *The New Grove*, vi, p. 397. Sorosina's letter suggests that he died in 1725 or 1726.
21   See Paoletti, *L'architettura*, part II, p. 187.
22   See P. Lauritzen and A. Zielcke, *Palaces of Venice* (Oxford, 1978), pp. 90f. I am grateful to Michael Talbot for drawing this book to my attention and for kind assistance when this essay was in typescript. On Durazzo, cf. *The New Grove*, v, pp. 746ff.

Palazzo Loredan a S. Barnaba sopra Canal Grande.

Plate 3   The Palazzo Loredan in the *contrada* of S. Barnaba, later known as the Palazzo Loredan dell' Ambasciatore, which was rented by George I during the 1720s.

It would seem from the attestation mentioned above that in the mid-1720s the palace belonged half to Giovanni Loredan and half to his nephews. The rent was collected by the nephews' agent, Antonio Novello, who gave half to Giovanni's agent, Antonio Rotta. Rotta affirmed that the money for payment had arrived from Hanover and that Sorosina had told him so, but that the latter had occasionally refused to hand it over until repairs had been completed; otherwise, Rotta had always found Sorosina very 'ponctual'. It was doubtless problems such as these that led Francesco Loredan to lay down such strict conditions when he let the palace to the Austrians in the 1750s.

On the question of the theatre boxes, Sorosina claimed in his 'relazione' that he had been ill in 1721–2 and unable to carry out his duties, and that he had then been smitten by an attack of apoplexy. In support of this claim he enclosed a certificate, dated 20 March 1726, from two doctors (Appendix, sect. IV, A). At first sight this appears quite convincing, but on reflection the words 'une Maladie tres dangereuse' seem suspiciously vague and one wonders whether these doctors had any knowledge of Sorosina in 1721–2. He also claimed that during his illness somebody else (unnamed) had looked after his affairs and that if they had deferred paying for the boxes or had altered any dates this was not his fault. All the money he had received from the 'Chambre Royale' had been spent on the proper rentals, as could be seen from the receipts that he had sent back from time to time. Nobody had profited during his term of office.

As evidence of his integrity with regard to S. Giovanni Grisostomo and S. Samuele, the theatres which involved the greatest expense, he submitted an affidavit from their proprietor, Vincenzo Grimani (Appendix, sect. IV, B). Grimani affirmed that Sorosina had normally paid the rentals on time but that he had defaulted once. Some years ago, all the other box-holders at S. Samuele had paid one half of their usual rental for the performance of an opera there, but Sorosina had said that he had not received any instruction on this matter from the court. This attestation presumably relates to one of the operas put on at Ascensiontide in 1720 or 1722–5, for there appears to have been no opera at S. Samuele in the carnival or autumn seasons of the early 1720s.[23]

Sorosina turned next in his 'relazione' to the question of S. Cassiano. He had suspended payment there in 1722 and 1723 because everybody else had done the same; and this was because the 'Entrepreneurs Commiques' at the time disposed of the boxes 'a leur fantasie avec prejudice, et desordre'. His claim was supported by an affidavit from Scipion Boldù (Appendix, sect. IV, C), a Venetian nobleman, who affirmed that in 1724 he

---

[23]   See G. Bonlini, *Le glorie della poesia, e della musica* (Venice, 1730/R1979), pp. 182–202; A. Groppo, *Catalogo di tutti i drammi per musica* (Venice, [1745]/R1977), pp. 112–21; and T. Wiel, *I teatri musicali veneziani del Settecento* (Venice, 1897/R1978), pp. 56–79.

had been asked to pay retrospectively for the two preceding years by contributing half of the rent that had been due from him for 1722; he had paid, but could not vouch for others. Sorosina had paid on the instructions of the 'cavagliere consaputo', according to his letter to Görtz, but his 'relazione' goes on to mention 'la déposition du S.' Castoreo', in which the rentals, presumably for S. Cassiano, were said not to have been paid; unfortunately, the deposition is not preserved with the documents under discussion and the identity of this particular 'S.' Castoreo' has still to be established.[24]

The same kinds of 'ritardo' and 'impedimenti', Sorosina told Görtz, had also occurred under his predecessors. Evidence of this was to be found in an attestation supplied by the singer Severo Frangioni (Appendix, sect. IV, F). Although this document is dated 1726, the events it describes presumably took place when Farinelli was George I's agent, i.e. before March 1720. It probably refers to autumn 1717 or Carnival 1718, the only two seasons when, according to Wiel, Antonia Gavazzi (or Cavazzi) sang at S. Cassiano.[25] Frangioni had sung at Hanover in 1689, presumably in Steffani's *Henrico Leone*, and was employed as an alto at St Mark's from 25 July 1694 to 1 December 1720;[26] this document sheds new light on his additional activity as a teacher. The meaning of the attestation is not entirely clear, but if the gender of 'les quelles' is correct it indicates that Frangioni accepted two boxes at the opera instead of 60 ducats as his fee for teaching Gavazzi her parts. If this is so, it is hard to see how his statement supports Sorosina's point about delays in payment for the boxes.

The three remaining affidavits (D, E and [G]) also relate to Sorosina's letter to Görtz rather than to his 'relazione'. Statements D and E were intended to demonstrate his 'pontualità' and 'zelo, per il Decoro, e grandezza di S[ua] M[aestà]' in the allocation of the boxes, and they appear to do so. Attestation D also reveals how difficult it could be to come by a box for a first performance of a new opera. The signatory, a certain Zuane Rosa, had been approached by a Venetian senator (discreetly unnamed) acting on behalf of a 'chevalier' (also unnamed) and appears to have made contact with Sorosina only after a long and arduous search. The latter, to his credit, demanded to speak to the 'chevalier' himself in order to give him the key to the box and impress upon him the nature of the privilege he was to enjoy; and we are assured that Sorosina refused to accept any money.

Attestation E is dated 18 March 1726 but refers, nevertheless, to 'le

24   There were librettists by the name of Bortolameo and Giacomo Castoreo in the mid seventeenth century (cf. Bonlini, op. cit., pp. 53, 55–6).

25   Wiel, op. cit., pp. 46, 52. The dates are corroborated by Bonlini, op. cit., pp. 176–9.

26   See Wallbrecht, op. cit., p. 191, and O. Termini, 'Singers at San Marco in Venice: the Competition between Church and Theatre (c1675–c1725)', *R.M.A. Research Chronicle*, xvii (1981), p. 86.

Carneval de l'annèe passèe 1724' and 'l'Ascension dans l'Ête passè 1725'. The earlier date is undoubtedly *more veneto* (*m.v.*) and the carnival in question that of December 1724 to February 1725 – the same year as the Ascension concerned. The statement shows that the king had boxes in 1725 in S. Samuele and other theatres and that some of them were put at the disposal of Bernardo Riva (for himself and other people), Giovanni Antonio Cossali (for himself and for Filippo and Agostino Nani) and Scipion Boldù. Like the Boldù, the Riva and the Nani were Venetian noble families; Cossali, as we shall see, was Schulenburg's agent.

The final affidavit, referred to as 'G' in the addendum to Sorosina's letter to Görtz, relates to the Teatro S. Moisè and was supplied by Sebastiano Mauro, its impresario in May 1725. He was presumably related to the stage-designer Antonio Mauro, who is mentioned in the attestation, and to some of the other Mauro employed in theatres at the time.[27] Sebastiano affirmed that Sorosina had always paid the rental on the king's box in S. Moisè, except in 1724, when Sorosina claimed that he had not received any remittance for the purpose. In 1725 he had paid Antonio Mauro, one of the 'interessès' of the theatre, who had given him a receipt. Later, the same rental had also been paid by Cavalier Querini to Pietro Balbi, an agent of the theatre, who knew nothing of Sorosina's payment. The affidavit establishes that Querini was the unnamed *cavaliere* mentioned in the addendum to Sorosina's letter to Görtz. There Sorosina said that the *cavaliere* had been given back his 30 ducats on returning to Venice and made clear that he felt that Querini's intervention had been a deliberate attempt to blacken his name. In view of this it seems very likely that Querini was also the person who 'invigilava' over Sorosina.

Proof of this is to be found in two letters of Steffani, who in 1722–5 lived in semi-retirement at Padua. Apart from revealing that the soprano Benedetta Sorosina was related to George I's agent,[28] Steffani's letter of 1 December 1724 to Signora Fiorenza Ravagnina[29] (Appendix, sect. VI)

[27]   Cf. N. Mangini, *I teatri di Venezia* (Milan, 1974), *passim*, and L. Moretti, 'Dopo l'insuccesso di Ferrara: diverbio tra Vivaldi e Antonio Mauro', *Vivaldi veneziano europeo*, ed. F. Degrada (Florence, 1980), pp. 89ff.

[28]   A further letter, of 8 March 1725, from Steffani to Giuseppe Riva, the Modenese Resident in London, reveals that Benedetta was Sorosina's daughter and that she was not a success when she sang in Handel's *Giulio Cesare* in early 1725 (see Appendix, sect. VII). It is clear that she wrote to Steffani about her experience; it also seems possible that he had recommended her for London and that some parties there desired or conspired that she should fail.

[29]   Signora Ravagnina was a Venetian noblewoman, born Fiorenza Riva, who had married Girolamo Ravagnin in 1674 (see *Nomi, cognomi, età, e blasoni . . . de' veneti patrizj viventi e de' genitori loro defonti . . . Libro d'oro* (Venice, 1714), pp. 180f). The Ravagnin family hailed from Treviso and was enrolled in the Venetian Nobility in 1657 (see E. A. Cigogna [Cicogna], *Saggio di bibliografia veneziana* (Venice, 1847), p. 486).

establishes immediately that the Querini in question was the Venetian nobleman Count Giacomo Querini, who had gone to Hanover in the reign of Ernst August and supervised the building of Herrenhausen. He was still 'Hofbau- und Gartendirektor' in 1709–10 but went to Venice in 1711.[30] It would seem from Steffani's letter that Sorosina had been defaulting on the payment of postal charges and had suspected Querini of trying to prevent him from receiving his mail. If he had been so prevented, this would have affected Steffani, for while he was in Padua most of his letters came to him via Sorosina in Venice. Sorosina therefore had good reason for asking Steffani, as he presumably did, to take steps to remedy the situation. Steffani's response was to ask Signora Ravagnina to make discreet enquiries of the 'Conte Tassis' – Prince Anselm Franz of Thurn and Taxis (1681–1739), who was responsible for postal services throughout the empire[31] – and to let him know the result. I have not discovered what this was, but in view of Sorosina's later dismissal it may not have been very favourable.

The second Steffani letter was written in Padua on 14 September 1725 and addressed to Sorosina himself:

. . . Per altro mi rimetto alla mia di hieri, e circa al consaputo Cavaliere, Io credo, che arriverà presto à Venezia, perch'è partito da Hannovera alli 27. del passato. Chi me lo scrive dice una cosa, che Io non intendo, perche dice precisam[en]te il Sig.^r Co: Querini è, Lode a Dio, partito lunedi passato di ritorno per Venezia, e questo è il giorno 27. di Agosto . . .[32]

Otherwise, I refer to my letter of yesterday; and on the 'consaputo Cavaliere', I believe he will soon arrive in Venice because he departed from Hanover on the 27th of last month. The person who wrote to me about this says one thing that I do not understand, because he/she says precisely that Signor Conte Querini left – thank God – last Monday to return to Venice, and this is 27 August.

The description of Querini as the 'consaputo cavaliere' suggests very strongly that he was the 'cavagliere consaputo' who had ordered Sorosina to pay for the boxes at S. Cassiano in 1722 and 1723 and that he had a reputation of some kind: everyone knew who this *cavaliere* was. He may have gone to Venice in 1711, but he clearly did not stay there, for at the time of Steffani's letter he was on his way back there from Hanover; it was presumably at the end of this journey that he was given back the 30 ducats that he had paid to Pietro Balbi for the box at S. Moisè. But the most instructive words in this letter are 'Lode a Dio', which show that Querini was heartily disliked by at least one person in Hanover; if he could inspire

---

30   Wallbrecht, *Das Theater des Barockzeitalters*, p. 101 n. 6.

31   *Allgemeine deutsche Biographie*, xxxvii (Leipzig, 1894), pp. 479–82.

32   Rome, Sacra Congregatio pro Gentium Evangelizatione seu de Propaganda Fide, Fondo Spiga, vol. 81, pp. 194–5.

this kind of sentiment and expression, there may have been some ground for Sorosina's suspicion that he was attempting to engineer his downfall.

Whatever Querini's role, it seems clear that Sorosina was not a success as George I's agent in Venice. His letter, 'relazione' and attestations constitute an impressive array of documents, most of which speak in his favour; but they also reveal that during his six years in office he frequently defaulted on payment of the rental for the palace and boxes, and Steffani's letter to Fiorenza Ravagnina suggests that he defaulted, too, on the payment of postal charges. There may have been good reason for some of these postponements, but Sorosina's claim that there had been similar delays under his predecessors, and that they had profited from their office, does nothing to strengthen his hand. He was, in his own words, 'surchargé de Famille, et environé de plus dures indigences', and it is hard to believe that he did not occasionally seek to take advantage of his position.

SOROSINA'S 'DISPOSITIONE'

It was because Sorosina foresaw 'qualche gran disgrazia', according to his letter to Görtz, that he kept a record of how he disposed of the boxes. From the documents discussed above it is clear that the king had one box in S. Moisè and a number of others in S. Cassiano, S. Samuele and S. Giovanni Grisostomo (including No. 25 in the first tier). All of this, and more, is confirmed in Sorosina's 'dispositione' which, so far as I am aware, is unique for the early eighteenth century in listing the names of the individuals to whom the boxes were allocated day by day (see Appendix, sect. V).[33]

The title of this remarkable document (cf. Pl. 4) reveals that Sorosina was commanded to draw it up by the king; it thus appears to contradict his letter to Görtz. He apparently received the order in 1724, though this date could be *m.v.* and refer to the start of the following year. The title also suggests, however, that the document was prepared after Sorosina's dismissal in 1726, a suggestion supported by the past tense of those entries that read 'andò vuoto' ('went empty') and by the curious entry for 30 January under S. Moisè, which must be a mistake. The explanation for this apparent contradiction is probably that the document is a fair copy, made in 1726, of the rough-and-ready list which Sorosina must have made at an earlier date when he was actually in the process of allocating the boxes.

The disposition itself almost certainly relates to 1725. It covers two seasons: the Carnival of January and February '1724' (cf. 'San Luca primo

---

[33]   The names of people with boxes in S. Moisè in 1686–7 are given by R. Giazotto, 'La guerra dei palchi', *Nuova rivista musicale italiana*, i (1967), p. 276; subscribers to many Venetian theatres in 1790 and 1792 are listed by Wiel, *I teatri musicali*, pp. [lxxxi]ff; and Wallbrecht, op. cit., p. 216, mentions a series of seating plans for the Schlosstheater at Hanover.

Lista della disposizione delle Logie neli Theatri di Venezia di Sua Maestà B.ᵃ
fatta da Giuseppe Sorosina Agente di Sua M.ᵗᵃ nel tempo, che ne ha havuto l'
ordine dalla Maestà Sua nell'anno 1724

Del Theatro di S. Gio Grisostomo Logia | Logia nel Theatro di S. Cassano nel primo
primo ordine n.º 25 | ordine n.º 28

14 Genaro andò vuoto	60 14 Genaro à S.E. Fiorenza Bauagnina
15 d. al Medico di S.E. Feld Marescial	15 d. à Dona Marina Giustiniana
16 d. à S.E. Fiorenza Bauagnina	16 d. à S.E. Becauitor di Malta
31 d. Prima vecita d'Opera neloua dato à S.E.	18 d. à S.E. Agostin Nani
Bauagnina si Servina à Duca di Massa Car-	19 d. à S.E. Bernardo Bina
rara	30 d. à S.E. Cecilia Cornera
2 Febraro à S.E. Cecilia Cornera	2 Febraro à S.E. Becauitor di Malta
3 d. al Sig.º Cossali Agente di S.E. Marescial	3 d. à S.E. Maria Bauagnina
4 d. à S.E. Maria Bauagnina	4 d. à Dona Marina Giustiniani
5 d. à S.E. Agostin Nani	5 d. à S.E. Antonia Michiel
6 d. à S.E. Antonio Loredan	6 d. à S.E. Agostin Nani
7 d. à S.E. Philippo Bon	8 d. à S.E. Benedetto Marcello
8 d. à S.A. Duchessa di Massa	8 d. à S.E. Giacomo Bina
12 d. à S.E. Contessa Coronini	9 d. à S.E. Fiorenza Bauagnina
13 d. andò vuoto	10 d. à S.E. Polo Benier
Logia in deto Theatro al secondo ordi-	11 d. à S.E. Contessa Coronini
ne n.º 32	12 d. à S.E. Giacomo Bina
24 Genaro andò vuoto	13 d. andò vuoto
25 d. andò vuoto	Logia nel deto Theatro secondo ord.ᵉ n.º 28
28 d. andò vuoto	14 Genaro al Sig.º Cossali
31 d. Prima vecita d'Opera nuova dato	15 d. Al Sig.ᵉ Fiorenzin Antoneti
à S.E. Contessa Coronini	16 d. à Sig.ª Nicolò Vanali
2 Febraro à S.E. Benedetto Marcello	18 d. à S.E. La Contessa Coronini
3 d. ada Sig.ª Durastante	19 d. à S.E. Becauitor di Malta
4 d. al Sig.º Pio Antonio Cossali	30 d. à Dona Marina Giustiniani
5 d. à S.E. Agostin Nani	2 Febraro al Sig.º Vicenzo Cassani
6 d. ada Durastante	3 d. al Sig.º Nicolò Vanali
7 d. al Sig.º Tomaso Giani	4 d. à S.E. Coronini
8 d. à S.E. Contessa Coronini	5 d. al Sig.º Bortolo Morandi
10 d. al Sig.º Nuevo Franzioni Musico	6 d. à S.E. Dama Muta S. Gio
11 d. à S.E. Polo Benier	7 d. à S.E. Contessa Coronini
12 d. à S.E. Co: Tassi	8 d. à Giuseppe Arrigida
13 d. ada Sig.ª Durastante	9 d. à S.E. Becauitor di Malta
	10 d. al Sig.º Cossali
	11 d. à Zuane Loredan
	12 d. al Sig.º Pellegrini
	13 d. andò vuoto

Plate 4   Sorosina's 'dispositione' for 1725

ordine nº 4') and the Ascension of May 1725. It would be very surprising if the document covered two isolated seasons over twelve months apart. There can be no doubt at all that 'May 1725' means what it says, but the date '1724' is doubtless *m.v.* and the carnival in question almost certainly that of 1725. If so, the 'dispositione' refers to the same two seasons as affidavit E. It appears from attestation B that the king normally had boxes in at least two theatres in the autumn season as well, but there is no mention of these in the 'dispositione'.

For the carnival season the king had ten boxes in five theatres – two each in S. Giovanni Grisostomo, S. Cassiano and S. Luca (i.e. S. Salvatore),[34] three in S. Samuele and one in S. Moisè. For the Ascension season he retained the three in S. Samuele. As one would expect, all the boxes were in the first or second tier. It would seem from the addendum to Sorosina's letter to Görtz and from affidavit F that the boxes at S. Moisè and S. Cassiano cost 30 ducats apiece, while attestation B suggests that those at S. Samuele at Ascensiontide cost half the usual amount. If all the other boxes cost 30 ducats each, which seems very unlikely,[35] the total cost of the thirteen boxes for the carnival and Ascension seasons would have been 345 ducats.

The repertory of operas known to have been performed in Venetian theatres in 1725 ties in very nicely with the theatres mentioned in the 'dispositione'; indeed, the fact that this repertory relates to the document more closely than does that of 1724 confirms that 1725 is the date of the carnival in question. For this season Bonlini and Groppo list three operas performed at S. Giovanni Grisostomo (Vinci's *Ifigenia in Tauride* and *Rosmira fedele* and Orlandini's *Berenice*), three at S. Moisè (Porta's *Agide, rè di Sparta*, Buina's *Li sdegni cangiati in amore* and the pasticcio *Il nemico amante*), two at S. Angelo (Zuccari's *Seleuco* and Porta's *Ulisse*) and one at S. Cassiano (Albinoni's *Didone abbandonata*); they also give one opera for S. Samuele at Ascensiontide (Francesco Brusa's *L'amor eroico*).[36]

If this repertory is compared with the list of the king's boxes given above, one or two discrepancies emerge. On the one hand, although there were operas at S. Angelo, the king did not have a box at that theatre. In this he appears to have copied his father and followed an established Hanoverian tradition. Why the Hanoverians eschewed S. Angelo remains an open question. On the other hand, the king had boxes for the carnival season at S. Samuele and S. Luca, for which Bonlini and Groppo provide no

[34]   'Segue il Nobilissimo Teatro di S. Salvatore, detto volgarmente S. Luca' (Bonlini, *Le glorie della poesia*, p. 24).

[35]   The figure is similar to prices at S. Giovanni Grisostomo in 1688–9 (when Ernst August was one of about ninety nobles who did not pay their subscriptions) but very much lower than those at S. Benedetto in 1750–60 (cf. Giazotto, op. cit., *Nuova rivista musicale italiana*, i (1967), p. 498, and iii (1969), pp. 931–2).

[36]   Bonlini, op. cit., pp. 196–9; Groppo, *Catalogo*, pp. 119–21.

repertory. This is because both theatres were used mainly for comedies and these were not included in their catalogues; when S. Samuele presented an opera, as it frequently did at Ascensiontide (cf. May 1725), Bonlini took care to record it. Allacci and Wiel cite a comic work performed at S. Luca, the libretto of which is dated 1725,[37] but Mangini says this date is *m.v.* and that the work was given in 1726.[38]

The boxes were allocated to a fascinating variety of people: Venetian and foreign nobles; singers, composers, painters and a librettist; agents; and a considerable number of Italians whose identity has still to be established. Several people had clear connections with Hanover or the Hanoverians, or with the Italian opera in London. Members of the nobility appear to be distinguished in the 'dispositione' by their title or the letters 'S.E.' (Sua Eccellenza). On this basis, the Boldù, Nani, Ravagnin and Riva, whom we have already met, are among at least fourteen Venetian noble families represented; the others are the Corner, Foscolo, Gradenigo, Loredan, Marcello, Michiel, Moro, Mula, Renier and Zambelli. The Giustiniani should probably be added to this list: 'Dona Marina Giustiniana' was almost certainly the Marina Capello who in 1671 had married Ascanio Zustinian of 'S. Salvador in Calle delle Acque';[39] the fact that he had died by 1714 may explain why his name does not appear in the 'dispositione'.

Most of the Venetian nobles can readily be identified by reference to the *Libro d'oro*, but 'S.E. Madama Moro' and 'S.E. Zambelli' cannot,[40] and several others are problematical. It is not clear which branch of the large Corner (or Cornaro) family 'Cecilia Cornera' belonged to: she may have been the Cecilia Gradenigo who in 1702 had married Zuane Battista Corner of the 'Ponte de' Nomboli, Rio, e Contrada di S. Polo', or Cecilia Marin, the bride in 1701 of Niccolò Corner of S. Basegio.[41] 'Pietro Gradenigo' was presumably the famous *erudito* of that name (1695–1776), the author–compiler of the *Commemoriali* (historical scrapbooks) and *Notatori* (journals) now preserved, together with the rest of Gradenigo's large collection of manuscripts, in the Museo Correr, Venice;[42] and 'Antonia

---

37   *Nerone detronato dal trionfo di Sergio Galba* (Venice, 1725): L. Allacci, *Drammaturgia . . . accresciuta e continuata fino all'anno MDCCLV* (Venice, 1755/R1961), col. 554; Wiel, *I teatri musicali*, p. 79.

38   Mangini, *I teatri di Venezia*, p. 113 n. 13.

39   *Libro d'oro* (see n. 29 above), pp. 226f.

40   'S. E. Madama Moro' is unlikely to have been the Venetian contralto Elisabetta Moro unless the latter was a noblewoman or the initials are a mistake. Elisabetta sang in nearly twenty operas between 1723 and 1741, including *Seleuco* and *Ulisse*, both at S. Angelo, in Carnival 1725: see Wiel, *I teatri musicali*; R. L. and N. W. Weaver, *A Chronology of Music in the Florentine Theater 1590–1750* (Detroit, 1978); and A. L. Bellina, B. Brizi and M. G. Pensa, *I libretti vivaldiani* (Florence, 1982).

41   *Libro d'oro*, pp. 66–9.

42   Extracts from the *Notatori* were published as *Notizie d'arte tratte dai notatori e dagli annali di N. H. Pietro Gradenigo*, ed. L. Livan (Venice, 1942).

Michieli' was presumably the Antonia Conti who had married Iseppo Michiel 'a' Tolentini, contrada di S. Pantalon' in 1696.[43] Whether 'Orsetta Mula' was the 'Dama Mula S. Vio' is not certain: the Mula (or Mulla) family came from S. Vio, but the *Libro d'oro* does not include an 'Orsetta'; in passing we should note that Antonio da Mula was an adjudicator at Ernst August's regatta in 1686[44] and that he was married to Isabetta Loredan.[45] 'Maria Ravagnina' was born Bonfadini and married Giulio Ravagnin in 1703.[46] She or Fiorenza Ravagnina had a box at S. Giovanni Grisostomo on 31 January 1725 'per servire il Duca di Massa Carrara': the duke in question, who also was a member of the Venetian nobility, was Alderano Cibo Malaspina (1690–1731), Duke of Massa and Prince of Carrara; the duchess (cf. S. Giovanni Grisostomo, 8 February) was Ricciarda Gonzaga, whom he had married in 1715.[47] The duke was the dedicatee of *Li sdegni cangiati in amore*, but neither he nor the duchess appears to have gone to S. Moisè to see it performed.

The names Canal, Carminati, Zini and Zuliani also belonged to Venetian noble families, but the absence from the 'dispositione' of the initials 'S.E.' suggests that the individuals listed were not members of them. There were instrumentalists by the name of Canal and Carminati in Venice in the early eighteenth century, but no 'Lorenzino' or 'Francesco' is known.[48] 'Pietro Zini' could conceivably have been related to the Zino family – 'marchands fabricants de laine à Venise. En plus, épices' – which was aggregated into the nobility in 1718,[49] or to the singer Maria Antonio Zini who took part in *L'oracolo in sogno* at S. Angelo in 1700;[50] while 'Benetto Zuliani' may have had some connection with the 'muranese' Giuliano Zuliani who sang at SS. Giovanni e Paolo in Carnival 1666–7[51] or with the sculptor Pietro Giuliani who worked at Osnabrück in the 1670s.[52]

The boxes were also given to nobles and dignitaries from other parts of Italy and abroad, such as the 'Conte' of Thurn and Taxis and the 'Contessa Coronini'. The latter was almost certainly Ursula Magdalena (1655–1727), widow of Lodovico Coronini, Count of Cronberg and Baron of Prebacina and Gradiscuta, who had died in 1700 and whose family seat was at Gorizia

43   *Libro d'oro*, pp. 136f.
44   Alberti, *Giuochi festivi*, p. 26.
45   *Libro d'oro*, pp. 154f.
46   Ibid., pp. 180f.
47   Freschot, *La nobiltà veneta*, pp. 169f; *Dizionario biografico degli italiani*, xxv (Rome, 1981), pp. 265–7.
48   See E. Selfridge-Field, 'Annotated Membership Lists of the Venetian Instrumentalists' Guild, 1672–1727', *R.M.A. Research Chronicle*, ix (1971), pp. 15–16.
49   J. Georgelin, *Venise au siècle des lumières* (Paris, 1978), p. 155.
50   U. Kirkendale, *Antonio Caldara: sein Leben und seine venezianisch-römischen Oratorien* (Graz, 1966), p. 29.
51   Mangini, *I teatri di Venezia*, p. 60 n. 16.
52   Tardito-Amerio, *Italienische Architekten*, p. 159.

in Friuli.[53] The Count Antonio Alberti who was at S. Samuele in May 1725 and the 'Cavalier Napolitano' who was there on 4 February have resisted identification, but not the 'Recevitor di Malta'. Receivers were officials appointed by the Grand Master of the Order of the Knights of St John, who governed Malta from 1530 to 1795, to collect revenues from European estates and remit the money to the island.[54] The official referred to in the 'dispositione' was presumably the receiver in Venice, Commendatore Fra Camillo, Conte di Pola.[55]

Field-Marshal von Schulenburg is mentioned frequently in the 'dispositione' (as 'S.E. Marescial' or 'Feld Marescial') but did not take a box himself because he was not in Venice at the time.[56] His agent, however, Giovanni Antonio Cossali, who is identified in an entry under S. Giovanni Grisostomo for 3 February, appears far more frequently than anybody else. Cossali was a versatile figure: in 1694 he published an oration (*Le glorie dell'esempio*) on the end of Alvise Foscarini's reign as *podestà* and *capitano* of Rovigo, and from 1734 to 1739 he was Venetian Resident for the republic of Graubünden in Switzerland.[57] Schulenburg's doctor and another member of his staff ('Zuane') were also given boxes. It appears that agents and servants enjoyed one of the privileges of their masters when the latter were not there. Sorosina and his family also took boxes on many occasions, and his predecessor Farinelli went to S. Samuele in May.

Among the most interesting names in the 'dispositione' are those of musicians and other artists. Only one librettist can be identified, Vincenzo Cassani, a Venetian who wrote the words of at least seven operas between 1711 and 1732 and a number of smaller works set by Benedetto Marcello and Albinoni.[58] Marcello, a Venetian nobleman, is one of the two composers named; the other is Antonio Lotti, who may have been born at Hanover when his father was Kapellmeister there. There are at least three singers: Margherita Durastanti, who had sung in London in 1723–4, Severo Frangioni, whom we met in attestation F, and Nicola Grimaldi ('Nicolini'), who was frequently in Venice in the 1720s and sang the role of

53   See the detailed family tree at the end of the first part of I. de Luca, *Das gelehrte Oesterreich* (Vienna, 1777–8).

54   See R. Cavaliero, *The Last of the Crusaders: the Knights of St John and Malta in the Eighteenth Century* (London, 1960), pp. 31ff.

55   I am grateful to Alison Hoppen for establishing the identity of this receiver with the aid of V. Mallia-Milanes, 'The Maltese Consulate in Venice during the XVIII Century', *Melita historica*, v (1971), p. 331. Michael Talbot informs me that Fra Camillo took up his post in January 1716, had his Public Entry on 10 February 1721 and left Venice in April 1730.

56   Schulenburg, *Leben und Denkwürdigkeiten*, p. 256.

57   See G. Soranzo, *Bibliografia veneziana, in aggiunta e continuazione del 'Saggio' di E. A. Cicogna* (Venice, 1885/R1968), p. 399, and *Repertorium . . . (1648)*, ii, p. 142.

58   See Allacci, *Drammaturgia, passim*, and M. Talbot, *Albinoni: Leben und Werk* (Adliswil, 1980), p. 56.

Enea in Albinoni's *Didone abbandonata* in the carnival season under consideration.[59]

The 'Sig^re Pellegrini' who took two boxes in February 1725 may have been the soprano castrato Valeriano Pellegrini, who had sung in operas by Steffani and Handel,[60] but he could equally plausibly have been the Venetian painter Giovanni Antonio Pellegrini (1675–1741), who had been brought to England with Marco Ricci by Lord Manchester in 1708–9, collaborated on the altar-piece in the Catholic church at Hanover (St Clemens) which Steffani had succeeded in getting built, and later worked in many other parts of Europe.[61] The latter possibility would seem to be strengthened by the fact that Ricci also appears in the 'dispositione'; this appealing landscape painter and scenographer was, like Pellegrini, a Venetian (Sorosina gives his name as 'Rizzi'), and six of his paintings were owned by Schulenburg.[62] It seems very likely that the 'Sig^r Francesco Monti' at S. Samuele on 16 May 1725 was also an artist: he was probably the Bolognese painter of that name whom Owen McSwiny (or Swiney) commissioned to help paint 'a series of allegorical tombs to commemorate the great men of England's recent history', a project on which Ricci also collaborated.[63]

The remaining figures can hardly be identified at all. Francesco Lorenzoni witnessed Vincenzo Grimani's signature on attestation B, but who he was is unknown. Tirabosco is described in the 'dispositione' as a 'Segretario di Senato', but his first name is not given, and it is not known whether he was related either to Antonio Tirabosco (1707–73)[64] or to Girolamo Tiraboschi, author of the celebrated *Storia della letteratura italiana*. Bortolo Morandi could conceivably be related to one of the three other Morandi mentioned by Robert Eitner,[65] and Doralice Rinaldi to the alto Antonio Rinaldi of Bologna, who sang in Florence between 1687 and 1699.[66] On the other hand, there were also many artists by the name of Morandi (or Morando) and Rinaldi – and Gentili and Viani;[67] unfortunately, none of them corresponds with the individuals mentioned in the

59   See Wiel, *I teatri musicali*, p. 75.
60   See *The New Grove*, xiv, p. 345.
61   See U. Thieme and F. Becker, *Allgemeines Lexikon der bildenden Künstler* (Leipzig, 1907–50), xxvi, pp. 359f, and Haskell, *Patrons and Painters, passim*.
62   See Haskell, op. cit., p. 314; also A. Blunt and E. Croft-Murray, *Venetian Drawings of the XVII and XVIII Centuries in the Collection of Her Majesty the Queen at Windsor Castle* (London, 1957).
63   See Haskell, op. cit., pp. 288ff.
64   See E. de Tipaldo, *Biografia degli italiani illustri nelle scienze, lettere ed arte del secolo XVIII* (Venice, 1834–45), ii, pp. 231–3.
65   *Biographisch-bibliographisches Quellen-Lexikon der Musiker und Musikgelehrten* (Leipzig, 1898–1904), vii, pp. 56f, and x, p. 431.
66   See Weaver, *A Chronology*, p. 368.
67   See Thieme and Becker, *Allgemeines Lexikon*.

'dispositione'. The 'Monsieur Patisel di Cà Venier' who took a box at S. Luca on 2 February is intriguing: was he a diplomat or a dancer, a musician or a chef – or was he the 'J. C. Patizel' who contributed to the *Componimenti poetici per l'ingresso di S.E. Almorò Barbaro Procuratore di San Marco a S.E. Cecilia Emo-Barbaro Procuratessa* (Venice, 1750)?[68] Four people remain – Lorenzino Antonetti, Antonio Moreschi, Bernardo Riosa and Nicolò Vanali – of whom nothing at all can be said.

The layout of the 'dispositione' reflects the relative social and artistic status of opera and comedy. At the top of the list are the Teatri S. Giovanni Grisostomo and S. Cassiano, the largest theatres presenting opera during Carnival. These are followed by S. Moisè and S. Samuele. The former also mounted opera but was smaller than the first two. S. Samuele was the larger of the theatres offering comedy, and it precedes S. Luca in the list. George I's boxes in the first tier at S. Giovanni Grisostomo and S. Cassiano, and box No. 3 in the first tier at S. Samuele, were almost invariably taken by nobles, but his other boxes were given to representatives of various social classes; one assumes that this was accepted practice, particularly since the 'dispositione' was intended for the king.

Although many Venetian noble families are represented in the list, many others – including notable ones such as the Contarini, Foscari, Grimani, Mocenigo, Morosini, Pasqualigo, Soranzo and Vendramin – are not; one wonders why. Since it could be difficult to come by a box (cf. affidavit D) and the king's were apparently free, it is surprising to find that they were not taken up on every available evening. There were only two dates left at Ascensiontide, when S. Samuele was the only theatre presenting opera, but there were plenty of vacancies during Carnival, particularly at S. Moisè, where the king, moreover, had only one box; this suggests that the standing of the theatre was comparatively low. The boxes were not always occupied by those to whom they had been allocated. It is clear from attestation E that Bernardo Riva took boxes 'non seulement pour moy, mais pour d'autres aussi' and that Cossali took them for himself and for Agostino and Filippo Nani (who also took them in their own names). Sorosina took one for his daughter at S. Moisè on 9 February, and on five occasions two boxes were given to one person (24 and 28 January, to Fiorenza Ravagnina; 3 February, to Nicolò Vanali; 5 February, to Agostino Nani; 6 February, to Margherita Durastanti). These people presumably gave or sold one of their boxes to somebody else; if they could do this, so could others: the path to corruption was clear.

It is doubtful whether the 'dispositione' materially affects the picture of Sorosina's competence painted above. On the one hand it demonstrates an ability to cope with detailed arrangements; on the other it suggests that he was not in touch with a very large proportion of Venetian society or of

68   Cited in Soranzo, *Bibliografia veneziana*, p. 318.

distinguished foreign residents or visitors. When the English Resident Doddington asked for boxes at SS. Giovanni e Paolo and S. Salvatore in 1671–2, his application said that 'he does not care for music, esteem poetry or understand the stage, but merely desires it for the honour of his office, as his predecessor and all other residents at present at the court enjoy the favour'.[69] This was presumably the main reason why George I retained his boxes – and the palace: if his agent could not use them to the monarch's advantage and was suspected, moreover, of incompetence or dishonesty, there was little reason why he should be kept on.

It was soon after his dismissal that Sorosina dispatched his letter, 'relazione' and affidavits to Görtz. He presumably also sent copies of these and of the 'dispositione' to Steffani, who had returned to Hanover in September–October 1725: this would explain why all these documents are among his papers today. Sorosina no doubt hoped that Steffani would put in a personal word for him at court. If he did, it was in vain. Sorosina was not reinstated, and one wonders whether he was given Farinelli's pension: the tone of his letter and 'relazione' suggests that he was deeply hurt by the treatment he had received.

What happened to the theatre boxes after Sorosina's dismissal remains to be established. If they were retained, as appears to have been the case, it seems very likely that responsibility for them was transferred to a person of higher rank, such as the British representative, John Law,[70] or possibly Count Giacomo Querini. If it was to this 'cavagliere consaputo', his victory – and Sorosina's humiliation – was complete. Be that as it may, Sorosina's years as George I's agent appear to have been an unhappy period in the history of the Hanoverians' relationship with Venice – a long and important relationship, both culturally and politically, on which further work clearly remains to be done.

APPENDIX

THE DOCUMENTS

This Appendix provides transcriptions of the documents on which the foregoing essay is based. I am grateful to Christoph Gieschen of the Niedersächsisches Hauptstaatsarchiv, Hanover, and to the archivist of the Sacra Congregatio pro Gentium Evangelizatione seu de Propaganda Fide,

---

[69]   Worsthorne, 'Venetian Theatres', p. 268.
[70]   See *British Diplomatic Representatives 1689–1789*, ed. D. B. Horn, Camden Third
        Series, xlvi (London, 1932), p. 84.

Rome, for supplying copies and microfilms of the documents in their collections. The transcriptions have been lightly edited: the letter 'u' is given as 'v' when appropriate, and some abbreviations have been expanded; otherwise, the original spelling, punctuation, capitals and accents have been retained.

I

Instructions of 10/21 March 1720 to Giuseppe Sorosina on his appointment as George I's agent in Venice (Hanover, Niedersächsisches Hauptstaatsarchiv, Hann. 92, LXXVII, 4, VI, 1, ff. 20f)

Noi Giorgio per la Gratia di Dio, Re della Gran-Bretagna

1. Ricevera l'Agente Nostro Sorosino Copia dell'Inventario de mobili, che si trovano nel Nostro Palazzo in Venezia, li quali gli saranno consegnati da nostro Agente Gio: Battista Farinelli.

2. Di più recevera le chiavi dei Palchi che habbiamo nei Theatri di Venezia, è le conservera appresso di se, per farne l'uso è la distributione che sarà più conforme alle nostre intentioni.

3. Doppo haver ricevuta la Consegna dei mobili e chiavi sodettes gli sarà libero d'entrar nel detto Nostro Palazzo ad alloggiarvi è ne havra cura come dei mobili sopr'accennati.

4. Havra esso Sorosino cura delle lettere, pieghi è di tutto cio che riceverà per nostra Commissione ò che potesse riguardar in modo veruno il nostro servizio, e dipender dai Nostri ordini.

5. Si manda qui annessa una Copia della Sua Patente di Nostro Agente in Venezia, la quale in luogo del giuramento solito à prestarsi da chi entra in carica, egli sottoscriverà di propria mano con promessa di sodisfar agli articoli in essa contenuti con esattezza è fede, è poi rimanderà quì questa Copia con la sottoscrittione è dichiaratione sodetta, per esser conservata nella Nostra Cancellaria.

In Fede di che habbiamo sottoscritte le presenti è fattovi apporre il Sigillo Nostro. Data dal Palazzo Nostro di S. Giacomo li 10/21 Marzo dell'Anno. 1720. del Regno Nostro il Sesto.

II

Letter of 5 April 1726 from Giuseppe Sorosina to Baron Friedrich Wilhelm von Görtz, Hanoverian *Kammerpräsident* (Rome, Sacra Congregatio pro Gentium Evangelizatione seu de Propaganda Fide, Fondo Spiga, vol. 2, f. 73r–v)

Eccellenza   Venezia 5 Aprile 1726
non havendo à questa corte altro apogio che il Padrocinio di V[ostra] E[ccellenza] Io ricorro con piena confidenza alla sua grande autorità perche

mi voglij difendere dalle insidie che sono state tornate contro la mia pontualità, questa, è causa di V. E., mentre solo doppo esser stato posto da lej nel merito di esser agente di S[ua] M[aestà] son stato perseguitato sin tanto, che anno procurato di farmi perdere con marche di disonore questo freggio, alle acuse dunque, che mi son fatte, io mando qui ingionto una relazione relazione [sic] giustificativa alla mia condotta, sostenuta da tre atestati giurati segnati A. B. C., et autenticati per mano di notaio Publico di questa Citta, et con questa S. E. V. resterà illuminata, che il merito di ben servire cautelatamente S[ua] M[aestà] S[erenissima] vien conversito in reità. tutte le acuse le vedrà dalli atestati stessi cancellate, et in oltre à questi, ogni dilacione de pagamenti, masime delle Logie di S. Cassano Teatro sottoposto à questa Corte, io ne ho sempre detto parte al S[ignor]e Barone di lei figlio, come mio protetore, acciò ne participasse à chi s'aspetta alla camera, per non essere una volta sottoposto ad una Taccia, come è succeduto al presente, in prova della verita, vedranno seguito lò stesso ritardo, et impedimenti anco sotto li miej predecessori, come vedrà da altro atestato segnato F., et quest'anno pure sucede lò stesso à chi tiene l'incombenza di pagare le loggie per il Teatro di S. Cassano per l'anno 1725, esendoli fatti seguestri in mano da diversi creditori. Vedrà pure S. E. V. dal atestato C. che per bon servizio di S. M. non devevo pagare perche non pagava[n] li altri, et sè pagai il 1722 un anno doppo lo feci perche mi fù comandato dal Cavagliere consaputo, fatto amico del proprietario del Teatro, et tanto lo feci per l'anno 1723 per lò stesso comando, e strepito, et sè avesse pagato pontualmente quel che non faceva[n] l'altri tutti sarei stato acusato d'infidele, et poco atento alli interessi di S. M., et di tutte queste cose ne hò avisato replicatamente a' tempi debiti il Sig^e Barone di lei figlio Vedrà pure S. E. V. due atestati segnati D., e E. con li quali comparirà la mia pontualità, et zelo, per il Decoro, e grandezza di S. M. nella dispositione delle loggie, et tanto posso farlo di tutte quelle che hò disposto à giorno per giorno, avendone una nota ben distinta cosi tenuta perche prevedevo da chi invigilava sopra di mè qualche gran disgrazia. quello che per altro non facevano li altri miej antessori, che con tal dispositione ne aprofitavano di molto, et veramente questa era una cosa molto contraria alla grandezza di S. M. Se io devo restare senza la carica almeno che non resti senza onore, et questo sarà l'impegno della bella anima di V. E. difendendo dall'opressione una creatura fatta sua per tanti Titoli. per le mie Fatiche poi per sei anni di servizio con l'asicuranze, che venendo à mancare il S^e Farinelli averej a[v]uto la sua pensione.

Conosciuta dalla M. S. la mia inocenza, non manca alla Sua grandezza modi di rilevarmi da questo precipitio, et intanto con pregar Idio per la conservatione di V. E. et della felicità della sua degna disendenza à lei con tutto rispetto, mi rasegno di V. E.

à S. E. Barone di Göertz Presidente della Camera de finance per S. M. Britanica in Hannover.

In oltre faccio vedere un altro atestato seg.^{to} G. col quale si fà conoscere à qual segno era gionta la persecutione per vedermi infelice avendo fatto quanto avevo saputo per far un pagamento del Palcho nel Teatro di S. Moise, volendo con la ricquita alla mano farmi credere alla Camera un omo impontuale. saputo questo feci fare questo atestato dal Impressario di D.^o Teatro, et mandato alla Camera il colpo andò voto, et al ritorno del Cavagliere à Venetia li fù ristituiti li suoi trenta Ducati dà Piero Balbi agente di Detto Teatro. mando qui unito un esemplare autentico di D.^{to} atestato, con la sua traducione fran[c]ese avendolo mandato con li sopra acennati à S. E. Presidente, mentre lo mandai l'anno pasato in originale, mà sarà bene Darlo anco adesso perche da questo si conosse quanto tempo erà che si andava machinando questa mia disgratia avanti anco del ricorso fatto à S. M. per il strapazzo fattomi in Palazzo Proprio si andava corendo questo mal animo contro di me. P. S. non mando l'originale perche non hò a[v]uto tempo di farlo ostare dal notaio, mà mando la traducione francese, che già l'originale lo mandai l'anno pasato.

III

Sorosina's account ('relazione giustificativa') of his conduct as George I's agent in Venice (Fondo Spiga, vol. 2, f. 62r–v)

Étant arrivé a moy Joseph Sorosina le malheur fatal d'être privé du grand honneur de servir a Sá Majestè Britannique en qualité de Son Agent dans cette Ville, j'ai dans moy même examiné quel faute pouroit m'avoir rendu coupable, et attirè cette disgrace dont la peine est pour moy estreme.

Quand je le recherche a ma conscience, a qui nulle crime peut être caché, je n'y retrouve aucun défaut dans ma ponctualitè, ni dans ma foy; rien dans mon zelle, ni dans l'empressement ardent de bien servire a un Si August, et Clement Monarque dont la bonté Royalle assuroit mes esperances, et mes services mon bonheur.

Quand je reflêchis sur quelques ommissions dont on veut me rendre criminel je ne puis de moins que d'être vivement toûché, et je me trouve dans la necessité de me justiffier, come je fais, avec la derniere soumission, et le respect le plus proffond.

Deux sont les chefs de mes accusations. Le premier d'avoir differè le payement du loyé du Palais de Sá Majestè. Le second d'avoir aussi posposè le payement dû pour les Loges que Sà Majestè tiene dans ces Theatres.

Il est vray que j'ai differè le payement du loyé du Palais; mais ce fût a cause que les Agents du Proprietaire trenoient [traînaient] les réparations necessaires; et j'ai crû faire l'interèt de Sá Majesté que de les obliger par ce moïen a s'acquiter de leur devoir en les obligeant a faire les portes, fenêtres, vitres, reparation du touois [toit], et autre dont le Palais avoit besoin, guardant l'argent entre mes mains jusques a ce qu'on eût fait ces reparations necessaires.

Preuve de la verité que je viens de dire. S. E. Feld Maressal Co[mte] de Solembourgh qui par permission de Sà Majestè loge dans ce Palais, a êtè contraint de remettre de son propre pour ces réparations necessaires; et il s'est trouvè dans le même cas a l'egard d'une maison attenant au Palais oú loge un partie du Monde a sa suite ayant été obligé de guarder l'argent du loyè jusques a ce qu'on eût fait les réparations necessaires. C'est un fait dont je ne doûte pas que S. E. voudra bien certiffier toute fois qu'il sera récherché, et faira valoir par son attestation une verité incontestable a l'avantage de ma pauvre personne oprimée.

Étant tres-evident tout ce que je dis a ma justiffication pour la premiere de mes accusations, mon innocence paroît dans toute sa clareté; d'autant plus qu'il est pratiqué dans cette Ville de Venise, e de coûtume de differer le payement du loyé jusques a ce que les Proprietaires de Maisons ayent répare aux besoins, et aux domages que les Bâtiments souffrent par le tems, l'eau salé, et l'aire de cette ville; même jusques a ce qu'ils ayent fait les commodites necessaires pour les habitans. Ce pour quoy bien souvent il arrivè que les Locataires en font les dèpenses pour être remboursés sur le Loyè.

Pour ce qui régarde la seconde de mes accusations qu'on voudroit agraver de circonstances dellicates je dirai en premier lieu:

Que dépuis l'année 1721 jusques a l'année 1722 j'ai été accablé de maux, et d'infirmites tres fâcheuses qui m'empêcherent de servir personnellement a Sà Majestè; apprés cette longe maladie je fûs surpris d'un Coup d'appoplexie qui me laissa plus mort qu'en vie, comme il est veriffié par le certificat autentique, et juré des Medecins. A.

Peut-être que ce lui qui faisoit mes affaires, et vaquoit a mes interêts dans un tems pour moy tres calamiteux ait differé de quelque mois le payement, et qu'il ait alteré les dattes; mais ce se peut par mêprise, ou par mêgarde, point a dessin, et je ne pouvois pas en avoir part, ni connoissance dans l'état deplorable où je me trouvois.

Il est constant pour tant que tout l'argent que la Chambre Royale m'a envoyè tant pour les Theâtres que pour le Palais a été entierement déboursé ayant été employè dans les payements des rentes dües, comme il paroît par les quitances que j'ai envoyè de tems en tems; et il n'y a personne qui peut pretendre un sold durant le tems que j'ai eu le maniment. Le certifficat ci joint .B. est une forte assurance de mon integrité aussi a l'égard des Theâtres de S.ᵗ Gio: Grisostomo, et S.ᵗ Samuel, qui sont ceux dont la dépense est la plus considerable. Pour le Theâtre de S.ᵗ Cassano on en suspendit le payement dans les années 1722, et 1723; parce que tous les interesses en firent de même: et la raison est que les Entrepreneurs Commiques d'allors disposoient des Loges a leur fantasie avec prejudice, et desordre comme il paroît du certificat .C. De plus la déposition du S.ʳ Castoreo est tres insusistante [?insuffisante] disant que faute de ponctualitè les Loges n'avoient pas êté payez; puisque dans les mêmes quitances des payements qu'on dépêcha a la Chambre avec les raisons de la dilation de d[i]ts payements il est prouvè tout le contraire.

De tout ce que je viens d'esposer tres-humblement il est facile de deduire que chache une des deux accusations sont entièrement détruites, et anneanties.

Dans le fait, e [et] la ponctualitè je ne puis pas certainement être attaquè, puisque toutes les rentes des Loges comme aussi du Palais sont entierement payés. de sorte qu'il ne peut pas y avoir aucun plaint, prejudice, ou pretension; Et si j'avois pû produire mes raisons en tems, je ne doûte nullement que ma justiffication auroit prevenu ma disgrace.

Je me soumette pourtant a tout ce qui plaira a Sá Majesté de disposer de moy, et du plus proffond de mon ame je seraj toujours résigné a ses Royalles dispositions, et je ne manquerai jamais de prier pour la conservation de Sá Sacrée personne, pour l'immortalité de sà gloire, et pour l'esaltation de sà Royale Famille.

Je me flatte pour tant qu'ayant pitiè de mon infortunée condition, attendu mes services de six années continuelles, Sá Majesté voudra bien par sa grande bontè rendre mon malheur moin sensible par l'agreement Royal de mon zelle, et de ma fidelitè qu'on a tâché en vain de trenir [?trahir]. La confusion, et l'affliction òn [où] ma disgrace m'a jetè est l'êtat le plus déplorable d'un homme, qui se trouve surchargè de Famille, et environè de plus dures indigences. Grace . . .

IV

Affidavits in support of Sorosina

A (Fondo Spiga, vol. 2, f. 65r)

C'est 20me Mars 1726 Venise

Nous soussignes Medecins, et Phisiciens de la Ville de Venise faisons foy juree que Monsieur Joseph Sorosina Agent de Sà Majestè Britanique, eut une Maladie tres dangereuse l'année 1721; par la quelle il fut contraint, pendant tout l'hyver de dèmeurer sans pouvoir s'appliquer d'aucune maniere. Le primtems en suite de l'annèe 1722 il fut surpris d'un Coup d'appoplexie qu'il le reduit impuissant, et incapable d'agire pendant toute la même année. Ce que nous affirmons, et certifions de propre main, et avec sarment.

Je Lorence Mattio Negri Med^{n} Phis^{n} affirme
Je Jacinte Grapiglia Med^{n} Phis^{n} affirme . . .

B (Fondo Spiga, vol. 2, f. 66r)

Ce 3me Mars 1726

Moy soussignè Certifie par pure veritè, que le Sieur Joseph Sorosina depuis qu'il est Agent de Sà Majestè Britanique, at toujours, et touts les Ans payé le loüage des Loges tenues a la disposition de S. M^{te} Britt^{que} et Ellect^e de Bransuich Luneburg, dans nos Theatres de St Gio: Grisostome, e St Samuel pour les recités de l'Autume, et du Carneval, ne nous ajant jamais donné occasion de faire du bruit contre sà ponctualitè; hormis pour la recite de l'Opera qu'on fait depuis quelques années dans le Theatre de St Samuel, et que pour tele Opera, tous les autres qui ont des Loges à loüages dans le dit Theatre payent une moitiée de l'autre loüage ordinaire des dites loges du dit Theatre, m'ajant respondu qu'il n'avoit recû jamais aucun ordre sur ce particulier de la Cour en foy de quoy

Vincent Grimani affermo

Veüe du Nob: Ho: q. Michel Grimani fù du q. Charles, e du Sr François q[uon]da[m] Sr Laurent Lorenzoni la susdite signature . . .

C (Fondo Spiga, vol. 2, f. 68r)

Par espression de veritè je soussignè declare, que les annees 1722 et 1723 l'on tent ouvert le Theatre de St Cassan pour en tirer le Loyè des Loges, faisant jouer des Compagnies Comiques; de sorte que la plus grand part de ceux qui tienent des Loges n'ont pas voulu payer le loyè. Et moy soussignè, qui en a une au premier rang, je ne paya pas non plus a l'exemple des autres le loyè.

L'annèe 1724 qu'on devoit joüer l'Opera dans ce Théatre l'on me pryà de vouloir payer aussi pour les deux annees precedentes avec le deboursement seul de la motiê du Loyè dù de l'annee 1722; ce que je fis. Pour ce qui les autres firent je n'en sçai rien. Tant je certifie par pure veritè

Je Scipion Boldù q[uonda]m Philippe certifie avec sarment . . .

Datum Venetiis hac Die 29 Mensis Martij 1726

D (Fondo Spiga, vol. 2, f. 69r)

A lumiere de la pure veritè, je soussignè declare, qu'ajant il y à quelques Annès la Comission d'un grand Senateur de cette Ville de trouver à force d'Argent une Loge dans le Theatre de St Gio Grisostomo pour la premiere soire d'une nouvelle Opera, et m'estant reussy vaines toutes les dilligences, il se trouva Monsr Joseph Sorosina Agent de Sà Majestè Britanique, qui avoit la loge n° 25 prem^r ordre, obligeament s'offrit de donner la Clef, mais à la propre persoñe à qui la Loge devoit servir. Je le fis parler avec le Chevalier, au quel presenta la Loge, et refusa l'Argent, disent que ces Loges devoient se ragaler par l'honneur de la magnanimitè de Son Soûrain, autant j'afferme de ma main. Io Zuane Rosa affirmo come cy dessus pour avoir ête présent âlors que le Sieur Sorosina refusá de recevoir aucun argent du Cavalier susd[i]t . . .

Datum Venetiis hoc die 18 M[en]sis Martij 1726

E (Fondo Spiga, vol. 2, f. 70r)

                              C'est le [18me] Mars 1726 Venise
Nous soussignez certifions avec sarment que Monsieur Joseph Sorosina
Agent de Sà Majestè Britanique, ayant la disposition des Loges, que Sà
Majestè tiene dans les Theatres de Venise dans le Carneval de l'année
passèe 1724 et pour l'Opera de l'Ascension dans l'Ête passè 1725 au Theatre
de St Samuel le d[i]t Sr Sorosina, m'a toujours gracieusement donnè toutes
les Loges dont je l'ai prié sans aucun interêt mais au contraire avec des
genereuses protestations, qu'elles devoient être regallez comme la gran-
deur de Son Souvrain le demandoit en foy de quoy
    Je Bernarde da Riva Certifie avec sarment, que l'année passèe 1724,
toutes les foies que j'ai prié le d[i]t Sr Agent de Sà Majestè Britanique de me
donner les Cleis des Loges tant de St Samuel que dans les autres Thèatres,
non seulement pour moy, mais pour d'autres aussi, il m'a fait le plaisir de
me les donner gracieusement
    Je Jean Anthoine Cossali Certifie avec sarment en tout, et par tout
comme ci dessus avoir reçu le mẽme plaisir tant en mon particulier que
pour leur Ex.^{ces} Messieurs Augustin, et Philippe Nani
    Je Scipion Boldù affirme tout ce qui est contenu dans le present
Certificat comme ci dessus, faisant justice a la bontè usè an vers moy par le
dit Sr Sorosina . . .
    Datum Venetiis hac die 18 M[en]sis Martij 1726

F (Fondo Spiga, vol. 2, f. 71r)

Par pure espression de verité je Severo Frangioni Musicien de la Ducale
Chapelle de St Marc, et çi devant de la Royal cour d'Hannover, declare,
comme ayant appris la musique a la Sig.^{la} Gavazzi Chanteuse, elle me
renonca pour recompense des mes peines comme son maître a reçevoir
soxisante ducats sur ses gages qu'elle devoit avoir comme Chanteuse du
Theatre de St Cassano pour quoy elle avoit dejà fait saisir le Loyè des deux
Loges entre les mains de Monsieur Farinelli pour les sud.^{ts} 60 Duc.^{ts} les
quelles je soussignè ai reçu aussi du d.^{t} Sr Farinelli, ce de quoy je certifie
avec sarment . . .
    Datum Venetiis hac Die 30 M[en]sis Martij 1726

[G] (Fondo Spiga, vol. 2, f. 72r)

                        1725 ce 25me May Venize/du Theatre de St Moise
Par pure veritè moy soussigné Impressaire Certifie comme Monsieur
Sorosina Agent de Sà Majestè Britanique que depuis qu'il est dans la
possession de tele Charge àt toujours pajèe d'année en Année la louyé de la

loge que S: M^{té} tient à sa disposition dans le même Theatre, et comme qu'il parroitrà des quittances, qui luy auroit êtès faites par plusieurs personnes, qui dans ces tems tennoient l'action sur tels louages; restant seul a payer l'annè 1724 disant que pour tel payement il n'a point recüe la remise; Je declare en outre que pour l'Anné 1725 le meme M^r. Sorosina paya le loüè au S^r. Antonio Mauro un des interessès du dit Theatre, du quel même luy fut faite la quittance. Declarant aussj que le dit pajement fût fait encore après par S. E. Monsr. le Cheva^r. Querini, e[n] main du S^r. Pierre Balbi facteur du dit Theatre, puisque le dit Balbi n'avoit aucunne conoissance du premier payement fait par le dit M^r. Sorosina restant pourtant le dit desbours de S. E. à sa disposition, pour luy être rendu en foy

   Je Sebastian Mauri Impressaire du Theatre de S^t. Moise manu prop. . . .

   Datum Venetijs hoc die Venerij 25 M[e]nsis Maij 1725

[H] (Fondo Spiga, vol. 2, f. 63r; Italian version on f. 64r–v)

Moy soussignè Agent de Son Ex^{ce} Monsieur Jean Loredan fût du S^r. Leonard, Certifie, que le Palais de S^t. Trovase tenu a loüage par Sà Majestè Britanique appartenant la moitiè à S. E. mon Maitre, et l'autre moitiée à L. L. E. E. [Leures Excellences] ses Neveux pour les quels estoit Agent le S^r. Antoine Novello, et come que luy S^r. Novello, en tirroit le louagè du dit Palais, me donnent ensuite la moitié, ainsi je declare par pure Verité, que Monsieur Joseph Sorosina Agent de Sà Majestè d'abord que l'argent remis, arrivoit de la Cour pour en faire ce payement, nous en avertissoit, mais quelque fois prostestoit aussi qu'il ne payera le dit loüage, le bon service de Son Maitre le voulant aussi, jusqu'a ce qu'on ne reparroit quelque essentiel besoin du dit Palais. Pour le reste j'ay toujours trouvé le dit Sr Sorosina homme très ponctual dans le soude des payes, et qu'il n'en demeura jamais defectif d'aucuñe. Rèllachant le presente a la requisition du même S^r. Sorosina, pour s'en prevaloir par tout, et ou il luy pourra être necessaire.

   Antoine Rotta Agent de S. E. affermo . . .

   Datum Venetijs die 4to M[en]sis Maij 1726

V

Sorosina's 'dispositione': list of people to whom Sorosina allocated George I's Venetian theatre boxes in 1725 (Fondo Spiga, vol. 2, ff. 60r–61v)*

---

*   The transcription follows the layout of the original, except that there the allocations for the second box at S. Luca appear below those for the first, not alongside.

Lista della dispositione delle Loggie nelli Theatri di Venezia di Sua Maesta B[ritanni]ca fatta dà Giusseppe Sorosina Agente di Sua M[aes]tà nel tempo, che ne hà havuto l' ordine dalla Maestà Sua nell'anno 1724

Del Theatro di S. Gio Grisostomo loggia pño ordine nº 25

24 Genaro	andò vuoto
25 dº	Al Medico di S.E. Feld Marescial
28 dº	a S.E. Fiorenza Ravagnina
31 dº	Prima recita di Opera nuova dato à S.E. Ravagnina per servire il Duca di Massa Carrara
2 Febraro	à S.E. Cecilia Cornera
3 dº	al Sigᵉ Cossali Agente di S.E. Marescial
4 dº	à S.E. Maria Ravagnina
5 dº	à S.E. Agostin Nani
6 dº	à S.E. Antonio Loredan
7 dº	à S.E. Fhilippo Nani
8 dº	à S.A. Duchessa di Massa
12 dº	à S.E. Contessa Coronini
13 dº	andò vuoto

Logia in detto Theatro al secondo ordine nº 32

24 Genaro	andò vuoto
25 dº	andò vuoto
28 dº	andò vuoto
31 dº	Prima recita di Opera nuova dato à S.E. Contessa Coronini
2 Febraro	à S.E. Benedetto Marcello

Loggia nel Theatro di S. Cassano primo ordine nº 18

24 Genaro	à S.E. Fiorenza Ravagnina
25 dº	à Dona Marina Giustiniana
26 dº	à S.E. Recevitor di Malta
28 dº	à S.E. Agostin Nani
29 dº	à S.E. Bernardo Riva
30 dº	à S.E. Cecilia Cornera
2 Febraro	à S.E. Recevitor di Malta
3 dº	à S.E. Maria Ravagnina
4 dº	à Dona Marina Giustiniani
5 dº	à S.E. Antonia Michiel
6 dº	à S.E. Agostin Nani
7 dº	à S.E. Benedetto Marcello
8 dº	à S.E. Giacomo Riva
9 dº	à S.E. Fiorenza Ravagnina
10 dº	à S.E. Polo Renier
11 dº	à S.E. Contessa Coronini
12 dº	à S.E. Giacomo Riva
13 dº	andò vuoto

Logia nel detto Theatro secondo ordᵉ nº 28

24 Genaro	al Sigᵣ Cossali
25 dº	Al Sigᵣ Lorenzino Antonetti
26 dº	Al Sigᵣ Nicolò Vanali
28 dº	à S.E. la Contessa Coronini
29 dº	à S.E. Recevitor di Malta
30 dº	à Dona Marina Giustiniani
2 Febraro	al Sigᵣ Vicenzo Cassani

3 d° alla Sig.la Durastante
4 d° al Sig.r Gio: Antonio Cossali
5 d° à S.E. Agostin Nani
6 d° alla Durastante
7 d° al Sig.r Tomaso Viani
8 d° à S.E. Contessa Coronini
10 d° al Sig.r Severo Frangioni Musico
11 d° à S.E. Polo Renier
12 d° à S.E. Co: Tassis
13 d° alla Sig.la Durastante

Loggia nel Teatro di S. Moise nel primo ordine n° 9

24 Genaro andò vuoto
25 d° Al Sig.r Antonio Moreschi
26 d° andò vuoto
29 d° à S.E. Lunardo Foscolo
30 d° à S.E. andò vuoto
2 Febraro andò vuoto
3 d° à Giuseppe Sorosina
5 d° al Sig.r Antonio Moreschi
6 d° alla Sig.la Durastante
7 d° andò vuoto
8 d° andò vuoto
9 d° à Giuseppe Sorosina per la figlia
10 d° al Sig.r Gerolimo Gentili
11 d° alla Sig.la Chiara Sorosina
12 d° al Sig.r Francesco Lorenzoni
13 d° non si fece Opera

3 d° al Sig.r Nicolò Vanali
4 d° à S.E. Coronini
5 d° al Sig.r Bortolo Morandi
6 d° à S.E. Dama Mula S. Vio
7 d° à S.E. Contessa Coronini
8 d° à Giusseppe Sorosina
9 d° à S.E. Recevitor di Malta
10 d° al Sig.r Cossali
11 d° à Zuane Loredan
12 d° al Sig.r Pellegrini
13 d° andò vuoto

Loggia nel Theatro di S. Samuel nel primo ordine n° 5

24 genaro à S.E. Fiorenza Ravagnina
25 d° andò vuoto
26 d° al Sig.r Cossali
27 d° alla Durastante
28 d° al Sig.r Gerolimo Gentili
29 d° à S.E. Giacomo Riva
30 d° al Cavalier Nicolà Grimaldi
31 d° à S.E. Bernardo Riva
2 Febraro à Giusseppe Sorosina
3 d° alla Sig.la Chiara Sorosina
4 d° ad un Cavalier Napolitano
5 d° andò vuoto
6 d° à S.E. Bernardo Riva
7 d° al Sorosina
8 d° à Zuane Loredan
9 d° al Sig.r Lodovico Gentili
10 d° à Giustina Sorosina
11 d° alla Sig.la Doralice Rinaldi
12 d° à Zuane di S.E. Marescial
13 d° à S.E. Bernardo Riva

Loggia nel Theatro S. Samuel
primo ordine n.º 3

24 Genaro	alla Sig.la Chiara Sorosina
25 d.º	à S.E. Bernardo Riva
26 d.º	à S.E. medessimo
27 d.º	à S.E. Giacomo Riva
28 d.º	à S.E. Fiorenza Ravagnina
29 d.º	à S.E. Polo Renier
30 d.º	à Dona Marina Giustiniani
31 d.º	à S.E. Scipion Boldù
2 Febraro	à S.E. Bernardo Riva
3 d.º	all'Abbate Riva
4 d.º	à S.E. Riva
5 d.º	al Sig.r Pellegrini
6 d.º	à S.E. Maria Ravagnina
7 d.º	à S.E. Fiorenza Ravagnina
8 d.º	à S.E. Giacomo Riva
9 d.º	all'Abbate Riva
10 d.º	à S.E. Recevitor di Malta
11 d.º	à S.E. Bernardo Riva
12 d.º	à Dona Marina Giustiniana
13 d.º	à S.E. Orsetta Mula

Loggia nel Theatro S. Luca primo ordine n.º 4

24 Genaro 1724	à Giusseppe Sorosina
25 d.º	al Sig.r Gerolimo Gentili
26 d.º	andò vuoto

Loggia nel Theatro di S. Samuel
primo ordine n.º 17

24 Genaro	alla Sig.la Durastante
25 d.º	à S.E. Cossali
26 d.º	alla Sig.ra Durastante
27 d.º	à S.E. Cossali
28 d.º	à Zuane di S.E. Marescial
29 d.º	à S.E. Cossali
30 d.º	à S.E. Fhilippo Nani
31 d.º	à S.E. Agostin Nani
2 Febraro	al Tirabosco Segretario di Senato
3 d.º	al Sig.r Vanali
4 d.º	à S.E. Fhilippo Nani
5 d.º	al Sig.r Cossali
6 d.º	à S.E. Polo Renier
7 d.º	al Sig.r Cossali
8 d.º	à S.E. Polo Renier
9 d.º	al Sig.r Tirabosco
10 d.º	alla Sig.la Antonia Michieli
11 d.º	à Pietro Zini
12 d.º	al Sig.r Cossali
13 d.º	al Sig.r Tirabosco

Loggia nel Theatro S. Luca secondo ordine Lettera .C.

24 Genaro	al Tirabosco
25 d.º	alla Durastante
26 d.º	andò vuoto

27 dº al Sigr Bernardo Riosa
28 dº à Dona Marina Giustiniana
29 dº alla medessima
30 dº à Giusseppe Sorosina
31 dº à S.E. Zambelli
2 Febraro à Monsieur Patisel di Cà Venier
3 dº al Sigr Cossali
4 dº à S.E. Ravagnina
5 dº à S.E. Giacomo Riva
6 dº à S.E. Benedetto Marcello
7 dº à S.E. Bernardo Riva
8 dº à Dona Marina Giustiniani
9 dº à S.E. Scipion Boldù
10 dº à S.E. Contessa Coronini
11 dº al Sigr Nicolò Vanali
12 dº à S.E. Bernardo Riva
13 dº à Dona Marina Giustiniani

Del Theatro di S. Samuel per le Recite dell'Opera della Assensione nel mese di Maggio 1725

Loggia primo ordine nº 17

9 Maggio al Sigr Cossali
10 dº à S.E. Fiorenza Ravagnina
11 dº al Sigr Antonio Lotti
12 dº al Sigr Farinelli
13 dº al Sigr Co: Alberti
14 dº al Sigr Vanali
15 dº à S.E. Recevitor di Malta
16 dº al Sigr Francesco Lorenzoni

27 dº al Sorosina
28 dº al Sigr Vanali
29 dº al Sigr Gerolimo Gentili
30 dº al Sigr Lorenzino Canal
31 dº al Sigr Girolamo Gentili
2 Febraro al Sigr Cossali
3 dº Sigr Zuane Loredan
4 dº S.E. Contessa Tassis
5 dº Al Sigr Francesco Carminati
6 dº al Tirabosco
7 dº al Cavalier Nicola Grimaldi
8 dº al Conte Tassis
9 dº al Sigr Girolamo Gentili
10 dº al Sigr Antonio Lotti
11 dº al Sigr Sorosina
12 dº à S.E. Madama Moro
13 dº S E. Ravagnina

Loggia nel detto Theatro primo ordine nº 3

9 Maggio à S.E. Co: Tassis
10 dº à S.E. Maria Ravagnina
11 dº à S.E. Fhilippo Nani
12 dº Al Sigr Cossali per S.E. Fhilippo Nani
13 dº à S.E. Fiorenza Ravagnina
14 dº à Dona Marina Giustiniani
15 dº à S.E. Maria Ravagnina
16 dº al Sigr Francesco Monti

17 d.°	al Sig.r Farinelli
18 d.°	à S.E. Maria Ravagnina
20 d.°	al Sig.r Antonio Lotti
21 d.°	à S.E. Bernardo Riva
22 d.°	à S.E. Fiorenza Ravagnina
23 d.°	à Zuane Loredan
24 d.°	à S.E. Scipion Boldù
25 d.°	al Sig.r Marco Rizzi
27 d.°	al Sig.r Co: Antonio Alberti
28 d.°	al Sig.r Cossali

Loggia nel Theatro S. Samuel primo ordine n.° 5

9 Maggio	à S.E. Contessa Coronini
10 d.°	à S.E. Recevitor di Malta
11 d.°	al Sig.r Gerolimo Gentili
12 d.°	al Sig.r Benetto Zuliani
13 d.°	à S.E. Fhilippo Nani
14 d.°	al Sig.r Cossali
15 d.°	à S.E. Contessa Coronini
16 d.°	andò vuoto
17 d.°	à S.E. Fhilippo Boldù
18 d.°	al Sig.r Cossali
20 d.°	à S.E. Recevitor di Malta
21 d.°	à S.E. Fhilippo Nani
22 d.°	à Dona Marina Giustiniani
23 d.°	à S.E. Contessa Coronini
24 d.°	à S.E. Recevitor di Malta
25 d.°	à S.E. Contessa Coronini
27 d.°	à S.E. Fhilippo Nani

17 d.°	à S.E. Fhillippo Nani
18 d.°	à S.E. Pietro Gradenigo
20 d.°	andò vuoto
21 d.°	S.E. Co: Tassis
22 d.°	à S.E. Fhilippo Nani
23 d.°	Cà Loredan
24 d.°	Conte Antonio Alberti
25 d.°	Sig.r Francesco Lorenzoni
27 d.°	S.E. Giacomo Riva

VI

Letter of 1 December 1724 from Agostino Steffani to Fiorenza Ravagnina (Fondo Spiga, vol. 79, pp. 379–81)

xmbre 1724/À S.E./La Sig.^{ra} Fiorenza/Ravagnina/Padova/1
. . . Il n[ost]ro Sig.^{r} Giuseppe [Sorosina] si lagna amaram[en]te delle persecuzioni che soffre dal Sig.^{r} Cav.^{r} Giacomo Querini. In effetto, quando sussista la sola metà di quel che dice, basta per rovinare ogni galantuomo. Per il male, che si ne può temere nei Paesi lontani, già si è fatto il bisogno per prevenirli con sicurezza di riuscire. Mà li colpi, che potrebbe ricever di quà, sono d'un altra natura. Io son informato, che V[ostra] E[ccellenza] può di molto sopra il Sig.^{r} Conte Tassis Padrone della Posta di Fiandra. M'importa infinitam[en]te sapere se il Sig.^{r} Cav.^{r} Querini habbia in quell'uffizio dato qualche avviso, ò fatta qualche istanza, che non si diano al Sig.^{r} Giuseppe le lettere che vengono à quella Posta sotto il di lui Nome, se non le paga. Se questo fosse, e che il pred[et]to Sig.^{r} Co: Tassis aderisse a questa istanza, Io ne haverei innocentem[en]te la mia parte del danno, ed una infinità del disturbo; attesoche la maggior parte delle mie lettere vengono sotto la coperta del Sig.^{r} Giuseppe, conche important[issi]me corrispondenze sarebbero arenate. V.E. dunque habbia la generosa bontà d'informarsi destram[en]te di questi fatti, e darmene lumi: e poi faccia la insigne carità di disporre il Sig.^{r} Co: Tassis a non abbadare alli Cattivi Uffizj, che potrebbero esser fatti al n[ost]ro Sig.^{r} Giuseppe; tanto più che il pred[et]to Sig.^{r} Co: può esser sicuro di nulla perdere; con che qualche mese di più o di meno, che li pagamenti restino indietro, non è per lui un grande incommodo. Oltre di che guardi Dio, che il n[ost]ro Sig.^{r} Giuseppe havesse qualche disgrazia per quella strada, V.E. può ben credere, che la n[ost]ra Sig.^{ra} Benedetta ne soffrirebbe la parte sua per consenso. Scusi l'E. V. il mio ardire, se per sorte è soverchio . . .

VII

Letter of 8 March 1725 from Agostino Steffani to Giuseppe Riva (Fondo Spiga, vol. 80, pp. 210–13: 210–11)

1725 Marzo./A/Mr Riva./Padova/8.
. . . la dolente storia della Sig.^{ra} Sorosina hà posto in angustie il di lei Padre, e data a me qualche amarezza. Il disgusto, che ne hà ricevuto quel Galantuomo è chiaro senza comentarj. Quello, che ne risento Io, è dall'aver di buona fede sempre asserito, che in ogni luogo, ove quella Figlia hà cantato, si è fatto ogni sforzo per riaverla: onde mi dispiacerebbe, che la di lei poco buona riuscita in quel paese, facesse torto, non dico al mio gusto nella musica, perche non importa nulla: ma alla mia ingenuità, ch'è stata

sempre illibata, e senza rimprovero. Per fortuna il Fratello della Figlia, hà fatta al Padre una relazione totalm[en]te conforme a quanto ella si è degnata scrivermi; aggiungendovi solo di più, che il Sig.ʳ Co: di Bothmer si trovi notabilm[en]te stomacato del procedere di cotesti Sig.ʳⁱ Direttori dell'Accademia. Io non ardisco scriverne oggi a quel degno Ministro, perche oltre al poco bisogno, ch'egli hà di perdere il tempo in queste bagatelle, mi trovo da qualche ordinario in quà privo delle di lui consuete grazie, onde non son senza timore, che o insolite occupazioni, o qualche alterazione della sua preziosa salute, gl'impediscono il dispensarmele. La conclusione si è, che quando non si può quel, che si vuole, convien voler quel, che si può. Hò consolato il Sig.ʳ Sorosina colla sicurezza della di lei protezione per la Figlia. Sopra il tutto gli potranno molto giovare le caute grazie, che gli dispenserà il nostro amabil[issi]mo Sig.ʳ Bononcini, al quale supplico portare le più vive proteste del mio costante desiderio di servirlo . . .

Vivaldi's and Handel's settings of Giustino

REINHARD STROHM

Handel's operas have not often been compared with settings of the same texts by other composers. The opportunity for such studies exists in at least sixteen cases, where we have complete scores or sufficient fragments of music for a libretto that Handel also used.[1] It is clear that careful examination of all these scores would reveal a great deal about Handel's position in the history of opera. This is not to say that we would discover the 'stylistic standards of *opera seria*' against which to measure Handel. These standards, sometimes called the 'opera seria conventions', may in fact not really exist, and the search for them may prove to be fruitless. But it is necessary to know how composers other than Handel reacted in similar situations, or what alternatives there were to what he chose to do. Besides, three out of the four existing comparisons of a Handel opera with one by a contemporary[2] have suggested that he not only knew but actually used the other composer's music, in differing degrees, for his own setting. One wonders what the twelve remaining cases might reveal.

Neither Handel nor Vivaldi is likely to be mistaken for that elusive animal, the 'average' Italian opera composer. Their relative independence in taste and career is perhaps the only thing they have in common (a feature that is perhaps also relevant to their instrumental music), but to compare them is legitimate because either composer could have chosen to be more similar to the other than he really was. Handel may have heard Vivaldi as a performer at the Pietà in Venice in 1708–10, and he was certainly aware of his concertos in London (as his Op. 3 might indeed

---

[1] The librettos and scores are identified in R. Strohm, 'Handel and his Italian Opera Texts', *Essays on Handel and Italian Opera* (Cambridge, 1985), pp. 34–79.

[2] The most important comparison is H. S. Powers, 'Il Serse trasformato', *The Musical Quarterly*, xlvii (1961), pp. 481–92, and xlviii (1962), pp. 73–92. See also J. M. Knapp, 'Handel's *Tamerlano*: the Creation of an Opera', *The Musical Quarterly*, lv (1970), pp. 405–30; Strohm, 'Francesco Gasparini's Later Operas and Handel', *Essays*, pp. 80–92; and C. Spitz, 'Die Opern "Ottone" von G. F. Händel (London, 1722) und "Teofane" von A. Lotti (Dresden, 1719): ein Stilvergleich', *Festschrift zum 50. Geburtstag Adolf Sandbergers* (Munich, 1918), pp. 265–71.

131

suggest). In this essay I aim to show that he knew the score of Vivaldi's *Giustino* (1724), and he must have seen others, for example during his stay in Venice during Carnival 1729. Four or five of Vivaldi's opera arias were sung in Handel's pasticcios,[3] and others seem to have been performed in concerts and operas in London around 1714–15.[4] Most important, Charles Jennens's admiration for Vivaldi and the meetings his agent Edward Holdsworth had with the composer himself in Venice in 1732–3 must have given Handel not only greater access to Vivaldi's music but also good reasons to study and perhaps re-use it.[5] The evidence for Vivaldi's awareness of Handel is somewhat slighter but is of some value when we consider how little Handel was known in Italy after about 1720. At the time of the success of *Agrippina* in Venice (1710), of course, the ambitious Vivaldi would have made a grave mistake had he not studied the work. Later, Handel's operas were available in print, and Vivaldi and Handel shared the publishers Roger and Walsh. They employed the same singers in some of their operas (although, in most cases, the singers did not return to Vivaldi after singing in London).[6] As far as we know today, Vivaldi was the only contemporary Italian to perform a Handel aria in one of his pasticcios after 1718.[7] Further links could have existed via common patrons such as Cardinal Pietro Ottoboni and Prince Ferdinando de' Medici or musicians such as Francesco Gasparini and Benedetto Marcello. The case of *Giustino* can, of course, only illustrate Handel's attitude towards Vivaldi, not vice versa.[8]

Vivaldi composed his *Giustino* for the carnival season of 1724 at the Teatro Capranica, Rome, having received the commission from the owner–impresario, Federico Capranica. The work was his fourth and last contribution to the Roman operatic stage. It was a culminating effort also in the sense that this is the last extant score where he is still totally faithful to the successful style of his earlier Venetian and Mantuan operas, and about half of the arias are, in fact, re-used from those earlier productions. His scores from 1727 onwards show the increasing influence of the so-called Neapolitan school – and it must have been in Rome in 1723–4 that he first heard operas by the Neapolitans Porpora and Vinci. The libretto of

---

3   See Strohm, 'Handel's pasticci', *Essays*, pp. 205, 210.
4   'Io sembro appunto' from *Ottone in villa* (1713) was performed in Haym's pasticcio *Arminio* (1714) and even printed in London, albeit under Alessandro Scarlatti's name.
5   See M. Talbot, *Vivaldi* (London, 1978), pp. 80f. Further on Jennens and on Holdsworth's activities in Italy, see the essay by John H. Roberts, below.
6   See Strohm, 'Vivaldi's Career as an Opera Producer', *Essays*, pp. 135–9.
7   'Gia risuonar d'intorno' from *Ezio*, with a parody text, in *Rosmira* (1738).
8   That Handel used Vivaldi's version of the libretto was recognized by Powers: 'Il Serse trasformato', p. 91. For a detailed description of Vivaldi's opera and its sources, see *Giustino*, ed. Strohm, Nuova edizione critica delle opere di Antonio Vivaldi (Milan, forthcoming), introduction.

Giustino was a Venetian product, having been written by Nicolò Beregan for Giovanni Legrenzi in 1683. It became one of the most famous and widely performed Venetian operas for several decades, and the music was still mentioned by Marcello in *Il teatro alla moda* (1720) as naturally familiar to young singers. Although Rome had heard a new setting (by Luigi Mancia) in 1695 and the source of Vivaldi's text was a revision by Pietro Pariati, first performed with music by Albinoni in Bologna in 1711, the choice of *Giustino* in 1724 may have had something to do with Vivaldi's wish to display loyalty to his native traditions. He knew that his music would be measured not only against that of Legrenzi but also against the style of Gasparini, his one-time superior at the Pietà, who had settled in Rome over ten years earlier and influenced a whole generation of singers and composers. At least two of Gasparini's pupils, Giovanni Ossi and Girolamo Bartoluzzi, sang in Vivaldi's opera (the roles of Anastasio and Leocasta respectively). Vivaldi's is the last-known use of the libretto in Italy; his music can be said to affirm the continuity of the Venetian tradition.

Handel set *Giustino* – using, as we have seen, Vivaldi's version of the libretto – twelve years later without any such traditional context. There are several other instances of his choosing old-fashioned opera texts, but most of these were still around in newer versions (for example *Giulio Cesare in Egitto* or *Partenope*). With *Giustino*, hardly anyone in the audience would even have heard of the drama, whether in London or on the Grand Tour in Italy. Neither external influences nor Handel's otherwise known priorities (a liking for the librettos of Antonio Salvi) help explain this particular choice of text. The external circumstances are, however, well worth considering. From about the time when Handel had to write the wedding opera for the Prince of Wales, *Atalanta* (performed on 12 May 1736), to the summer of 1737, Handel and John Rich produced no fewer than nine operas, four of them newly composed, plus four oratorio revivals in Lent 1737. They must have acted at least on the promise of large grants from the new royal couple, who commanded several productions and individual performances.[9] In fact, newspaper reports of spring 1736 suggest that a series of eight operas was being planned for the 'Entertainment of Her Royal Highness the future Princess of Wales' (Princess Augusta of Saxe–Gotha).[10] Whereas *Atalanta*, as the *pièce d'occasion*, might even have been suggested from the Saxon end of the court, it is still clear that Handel's *Arminio* and *Berenice* were at least very suitable to celebrate the royal couple (and the revived *Alexander's Feast* and *Il Parnasso in festa* could pass as topical too). These circumstances

9   See O. E. Deutsch, *Handel: a Documentary Biography* (London, 1955/R1974), pp. 404–39.

10   Ibid., p. 404.

mattered for Handel also in that he was able to employ the famous and expensive new castratos Gioacchino Conti and Domenico Annibali, changing his vocal writing accordingly. Annibali arrived from Dresden only about 5 October 1736, but Handel must have known his range and singing style from the Venetian carnival season of 1729.

It is curious, therefore, that his score of *Giustino*, on which he worked with his usual speed between 14 August and 7 September, was left unfinished until after the completion of *Arminio* (composed between 15 September and 14 October) and was 'ausgefüllet' between 15 and 20 October.[11] No evidence in the score of *Giustino* suggests that the delay was due to the late arrival of Annibali, who was to sing the title role. Moreover, *Arminio* was also performed before *Giustino*, on 17 January 1737, and by the time *Giustino* reached the stage, on 16 February, even *Berenice* had been completed. The delay was surely due in part to technical difficulties, but the preference given to *Arminio* must have resulted from a royal command (perhaps of early September 1736) which imposed this subject on Handel. One might even say that *Giustino* was the one opera of the whole season that the Prince of Wales, Handel's new patron, did not explicitly want. This is significant in a period when Handel damaged his finances as well as his health in order to justify such patronage. We can be satisfied that he wrote *Giustino* for himself – that his personal artistic aims were involved here. No mistaken conclusions should be drawn from the fact that the first newly composed opera of the season at the Opera of the Nobility, *Demetrio* by Metastasio and Pescetti, was staged just four days before *Giustino*, presenting the very same dramatic idea: the meteoric social ascent of a peasant who is later revealed to be of royal birth. This was surely because his rivals had spied out Handel's plans and pre-empted his own opera subject, as they had already done with the *Arianna* operas in 1734. Handel's motive for composing *Giustino*, on the other hand, came to him from the past. (We do not know when and where he had first seen Vivaldi's libretto, but arguably it was in Rome in 1729.) This corresponds to the fact that the opera starts a whole group of late works which contain unambiguous borrowings from other composers' music.

A comparison of the two librettos of *Giustino* in Vivaldi's version ('1724') and Handel's ('1736') will not only illustrate Handel's dramatic intentions but also help clarify his working procedure. It seems that in 1736 no libretto was consulted other than 1724. The 1736 text owes nothing to Pariati's (five-act) version of 1711 that is not also present in 1724. That Beregan's original was consulted by Handel is possible, but this

---

11   The autograph score is British Library MS R.M. 20.b.4; see W. B. Squire, *Catalogue of the King's Music Library*, I: *The Handel Manuscripts* (London, 1927), pp. 36f. I am not sure whether 'ausgefüllet' here should not rather be read as 'ausgeführt'. The work referred to seems mainly to have been the composing of recitatives, not the 'filling in' of inner parts.

cannot be demonstrated from his text. Handel's librettist was probably either Giacomo Rossi or Angelo Cori. Paolo Rolli wrote a satirical epigram, datable to c1735–6, in which he states that both men were then working for Handel.[12]

The biggest task facing the librettist was to shorten the whole text of 1724, whereby the recitatives were reduced to less than a third of their original length. This was common practice with Handel's London operas (except with the librettos arranged by Rolli) and need not further concern us here, at least when the dramatic content was not seriously altered. One character of 1724, Andronico, was completely eliminated, resulting in the omission of several scenes. That these all involved a degree of erotic interest may account for the removal of this particular role, but the reduction from nine to eight characters must have been a practical necessity for Handel in any case.[13] Most of the other changes, which involve scenic and musical elements – there are cuts, additions, substitutions and transfers of text – were surely initiated by Handel himself, for two reasons: he took a personal interest in the text, and his librettist was clearly a subordinate partner who showed no poetic initiative. Some of the changes are connected with the musical plan.

The following summary of the complicated plot is set out not according to individual scenes as defined by entrances and exits of characters but according to large scenic units as defined by stage sets.[14] These are the only safe guide through the labyrinth of the plot – which offers the spectator a variety of blind alleys, loops and trap-doors.

In the plot summaries for each scenic unit, changes in 1736 are shown in round brackets. The arias and other vocal numbers are listed in separate columns for 1724 and 1736 under the description of each unit; '*': exit aria, '—': corresponding text missing.

> Characters:
> ARI: Arianna, empress
> ANA: Anastasio, emperor
> GIU: Giustino, peasant, then co-regent
> LEO: Leocasta, sister of Anastasio, in love with Giustino
> VIT: Vitaliano, rival king, later revealed to be Giustino's brother
> POL: Polidarte, his general
> AM: Amanzio, Anastasio's general
> AND: Andronico, Vitaliano's brother, disguised as a girl for love of Leocasta (omitted in 1736)
> FOR: the goddess Fortuna

12 See Strohm, *Essays*, p. 278 n. 83.
13 It should be noted that the role of Andronico was first intended for Maria Caterina Negri. Her part in the autograph (Amanzio) was originally written for bass, so that she would have been available for Andronico.
14 The two types of unit are discussed in Powers, 'Il Serse trasformato', under the designations 'internal structure' and 'external structure' respectively.

Act 1, scenic unit a
Luogo maestoso (Sala maestosa). Grand coronation scene at the Imperial court of Byzantium. The enemy's ambassador (Polidarte) is received and rebuffed; war is to follow. Pride and mutual devotion of Anastasio and Arianna.

1724	1736
CORO, ARI, ANA: Viva Augusto	CORO: (no soli) Viva Augusto
*ANA: Un vostro sguardo	*ANA: Un vostro sguardo
*ARI: Da tuoi begl'occhi impara	*ARI: Da tùoi begl'occhi impara

1b
Campagna con alberi fruttiferi. Pastoral scene with Giustino as a ploughman, who day-dreams of honour and glory, then falls asleep. *Al suono d'allegra sinfonia s'illumina la scena . . .*: Fortuna appears on a turning wheel (*machina*), predicting glory to Giustino. Leocasta enters, pursued by a bear, which is killed by Giustino. She promises to help him to a career at court.

GIU:	Misero è ben colui (traditional *ottava rima*, no music notated)	GIU:	Può ben nascer tra li boschi
GIU:	Bel ristoro de' mortali (sleep aria)	GIU:	Bel ristoro de' mortali
Sinfonia		FOR:	Corri, vola
FOR:	recit. accompagnato	FOR	recit. accompagnato
*FOR:	Della tua sorte	*CORO:	Corri, vola (music as above)
—		GIU:	Se parla nel mio cor
*LEO:	Nacque al bosco	*LEO:	Nacque al bosco

1c
Camera. Private Imperial rooms. Anastasio, Arianna, Amanzio about to start on military campaign against Vitaliano (1736: Amanzio alone, disclosing treacherous plans to the public). Andronico in disguise, then Leocasta and Giustino enter; Anastasio, returning, laments Arianna's capture by the enemy and takes Giustino with him for help (1736: only Anastasio and Giustino on stage, setting out for war). Leocasta and her disguised suitor, Andronico, exchange light-hearted 'girls' talk' (omitted in 1736).

*ARI:	Sole degl'occhi miei	—	
*AM:	La gloria del mio sangue	*AM:	È virtute in sin la frode
*ANA:	Vedrò con mio diletto	—	
*ANA:	Non si vanti un'alma (not set by Vivaldi)	*GIU:	Allor ch'io forte avrò
*GIU:	Allor che mi vedrò	*ANA:	Non si vanti un'alma
*LEO:	Nò, bel labbro	—	
*AND:	È pur dolce	—	

1d

Vasta pianura sotto Costantinopoli. Battlefield with Vitaliano and Polidarte. Arianna captured. She rejects Vitaliano's amorous entreaties; he orders her to be exposed as prey to a sea monster. She sings a farewell aria to Anastasio.

VIT:	All'armi, guerrieri	VIT:	All'armi, guerrieri
*VIT:	Vanne, sì, superba	*VIT:	Vanne, sì, superba
*ARI:	Mio dolce amato sposo	*ARI:	Mio dolce amato sposo

Act 2, scenic unit a

Bosco aperto con veduta di mare. Anastasio and Amanzio (1736: Anastasio and Giustino), shipwrecked, seek refuge in a hut on the shore. Polidarte enters with Arianna, who is chained to a cliff. As the monster appears, Giustino is alerted by Arianna's cries and kills it. Anastasio and Arianna are reunited; they all sail away. Vitaliano remorsefully returns to the scene in search of Arianna.

*ANA:	Sento in seno (text not in libretto)	—	
*POL:	Ritrosa bellezza	*POL:	Ritrosa bellezza
ARI:	Per me dunque – Ah, Signor (echo arioso)	ARI:	Per me dunque —
ARI/ANA:	Mio bel tesoro	ARI/ANA:	Mio bel tesoro
*ARI:	Per noi soave e bella	CORO of sailors:	Per voi soave
*VIT:	Quel torrente		(recitative only)

2b

Giardino. Leocasta and Andronico, then Arianna, enjoying flowers, soft breezes, birdsong (1736: Leocasta alone, lamenting separation from Giustino).

*AND:	Più bel giorno	—	
*LEO:	Senti l'aura che leggiera	*LEO:	Sventurata navicella
*ARI:	Augelletti garruletti	—	

2c

Camera (Stage direction inadvertently omitted in 1736). Anastasio victorious: Giustino presents the captured Vitaliano. Amanzio makes Anastasio suspicious of Giustino's loyalty (1736: this dialogue first at the end of 2c, then moved to 3a in performance). Arianna announces revenge to the imprisoned Vitaliano. (Remainder omitted in 1736.) Anastasio, suspicious of Arianna's faithfulness, gives her Vitaliano's crown jewels.

ANA:	Verdi lauri	ANA:	Verdi lauri
*GIU:	Su l'altar di questo	*GIU:	Su l'altar di questo
*AM:	Candida fedeltà	—	

*ANA: Taci per poco ancora,   —
     o fiero e rio sospetto
*VIT: Quando serve alla ragione   *ARI: Quel torrente che s'inalza
*ANA: Se all'amor   *ANA: O fiero e rio sospetto
     (in original version 1736)
*ARI: Dalle gioie del core   —

2d   (omitted in 1736)

Bosco. Andronico has persuaded Leocasta to follow him to the battlefield, then tries to rape her. Giustino rescues her and arrests Andronico.

*LEO: Sventurata navicella
*GIU: Ho nel petto un cor sì forte

Act 3, scenic unit a

Bosco suburbano con torre. Vitaliano and Andronico (omitted in 1736) have escaped from prison, planning revenge.

*VIT: Il piacer della vendetta   *VIT: Il piacer della vendetta
     (This stage set eliminated in performance, 1737; scene starts as *Cabinetto*, with Anastasio: 'O fiero e rio' from 2c, then Vitaliano's escape indoors.)

3b

Camera. Arianna presents the crown jewels to Giustino, watched by Amanzio, who reports this to Anastasio; the latter incriminates Arianna and arrests Giustino. Leocasta and Giustino lament their fate (1736: Leocasta and Arianna). Amanzio rejoices over the success of his design.

*GIU: Zeffiretto che scorre   *GIU: Zeffiretto che scorre
*ARI: Quell'amoroso ardor   —
*ANA: Di Re sdegnato   *ANA: Di Re sdegnato
     (not set by Vivaldi)
*GIU: Il mio cor già più   *ARI: Il mio cor già più
*LEO: Senza l'amato ben   *LEO: Augelletti garruletti
*AM: Sì vo' a regnar   *AM: Dall'occaso all'oriente

3c

Orrida montuosa. Giustino, freed by Leocasta but a fugitive, remonstrates with Fortuna and falls asleep. Vitaliano enters; as he moves to kill Giustino, the voice of his father from a mausoleum stops him, revealing that they are brothers. They set out to rescue Anastasio and Arianna from Amanzio's palace coup.

(only recitative)   *GIU: Sollevar il mondo oppresso

3d
Camera. Leocasta and Arianna are in fear of Amanzio. (1736: *Deliziosa con machina in prospetto*; scene with Leocasta and Arianna omitted.) Amanzio has crowned himself emperor. Anastasio and Arianna enter in chains but are rescued by Giustino and Vitaliano, entering with soldiers. Anastasio and Arianna reconciled. Leocasta arrives late, receiving the news from Polidarte (this is omitted in 1736, where Leocasta shares Arianna's fate). Giustino marries Leocasta and is crowned co-emperor; *machina maestosa* representing the Temple of Fame.

AM:	Or che cinto ho il crin	AM:	Or che cinto ho il crin
ARI/ANA:	In braccio a te	ARI:	Ti rendo questo cor
*LEO:	Lo splendor	—	
CORO:	Dopo i nembi e le procelle	SOLI, CORO:	In braccio a te . . . Siam lieti in questo giorno

1736 has one stage set less than 1724 (2d, *Bosco*). The cutting of this episode with Andronico was easy, though it was not a saving of expense since the stage set was available anyway. The end of Act 2 and the beginning of Act 3, however, were significantly altered – the only major change made after the completion of Handel's original score.

The succession of scenes and exit arias in 2c was awkward in 1724, partly because the old-fashioned libretto structure was not suitable for a string of exit arias, partly because Vivaldi had inserted several unnecessary arias taken from his earlier works. After Giustino's exit with 'Su l'altar', Amanzio makes Anastasio suspicious of him and of Arianna – in her absence, of course – while protesting his own faithfulness ('Candida fedeltà'). He gives the crown jewels to Anastasio, who leaves with his 'suspicion' aria 'Taci per poco ancora'. Then Arianna and Vitaliano enter – a break in the *liaison des scènes* – and the latter leaves defiantly ('Quando serve'). Arianna is joined by the returning Anastasio and Amanzio and is presented with the crown (as a test of her fidelity); then Anastasio and Arianna leave with their respective arias. The exit direction for Amanzio is missing.

Handel moved the dialogue between Anastasio and Amanzio to the end of 2c and thus to the end of the act, as 2d was cut. Anastasio and Amanzio therefore must first leave without motivation to make room for Arianna and Vitaliano and then return for the dialogue – two breaks in the *liaison*. Moreover, there is now no opportunity for giving the crown to Arianna because she and Anastasio never meet in 2c. This could have been avoided if the dialogue had been left in its original place, followed by a recitative scene for Anastasio and Arianna and then the final scene for Arianna and Vitaliano. I am inclined to suspect that this was Handel's original plan. It would have placed Arianna's heroic simile aria 'Quel torrente' at the end of the act and would have produced a good key sequence: C–B♭–A–E ('Quel torrente' as originally written). As it is, Act 2 ends in the autograph with 'O fiero e rio', and the preceding 'Quel torrente' is transposed to D, obviously to avoid the clash between B♭ and E. The ending with the siciliano about 'suspicion' instead of the heroic simile for Strada is not un-Handelian but may simply have been requested by Conti. The thread of Anastasio's suspicion is taken up in 3b, but only Handel's libretto tells us that the crown had meanwhile been given to Arianna.

Chrysander must have been puzzled by all this when editing the score,[15] and he naturally consulted the sources in his own collection – the libretto and the conducting score. These show the version as performed: 'Quel torrente' concludes Act 2, and the 'suspicion' scene is transferred to the beginning of Act 3 (stage set: *Cabinetto*). Vitaliano's scene and aria are squeezed in after that, curiously taking place in the same *cabinetto*. His escape scene, however – in which John Beard had to climb down from a high tower – was omitted, together with its expensive stage set and its splendid sinfonia. Chrysander must have regretted this loss, for he also printed the escape scene with the sinfonia, causing a conflation between the autograph and performance versions. Scholars have censured him for this,[16] nobody apparently realizing that a simple omission of the escape sinfonia (p. 85) would make the score agree with the version as actually performed. In neither version is the path of the crown jewels sufficiently clear, and the dramaturgy jumps back and forth between different threads of the plot even without changes of scenery. Whereas the jealousy motif reminds one very much of *Othello*, the dramaturgy is Shakespearean only unwittingly.

In considering now the other major changes of text made in 1736, I shall pay more attention to the reinterpretation of the characters of the drama, adducing evidence from Vivaldi's and Handel's music as well.

1a is not changed except that the opening number in 1724 has solos for the newly wed Imperial couple (it is ironic that 1736 removes any allusion

15   *Georg Friedrich Händel's Werke: Ausgabe der Deutschen Händelgesellschaft* [HG] (Leipzig and Bergedorf, 1858–1902, reprinted Farnborough, 1965), ed. F. Chrysander, lxxxviii. Music examples, below, from Handel's *Giustino* are taken from this edition.
16   See, for example, H. Dütschke, 'Ein Eingriff in eine Händelpartitur', *Händel-Jahrbuch*, i (1928), pp. 68–70. The conducting score is Hamburg, Staats- und Universitätsbibliothek, MS MA/1020 – see H. D. Clausen, *Händels Direktionspartituren ('Handexemplare')* (Hamburg, 1972), p. 154 – and the libretto in Chrysander's collection has the shelf-mark MA/401.

to the wedding). Vivaldi set the number in rondeau form. Strangely enough, Handel has only chorus here but he turned the final number of *Giustino* into a rondeau with solos where Vivaldi has only chorus.

1b, the pastoral episode, is the only unit actually lengthened in 1736. The new entrance aria 'Può ben nascer' occupies a place where Vivaldi's score (but not the libretto) requires Giustino to sing, with the stage direction 'Giustino coll'aratro cantando'. But Vivaldi copied only the text of the song, an *ottava rima* which Giustino may have performed according to non-written, improvised tradition, in the manner of an *aria da cantar ottave rime* over a ground. This would have been quite unique for Vivaldi's time; but since the song is not in the libretto it may not have been performed. The sleep aria 'Bel ristoro' is a pastoral siciliano in 1724 but a surprisingly serious Largo e staccato in 1736, similar in some respects to 'Di Re sdegnato' (3b). The gloom is interrupted by Fortune's 'allegra sinfonia' and *machina*. The new text here is intimately connected with the musical idea (see below). 1736 makes Giustino respond with a joyful, heroic aria which antithetically corresponds to 'Bel ristoro'. Then 'Nacque al bosco' corresponds to 'Può ben nascer'. The whole unit is symmetrical, with Fortune's accompagnato as centre. Handel's construction must have started with the topos of ignoble birth. (This main idea of the drama is also expressed in Metastasio's *Demetrio*, by the aria 'Alma grande e nata al regno'.) Handel inserted 'Può ben nascer' to match 'Nacque al bosco' possibly because he saw the *ottava rima* 'Misero è ben colui che dopo nato' in Vivaldi's score.

In 1c Vivaldi has mostly *galant* arias in somewhat random order, partly as a result of the insertion of re-used items. It is interesting how precisely Handel avoided these texts. The dramaturgical problem in 1724 was that Arianna leaves and gets captured by the enemy only minutes before Anastasio returns with the bad news. This is remedied in 1736 by Arianna's not appearing in 1c at all, so that her exit aria in 1a marks the time of her departure. As for characterization, Vivaldi did not set the heroic text 'Non si vanti' for Anastasio but the very sentimental 'Vedrò con mio diletto'; Handel chose the former. Giustino has about the same musical identity in both scores, although his 'Allor che mi vedrò' in 1724 is a brilliant gigue, pleasing rather than proud. An important change concerns Amanzio, who is given a separate solo scene at the beginning of 1c in 1736. This reveals him as the villain of the plot, making further characterization of him in arias unnecessary. In 1724 he keeps his mask, with the fake-heroic 'La gloria del mio sangue' (1c) and the shameless lie of 'Candida fedeltà' (2c). At the end of 1c, 1736 omits the intermezzo–like girls' scene. Nothing in Handel's entire score is as simple and charming as the two arias that Vivaldi gave here to Leocasta and Andronico.

The text of 1d is basically the same, but Arianna's aria at the end, 'Mio dolce amato sposo', is *cantabile* and overloaded with virtuoso *rocaille* in Vivaldi, serious and sorrowful in Handel.[17]

Vivaldi's opening aria in 2a is so tearful that Anastasio is unequivocally marked down as a coward. (This is a last-minute insertion for the sake of its haunting music, in E minor.) Afterwards, the versions are analogous until 'Per noi soave', the song to the soft breezes. Handel takes away from the heroine Arianna the pastoral topos of the happy sea voyage – foreshadowing 'Soave sia il vento' in *Così fan tutte* – and gives it to a sailors' chorus. The duet of the reunited couple, with the clearing of the sky and a happy voyage, exactly matches the end of the opera. In 2a, Handel lets the duet and the chorus stand as separate items, as Vivaldi did at the end, whereas Handel's final number, with its rondeau structure, matches Vivaldi's opening number. That the scene with the returning Vitaliano is deprived of the aria may be a loss. Vivaldi's 'Quel torrente' expresses 'boundless desire' – this becomes 'boundless rage' when transferred to 2c for Arianna in 1736. The passionate affection, taken away from Vitaliano, is given to Arianna.

2b is a pastoral island in 1724, with a sort of 'nature-song contest' between Andronico, Leocasta and Arianna. For illustrative beauty 'Senti l'aura', originating as a slow concerto movement, is outstanding. Handel replaced the whole scene with a single episode for Leocasta alone, comparable to that for Amanzio in 1c; she straightforwardly reveals to the audience that she loves Giustino and suffers from her separation from him. This dispenses with the need for an actual love dialogue such as 1724 has at the end of the act. The new solo scene condenses much of 2b and 2d, using Leocasta's aria text from 2d. But why? The simile of the little ship in the stormy sea may fit her emotional state in the 1724 version – she is shaken after Andronico's hideous attack – but not her situation in 1736, where she is simply longing for the return of Giustino. The reason is pictorial, as it were: Leocasta, left alone at home, experiences in her heart the very things that Arianna, Anastasio and Giustino experience in reality – shipwreck, sea monster, battle and, finally, happy voyage. The simile aria counterbalances the whole story of 2a and may be imagined as happening simultaneously ('Meanwhile, back home . . .'). The imagery of the aria is eminently suitable here, more so than in its original position in 1724.

2c has already been discussed, but a word should be added about the heroic figure of Giustino. Beregan had drawn him as a militarist, initially averse to love. 1724 softens this characteristic but still has only heroic aria texts for him in Act 2. Vivaldi set 'Su l'altar' in a purely heroic vein but 'Ho nel petto' (in 2d) in a most unusual, almost exotic fashion – in E minor, with concertante psaltery and pizzicato strings. In 1736, the only aria for

17   On the progressive nature of Vivaldi's aria, see H. C. Wolff, 'Vivaldi und der Stil der italienischen Oper', *Acta musicologica*, xl (1968), pp. 179–86.

Giustino is 'Su l'altar', and, not surprisingly, Handel tries to say everything about him in it. There is the exceptional occurrence of a heroic march in slow 3/4, but this is simply old-fashioned, going back to Lully's 3/4 marches and sarabands. There are the dotted rhythms, denoting aspiration to royal glory, and the harshly dissonant progressions, signifying stubbornness and the rejection of tender affections. The descending semiquaver figuration, mostly in the bass, is actually taken from Vivaldi's setting of this aria. Vivaldi uses this figuration in his ritornello (in the top line as well as in the bass), and he refers to it at the words 'mille rai' (see Ex. 1). The crowded, repetitive note-pattern illustrates the words 'mille' and 'cento' in this aria, suggesting multitudes.

More will be said below about the arias of Vitaliano and Amanzio in Act 3. 3b has the only pastoral aria for Giustino in this act. Vivaldi's and Handel's settings of 'Zeffiretto' are quite different – the former in B♭ and fresh and energetic, the latter in E♭ and superbly illustrative – because they balance different opposites, Vivaldi's the touching, sentimental 'Il mio cor' in E and Handel's the triumphant gigue 'Sollevar' in D. Handel gives 'Il mio cor' to Arianna and transforms its easy self-pity into deep pathos. In fact, her heroic self-control in deepest misery is the actual theme of the aria. The royal dotted rhythms of the saraband give way to mounting pain (note the bass ascent from A to d♭) and to a flowing accompaniment as she can no longer hold back her tears. In the B section there is similar imagery about repressed sighs and internal weeping. The aria has affinities with both Giustino's heroic 'Su l'altar' and a moment in the final *ciacona* when Arianna can at last 'enjoy happiness and peace'.

The only Largo e staccato in Vivaldi's score is given over to the simpler grief of Leocasta. 'Senza l'amato ben' corresponds to 'Il mio cor' in Handel. The purely melodic chromaticism of Vivaldi's lament contrasts with the broad harmonic feeling of Handel's orchestra (see Ex. 2). The other arias in 1724 are fillers, including two love-songs for Arianna, one of which, 'La cervetta', was used by Handel in his pasticcio *Catone* in 1732.[18]

Vivaldi's weakling, Anastasio, has nothing to say in Act 3, because he is spared the aria 'Di Re sdegnato'. Handel, of course, did set the text, again using ideas from Vivaldi's 'Su l'altar' (see Ex. 1). He handles these musical ideas as separate entities, transferring them from one character to the other. It is not Handel's score that needs padding out with Vivaldi's motifs, but Anastasio's heroism with Giustino's. The motifs are also treated 'dialectically' – inverted, ironicized. The one consisting of pairs of legato quavers in the violins, for example, could come ultimately from an anonymous pastoral aria, 'Vaghi fiori' (possibly by Giovanni Bononcini), but Handel also uses it in Vitaliano's 'Vanne, sì' in 1d at the words 'se per

[18]   See Strohm, *Essays*, p. 205. This use of it does not prove that Handel had access then to the complete score of Vivaldi's opera.

Ex. 1

(a) Vivaldi

GIUSTINO

Su l'al - tar   di que - - sto nu - me

Basso

tu ve - drai   mil - le, mil - le   rai a ba - le - nar

Final ritornello:

Vlns

Basso

(b) Handel

Ex. 2

(a) Vivaldi

Largo, e staccato

Sen - za l'a-ma-to ben, l'a-ma-to ben vi - ve-re

Basso [Vla]

que-sto sen non può, non sà, non può, non sà,

vi - ve - re que - - sto sen non può, non sà.

(*b*) Handel

me non senti amor' – superb irony, if one considers the relationship between Arianna and Anastasio at the moment of 'Di Re sdegnato'.[19]

Handel's *Giustino* contains a considerable number of borrowings from, or – perhaps a better word – re-uses of, other music. Many of these have been identified by John H. Roberts, to whose generosity I owe my knowledge of them.[20] He has discovered many 'new' re-uses of material in Handel's later works, and again the old question why Handel indulged in this habit becomes pressing. *How* he did so has been somewhat better investigated, for example by Harold S. Powers in the case of *Serse*.[21] Obviously, there is a connection between the why and the how, which can best be studied in a case like *Giustino* where we know the source material with which Handel worked.

That Vivaldi's setting was to some degree a model for Handel should be clear from the examples quoted above – though they are few and somewhat concealed. The simplest borrowing technique, that of using a text from the source libretto together with its music, is the rarest in *Giustino*, whereas it is the normal (perhaps the only) method in *Serse*. More often, Handel replaced the text found in 1724 by another suiting both the dramatic situation and the prosody of the music, which he took from elsewhere. Quite often he managed to keep the original text while drawing on music from external sources, sometimes more than one at a time. The why (dramatic versus musical goals) and the how (various forms of elaboration and recombination) are woven together. In 'Di Re sdegnato', for example, Handel did not borrow a ready-made combination of text and music – there was none in Vivaldi – but transferred ideas from another aria in Vivaldi's score (this could be called 'cross-borrowing') and from yet another in his own score (see above). This is different from a re-use of totally external material because Giustino and Anastasio are figures in the same drama, and the transfer between them strengthens the network of musico-dramatic images.

Some arias in *Giustino* seem to be based on purely external material but also from more than one source. 'Un vostro sguardo' has nothing in common with Vivaldi but uses perhaps two different motifs from arias by Francesco Gasparini. 'Se parla nel mio cor' has material in common with an aria by Alessandro Scarlatti, and the initial tune is reminiscent of another by Gasparini. 'Può ben nascer' is derived from an aria in Bononcini's *Serse* but

---

[19]   See also the essay by John H. Roberts, pp. 164 (aria No. 11) and 196 (item No. 25), below (Ed.).

[20]   Unless otherwise stated, all further references to re-uses of other material in Handel's *Giustino* are based on Dr Roberts's suggestions. (He discusses instances in other works, notably *Faramondo*, in his own essay, below (Ed.).)

[21]   See 'Il Serse trasformato', pp. 73–90.

shares other features with a Gasparini piece.[22] None of these motifs is particularly original in character, nor even important in Handel's context. Are these really borrowings, or are they, rather, commonplace motifs the occurrence of which is simply a coincidence? It might be argued that they are commonplace motifs not in the operatic style of Handel's contemporaries but in that of his important predecessors and their 'moderate and mixed' style, cultivated mostly in Roman opera until about 1720. Handel evokes a stylistic sphere which meant a lot to him. This is fresh, *galant* but not yet sentimental music. Handel, in the first act of *Giustino*, suggests a particular atmosphere of the past by consciously quoting its commonplaces.

The presence of musical images – or emblems, since there is usually an aria text to give them a meaning – is the key also to those cases where the technique of re-use is somewhat cruder. After completing his setting of 'Nacque al bosco' Handel replaced it with a beautiful duet by Carl Heinrich Graun, whose primary motifs suited his text perfectly. His own setting was related in rhythm, mode and mood to his 'Su l'altar' and even 'Il mio cor'. This was because 'Nacque al bosco' was sung by Leocasta as an allegory of Giustino's fate. Graun's aria, on the other hand, expresses the innocence and devotion of the loving soul who is hoping to be united with Jesus. Thus 'Nacque al bosco' makes Leocasta speak of herself – she is the innocent soul, the flower of the fields. Certain characteristics of Graun's aria recur also in Vivaldi's 'Nacque al bosco' and in his last aria for Leocasta, 'Lo splendor'. Even Handel's own 'Nacque al bosco' is a distant relative. The common musical image is the minuet – with saraband elements – embellished by triplet figuration and French trills. The poetic topos is the pastoral idea – the princess as a shepherd girl and bride, the child, the flower.

In 'Dall'occaso all'oriente' Handel used Graun's aria 'Mein Knecht der Gerechte' for the most sinful of his characters, Amanzio. The contrafactum text, which replaces Vivaldi's 'Sì, vo' a regnar', has the same peculiar metrical scheme as Amanzio's aria 'È virtute in sin la frode' (*ottonari* with interspersed *quaternario*). This connection may be just the last member of a whole concatenation of textual–musical images. 'Dall'occaso', a gavotte in G minor, is surprisingly similar to Vitaliano's revenge aria 'Il piacer della vendetta'. This piece is a re-use of an aria in *Almira* which also occurs in the motet *Coelestis dum spirat aura*, drawing on features of both of them.[23] But

22   For the borrowing from Bononcini and Scarlatti I cite suggestions by John H. Roberts (and again see his essay, below, p. 196, item No. 23 – Ed.); for the others, see Strohm, *Essays*, pp. 87f, including music examples.

23   See B. Baselt, *Händel-Handbuch*, i: *Thematisch-systematisches Verzeichnis: Bühnenwerke* (Leipzig, 1978), p. 450.

there is also a very similar revenge aria in *Silla*, 'La vendetta è un cibo al cor'. The aria text of 1724, 'Il piacer della vendetta', must have led Handel to his *Silla* aria, and this, in turn, triggered off the musical borrowings.

Vivaldi's delightful setting of 'Il piacer', however, impressed Handel with its different musical image. He gave this image to Amanzio instead (see Ex. 3). This 'walking' theme over a descending bass is, after all, a commonplace of Handel's own period. It is familiar from comic arias, mostly for buffo basses, beginning with Handel's own Polyphemus ('O ruddier than the cherry', derived from Keiser), but is most often found in *intermezzi comici* (whence it entered the motivic repertory of Vivaldi's concertos). The consequent motif in the violins over the same descending bass with the characteristic, dissonant seconds reminds us of Pergolesi via Stravinsky's *Pulcinella*. The clumsy puppet-like movements of the lewd, self-satisfied villain were captured by Vivaldi in his 'Il piacer della vendetta' – he added exquisite concertante diminutions in the violins as if to make the dish of sweet revenge even more appetizing. In Handel it is Amanzio who is licking his lips.

Handel's *Giustino* contains some arguably inferior arias which stand outside the rich network of images found in the items with re-used music. Are they borrowed, then? 'Sollevar il mondo oppresso' and 'Ti rendo questo cor' both have texts not found in 1724 and are not to Handel's usual standard. They remind one of younger Italian composers like Porta or Orlandini, and the later Keiser also approached this facile north Italian style. 'Da tuoi begl'occhi' and 'Sventurata navicella' are more reminiscent of Neapolitans like Domenico Sarro, especially the second of them, which would be quite at home in an intermezzo. They could be Handel imitations – if they are borrowed they probably do not come from Vivaldi.[24] In any case, they are padding, not enrichment of the drama.

The two most wonderful pieces in Handel's *Giustino* owe their richness of meaning to the multitude of poetic–musical images that they weave together. The combinatory technique *par excellence* is, of course, the fugue, and 'Corri, vola' is a concerted fugue. 'Run, fly' is a command that the musical voices in this 'flight' are only too keen to obey, trying to involve Giustino in their lively, easy-to-follow rhythm. Fortune on her wheel (which turns like clockwork) and her company of flying geniuses who divide two fugal statements between them, are parts of a greater whole, the 'allegra sinfonia'. All this is only a *machina* (a dream of Giustino) whose details are fitted together with consummate craftsmanship. The opening of Bononcini's sinfonia for *Serse* provides the details of the tic-tac quavers, rising through the triad, and of the concluding runs which circle in on the

[24]   On 'Sollevar il mondo oppresso', also see p. 191, below; and in the case of 'Sventurata navicella' Dr Roberts claims specific borrowing, from Sarro: see below, p. 196, item No. 26 (Ed.).

Ex. 3

(*a*) Vivaldi

(*b*) Handel

AMANZIO

Or che cin-to ho il crin d'al - lo - - - - [ro]

cadence.[25] The semiquaver subdivisions, especially on each fourth quaver, come from Vivaldi – from his most popular tune, in fact (see Ex. 4). This tune (at the top of the texture, significantly) is quoted here not from the 'Primavera' concerto but from its earlier occurrence as the 'allegra sinfonia' in *Giustino*. In Handel's score, these ideas fit together in more than one way, including inversion, as is fitting for Fortune's wheel. The text had to be newly made up, the idea of 'running' being derived from the repeated pitches and semiquavers in Vivaldi. In the second, ensemble statement, which corresponds in position to the aria 'Della tua sorte' in Vivaldi, Handel goes so far as to quote the opening motif of 'Della tua sorte' in a rather hidden place; this motif is also akin to the sinfonia tune (see Ex. 5). It is almost as if Handel wanted to assure us that he knew the aria too.

The last piece to be discussed is the final number of the opera, like 'Corri,

25   This re-use was recognized by Powers: op. cit., p. 91. It is noteworthy how often Handel comes close to Bononcini's style when writing active, repetitive basses.

Ex. 4
(a)   Vivaldi (transposed from E major)

(b)   Handel

(c)   Bononcini

Ex. 5
(a)   Vivaldi (transposed from A major)

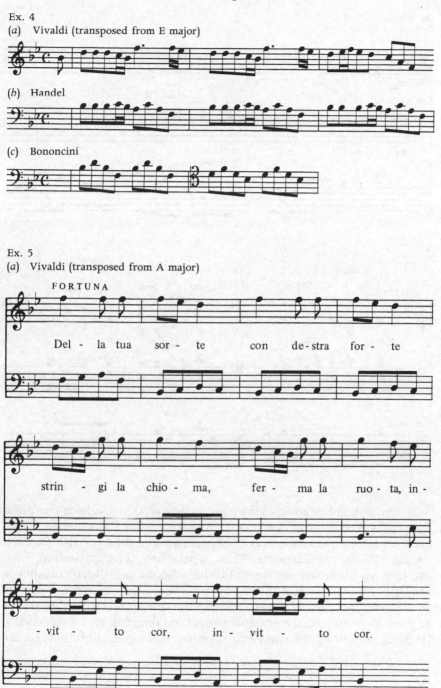

FORTUNA

Del - la tua   sor - te   con de-stra   for - te

strin - gi la chio - ma,   fer - ma la   ruo - ta, in -

- vit -   to   cor,   in - vit -   to   cor.

(b) Handel

vola' not an aria but an ensemble. But, whereas 'Corri, vola' is one piece
with two statements, 'In braccio a te' is two pieces in one, a minuet which
expands into a chaconne.[26] Vivaldi had first the duet for the reunited
couple, 'In braccio a te la calma'. Then, separated by a curious episode with
a re-used aria, followed the 'scena ultima' with the *coro* 'Dopo i nembi e le
procelle'. Handel saw that the two texts were related – clouds and storms
are followed by calm and peace – and that the episode was superfluous (but
he must have noticed the graceful minuet–saraband in it, 'Lo splendor').
He decided to bring the two items together, making his librettist rewrite

[26] This and other compound finales in Handel are discussed in W. Dean, *Handel and the
Opera Seria* (Berkeley and Los Angeles, 1969), pp. 148ff. See also his important
remarks on 'Corri, vola' (pp. 173ff) and 'Può ben nascer' (p. 197).

the duet text for the ensemble Arianna–Anastasio, Leocasta–Giustino plus Vitaliano. The ten lines of this text (3 + 3 + 3 + 1) matched the two stanzas (5 + 5) of the actual *coro* which immediately follows. The common final line of both halves is 'rinasce il secol d'or', which is not only isolated metrically but contains the textual idea newly introduced by Handel – the 'rebirth of the golden ages of the past'. The Golden Age is, of course, a commonplace but one that particularly distinguishes Handel's *Serse*, which is so programmatically retrospective.[27]

Handel's minuet, 'In braccio a te la calma', is woven together from two musical sources, Alessandro Scarlatti's *Il Pompeo* and Vivaldi (see Ex. 6). The beginning of Handel's melody connects both predecessors: the 5–3 step comes from Vivaldi, the 5–6 step from Scarlatti. Vivaldi's piece is a passepied (in 3/8), Scarlatti's a gigue (in a fast 3/4 with dotted rhythm – note the position of the bar-lines). Handel finds a common denominator in the minuet–saraband, with bar-lines shifted against Scarlatti's version so that the cadence falls on beats 1 and 2. Thus the first beat can become a dissonance, for example by suspension. Suspended dissonances are used in Vivaldi's duet and resolved with the running figure first heard in bar 10, which also imitates the initial rhythm. Handel uses both the rhythmic and the contrapuntal device in various guises for his pairs of characters (see HG, pp. 115f). Only at the fugal entries of the last line ('rinasce') does the first beat become consonant again, in a passage reminiscent of Bach. Suspended dissonance on the first beat of 3/4 is a common feature of that queen of dances, the chaconne. This is also a climactic, multi-sectional type of music, where the later sections increase the density of rhythmic figuration as is fitting for variations over a ground. Vivaldi's setting of the *coro* is in fact such a chaconne, for in it he gradually introduces suspensions over the descending bass and increases the rhythmic activity. The climax is at his bars 36–43 (see Ex. 7).

Handel concluded almost all his operas with a French dance movement, just as he almost always began them with a French overture. His final *cori* are gavottes, passepieds, rigaudons and minuets. The chaconne is rare, but here it was the only proper solution: it 'answered' both the preceding minuet–ensemble and Vivaldi's final chorus. At the same time, Handel lets the main tune recur in rondeau fashion, a structure applicable to all dance types. He therefore has a bass line which is not an ostinato. The ostinato idea is transferred to the rondeau-like recurrence of the tune itself which unifies the ensemble and the tutti. The chaconne characteristics start, as a climax, at 'Cessate le procelle' with the violin figurations. At 'Del fato abbiam la palma', the hammering bass rhythm begins to resemble Vivaldi's

---

[27]   For this important topos in *Serse*, see W. Osthoff, 'Handels "Largo" als Musik des Goldenen Zeitalters', *Archiv für Musikwissenschaft*, xxx (1973), pp. 175–89.

Ex. 6

(a) Vivaldi

(b) Scarlatti

Bel - lez - za   che s'a - ma   e gio - ia   del   co - re

(c) Handel

In   brac - cio a te   la   cal - ma   del   cor, del sen, del - l'al - ma,   In   brac - cio a te   la   cal - ma   *etc.*

etc.

climactic passage quoted as Ex. 7, but the descending chaconne bass is converted into an ascent (see HG, pp. 118f). Whereas Vivaldi's conclusion appears to be unique in his operas, the chaconne has a different meaning for Handel. He refers back not only to the court of Louis XIV, the model for all royalty, but more specifically to its German derivatives in Hamburg and Hanover and to the music of Keiser and Mattheson: the royalty in Handel's Covent Garden boxes were all Germans.

When clouds and storms clear away, the *machina in prospetto* dominates the view again. It represents the Temple of Fame (*Ruhm, gloire*). With Handel, this is like a look into the past. As he gives new life to the fame of

Ex. 7   Vivaldi

the ancient heroes on his stage (even if apparently born in humble conditions), the Golden Age is reborn. At the beginning of the drama Giustino's Constantinople is called 'la nuova Roma', and a renaissance of the 'secol d'oro' is to take place there. London is the 'new Rome' of the eighteenth century. But musically speaking it is his own Golden Age, his youthful years in Germany and Rome, that Handel glorifies.

Handel and Charles Jennens's Italian opera manuscripts

JOHN H. ROBERTS

'Friend of Handel' is how the *Dictionary of National Biography* epitomizes Charles Jennens (1700–73). This, we have learnt, does him less than justice, for though he never lived up to his inflated pretensions as a poet and editor of Shakespeare, he deserves a place of some honour in the history of music. The librettos he wrote or compiled for Handel inspired four of the composer's greatest masterpieces, *Saul* (1738), *L'Allegro, il Penseroso ed il Moderato* (1740), *Messiah* (1741) and *Belshazzar* (1744), and the large music library he assembled has proved, increasingly, an immensely rich resource for modern scholarship. He was, first and foremost, a Handel collector. 'He subscribed to all his works published on subscription, and had a standing order for copies of the scores and parts of his compositions, including revised, unperformed and unfinished pieces.'[1] But Jennens also amassed a formidable collection of manuscript and printed music by other composers, chiefly Italian.[2] For this he was in large part indebted to his friend Edward Holdsworth (1684–1746). A non-juror, like Jennens, and hence barred from pursuing a promising academic career as a classicist, Holdsworth spent much of his time accompanying young gentlemen on the Grand Tour, giving him ample opportunity to purchase music in Italy and elsewhere. An extensive correspondence between the two men covering the years 1729–46, auctioned at Christie's on 4 July 1973 and now in the collection of Gerald Coke, allows us to trace in considerable

---

[1] W. Dean, 'Jennens, Charles', *The New Grove*, ix, p. 599.

[2] Much important work has recently been done on Jennens's non-Handelian manuscripts by Michael Talbot and Paul Everett. See especially Talbot, 'Some Overlooked MSS in Manchester', *The Musical Times*, cxv (1974), pp. 942–4; idem, 'Vivaldi's "Manchester" Sonatas', *Proceedings of the Royal Musical Association*, civ (1977–8), pp. 20–9; idem, 'Charles Jennens and Antonio Vivaldi', *Vivaldi veneziano europeo*, ed. F. Degrada (Florence, 1980), pp. 67–75; Everett, 'A Roman Concerto Repertory: Ottoboni's "what not"?', *Proceedings of the Royal Musical Association*, cx (1983–4), pp. 62–78; and idem, 'Vivaldi Concerto Manuscripts in Manchester', *Informazioni e studi vivaldiani*, v (1984), pp. 23–52, and vi (1985), pp. 3–56.

detail the course of Holdsworth's collecting on Jennens's behalf.[3] His greatest coup came in 1742 when he bought for some 40 shillings a substantial portion of the music library of Cardinal Pietro Ottoboni, the munificent Roman patron of Corelli, Alessandro Scarlatti and Handel who had died two years previously.

When Jennens died in 1773 he bequeathed his music to his cousin Heneage Finch, 3rd Earl of Aylesford, who (as Lord Guernsey until 1757) had likewise been a friend of Handel's. For a hundred years this precious legacy remained in the possession of the successive earls, apparently with few additions. Then, on 25 August 1873, a small and comparatively unimportant selection was sold at auction by Puttick & Simpson, and the rest met the same fate at Sotheby's on 13 May 1918. In this second, crucial sale almost everything went to dealers, often for absurdly low prices. Later, Newman Flower (not yet knighted) acquired the lion's share of the Handel material and various other items, which today constitute the bulk of the Newman Flower Collection in the Henry Watson Music Library, Manchester. The remaining Aylesford manuscripts were widely dispersed, but many can still be located, mainly in British and American libraries.[4]

This essay principally concerns a small group of Italian opera manuscripts sent to Jennens by Holdsworth in 1732, all intimately linked to Handel. They are described with unusual exactness in Holdsworth's letter from Rome of 17 April 1732:

As to your musick, I have purchas'd Vinci's Artaserse, which was his last and most admir'd performance; The Saxon's Fabricio, which was acted here the last Carneval with great applause; Three operas of Scarlatti; and some Airs of Porpora and others. value in all about 8^L: 15^{sh}: Vinci's opera and one of Scarlatti's you have entire, both Songs and Recitativo, as I was advis'd to take them, so that if you think they deserve it, you may have them perform'd on the English Theater.

Vinci's *Artaserse* had received its first performance in Rome on 4 February 1730, a few months before his early death. Holdsworth reported on 24 August 1730 that he was having copied 'the Overture, Songs and Symphonies', and only his absence from the city prevented his dispatching the score to Jennens. 'The Saxon's Fabricio' was Hasse's *Cajo Fabricio*, heard for the first time on 12 January 1732. With the help of the Sotheby's sale catalogue we can also identify the three other operas as Alessandro

3   An overview of the Jennens–Holdsworth correspondence, with extensive quotations, is provided in the sale catalogue, *Autograph Letters of George Frideric Handel and Charles Jennens* (London, 1973), pp. 19–28. Christopher Hogwood has also included many extracts in his *Handel* (London, 1984). I am grateful to Mr Coke for kindly allowing me to quote several previously unpublished passages, and to Anthony Hicks for making available his transcripts of the relevant letters.

4   For a somewhat fuller account of the history of the Aylesford collection, see the essay by Anthony Hicks, below, p. 208 (Ed.).

Scarlatti's *Dafni* (Naples, 1700), *Marco Attilio Regolo* (Rome, 1719) and *Griselda* (Rome, 1721).[5]

Fortunately all five scores can be tracked from the 1918 sale to their present locations. The three Scarlatti manuscripts were bought by the music dealer Harold Reeves and sold shortly thereafter to W. Barclay Squire of the British Museum. Distressed over the dispersal of the Aylesford Collection, Squire made it his business to retrieve a number of the more unusual manuscripts from the dealers and sell them to appropriate libraries – as well as donating several volumes to the Museum and the King's Music Library, then on deposit there. As a permanent home for *Dafni* and *Attilio Regolo* he selected the Fitzwilliam Museum, Cambridge, presumably because of Edward Dent's interest in Scarlatti;[6] *Griselda* was consigned to the Library of Congress. The original purchaser of *Artaserse* and *Cajo Fabricio* was one Hunt, apparently a dealer. Some time before 1940, however, they too came into the hands of Reeves, who then sold them to the Sibley Music Library of the Eastman School of Music, Rochester, New York, and the Newberry Library, Chicago, respectively.

Jennens had received the manuscripts by the time he wrote a letter to Holdsworth, now lost, on 27 November 1732.[7] He must have shown them to Handel not long afterwards, for the oratorio *Athalia*, completed on 7 June 1733, contains material derived from *Dafni* and probably also *Griselda*. Borrowing from all three Scarlatti works continued regularly up to 1738, but the two newer operas, representing the latest Italian fashion, were turned to a very different purpose. In December 1733, Handel brought out at the King's Theatre *Caio Fabbricio*, a pasticcio version of Hasse's opera, and little more than a month later, in January 1734, he offered an adaptation of *Artaserse* under the title *Arbace*. Many pencilled changes in his hand in the Aylesford scores reveal that he used these manuscripts as the basis of his arrangements.

A brief description of the five manuscripts is given below. Many Aylesford scores still retain their original shelf-marks, consisting of two capital letters over a number, separated by a horizontal line; these shelf-marks may appear on a circular label near the top of the spine or, occasionally, inside the volume. In addition, items included in the 1918 sale usually display, typically on the inside of the front cover, a stock number in bright red crayon, not corresponding to the lot number.

5   Jennens also owned the autograph of Scarlatti's *La fede riconosciuta*, described in E. J. Dent, 'A Pastoral Opera by Alessandro Scarlatti', *The Music Review*, xii (1951), pp. 7–14. But this manuscript is of Ottobonian provenance and so could not have come to him until after the cardinal's death in 1740.

6   Squire's letter of 4 November 1918, offering the manuscripts to the Fitzwilliam Museum and mentioning his rescue efforts, is printed in *Marco Attilio Regolo*, ed. J. Godwin, The Operas of Alessandro Scarlatti, ii (Cambridge, Mass., 1975), p. 11.

7   This is evident from Holdsworth's reply dated 13 February 1733.

Sometimes one also finds the lot number written in dark red crayon, with the number of volumes in the lot inscribed below a horizontal line. Whenever a manuscript carries such distinguishing marks, they are duly noted. Since I have not had an opportunity to examine most of the manuscripts directly, I have not attempted to provide information about their physical characteristics.[8]

A   Sibley Music Library, Eastman School of Music, Vault M1500.V777A

       3 vols., without foliation. A complete score of Vinci's *Artaserse*, conforming to the printed libretto of 1730. One folio, bearing the last $10\frac{1}{2}$ bars of the aria 'Su le sponde' in Act 1 scene 3 and the first $4\frac{1}{2}$ bars of recitative in scene 4, is missing, though it must have been present when Handel's conducting score was copied. A fragmentary Aylesford label on Vol. 3 is illegible. Stock numbers: 527, 525 and 502.

B   Newberry Library, MS VM 1500 H35c

       234 unnumbered fols. Twenty-eight arias from the 1732 version of Hasse's *Cajo Fabricio*. The aria 'Nocchier che teme assorto' is attributed to 'Sig:[r] Porpora', all the others being specifically ascribed to Hasse. Porpora may well have contributed this number to Hasse's opera; his own *Germanico in Germania* had its first performance at the same theatre, the Teatro Capranica, a few weeks later. Stock number: 534. Lot number: $\frac{311}{1}$.

C   Fitzwilliam Museum, MS Mus. 227 (formerly 24-E-8)

       125 fols. A complete score of Scarlatti's *Dafni*, conforming (except for omission of a dedicatory prologue) to the printed libretto of 1700. The title-page, however, calls the opera 'Dafni, e Galatea' and refers to an otherwise unknown performance in Naples in 1723 ('1723 in Napoli/opera molta gradita'). On the last page of music the copyist noted: 'scritta li ii mag$^{\underline{o}}$ 1724.' This is the only recorded score of *Dafni*. Stock number: 253.[9]

D   Fitzwilliam Museum, MS Mus. 228 (formerly 24-E-9)

       245 fols. Fifty-one numbers from Scarlatti's *Marco Attilio Regolo*, including forty arias (three of them alternatives), five duets, one trio, one quartet, two accompanied recitatives and two simple recitatives.[10] Stock number: illegible.

[8]   For providing first-hand information about these manuscripts I am indebted to Damaris Naylor of the Fitzwilliam Museum, Lucille Wehner of the Newberry Library, Louise Goldberg of the Sibley Music Library, and Lowell Lindgren.

[9]   The stock number was removed when the volume was 'restored' but can still be seen on the microfilm copy currently available from the Fitzwilliam Museum. A facsimile edition of this manuscript has appeared as *Handel Sources*, vii, ed. J. H. Roberts (New York, 1986).

[10]   In the numbering of Godwin's edition (see note 6 above) the contents of the manuscript are as follows: Nos. 6, 9, 12, 14, 16, 18, 20, 22, A2, 25, 27, 29, 31, 39, 41, 43, 45, 47, 48 (no recitative), 51, 49, 53 (no recitative), 55, 57–9, 61, 63, 66, 68, 70–1, 77, 79, 81–3, 86, 88, 90–2, 94, 96, 98, 100, A4, 102, 107, 109 and A1.

E   Library of Congress, M1500.S28G5

180 fols. Twenty-four numbers from Scarlatti's *Griselda*, including twenty arias, two duets, one quartet and one accompanied recitative (ff. 1r–135v); and eight arias and three duets by other composers (ff. 136r–180r).[11] Aylesford shelfmark (on spine): $\frac{ND}{2}$.Stock number: 254.

Though all of Roman provenance, these manuscripts are clearly the products of two different groups of copyists working at different times. Of the three music hands in *A* two also appear in *B*, along with four others, and one of the three text hands in *A* copied all the words in *B*. None of these copyists, however, wrote any part of the three Scarlatti manuscripts, *C*, *D* and *E*, which are largely the work of a single individual. Only on folios 1r–56r of *E* do we encounter two other hands. These three scores belong to an earlier period than the other two: *C* is dated 1724, *D* was probably copied not long after the première of *Attilio Regolo* in 1719, and the repertory of *E* implies a copying date of 1721 or 1722. We may assume that Holdsworth acquired these manuscripts second-hand, already bound in their present vellum.

As is usually the case in miscellaneous aria collections, the eleven pieces at the end of *E* are very imperfectly identified by the copyist. With the generous and very extensive help of Reinhard Strohm, I have been able to place most of them:

1.   Domenico Sarro, 'Placida auretta' (soprano, A major), ff. 136r–138r. 'Del Sr Dom.^{co} Sarro./Di Napoli/in Roma 1721'. Originally composed for Sarro's *Ginevra Principessa di Scozia*, Naples, Teatro S. Bartolomeo, 20 January 1720, and included in the pasticcio *Artaserse*, Rome, Teatro Alibert, Carnival 1721.

2.   Nicola Porpora, 'Resta crudele à piangere' (soprano, E minor), 138v–139v. 'Aria Del Porpora/Prima D'Alibert/1721.' Also in the pasticcio *Artaserse*.

3.   Francesco Gasparini, 'Un non sò che mi sento' (soprano, G major), 140r–142v. 'Del Gasperini/2.ª della Pace/1721.' From Gasparini's *La Zoe*, Rome, Teatro della Pace, Carnival 1721 (originally *Il comando non inteso ed ubbedito*, Florence, Teatro in via del Cocomero, autumn 1715).

4.   Pietro Auletta, 'Ferma ingrato' (soprano duet, G minor), 143r–[143ᵃv]. 'Sig.^r Pietro/Auletta'. From a cantata? Auletta (*c*1698–1771) is not known to have composed any operas before 1725.

5.   Giuseppe Vignati, 'Sciolta dal lido' (soprano, F major), ff. 144r–153r. 'Del Sr Giuseppe Vignati di Milano/Cantata in detta Città dà Faustina/Con li suoi modi scritti come la/Cantava Nel Carnevale 1720.' From a composite

11   The Scarlatti numbers are all included in *Griselda*, ed. D. J. Grout, The Operas of Alessandro Scarlatti, iii (Cambridge, Mass., 1975). In Grout's numbering the manuscript contains the following: Nos. 5, 24, 36, 46, 51, 58, 73, 81, 43, 29, 37, 49, 55, 79, 71, 11, 53, 39, 27, 82, 89, 86, 60 and 93 (bars 51–98). The eleven pieces at the end of the manuscript are published in *Handel Sources*, ix (New York, 1987).

Ambleto, Milan, Teatro Regio Ducale, 1719. This example of Faustina Bordoni's ornamentation has been extensively discussed by George Buelow and by Howard Mayer Brown, who was able to identify the opera to which the aria belongs from a manuscript in his personal collection.[12]

6.   Andrea Stefano Fiorè, 'Scherza di fiore in fiore' (soprano, D minor), ff. 154r–159r. 'Fiorè/in Turino/1720'. Not further identified.

7.   Giuseppe Maria Orlandini, 'Mi fien care' (soprano, G major), ff. 160r–166v. 'Vignati'. From Orlandini's *Paride*, Venice, S. Giovanni Grisostomo, Carnival 1720.

8.   Fiorè(?), 'Rondinella sconsolata' (soprano, B minor), ff. 167r–170v. 'Aria/Cantata in Venezia/Dalla S.ra Marg.a Zani/1720.' Reinhard Strohm informs me that this aria was sung by Zani in the pasticcio *Alessandro cognominato Severo*, Mantua, Carnival 1720. A very different version of the text, beginning 'Rondinella che nel nido', is found in the libretto of Fiorè's *Il pentimento generoso*, Venice, Teatro S. Angelo, Carnival 1719, for a character sung by Zani.

9.   Giovanni Bononcini, 'Così piangendo e mesta' (soprano duet, B♭ major), ff. 171r–173r. 'Gio. Bononcini.' From Bononcini's *Erminia*, Rome, Teatro della Pace, Carnival 1720.

10.   Bononcini, 'Hai begl'occhi' (soprano duet, G major), ff. 173r–174v. 'Bononcini'. Also from *Erminia*.

11.   Anon., 'Vaghi fiori con cifre odorose' (soprano, C major), ff. 175r–180r. This unidentified aria also appears, like No. 8, in Bibliothèque Nationale, fonds du Conservatoire, MS D.1348.

It might be supposed that these eleven pieces correspond to the 'Airs of Porpora and others' mentioned by Holdsworth in April 1732, but this seems unlikely. The binding of *E* is undoubtedly Italian, and Holdsworth's later remark that he was 'sorry that the loose airs which I sent you from Rome were not to your mind' indicates that the arias in question were unbound.[13] We will probably never know precisely what became of these unacceptable offerings. But it is worth noting that an Aylesford manuscript in the Newman Flower Collection (MS Q520 Vu51), a composite of Italian and English music copied at various times and places, contains, on folios 1r–6v, an Italian copy of one of the arias Handel interpolated into the pasticcio *Caio Fabbricio*, 'Per amor se il cor sospira' from Vinci's

---

12   G. J. Buelow, 'A Lesson in Operatic Performance Practice by Madame Faustina Bordoni', *A Musical Offering: Essays in Honor of Martin Bernstein*, ed. E. H. Clinkscale and Claire Brook (New York, 1977), pp. 79–96; and H. M. Brown, 'Embellishing Eighteenth-Century Arias: on Cadenzas', *Opera & Vivaldi*, ed. M. Collins and E. K. Kirk (Austin, 1984), pp. 258–76.

13   Letter to Jennens, 13 February 1733.

Astianatte (Naples, 1725).[14] Another aria, on folios 45r–48v, 'Non può più saldarsi' from Orlandini's *Paride*, also has a Handelian connection, since ideas from it turn up in the rejected air for *Saul* 'The time at length is come'.[15] He re-used parts of the air, including the borrowed incipit, in the aria 'In mezzo a voi dui' in *Imeneo* (begun in September 1738, during the composition of *Saul*, but completed only in 1740). The Manchester copy of 'Non può più saldarsi' may not have been his source, however; for another aria from the same Orlandini opera found in *E*, 'Mi fien care' (No. 7 of the miscellaneous pieces), also served as the basis of a number in *Saul*, the duet and chorus 'Oh fairest of ten thousand fair'. Especially as this is the only apparent borrowing in the oratorio from any of our five Aylesford manuscripts, one suspects that Handel actually worked from some fuller score of Orlandini's *Paride*.

Between 1725 and 1737 Handel offered the London public nine pasticcio operas consisting of music by other composers.[16] At first he merely culled arias from various sources and applied them to an existing libretto, but beginning with the fourth pasticcio, *Lucio Papiro* (1732), he took to adapting a single opera, albeit with many insertions. His own musical contribution always remained limited to the composition or reworking of recitatives and occasional revisions in arias. The season of 1733–4 was exceptional, because, after presenting one pasticcio a year since 1730, he suddenly mounted three in quick succession: *Semiramide* (based on Vinci's *Semiramide riconosciuta*) on 30 October 1733, *Caio Fabbricio* on 4 December and *Arbace* on 8 January 1734. Strohm is unquestionably right in seeing this as part of a major counter-offensive against the newly formed rival company, the so-called Opera of the Nobility, which opened its doors on 29 December 1733 with Porpora's *Arianna in Nasso*. That Handel expanded his repertory with works by Hasse and Vinci rather than himself because 'he wanted to confront Porpora with superior examples of Porpora's own kind of music' may, however, be doubted.[17] More likely he was simply too busy assembling and training an almost entirely new troupe of singers to

14   For a summary account of this manuscript see Talbot, 'Some Overlooked MSS', pp. 942–3. Of the fifteen Italian arias, ten are Italian copies, five English. One aria is specifically attributed to Porpora, 'Dalla cuna intorno al core' from his *Siface* (Venice, 1726) on folios 23r–26v, but the clear Venetian provenance of the copy argues against its having been among the arias Holdsworth sent from Rome. I am again much obliged to Reinhard Strohm for assistance in identifying these arias.

15   The air is printed in *Hallische Händel-Ausgabe*, I/xiii, *Kritischer Bericht* (Kassel etc., 1964), pp. 164–75. Its relationship to Orlandini's aria is most evident in the opening idea and the cadence figure in bar 12 (cf. Orlandini, bar 14).

16   The following account of two of Handel's pasticcios owes a large debt to Reinhard Strohm's pioneering study, 'Handel's pasticci', *Essays on Handel and Italian Opera* (Cambridge, 1985), pp. 164–211, and to H. D. Clausen, *Händels Direktionspartituren ('Handexemplare')* (Hamburg, 1972).

17   Strohm, op. cit., p. 183.

compose more than one new opera for the season – *Arianna*, completed on 5 October 1733. And the ready availability of *Cajo Fabricio* and *Artaserse*, which had probably been in his possession since the previous spring, made them obvious choices for production.

Our principal sources of information about the pasticcios *Caio Fabbricio* and *Arbace* are Handel's conducting scores, both in the Staats- und Universitätsbibliothek, Hamburg.[18] These manuscripts were extensively altered after their initial copying, but, with the help of the Aylesford scores, we can largely determine their original form. Comparison with Handel's sources also allows us to see exactly what changes he made in the operas before the conducting scores were copied. In neither case do his annotations provide anything like a full prescription for copying the first version of the pasticcio. For many changes the copyists must have received additional instructions, written or oral. At the same time we find some directions that were not followed in the original copying of the Hamburg score and which therefore probably date from a later stage of the proceedings. In one aria the Aylesford manuscript furnishes unique testimony concerning what was actually performed.

Handel's first versions differed very considerably from the final ones, standing much closer to Hasse and Vinci. He retained the great majority of the numbers in both Aylesford scores, twenty-two out of twenty-eight in *Caio Fabbricio*, twenty-four out of thirty-two in *Arbace*. Very few pieces from other operas were inserted at this stage. An opening sinfonia and final chorus for *Caio Fabbricio* had to be taken from elsewhere to fill the gaps in Jennens's manuscript; otherwise the sole interpolation was a final aria for the *primo uomo* Carestini, 'Vorrei da lacci sciogliere' from Leo's *Demetrio* (1732), an outright addition. In *Arbace* Handel made only one insertion, replacing the other castrato Scalzi's third-act aria 'Nuvoletta opposta al sole' with 'Se l'amor tuo mi rendi' from Hasse's *Siroe* (1733) and moving it to a position preceding rather than following Carestini's 'L'onda del mar'. But this substitution (though not the change of position) took place after the manuscript had been partially copied. As with the insertion of Carestini's aria in *Caio Fabbricio*, one suspects the singers had already begun to make demands.

Six of Hasse's arias and seven of Vinci's seem never to have been copied at all. These omissions served a dual purpose. On the one hand, they shortened the operas to conform with prevailing London standards. On the other, they allowed Handel to give the greatest prominence to his strongest singers. Thus in Vinci's *Artaserse* the six roles had been nearly equally balanced, each having five solo arias, except Arbace with six and Megabise with three. By taking nothing from Arbace, Artaserse or Mandane – sung

18   *Caio Fabbricio* has the shelf-mark MA/1011, *Arbace* MA/1004.

by Carestini, Scalzi and the prima donna Strada – and reducing Artabano and Semira to three arias each and Megabise to one, Handel radically altered the relative importance of the characters. In Hasse's opera the parts were less equal to start with, and Strada did have to give up one aria. But the title role, conceived for the great castrato Annibali and now assigned to the mediocre bass Waltz, was deprived of three of its five arias.

Rehearsals brought many further additions and a few more cuts. Eight numbers in *Caio Fabbricio* were replaced (including the added sinfonia), as were six numbers in *Arbace*, though one replacement was later dropped. Carestini gained a final aria in *Arbace* but lost the second half of his extended arioso 'Perche tarda'. Two arias were excised from *Caio Fabbricio*. The impetus for most of the insertions certainly came from the singers. Symptomatically, all the interpolations in *Arbace* involved the three principals; in *Caio Fabbricio* Durastanti and Maria Caterina Negri also received new arias, probably to compensate them for having to trade roles. The *Arbace* sinfonia had to be replaced and Waltz's aria 'Non sempre oprar' in *Caio Fabbricio* omitted, because in the meantime Handel had introduced both pieces into *Semiramide*. Yet even with all the changes a majority of the numbers in both pasticcios derived from the Aylesford scores.

In tailoring these two operas to his company Handel altered to a greater or lesser extent the ranges of most of the roles. Besides transforming Fabbricio from an alto into a bass he also converted the tenors Cinea (*Cajo Fabricio*) and Artabano (*Artaserse*) into mezzo-sopranos. Strohm asserts that not all the necessary transpositions are shown in the conducting scores,[19] but I find no clear evidence of this. The most surprising discrepancy between the range of a part and a singer's supposed compass involves the role of Turio in *Caio Fabbricio*, ultimately taken by Maria Caterina Negri, which rises to g'', whereas in his own works Handel never required her to go above e''. The aria containing the g'', 'In così lieto giorno', had been transposed up for Handel's original singer, Durastanti. But he had also given Negri an aria with a g'' in her original role of Bircenna, and the new aria he inserted for her as Turio, 'È grande e bella', goes up to f''.

The conducting score of *Arbace* does, however, display some curious inconsistencies in the vocal parts. Most of the role of Artabano is notated in the soprano clef, but in the recitatives of Act 1 scenes 2–3 and his aria 'Non ti son padre' in scene 11 he appears as a bass. Semira, an alto, is a soprano in her first recitative in Act 1 scene 5, and her 'Bramar di perdere' in scene 7 also uses the soprano clef, though the aria has obviously been transposed down for an alto. The explanation of this bizarre situation seems to be as

---

19   See op. cit., pp. 185–6.

follows. Handel initially intended the role of Artabano for the bass Waltz; the mezzo-soprano Durastanti, whose parts were always written in the soprano clef, would have sung Semira, the alto Maria Caterina Negri, Megabise. But Waltz apparently became ill – he was also eliminated from *Semiramide* after the copying of the conducting score – and Handel recast Durastanti as Artabano and Maria Caterina Negri as Semira. This occurred after the chief copyist, John Christopher Smith senior, had written out the recitatives of Act 1 scenes 1–5. Handel therefore corrected Semira's part in scene 5, but he left intact Waltz's recitatives, which would have required only octave transposition for Durastanti. From scene 6 onwards Smith, who was copying the clefs and words of the recitatives (Handel later filled in the notes), conformed to the final distribution. He probably assumed that when his assistant, the copyist known as S1, came to transcribe the arias he would notate the voice part in the clef indicated by the preceding recitative, but instead S1 must have looked at the character's first appearance in the opera. It was not until some time between the copying of 'Non ti son padre' and Artabano's 'Così stupisce' at the end of Act 2 that Smith discovered the misunderstanding. To guard against further confusion he entered the initial clefs and key signatures of most of the arias in Act 3 himself.

All Megabise's music is notated in the alto clef. This would seem to imply that after the role was relinquished by Maria Caterina Negri it passed to another contralto. Yet the only other singer Handel is known to have employed in opera at this time was her sister Maria Rosa Negri, a mezzo-soprano whose parts were written in the soprano clef. If he did avail himself of her dubious talents on this occasion (no printed libretto of *Arbace* survives to establish the cast), she would have had no trouble with the range, which does not exceed the octave d'–d''.

There is also an apparent contradiction in the conducting score of *Caio Fabbricio* regarding Scalzi. To begin with, Handel put his aria 'Nocchier che teme assorto' down a tone, sparing him a b'', but left him with a b♭'' in 'Scherza talor'. A note in Smith's hand shows that the latter aria was subsequently taken down a minor third, and this accords with the situation in *Semiramide*, where Scalzi was unable to sing the part composed for him in 1729 without similar transpositions. Later, however, Handel replaced 'Scherza talor' with the extraneous 'Per amor se il cor sospira', which includes a b♭''. Possibly additional transpositions were made; more probably Scalzi had simply recovered from a temporary indisposition (had he caught something from Waltz?), especially since he apparently sang a b♭'' in Handel's *Arianna* in late January 1734.

In all, ten arias in *Caio Fabbricio* and five in *Arbace* were transposed at one time or another. Incompatibility of range was not the only reason. Strada, for example, could easily have sung her 'Caro sposo' in *Caio*

Fabbricio as it stood, but from the first Handel raised this concluding aria of Act 1 a tone for greater brilliance. The Aylesford manuscripts contain many directions for transposition (always in the characteristic form 'ex A', meaning 'transpose into A'), including some for arias never copied. In *Arbace* all transpositions needed for the first version are indicated. In *Caio Fabbricio* Handel marked only the three arias of Bircenna (Maria Caterina Negri) and one of Volusio (Scalzi), though five further transpositions were made in copying the conducting score.

Considerations of range must also have played a part in the discarding of certain numbers, particularly for Carestini. Although he had created the role of Arbace for Vinci in 1730, his voice had somewhat lowered in the intervening years. This presumably led Handel to replace his one aria with a b♭'', 'Mi scacci', and to cancel the second half of the arioso 'Perche tarda', which also contains this note – otherwise a perplexing cut, since it saved only eleven bars and caused the piece to end in the relative major. In *Caio Fabbricio* it was an act of singular optimism to have Carestini's 'Se tu non senti' copied at all, for it not only rises to c'''' but descends to a, ruling out transposition as a means of accommodation; it was supplanted by an aria of Albinoni moving between d' and g''.[20] Scalzi too may have rejected an aria because of a note beyond his reach: 'Nuvoletta che opposta al sole', discarded during the copying of *Arbace*, called for an a'', the only one in his original role.

One ill-fitting aria in *Arbace* received a different sort of treatment. This was Artabano's impressive 'Così stupisce', which ends Act 2. As written, the vocal line lay too high for either Waltz or Durastanti, frequently reaching a'', yet the aria could not be transposed downwards without completely rewriting the violin figuration. This aria was copied into the conducting score just as Vinci wrote it. But in the Aylesford manuscript Handel extensively retouched the voice part, lowering the tessitura and bringing the high note down to g''. Whether an accident-prone S1 overlooked the lightly pencilled changes (except in one passage only the note-heads were added) or, as seems more likely, the revisions are of a later vintage, this example plainly demonstrates the danger of assuming that the version in the conducting score is the final one.

Internal cuts were made in seven arias in *Caio Fabbricio*, half those retained from the Aylesford score. Only two of these excisions antedate the copying of the conducting score; the rest appear as cancellations or paste-overs. And yet most of the cuts are clearly prescribed in the Aylesford manuscript, the strongest indication we have that Handel continued to use it to record his intentions even after the conducting score was completed. He cannot indeed have communicated his original cuts to the copyist solely

[20]   Carestini did sing one b♭'' in *Caio Fabbricio*, a quaver just before his final cadence in the A section of 'Vedrai morir'.

through the Aylesford manuscript, because it shows no trace of his first small deletion in the opening ritornello of 'Nocchier che teme assorto' but only of the later larger cut. These abridgements are not without musical interest. While some may have been designed merely to reduce the opera's overall length, in certain cases at least they clearly bespeak a desire on Handel's part to tighten up what seemed to him long-winded. From Volusio's 'Varcherò la flebil onda', for example, he removed two 3/8 bars of repetition near the end of the opening ritornello, not surely to save a few seconds in a long evening but to forestall monotony when the same repetition is heard again in the body of the A section and the abbreviated closing ritornello. Most of the cuts, in fact, are in ritornellos, which are sometimes disproportionately long by Handel's standards. The A section of 'Giovani cori amanti' has seventy-six bars of ritornello as against sixty-eight vocal bars – an imbalance not justified by any instrumental display. Handel trimmed the ritornellos by twenty-one bars, the vocal portions not at all.[21]

Because the Aylesford manuscript of Hasse's opera entirely lacked recitatives Handel composed his own, setting a drastically abridged text that then suffered further mutilation. London audiences, as Giuseppe Riva observed in 1726, liked 'few verses of recitative and many arias'.[22] In *Arbace*, Handel based his recitatives on those of Vinci, retaining a remarkable number of notes considering the many discrepancies of vocal range and the heavy textual cutting. Two of the accompanied recitatives in *Artaserse* he took over unchanged, including the partial reprise of 'Lucido Dio' in Act 3; the third he scrapped altogether. At first he pencilled his cuts and revisions into the Aylesford manuscript. After preparing the first five scenes he apparently gave the score to Smith to begin copying – a striking illustration of how the activities of composer and copyist often overlapped and intertwined. Then came the change of casting precipitated by Waltz's departure, making it more expedient to write the revised recitatives directly into the conducting score.

In his adaptations of Hasse's *Cajo Fabricio* and Vinci's *Artaserse* Handel functioned essentially as an impresario and performer. Except perhaps in making internal cuts in the former opera, he evinced no urge to tamper with these works. Almost every change seems to have been forced upon him by the circumstances of performance, the demands of singers, the limitations of his source. When a number had to be replaced he did not compose a new one, or even insert an old one of his own, but always introduced a ready-made piece by someone else. He provided recitatives for *Caio Fabbricio* simply because they were lacking in the Aylesford score.

---

[21]   The arias with internal cuts, in addition to those already mentioned, are 'Caro sposo', 'Non mi chiamar crudele', 'Volgi a me' and 'Lo sposo và à morte'.

[22]   O. E. Deutsch, *Handel: a Documentary Biography* (London, 1955/R 1974), p. 197.

He revised the recitatives and one aria in *Arbace* for equally practical reasons. It was in a totally different spirit that he approached Jennens's three Scarlatti manuscripts.

Since 1707, if not before, Handel had been regularly taking ideas from other composers and incorporating them in his own music. In the early days the balance between spontaneous recollection and deliberate searching is not entirely clear, but from 1727 at the latest – the year he began borrowing from Telemann's cantata cycle *Harmonischer Gottes-Dienst*[23] – we know he usually had in hand one or more foreign works or collections he systematically perused for promising material. This is what he did with the manuscripts of *Dafni*, *Attilio Regolo* and *Griselda*. From the first he seems to have treated them as a unit, normally quoting from at least two at a time, sometimes from all three. Direct borrowing was confined to seven or eight major scores, composed during three comparatively brief periods: *Athalia* and *Arianna* in May–October 1733; *Atalanta*, *Giustino* and *Arminio* in April–October 1736; and *Faramondo*, *Serse* and possibly *Saul* in November 1737–February (or September) 1738. By any reckoning there are several dozen separate appropriations from these three sources; *Faramondo* alone has no fewer than nineteen. The principal relationships I have found are listed in Appendix I, pp. 193–201, below. After 1738, apparently, Handel never again drew directly on this particular fund of inspiration – though 'He was despised' in *Messiah* derives in part from *Griselda* by way of *Arminio*. Perhaps he felt he had by then exhausted its potential, or perhaps it was at this time that he returned the manuscripts to their rightful owner. We may imagine Jennens, on one of his visits to Brook Street during the composition of *Saul*, catching sight of his long-lost possessions and seizing the opportunity to reclaim them.[24]

Like Handel's borrowings in general, those from the Aylesford Scarlatti manuscripts vary greatly in size and exactness. Never did he take over an entire movement unaltered. Even when he appropriated some 45 bars of 'Vi respiro aurette placide' in *Dafni* for 'Un aura placida' in *Faramondo* he extensively rearranged and elaborated Scarlatti's material, expanding the original 88 bars into 284 (including the da capo). On the whole, the relationships of 1733 are more limited than those of 1736–8, confirming an impression gained from other examples that in the course of the 1730s Handel's borrowing habits underwent a major change. In the earlier group, for instance, we do not find him drawing on the B section of a model, whereas later this becomes quite common. Almost always the old ideas are significantly transformed. The one literal quotation of any length

[23]   See Roberts, 'Handel's Borrowings from Telemann: an Inventory', *Göttinger Händel-Beiträge*, i (1984), pp. 147–71.

[24]   Handel also borrowed systematically from Scarlatti's *Il Pompeo* (1683) – of which Jennens is not known to have owned a copy – between 1731 and 1744. *Il Pompeo* has been published as *Handel Sources*, vi (New York, 1986).

to which one can point (in the aria 'Nella terra' in *Faramondo*) occurs at the beginning of a B section, that dark side of the da capo form, in which Handel so often seems to be merely marking time before the main action resumes.

Three examples seem to me particularly important for our understanding of Handel's borrowing and composing process. The relationship between the arias 'Son qual nave' in *Attilio Regolo* and 'Combattuta da due venti' in *Faramondo* is remarkable, above all, because Handel availed himself not only of Scarlatti's music but also of his text. Retaining or rewriting the words of an aria when transferring it into a new context was a standard practice of the period and one frequently employed by Handel in borrowing from his own works and in shuttling pieces from opera to opera for revivals. No other instance has yet been noted, however, of his adopting this strategy in his borrowing from other composers. A comparison of the two texts leaves no doubt as to their kinship (my italics):

Attilio Regolo	*Faramondo*
Son qual nave in mezzo al onde,	Combattuta da due venti,
Che in funesta Ria tempesta	*Son qual nave in mezzo all'onde,*
Già dispera	E le sponde
Il cammino *a ritrovar.*	*Già* sospiro *a ritrovar.*
Tocca alfin l'amate sponde,	Approdar mi pare il *lido,*
Ma dal *lido Vento infido*	*Ma* un nemico *vento infido*
La *respinge a naufragar.*	Mi *respinge a naufragar.*

Although the new aria text does not differ greatly in content from the old, its insertion into the libretto Handel was adapting, a much altered version of Zeno's drama set by Francesco Gasparini for Rome in 1720, entailed a small but not insignificant change of plot. At this point in the opera the hero Faramondo has fallen into the hands of his arch-enemy Gustavo. In Gasparini, Faramondo's sister Clotilde, for whom Gustavo has contracted an unwelcome passion, decides to go to him and plead for clemency. She will offer to die in her brother's place, but if that fails she is prepared (as the recitative makes clear) to submit to Gustavo's lechery:

> Sì, andrò a pregare, e piangere,
> E tentarò di frangere
> D'un Rè la crudeltà.
>
> Mà,
> Se al misero mio cor
> Hà da costar amor
> Non chiederò pietà.

In Handel, her intentions become at once vague and vacillating: the revised recitative has her say only 'Io vado . . .', and the aria, with its

Ex. 1

(a)   Scarlatti, *Attilio Regolo*, 'Son qual nave', bars 3–4 (viola and bass omitted)

(b)   Handel, *Faramondo*, 'Combattuta da due venti', bars 1–4 (bass omitted)

imagery of conflicting winds, suggests uncertainty whether to sacrifice Faramondo or her maidenly virtue. It may be that the original version was thought too compromising for such a noble character. More probably, the composer simply wanted to give Francesina a better vehicle for vocal display than Gasparini's pathetic verses warranted.

The revisions in Scarlatti's text are intriguing in that they seem, in places, to have been inspired by Scarlatti's music. The close canon between the two treble parts in bars 3–4 of 'Son qual nave' must have prompted the metaphor of the two winds in the new first line, which Handel depicts with an expanded form of that idea (see Ex. 1). And one strongly suspects that

Ex. 2

(a) 'Son qual nave', bars 30–1 (orchestra omitted)

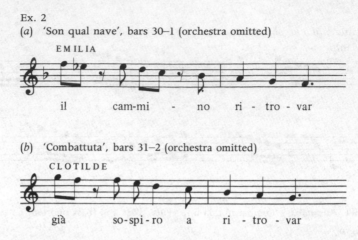

EMILIA

il   cam-mi - no   ri - tro - var

(b) 'Combattuta', bars 31–2 (orchestra omitted)

CLOTILDE

già   so-spi-ro   a   ri - tro - var

the word 'sospira' was placed in the fourth line of 'Combattuta' specifically in order to match the halting figure associated with the corresponding line of Scarlatti's text (see Ex. 2). Either Handel gave precise instructions about what he wanted in the revised verses, or he wrote them himself. Strohm has concluded from his study of *Berenice* and the pasticcio *Didone* (both 1737) that at this stage in his operatic career Handel had no regular literary collaborator on whom he could depend.[25] The libretto of *Faramondo* lends support to this hypothesis, containing as it does only two other aria texts not based on the Gasparini version.

Musically, Handel did not follow Scarlatti as closely as one might expect. Several ideas in both the A and B sections of 'Combattuta' derive from 'Son qual nave', but everything is greatly transformed, amplified and newly elaborated. Obviously he was not simply re-using an old piece, words and all, to save himself the trouble of composing a new one. Rather he had realized that some of the works from which he was taking musical raw material could also help supply his textual needs. In his next opera, *Serse*, he went a step further, resetting the entire libretto of an opera whose score he had been despoiling for the past several years.

Another aria in *Faramondo* with ties to Scarlatti, 'Vanne, che più ti miro', exists in three quite different versions, two of them never finished. The first, found in the main autograph in the British Library (MS R.M. 20.a.13, ff. 13r–v and 16r–18r), is completely drafted but only partly filled up. The second, on a stray leaf in the Fitzwilliam Museum (MS Mus. 262, pp. 45–6), breaks off after twelve bars, of which the first nine are fully scored. Handel seems to have had some difficulty hitting upon the right dramatic tone for this aria, sung by Gustavo's daughter Rosimonda at the end of her first encounter with Faramondo, the supposed murderer of her brother. Duty-

---

25   *Essays*, pp. 75, 198.

Ex. 3   Handel, *Faramondo*, 'Vanne, che più ti miro'

(*a*)   first version, bars 11–15

bound to hate him, she finds him disconcertingly good-looking. In the A section of the aria she gives vent to virtuous outrage; in the B section she hints at guilty inclinations:

> Vanne, che più ti miro
> Più cresce il mio dolor.
>
> Sento novo tormento
> Per novo mal sospiro
> Ne lo conosce il cor.

Initially Handel appears to have taken the words of the A section more or less at face value. Rosimonda denounces Faramondo in accents of righteous indignation tinged with grief — just the sort of thing one would expect from a typical *opera seria* heroine confronting her brother's assassin (Ex. 3a). But in his second version, the composer clearly made an effort to

(*b*) second version, bars 1–3

depict the flustered state into which Rosimonda's nascent attraction to
Faramondo has thrown her. Beginning without instrumental introduction
(where the first version has ten bars of ritornello), she declaims the text
nervously, with many abrupt changes of direction, while the no less
nervous accompaniment figuration registers the palpitations of her uneasy
heart (Ex. 3b). Handel sharpened the point still further in the final version,
which begins with a revision of the second: the setting of 'che più ti miro'
in bar 1 was replaced by a more energetic, upward-thrusting figure, and
two bars of heightened agitation were interpolated following the first half
of bar 3 (Ex. 3c).

(c)   final version, bars 1–5

Ex. 4

(a) Scarlatti, *Attilio Regolo*, 'Deh per pietade', bars 16–18

Moderato

(b) Handel, *Faramondo*, 'Vanne, che più ti miro', first version, bars 34–6

(c) 'Vanne, che più ti miro', final version, bars 14–16

In the first version of 'Vanne, che più ti miro' Handel borrowed fairly extensively from the aria 'Corri, vola alla vendetta' in Scarlatti's *Attilio Regolo*. This was his source for the exclamatory incipit and the bulk of the B section, though the latter underwent a drastic metamorphosis; most of this material survives in the final version. More remarkable are his appropriations from a second *Attilio Regolo* aria, 'Deh per pietade'. Often in attempting to trace Handel's debt to his predecessors one comes across resemblances so vague or so brief that one is inclined to dismiss them as unconscious, if not entirely fortuitous. By comparing the three versions of 'Vanne, che più ti miro' with 'Deh per pietade', however, we can see clearly that at least some of these shadowy relationships do have psychological significance. Only one idea in the first version has any tangible connection with Scarlatti's aria: a phrase illustrating the words 'più cresce il mio dolor' in bars 34–8 that faintly echoes the climax of a pre-cadential melisma in bars 16–18 of 'Deh per pietade' (Ex. 4a–b).[26] The correspondence is slight enough – a matter of three chords over a pedal point and five notes of melody. Yet the dependence of Handel's aria on Scarlatti's is conclusively demonstrated by its subsequent history. In the second version the borrowed phrase already assumed a more readily recognizable form, and in the third version, just where he had broken off in the second, Handel introduced an expanded and quite unmistakable quotation from Scarlatti's melisma (Ex. 4c).

Still more revealing is the role played by borrowing in the transformation of the second version of 'Vanne, che più ti miro' into the opening of the third. The new second phrase in bar 1 of the third version in fact derives from the vocal incipit of 'Deh per pietade' (Ex. 5a), while the falling fifths in bars 3–4, heard first in the voice and then in the orchestra, can be traced back to bar 8 of the same source (Ex. 5b). Handel's continuation

[26]   A variant of this idea also appears in bars 5–8 of Handel's ritornello.

Ex. 5

(a) Scarlatti, *Attilio Regolo*, 'Deh per pietade', bars 3–4

(b) 'Deh per pietade', bars 7–10

(c)   Handel, *Faramondo*, 'Vanne, che più ti miro', first version, bars 19–22

from the latter figure also bears some resemblance to what follows in Scarlatti, but it looks even more like bars 19–22 in the first version of 'Vanne, che più ti miro' (Ex. 5c). One scarcely knows which to wonder at more, Handel's ability to see the expressive potential in these miscellaneous scraps or the need that impelled him to seek them out rather than relying on spontaneous invention.

Naturally one should not infer from this example that every fugitive similarity one sees reflects a conscious act of appropriation. More scepticism in these matters, not less, is currently needed. But it should be recognized as a general principle that Handel did deliberately borrow small and seemingly inconsequential details as well as larger musical units, and that he sometimes so transmuted them in the process of composition that the relationships became virtually invisible to the analytical eye. For this reason we can never be very confident that we have fully comprehended his use of any particular source.

'Vanne, che più ti miro' is by no means the only piece in which Handel brought together pre-existing materials of diverse origin. *Faramondo* includes at least four other numbers with more than one Aylesford ancestor; the aria 'Poi che pria di morire' has three. The most complex case of all, however, is that of the aria 'Sì, la voglio' in *Serse*. Here too the autograph contains a partly completed first version very different from the final one (B.L. MS R.M. 20.c.7, ff. 56v–57v). Handel wrote out the vocal line up to the final cadence of the A section in bar 35; the bass and the topmost instrumental part he carried through only to bars 23 and 21. Surprisingly, this draft does not appear to have been significantly influenced by Giovanni Bononcini's setting of the same text in *Il Xerse* (1694), the principal source of Handel's score as a whole.[27] It does owe a modest debt to both the 1707 and 1737 versions of the aria 'Voglio cangiar desio' in *Il trionfo del Tempo* – including the initial setting of the words 'la voglio', which obviously triggered the recollection – and thus indirectly to an aria in Keiser's *Claudius* (1703). The cadence in bars 33–4, which became bars 22–3 of the final version, is almost pure Keiser.[28]

As with Rosimonda's aria in *Faramondo*, Handel probably abandoned his first version of 'Sì, la voglio' because he had become dissatisfied with it dramatically. For Arsamene, infuriated at Serse's persistent refusal to believe he loves Romilda and determined not to let his capricious master take her away from him, he wanted something more impetuous and forceful. (The preceding recitative ends with Serse insisting, 'Non la volete' – 'You do not want her'; to which Arsamene responds, 'Sì, la voglio, e la otterrò' – 'Yes, I want her, and I shall have her'.) The autograph of the second version (which follows the first on fols. 58r–59v) contains sixteen additional bars cut before filling up. It is this longer version that we must primarily consider in studying the aria's genesis. In composing his second version Handel made extensive use of his rejected draft, but he also turned to four other sources: Bononcini's setting, the *Trionfo* aria laid under contribution in the first version, and two Scarlatti arias. The intermingling of antecedents is particularly intense in the first ten bars, shown in Ex. 6 together with the relevant portions of the sources. Where the first version had begun with Arsamene affirming his love in measured tones, in the second he comes directly to the point. The original opening $3\frac{1}{2}$ bars (Ex. 6b) were compressed into $1\frac{1}{2}$ and at the same time amalgamated with Bononcini's first bar (Ex. 6c). Then, instead of continuing with syllabic declamation against a running instrumental line, Handel inserted a bristling ritornello modelled on bars 2–5 of 'Tutta sdegno' in *Attilio Regolo* (Ex. 6d). The ensuing vocal section is a compilation of material from bar 2 of Bononcini's setting, bars 8–10 of Handel's first version and bars 10–13 of 'Tutta sdegno' (Ex. 6e).

[27]   On Handel's use of Bononcini's score generally, see H. S. Powers, 'Il Serse trasformato –II', *The Musical Quarterly*, xlviii (1962), pp. 73–92; the score is published as *Handel Sources*, viii (New York, 1986).

[28]   The *Trionfo* aria has a complicated history of its own. As I have shown in 'Handel's Borrowings from Keiser', *Göttinger Händel-Beiträge*, ii (1986), pp. 57–9, 70, Handel based his 1707 setting largely on 'Caro, son tua' in *Claudius* but replaced the original incipit with one from an aria in Keiser's *Adonis* (1697), 'Es wird doch endlich'. On revising the work in 1737 he superimposed the *Claudius* incipit on his 1707 opening, apparently to avoid redundancy with the air 'Tears, such as tender fathers shed' in *Deborah*, a revival of which was planned for the Lenten season of 1737 but never took place. It is the 1737 incipit that Handel echoed in the first version of 'Sì, la voglio'.

Ex. 6

(a) Handel, *Serse*, 'Sì, la voglio', second version, bars 1–10

Allegro

(b) 'Sì, la voglio', first version, bars 1–11

sì,   sì,   la   vo - glio e l'ot - te - rò,   sì,

sì,   la   vo - glio e l'ot - te - rò

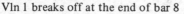

Vln 1 breaks off at the end of bar 8

(c) Bonocini, *Il Xerse*, 'Sì, la voglio', bars 1–3

(d) Scarlatti, *Attilio Regolo*, 'Tutta sdegno', bars 2–5 (voice omitted)

(e) 'Tutta sdegno', bars 10–13

The rest of the A section brings four further direct quotations from the first version and two more from 'Tutta sdegno'. A cadential phrase from 'Voglio cangiar desio' (either version) also appears in bars 26–7 – a connection that might well be discounted were it not for the unquestionable link between the first version of 'Sì, la voglio' and the *Trionfo* aria. And finally, at bar 29, comes a remarkably faithful reproduction of seven bars from a second aria in *Attilio Regolo*, 'Voglio a terra' (Ex. 7). The intricate chain of interlocking borrowings in 'Sì, la voglio' is summarized in Appendix II.

What are we to make of this astonishing example? It is tempting to treat it as a rare aberration, the response of a man driving himself to produce at his usual prodigious rate while still recovering from a serious illness. Handel had returned from taking the cure at Aix-la-Chapelle, after an apparent stroke, around the beginning of November 1737 and had composed *Faramondo* and the Funeral Anthem for Queen Caroline before starting work on *Serse* on 26 December. The abnormally large number of changes in the *Serse* autograph testify to a particularly arduous creative struggle, and many, like Burney, have interpreted the state of this 'foul score' as evidence of 'a mind disturbed, if not diseased'.[29] Yet combinations hardly less manifold than that in 'Sì, la voglio' have been found in arias of Handel's Italian period. 'Volo pronto' in *Agrippina* (1709) incorporates fragments from four earlier arias, three by Keiser and one by Handel himself, while 'Vaghe perle' in the same opera includes seven excerpts from four distinct, though interrelated, sources.[30] It may be doubted that at any period of his life Handel routinely patched together entire movements in this way. But we have ample evidence that he often drew on two or more sources at once, a point that should always be borne in mind in analysing single relationships. What appears to be a free continuation or a fresh development may actually be a quotation from somewhere else.[31]

At least one other Italian opera manuscript belonging to Jennens passed through Handel's hands. This was a copy of Vinci's *Didone abbandonata* (Rome, 1726), now in the Newberry Library, which purchased it from Reeves along with the Aylesford score of *Cajo Fabricio*. The 1918 sale catalogue does not list it specifically – it must have been subsumed in one of the large miscellaneous lots – but its provenance is definitely established by a dealer's note and the characteristic Sotheby's stock numbers.[32] Presumably procured by Holdsworth during one of his visits to Rome (though it is not mentioned in his correspondence with Jennens), it emanated from the same *copisteria* as *Artaserse* and *Cajo Fabricio*. The music of Act 1 is in a hand familiar from both those manuscripts; the words were written by the text copyist of *Cajo Fabricio* and of the arias in *Artaserse*.

This time Handel steered a changing course in his treatment of Jennens's score, giving rise to some interesting complications. As Howard Mayer Brown first suggested, in his introduction to a facsimile edition of this manuscript,[33] Handel used it in preparing his last pasticcio *Didone*, first

---

29   C. Burney, *A General History of Music* (London, 1776–89), ed. F. Mercer (London, 1935/R1957), ii, p. 823.

30   See Roberts, 'Handel's Borrowings from Keiser', pp. 66–9.

31   This may be true even when it appears most unlikely. Comparing the aria 'Poi che pria di morire' in *Faramondo* with its primary model 'Occhi belli' in *Griselda*, anyone would naturally suppose that the setting of 'mi beo, pupille care' in bars 15–16 is a direct outgrowth of bars 2–3, which in turn come from 'Occhi belli'. But in fact bars 15–16 form part of a larger borrowing from another *Griselda* aria, 'In voler ciò che tu brami'.

32   The stock numbers on the three volumes are 526, 514 and 453. I thank Bernard Wilson of the Newberry Library for providing me with this information.

33   Vinci, *Didone abbandonata*, Italian Opera 1640–1770, xxix (New York, 1977).

Ex. 7

(*a*) Scarlatti, *Attilio Regolo*, 'Voglio a terra', bars 22–9

- - - - - - ra

(b)   Handel, *Serse*, 'Sì, la voglio', second version, bars 29–36

la   vo - glio,   sì,   la   vo - glio   e

la ot - te - rò

performed at the King's Theatre on 13 April 1737. In it we find pencil
annotations similar to those in the Aylesford *Artaserse* and *Cajo Fabricio*,
though we cannot follow the evolution of this pasticcio in comparable
detail, because the conducting score (B.L. Add. MS 31607) was not copied
until after most of the changes had been made. But previously, apparently
with no thought of a London production of *Didone*, Handel had borrowed
ideas from several of the arias for his *Giustino* and *Arminio*, composed in
curious alternation between August and October 1736. The relationships
are neither very numerous nor very substantial, but taken together there
can be no doubt as to their authenticity.

What makes these borrowings especially noteworthy is that when
Handel decided, after all, to mount *Didone* in his 1736–7 season along with
Giustino and *Arminio* he methodically altered Vinci's opera to conceal the
resemblances. This is particularly apparent in the aria 'Se vuoi ch'io mora',
on which he had drawn in two *Giustino* arias. Vinci's incipit, which had
become the second idea of 'Mio dolce amato sposo', was radically altered;
in the B section, a passage paraphrased in 'Zeffiretto, che scorre nel prato'
was rewritten with a net loss of three bars. Likewise, a phrase in 'Se dalle
stelle' that had gone into the A section of 'Zeffiretto' was consistently
reshaped or, in one case, excised. The only other internal cut in a Vinci
aria, the removal of bars 113–24 of 'Son quel fiume', eliminated a not very
conspicuous parallel with 'Sollevar il mondo oppresso' in *Giustino*.[34]
Lastly, Handel replaced altogether Didone's 'Prende ardire', which makes
much of a figure also prominent in 'Fatto scorta' in *Arminio*. In the end
nothing remained that might have ignited a flash of recognition in the
London audience of 1737. The oft-repeated statement that Handel made no
effort to hide his borrowings, fearing no censure and perhaps even

[34]   Also see the essay by Reinhard Strohm, p. 150, above (Ed.).

expecting them to be savoured by *cognoscenti*, obviously needs re-examination.[35]

Handel did not altogether escape detection, however. This is revealed by a letter from Jennens to Holdsworth on 17 January 1743, soon after the arrival of the Ottobonian collection. 'I told you before', he writes, 'that one of the Composers in my Box was good, I mean Scarlatti: & I shall not condemn the rest without a fair Trial. Handel has borrow'd a dozen of the Pieces & I dare say I shall catch him stealing from them; as I have formerly, both from Scarlatti & Vinci.'[36] Almost certainly Jennens was referring to some of the manuscripts discussed in this essay. He is not known to have owned any music by Vinci except *Artaserse*, *Didone* and the one aria in the Manchester miscellany, and none of his other Scarlatti manuscripts seem to have been exploited by Handel.[37] But what of the 'dozen pieces' that Handel took away in 1743? Was Jennens right in suspecting the purity of his motives? Perhaps among the scattered treasures of the Aylesford collection we may one day find an answer.

APPENDIX I

Borrowings from Jennens's Scarlatti Manuscripts

ABBREVIATIONS

HG *Georg Friedrich Händels Werke: Ausgabe der Deutschen Händelgesellschaft*, ed. F. Chrysander
HHA *Hallische Händel-Ausgabe*
OAS *The Operas of Alessandro Scarlatti*, ed. D. J. Grout

Entries consist of the name of the Handel movement and its location in HG or HHA or in manuscript (unless otherwise stated, incipits refer to arias or

---

[35]   This entire matter is covered more fully in my article 'Handel and Vinci's *Didone abbandonata*: Revisions and Borrowings', *Music & Letters*, lxviii (1987).

[36]   *Autograph Letters*, p. 23.

[37]   Other Aylesford manuscripts containing music by Alessandro Scarlatti are in the British Library; the Fitzwilliam Museum; the Rowe Music Library, King's College, Cambridge; the Newman Flower Collection; the Beinecke Library, Yale University; the Morristown National Historical Park Library, Morristown, New Jersey; and the Frank V. de Bellis Collection, San Francisco State University. The Beinecke manuscript is described by Reinhard Strohm in his paper 'Scarlattiana at Yale', read at the conference 'Haendel e gli Scarlatti a Roma', Rome, 12–14 June 1985 (proceedings forthcoming).

airs); the source of the borrowing and its location in OAS or manuscripts *C* or *E* (see above pp. 162–3); and the bar numbers of the principal correspondences, together with other information about the relationship as appropriate. Bar numbers for Handel are given first, then those for the source, in parenthesis. To facilitate use of HG, which lacks bar numbers, I have sometimes interpolated a second Handel citation, introduced by ' = ', in the form page/brace/bar.

ATHALIA (completed June 1733)

1 Air and chorus 'Tyrants would in impious throngs' (HG 5:19). Cf. *Parnasso in festa*, aria and chorus 'Deh! cantate un bell'amor' (HG 54:11).

   Dafni, 'Son ben tenera' (*C*, f. 61r)

   17–28 = 20/1/5–2/8 (1–12). Same key (B♭ major). Cf. No. 44.

2 Air and chorus 'Oh Lord, whom we adore' (HG 5:44). Cf. *Parnasso in festa*, aria and chorus 'Hò perso il caro ben' (HG 54:81).

   Dafni, 'Arderò si nel mio foco' (*C*, f. 13r)

   3–4 (6–8). Questionable. The same idea is used in *Serse*, 'Sì, sì, mio ben' (HG 92:17; HHA II/39:27), bars 19–20 = 18/3/3–4/1.

3 'Faithful cares' (HG 5:78). Cf. *Parnasso in festa*, 'Quanto breve è il godimento' (HG 54:34).

   Dafni, 'Incomincio à rimirarvi' (*C*, f. 112r)

   6–9 (7–17). Same key (B♭ major).

4 'Through the land', 1st setting (HG 5:125). Cf. *Parnasso in festa*, 'Nel spicgar' (IIG 54:56).

   Dafni, 'Tortorella smarrita' (*C*, f. 33v)

   21–26 = 125/3/6–126/1/3 (23–28)

5 'Hark! hark! His thunders round me roll' (HG 5:195). Cf. *Parnasso in festa*, 'Già, già le furie' (HG 54:78); *The Triumph of Time and Truth*, 'Like clouds', B section (HG 20:156).

   Griselda, 'Figlio! tiranno!' (OAS 3:121)

   1–4 (1–3). Questionable.

ARIANNA (completed October 1733)

6 'Deh! lascia un tal desio' (HG 83:15)

Attilio Regolo, 'Vorrei senza dolor lasciarti' (OAS 2:52)

3–4 (7–9), 19–20 = 16/2/2–3 (20–22)

7 'Nel pugnar col mostro infido' (HG 83:18)

Attilio Regolo, 'Non mi abbatte la fierezza' (OAS 2:234)

1–2 (1–2, 4), 49–51 = 21/2/4–3/1 (26–28), 53–54 (28–29), 58–60 (30–32). Cf. Nos. 9, 29 and 41.

8 'Sdegnata sei con me' (HG 83:32)

Griselda, 'Che bella tirannia' (OAS 3:80)

2 (2)

9 'Non ha difesa' (HG 83:52)

Attilio Regolo, 'Non mi abbatte la fierezza' (OAS 2:234)

3–5 (36–38). Cf. Nos. 7 and 29.

10 'Qual leon, che fere irato' (HG 83:58)

Griselda, 'Come va l'ape' (OAS 3:199)

1 (1–2), 46 = 62/1/5 (14–15). Both arias use horns in F.

11 'Narrargli allor saprai' (HG 83:66)

Griselda, 'Di', che sogno o che deliro' (OAS 3:84)

1 (1–2). Questionable.

12 'Al fine amore' (HG 83:68)

Griselda, 'Non vi vorrei conoscere' (OAS 3:74)

1–2 (1–2), 7–10 (16–19), 63–66 = 69/4/6–9 (32–35), 67–70 (38–41), 121–26 = 70/4/1–6 (49–53). The idea in bars 67–70 also appears in *Alcina*, 'È gelosia' (HG 86:32), bars 14–15 = 33/1/1–2.

13 Duet 'Bell'idolo mio' (HG 83:80)

Attilio Regolo, 'Se brami, che io t'ami' (OAS 2:118)

1–2 (1–2). Questionable. Cf. No. 17.

14 'Se nel bosco' (HG 83:82)

Fiorè(?), 'Rondinella sconsolata' (*E*, f. 167r)

1–2 (1–4), 25 = 83/4/1 (17–20), 34–35 = 84/1/5–6 (9–12), 63–64 = 85/2/5–6 (106–9).

15 'Un tenero pensiero' (HG 83:87)

[1] Handel, *Admeto*, duet 'Alma mia!' (HG 73:111)

1–2 (1–2)

(2) *Dafni*, duet 'Gran difesa' (*C*, f. 38v)

1–2 (1)

16 'Turbato il mar' (HG 83:99)

Griselda, 'Se il mio dolor' (OAS 3:192)

1–2 (3–6), 13–15 = 100/1/3–5 (7–11), 23–29 = 100/3/3–4/4 (22–32). Same key (A major). Cf. No. 39.

17 'In mar tempestoso' (HG 83:102)

(1) *Attilio Regolo*, 'Non è una pazzia' (OAS 2:190)

1–2 (1–2). Same key (D major). Questionable. Handel uses a similar idea in *Ariodante*, 'Dover, giustizia, amor' (HG 85:105), bars 1–2.

(2) Ibid., 'Se brami, che io t'ami' (OAS 2:118)

55 = 105/3/1 (1). Questionable. Cf. No. 13.

18 Aria and chorus 'Bella sorge' (HG 83:114)

Vignati, *Ambleto*, 'Sciolta dal lido' (*E*, f. 144r)

1–6 (1–10)

Atalanta (completed April 1736)

19 'Al varco, oh pastori!' (HG 87:18)

Dafni, 'Io t'invoco' (*C*, f. 3v)

1–2 (1–2), 8–9 (4–6), 27 = 19/3/4 (10–11). Same key (C major).

20 'Riportai gloriosa' (HG 87:21)

Dafni, 'Lascia l'armi' (*C*, f. 8r)

1 (1), 5–8 (3–6), 12 = 21/3/1 (7), 14–16 (8–10), 39–42 = 22/1/1–4 (11–14). Same key (A major).

21 'M'allontano, sdegnose pupille' (HG 87:51)

Sarro, *Ginevra Principessa di Scozia*, 'Placida auretta' (*E*, f. 136r)

1–3 (1–5). Cf. No. 26.

22 Sinfonia before Act 3 (HG 87:58)

Dafni, Overture ('Preludio'), 1st movement (*C*, f. 1v)

1–16 (1–15)

GIUSTINO (August–October 1736)*

23 'Se parla nel mio cor' (HG 88:28)

(1) *Attilio Regolo*, 'Vieni, o bella' (OAS 2:127)

1–2 (2–4)

(2) *Dafni*, 'Quel ch'hà di dolce amor' (C, f. 68r)

5–7 (2–4), 38–40 = 29/3/3–5 (8–10), 60–62 = 30/2/5–3/3 (19–21)

24 All'armi, o guerrieri' (HG 88:50)

Dafni, 'Ti conosco' (*C*, f. 71v)

1–3 (1–3). Same key (D major).

25 'Vanne sì' (HG 88:54)

Anon., 'Vaghi fiori' (*E*, f. 175r)

1–4 (1–4)

26 'Sventurata navicella' (HG 88:71)

Sarro, *Ginevra Principessa di Scozia*, 'Placida auretta' (*E*, f. 136r)

1 (1), 2 (6), 11–14 (60–64), 16–20 (29–38), 31–34 = 72/4/3–5/1 (73–77),
43–48 = 72/6/4–7/3 (80–90). Cf. No. 21.

27 'Quel torrente che s'innalza' (HG 88:80)

[1] Vinci, *Didone abbandonata*, 'Quando l'onda' (*Italian Opera 1640–1770*, xxix, f. 175v)

1–2 (1–4). Questionable.

*Also see Reinhard Strohm's essay, above, *passim* (Ed.).

(2) Fiorè, 'Scherza di fiore in fiore' (*E*, f. 154r)

1–2 (1–4), 5–6 (5–8), 12–13 = 80/3/2–3 (10–13), 28–31 = 81/2/2–5 (54–61), 44–47 = 82/1/3–2/1 (43–50), 56–64 = 82/4/1–83/1/5 (72–78), 87–90 = 84/3/1–4 (105–8). Same key (D major).

ARMINIO (September–October 1736)

28 'Durri lacci!' (HG 89:40)

Attilio Regolo, 'Ombre cieche' (OAS 2:136)

1–2 (1–2)

29 'Quella fiamma' (HG 89:52)

Attilio Regolo, 'Non mi abbatte la fierezza' (OAS 2:234)

25–28 = 54/1/1–4 (11–13), 34–38 (14–19), 63–71 = 56/1/3–3/1 (35–43), 99–102 = 58/1/1–4 (51–55), 116 = 58/4/1 (69), 117–18 (66–68), 119–20 (70–71). Same key (C major). Cf. Nos. 7 and 9.

30 'Vado a morir' (HG 89:60)

Griselda, 'Ho in seno due fiammelle' (OAS 3:195)

5 (1), 13–16 = 61/1/5–2/3 (13–14, 28–30), 27–29 = 62/1/1–3 (22–23), 31–32 (25), 32–34 (28–30). Same key (E♭ major). Bars 13–16 were later adapted as *Messiah*, 'He was despised' (HG 45:122; HHA I/17:97), bars 34–38 = 124/3/1–125/1/1.

FARAMONDO (November–December 1737)

31 'Chi ben ama' (HG 91:14)

(1) *Attilio Regolo*, 'È un inganno' (OAS 2:77)

1–4 (1–4), 35–36 = 15/1/9 (7–8). Same key (G major).

(2) Ibid., 'Se del fiume' (OAS 2:199)

9–10 (1–2), 90–100 = 16/3/5–4/4 (65–75), 124–35 = 17/2/6–3/6 (90–101). Bars 95–100 were later adapted as *Saul*, 'Birth and fortune' (HG 13:67; HHA I/13: 75), bars 84–90 = 68/3/15–69/1/5.

32 'Vanne, che più ti miro', 1st version (B.L. MS R.M. 20.a.13, ff. 13r–v, 16r–18r)

(1) *Attilio Regolo*, 'Corri, vola' (OAS 2:56)

11–12 (6–7), 56–58 (31–34), 59–60 (36), 67–68 (37), 70–71 (39). Same key (A minor).

(2) *Attilio Regolo*, 'Deh per pietade' (OAS 2:80)

35–36 (17–18)

33 'Vanne, che più ti miro', 2nd version (Fitzwilliam MS Mus. 262, p. 45)

[1] 1st version

1 (11), 4 (35–36), 8–12 (39–43)

(2) *Attilio Regolo*, 'Deh per pietade' (OAS 2:80)

4 (17–18)

34 'Vanne, che più ti miro', final version (HG 91:19)

[1] 2nd version

1–3 (1–3), 5–14 (3–12)

(2) *Attilio Regolo*, 'Deh per pietade' (OAS 2:80)

1 (3), 3–5 (8–9), 15–16 = 20/1/4–2/1 (17–18)

[3] 1st version

4–5 (19–21), 22 = 20/3/2 (3), 25–40 = 20/4/1–21/3/4 (56–71, 75–77)

35 'Rival ti sono' (HG 91:23)

Attilio Regolo, 'Vado sì' (OAS 2:38)

1–5 (1–5), 21 = 24/1/4 (5), 48–49 = 25/3/4–5 (36–37). Cf. No. 48.

36 'Voglio che mora' (HG 91:26)

Attilio Regolo, 'Sponde amiche' (OAS 2:46)

1–6 (1–5)

37 'Vado a recar la morte' (HG 91:38)

Attilio Regolo, 'Se non sà' (OAS 2:139)

2–5 (1–3)

38 'Mi parto lieta' (HG 91:40)

Attilio Regolo, 'Vanne infida' (OAS 2:110)

7 (17–18), 33–37 = 40/6/5–41/1/3 (26–33), 41–42 (40–42)

39 'Sì l'intendesti, sì' (HG 91:51)

Griselda, 'Se il mio dolor' (OAS 3:192)

4–12 (3–12). Questionable. Cf. No. 16.

40 'Poi che pria di morire' (IIG 91:60)

(1) Griselda, 'Occhi belli' (OAS 3:182)

1–3 (1–4), 10–12 (10–12)

(2) Ibid., 'In voler ciò che tu brami' (OAS 3:30)

14–16 (21–22)

(3) Ibid., 'Amanti che piangete' (OAS 3:97)

21–24 = 61/2/3–3/2 (6, 8–11)

41 'Combattuta da due venti' (HG 91:62)

(1) Attilio Regolo, 'Son qual nave' (OAS 2:83)

1–2 (3–4), 15–16 = 62/6/5–6 (30–31), 19–20 (9–10), 28–30 = 63/3/
1–3 (17–19), 99–100 = 67/1/4–5 (44–45), 105–6 (49–51). Handel's
text is a revision of Scarlatti's.

[2] Handel, Arianna, 'Nel pugnar col mostro infido' (HG 83:18)

25–26 = 63/2/3–4 (31–32 = 20/2/3–4). Cf. No. 7.

42 'Sc a' picdi tuoi morrò' (HG 91:68)

Dafni, 'Sconsolato rusignuolo' (C, f. 92v)

1–2 (1–2), 4–6 (15–18). Cf. No. 43.

43 'Nella terra' (HG 91:76)

(1) Dafni, 'O lasciate ch'io mi sveni' (C, f. 110r)

1 (1), 43–45 = 77/4/1–3 (17–19), 62–68 = 78/1/1–2/3 (3–9)

(2) Ibid., 'Sconsolato rusignuolo' (C, f. 92v)

8–10 (9–11). Same key (C minor). Cf. No. 42.

44 Duet 'Vado e vivo' (HG 91:80)

(1) Attilio Regolo, 'Nella procella' (OAS 2:168)

1–2 (11–12). Questionable.

(2) *Dafni*, 'Son ben tenera' (*C*, f. 61r)

1–2 (1–2), 49–53 = 81/1/8–2/2 (9–13), 85–89 = 82/1/1–4 (17–20). Cf. No. 1.

45 Duet 'Caro/cara, tu mi accendi' (HG 91:86)

(1) *Dafni*, 'Sempre aggiungi ò ciel tiranno' (*C*, f. 115r)

1–2 (1–2). Questionable.

[2] Handel, Organ concerto in D minor, Op. 7 No. 4, Adagio (HG 28:115). Cf. alternative version of this movement in HG 48:51 and HHA IV/12:87.

2–4 (15–18 = 115/3/5–116/1/2). The concerto movement may postdate *Faramondo*.

46 'Così suole' (HG 91:90)

(1) *Dafni*, 'So ben io' (*C*, f. 98v)

1–4 (1–4), 9–10 (5–6)

(2) Ibid., 'Sono amante' (*C*, f. 32r).

17–24 = 91/1/8–2/5 (8–16), 59–64 = 91/6/1–6 (17–22)

47 'Un aura placida' (HG 91:109)

Dafni, 'Vi respiro aurette placide' (*C*, f. 47r)

1–2 (1–2), 3–4 (19–20), 5–6 (6–7), 14–16 (3–5), 21–28 = 110/2/1–8 (8–16), 29–32 (1–2, 17–20), 71–72 = 112/1/1–2 (22–23), 77–80 = 112/1/7–2/3 (25–28), 84–86 (29–31), 99–100 = 113/1/2–3 (33–34), 104–6 (37–39), 127–34 = 114/1/1–8 (43–49), 141–44 = 114/2/7–3/2 (51–54). Same key (A minor).

SERSE (December 1737–February 1738)

48 'Più che penso' (HG 92:34; HHA II/39:49)

[1] Giovanni Bononcini, *Il Xerse*, 'Più che penso' (*Handel Sources*, viii, p. 85)

8–11 (4–9)

(2) *Attilio Regolo*, 'Vado sì' (OAS 2:38)

> 39–41 = 36/1/2–4 (22–23). In the autograph (B.L. MS R.M. 20.c.7, f. 25r), bar 41 was originally followed by one derived from Scarlatti's bar 23. Handel deleted a total of seven bars at this point before filling up.

49 'Sì, la voglio', 2nd version (HG 92:76; HHA II/39:108)

See Appendix II

SAUL (July–September 1738)

50 Duet and chorus 'Oh fairest of ten thousand fair' (HG 13:143; HHA I/13:175)

Orlandini, *Paride*, 'Mi fien care' (*E*, f. 160r)[†]

2–3 (3–6), 35–36 = 145/1/3–4 (9–12), 45–48 = 146/1/1–4 (20–27). Same key (G major).

[†] Concerning the possibility that Handel knew this aria from some other source, see above, p. 165.

APPENDIX II

Sources of the Aria 'Sì, la voglio' in *Serse*

The following table of corresponding bars summarizes the relationships between the second and final version of 'Sì, la voglio' and seven earlier arias:

A   1st version (B.L. MS R.M. 20.c.7, f. 56v)
B   Bononcini, *Il Xerse*, 'Sì, la voglio' (*Handel Sources*, viii, p. 178)
C   Scarlatti, *Attilio Regolo*, 'Tutta sdegno' (OAS 2:124)
D   Keiser, *Claudius*, 'Caro, son tua' (Berlin, Staatsbibliothek
       Preussischer Kulturbesitz, Mus. ms. 11485, p. 90)
E   Handel, *Il trionfo del Tempo e del Disinganno*, 'Voglio cangiar
       desio' (HG 24:78)
F   Handel, *Il trionfo del Tempo e della Verità*, 'Voglio cangiar
       desio' (HG 20:140, as 'Pleasure thy former ways resigning')
G   *Attilio Regolo*, 'Voglio a terra' (OAS 2:66)

Bar numbers in the first column refer to Handel's original draft of the second version in B.L. MS R.M. 20.c.7, ff. 58r–59v, those in the second column to the shortened aria ultimately filled up.

Draft Version	Final Version	Source
1–3	1–3	A, 1–5; B,1
3–5	3–5	C, 2–5
6	6	A, 8–9; B, 2
7		A, 10
8		C, 10–11
9–10	7–8	C, 11–13
10–14	8–12	A, 16–19
19–20	13–14	A, 21–23
21		A, 24
22–23		C, 16–17
26–27		D, 12; E, 15–16;
		F, 13–14
27–28		B, 1–2
29–30		G, 22–24
31–35	15–19	G, 24–29
37–39	21–23	A, 32–34; D, 14–15;
		E, 18–19; F, 15–16
39–41	23–25	C, 25–26
42	26	A, 35

Handel, Jennens and Saul: *aspects of a collaboration*

ANTHONY HICKS

So thoroughly and carefully has Winton Dean explored the works he covered in his great study *Handel's Dramatic Oratorios and Masques*[1] that few additions – and fewer corrections – are required even after the lapse of nearly thirty years. It is, however, possible to add something to Dean's account of the textual history of *Saul*, mainly because sources not accessible to him in the 1950s can now be examined and other new information can be taken into account. Some of the interesting questions raised by Dean which could not be answered on the evidence available can now be tackled, and much more can be said of the role of the librettist Charles Jennens in supplying ideas for 'improving' the oratorio. It might have been hoped that these matters would have been adequately treated in the Halle edition of *Saul*,[2] which made use of important manuscript sources not available to Dean, but regrettably that is not the case. The edition cannot be ignored, because its critical report contains much music and information not published elsewhere, but it is difficult to make references to it responsibly without also drawing attention to its errors. Perhaps the comments made here will help to encourage the production of an entirely new Halle edition of *Saul*; a modern scholarly edition worthy of the work is in any case long overdue.

We still do not know for certain when Handel first received the libretto of *Saul* from Jennens or the precise form in which it was presented to him.[3]

---

[1] London, 1959.

[2] *Hallische Händel-Ausgabe*, I/xiii, ed. P. M. Young (full score, Kassel etc., 1962 [HHA]; *Kritischer Bericht* (Kassel etc., 1964) [KB].

[3] A manuscript wordbook was presumably supplied to the Inspector of Stage Plays, but no copy of it exists in the Larpent collection of plays at the Huntington Library, San Marino, California, which contains most of the surviving copies of such wordbooks, including complete versions or fragments of twelve Handel oratorios. *Messiah* is also absent. The manuscript wordbooks of the other Jennens oratorios, *L'Allegro* (Larpent MS 26) and *Belshazzar* (Larpent MS 52), are both fair copies in the hand of John Christopher Smith the elder and present texts close to the version of first performance. The corresponding wordbook of *Saul* is therefore unlikely to have been a working copy actually used by Handel.

Handel's first extant letter to Jennens, dated 28 July 1735,[4] acknowledges the receipt of an 'Oratorio' which gave the composer 'a great deal of Satisfaction' on first reading, but the letter gives no clue to the subject of the work. The frequently made assumption that the libretto was *Saul* is plausible but open to question, because Handel's first draft of the oratorio incorporates a substantial portion of the anthem *The ways of Zion do mourn*, adapted to form the Elegy for Saul and Jonathan in the final act. Since this work was composed for the funeral of Queen Caroline in December 1737 its text cannot have been present in the libretto prepared by Jennens in 1735. If the latter was *Saul*, the Elegy must either have been the text finally set by Handel, or some other text. If it was the text as finally set, then we should have to assume that Handel at first rejected it in favour of the funeral anthem adaptation but later reinstated it at Jennens's insistence – in which case it is remarkable that Jennens later complained only of Handel's displacement of a 'Hallelujah'. If, on the other hand, the 1735 libretto did not contain the text of the Elegy as finally set, then we should have to conclude that Handel did indeed reject what Jennens had provided; that Jennens accepted the rejection and supplied a new text to replace it; and that Handel finally set this new text. While these scenarios are perfectly possible, the simplest explanation of the facts is that the 1735 libretto had nothing to do with *Saul*. However, no firm conclusion can be drawn in the absence of more concrete evidence.

For his account of the textual history of *Saul* before its first performance at the King's Theatre on 16 January 1739 Dean had to rely almost entirely on the autograph[5] and on information provided by Jennens in a letter to his young relative Lord Guernsey, written on 19 September 1738.[6] A useful description of the autograph had previously been provided by Barclay Squire.[7] Though the present state of the autograph is highly confused as a

4   O. E. Deutsch, *Handel: a Documentary Biography* (London, 1955/R 1974), p. 394.
5   British Library, MS R.M. 20.g.3.
6   Deutsch, op. cit., pp. 465–6. The letter (preserved in the archives of the Earl of Aylesford at Great Packington, Meriden, Warwickshire) was first published in N. Flower, *George Frideric Handel* (London, 1923), both in facsimile (plate facing p. 250) and in a slightly inaccurate transcript (pp. 251–2). (The facsimile, regrettably omitted from subsequent editions of the book, is faked to the extent of presenting two pages of the letter as if they were one: the final page of the letter begins with the line 'words would have bore as Grand Musick as . . . '). The significant error of Flower's transcript (which Deutsch unfortunately reproduces) is the substitution of 'constructed' for 'contriv'd' in the sentence beginning 'This Organ, he says, is so contriv'd . . . '; otherwise the inaccuracies are those of capitalization and punctuation. Thanks to the kindness of the present Earl of Aylesford, Donald Burrows and I were able to check the original document at Great Packington in May 1984. Lord Aylesford has no other letters of Jennens.
7   W. B. Squire, *Catalogue of the King's Music Library*, I: *The Handel Manuscripts* (London, 1927), pp. 71–6.

result of losses and misbinding during the eighteenth century, Handel's own numbering of the four-sheet gatherings of the first composition draft enables most of the original scheme for the work to be reconstructed. The most serious losses are the group of gatherings 11–15 – covering the end of Act 1 and the start of Act 2 – and the final page of the 'Hallelujah' with which Handel originally ended the oratorio. As a result, the dates of completion of Act 1 and of the first draft of Act 3 are missing, and the original arrangement at the start of Act 2 is not apparent, since the autograph resumes in the middle of an aria, 'Love from such a parent sprung',[8] which found no place in Handel's later revisions and whose context is not immediately clear.

Jennens's letter, reporting a visit to Handel on 18 September 1738, deals with the placing of the 'Hallelujah'. Having drawn attention to two 'Maggots' or foolish ideas dreamt up by the composer (i.e. the introduction of a carillon and a new organ), he continues:

His third Maggot is a Hallelujah which he has trump'd up at the end of his Oratorio since I went into the Country, because he thought the conclusion of the Oratorio not Grand enough; tho' if that were the case 'twas his own fault, for the words would have bore as Grand Musick as he could have set 'em to: but this Hallelujah, Grand as it is, comes in very nonsensically, having no manner of relation to what goes before. And this is the more extraordinary, because he refus'd to set a Hallelujah at the end of the first Chorus in the Oratorio, where I had plac'd one & where it was to be introduc'd with the utmost propriety, upon a pretence that it would make the Entertainment too long.

From this information and the dates which can still be found in the autograph, a rough timetable for the composition of the oratorio may be drawn up. Handel began the opening chorus of Act 1 on 23 July 1738. (There is no means of telling exactly when the overture was composed, but it is clearly contemporary with the rest of the oratorio.[9]) Act 2 was completed on 8 August and filled in on the 28th, presumably after Act 3 had been drafted. Handel must have finished this preliminary version of the oratorio by 9 September, when he began the opera *Imeneo*, the draft of

---

8   Not in Friedrich Chrysander's edition *George Friedrich Händel's Werke: Ausgabe der Deutschen Händelgesellschaft* (Leipzig and Bergedorf, 1858–1902, reprinted Farnborough, 1965), xiii [HG]. It will be found in KB, pp. 158–61, and in the appendices of the old English editions of *Saul*, including Vincent Novello's vocal score (c1858).

9   This conclusion is derived from the preliminary examination of the rastra patterns and watermarks of Handel's 'English' autographs undertaken by Donald Burrows and reported by him in the typescript document *A Handlist of the Paper Characteristics of Handel's English Autographs* (1982). The Cx watermark which the paper of the overture shares with the rest of the *Saul* autograph occurs only in works of the period 1738–9. The trio sonata on which the overture is based (autograph, Cambridge, Fitzwilliam Museum, MS 259, pp. 1–14) appears to be slightly earlier, c1737.

which was completed on the 20th.[10] He then resumed work on *Saul*, having had the benefit of at least one discussion with Jennens, and completed the composition of the Elegy on the 27th. In this section he was able to re-use some existing music which he must have already decided to abandon in its original context: the third verse of the Elegy ('From this unhappy day') does not appear in its expected place but is simply referred to with the cue 'la stanza 3za vide nell atto 2do'. (Dean observes that it may have appeared with different words in the early part of Act 2, now missing from the autograph.[11]) The 'Hallelujah' was moved to the end of the opening chorus of Act 1, where Jennens had intended it to be, and it was no doubt this action that loosened the first and last pages of this portion of the autograph and caused their subsequent loss.

Dean himself was later able to supply some of the missing dates in the timetable from the marginalia added by Jennens to his copy of John Mainwaring's *Memoirs of the Life of the Late George Frederic Handel*.[12] Against the entry for *Saul* in Mainwaring's list of Handel's works Jennens noted that Act 1 had been completed on 1 August 1738, Act 2 started on the 2nd and Act 3 (obviously in its first draft) completed on the 15th. In recording these dates Dean drew attention to the three-volume manuscript full score of *Saul* formerly belonging to Jennens and now in the Flower Collection at Manchester Central Library.[13] The dates for the end of Act 1 and the start of Act 2 were, according to Dean, 'found' by Jennens in this copy. Here Dean was unfortunately relying on second-hand information: in fact the dates were entered in the score by Jennens himself, and were probably obtained by him from direct consultation of the autograph. This score and the sets of parts that accompany it in the same collection throw a good deal of light on the early history of *Saul* and, studied in conjunction with Handel's autograph, provide some fascinating insights into Jennens's own role in attempting to revise the work.

Our investigation begins with a feature of the autograph noticed by Squire and Dean but not completely appreciated by them: the presence of handwritings other than that of Handel himself. There are in fact two 'foreign' hands in the autograph, and thanks to the pioneering study of

---

[10]   The first page of the overture to *Imeneo* was re-used by Handel in the concerto Op. 6 No. 9 and so appears among the autographs of the Op. 6 concertos (British Library, MS R.M. 20.g.11, f. 122; it is dated 'den 9 Sept. 1738. Sonabend'. The other date is found in the main *Imeneo* autograph (R.M. 20.b.5, f. 62): 'Fine dell'Opera den 20 Septembr 1738'.

[11]   *Handel's Dramatic Oratorios and Masques*, p. 309 n. 1.

[12]   'Charles Jennens's Marginalia to Mainwaring's Life of Handel', *Music & Letters*, liii (1972), pp. 160–4.

[13]   Discussed below.

Handel copyists provided by Jens Peter Larsen in his book on *Messiah*[14] (published too late to be taken much into account by Dean) they can both be identified. One is that of the younger John Christopher Smith, Handel's amanuensis and collaborator in the years of the composer's blindness, who added a new set of words to Jonathan's air 'Wise, valiant, good', one of the items Handel removed from *Saul* before first performance. (It was replaced by Merab's 'What abject thoughts', based on similar musical material.) This addition to the autograph was made in 1759 when the air in Smith's revised version ('Wise, great and good') was included in a revival of *Solomon*; it is not relevant to any version of *Saul*.[15]

The other hand turns out to be that of Jennens himself. His annotations are not only striking testimony of his intense involvement with the substantial revision of the oratorio in the period between the completion of the first composition draft and the first performance, but also demonstrate Handel's own respect for Jennens as a collaborator. By no means all of Jennens's suggestions were accepted by the composer, but the very fact that Jennens was allowed to go through the autograph score and enter his own alterations, both verbal and musical, is clear proof that Handel was genuinely interested in his views, at least in the early stages when his own ideas were still unsettled. Jennens had further opportunity to study the music of *Saul* in the full score and partbooks mentioned earlier, prepared for him by the copyist known as S2.[16] These also contain significant annotations by Jennens (apart from the dates already noted) and were undoubtedly copied directly from the autograph before Handel had completed his pre-performance revisions, since they preserve several numbers or versions of numbers which found no place in the version of the first performance.[17] In addition a second set of partbooks (and probably a corresponding full score, now lost) was prepared for Jennens at a slightly later stage, to cover items already discarded when the main material was copied, or items composed subsequently.

[14] *Handel's Messiah: Origins, Composition, Sources* (London, 1957, rev. 2/1972).

[15] The air is printed in the appendices of the old English editions and in Chrysander's appendix in its *Solomon* version, though Chrysander also includes the original *Saul* words in small print above the voice stave. In KB, pp. 137–41, the musical text follows the *Saul* autograph, but only the *Solomon* words are shown; the original words are relegated without explanation to the commentary (ibid., p. 88). There is nothing in the commentary to indicate that the *Solomon* words added in the autograph were not written by Handel.

[16] Larsen's designation.

[17] The version of first performance can be determined with a fair degree of confidence from the conducting score, the first printed wordbook (dated 1738) and Walsh's print of the overture and songs issued shortly after the first run of performances had finished. In essentials it is the version presented in the main body of the old English editions. The conducting score (Hamburg, Staats- und Universitätsbibliothek, MS M C/257) is described in H. D. Clausen, *Händels Direktionspartituren ('Handexemplare')* (Hamburg, 1972), pp. 216–20.

Since the material prepared for Jennens is imperfectly described in the Halle edition a list with basic bibliographical details is here set out in Table 1. (The supplementary volume in the British Library is not of special interest and will not be further considered.) The manuscripts once formed part of the great collection of Handel's music formed by Jennens, known as the 'Aylesford' Collection because it passed on Jennens's death in 1773 to the 3rd Earl of Aylesford (the recipient of Jennens's letter of September 1738, written before the earl had succeeded to the title). It is no longer an integral collection: a few items were sold in 1873 and the remainder at Sotheby's on 13 May 1918,[18] but the subsequent dispersal was fortunately not as disastrous as might have been expected. An important group of miscellaneous manuscripts was secured by Barclay Squire for the British Museum and added to the Royal Music Collection,[19] and a large number of manuscripts and early printed editions were acquired by Newman Flower, who published a summary catalogue of them around 1920.[20] (Flower later allowed several scholars access to his collection but denied it to Larsen and Dean, the two men who would have made best use of it.) After Flower's death in 1964 his collection (which by then had been augmented with many items not connected with the Aylesford Collection) was purchased for Manchester Central Library. A useful catalogue of the Manchester holdings was issued in 1972,[21] but unfortunately it describes all the manuscript items as 'The Aylesford Manuscripts' and thus perpetuates a long-standing confusion. (The notional reconstruction of the contents of the Aylesford Collection before its dispersal remains a major bibliographical challenge.) Thus of the two manuscript full scores of *Saul* now at Manchester only that listed in Table 1 is actually an 'Aylesford manuscript'.

Certain features of the partbooks in the main Aylesford material for *Saul* show that S2 began copying them even before Handel had finished composing the music. The Canto I, Alto and Cembalo parts include in the duet 'O fairest of ten thousand fair' a passage of seven bars (following bar 54)[22] which Handel deleted in the autograph and never orchestrated. (The bars were subsequently cancelled in the parts with the note 'NB this is not

---

18   See A. H. King, *Some British Collectors of Music c1600–1960* (Cambridge, 1963), pp. 58, 72, 138, 141.

19   In Squire's catalogue (see n. 7) items from the Aylesford Collection are generally indicated as such, but the indications are not entirely reliable: MS R.M. 19.c.9, for example, bears annotations in Jennens's hand and must be an Aylesford manuscript; but it is not so described in ibid., p. 136.

20   *Catalogue of a Handel Collection Formed by Newman Flower* (Sevenoaks, n.d.).

21   A. D. Walker, *George Frideric Handel: the Newman Flower Collection in the Henry Watson Library: a Catalogue* (Manchester, 1972).

22   Printed in KB, pp. 68–9. The presence of these bars in the Aylesford partbooks is not mentioned.

Table 1 *The Aylesford manuscripts of* Saul

Description	Library and shelf-mark	HHA designation
MAIN GROUP		
Full scores:	Manchester Central Library, Henry Watson Music Library,	
Act 1	MS 130 Hd 4 v. 269 ⎫	
Act 2	270 ⎬ L	
Act 3	271 ⎭	
Vocal parts (bound with parts for *Samson*):		
Canto I (Michal)	MS 130 Hd 4 v. 283	
Canto II (Merab)	284	
Alto (David)	285	
Tenore I (Jonathan)	286	
Tenore II (High Priest)	287	
Tenore III (Abner, Witch, Amalekite, Abiathar)	288	
Basso I (Saul)	289	
Basso II (Samuel, Doeg)	290	
		N
Instrumental parts (bound with parts for *Samson*):		
Oboe I	MS 130 Hd 4 v. 280	
Oboe II (with Flutes)	281	
Basson I, II	282	
Violino I	276	
Violino II	277	
Viola	278	
Violoncello, Contrabasso	279	
Tromba I (with parts for other works)	247 ⎫	
Tromba II (with parts for other works)	248 ⎬ not mentioned	
Timpani (with parts for other works)	353 ⎭	
Cembalo	275	O
Carillon (see below)		
ADDITIONAL SONGS		
Instrumental parts (bound with other works):		
Violino I	MS 130 Hd 4 v. 240	
Violino II	241	
Viola	242 ⎬ not mentioned	
Violoncello	243	
Oboe I	245	
Oboe II	246	
Cembalo (with main carillon part)	249	P
SUPPLEMENT		
Carillon part for recitative and scores of two airs	British Library, MS RM 18.c.11, ff.131-6	H

plaid'.) Thus S2 must have begun his work by copying the voice parts and instrumental bass from Handel's preliminary, unorchestrated draft; there are a number of other places where the parts preserve a reading earlier than that of the corresponding full score.[23] Although Jennens's partbooks were presumably not intended to be used in performance (except perhaps for occasional domestic concerts) it is highly likely that this early preparation of vocal parts from the composition draft was common practice in this period (as later) because it gave the singers something to work on at the earliest possible moment, allowing them to learn their parts and make any requests for revisions in good time. Changes made by the composer when completing the orchestration would be dealt with simply by amending the parts.

Another remarkable feature of the main Aylesford material is that it meticulously follows Jennens's annotations in the autograph, which in some respects can be seen as instructions to the copyist. The oddest case is that of 'While yet thy tide of blood runs high', a strophic air in three stanzas for the High Priest. The autograph shows two versions, the first of which was never fully orchestrated and remained as a sketch for voice and continuo, with a first violin part in the ritornellos only. The second version is the published one, though with the last three bars cancelled and replaced with an extended cadence involving a repetition by the singer of the last line of each stanza.[24] Jennens was clearly unhappy with the completed version of this piece – presumably he found it rather dull, but if so the blame lies as much with him as with Handel – and sought to enliven it with a scheme of varying ritornellos incorporating a fragment of the sketch and the revised cadence of the completed version. Under the violin line of the closing ritornello of the sketch Jennens wrote 'this Symphony after the 1st Stanza', and against the new closing ritornello of the completed version he wrote 'this Symphony after the 2nd Stanza'. The purpose of these instructions can be seen from the Aylesford score and parts, in which the three stanzas of the air are fully written out, with the two ritornellos annotated by Jennens appearing as links between the

23   Another example occurs in the opening bar of 'O let it not in Gath be heard', where the third note in the Aylesford Tenore I part is b♭, which is what Handel first wrote, though he had changed it to e'♭ (as printed) by the time the Aylesford score was copied. The partbook reading is conjectured to be a copyist's error in KB, p. 80.

24   Printed in KB, p. 53, where it is incorrectly referred to as 'diese gestrichene Stelle'; it is the passage that it replaces that is crossed out. Since this amendment was made before the first performance and appears to be Handel's final thought for the air, it is not immediately clear why it was not adopted in the conducting score (which has the published version without alteration). The revised close may be connected with Handel's instructions for transposing the air to F♯ minor, possibly for counter-tenor, a version perhaps sung in the early performances but later abandoned. There are signs in the conducting score that at some time the air was pasted over with an alternative version, not now extant.

Ex. 1

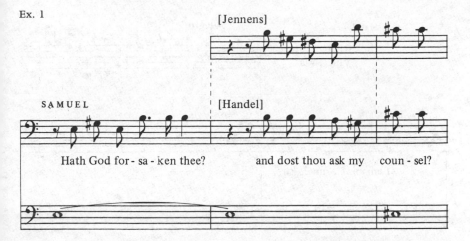

stanzas. (The original ritornello of the completed version is retained at the close.) Unfortunately Jennens's amendments do nothing to improve the air, and it is not surprising to find his annotations in the autograph heavily cancelled, presumably by Handel himself.[25]

Jennens proposed two other specifically musical improvements, both in Act 3. The first concerns a point of verbal accentuation, a subject on which Jennens, as librettist, had every right to express a view. In the scene in which the Apparition of Samuel appears to Saul, the ghost responds ironically to Saul's plea for help: 'Hath God forsaken thee? And dost thou ask/My counsel?' Handel's setting of this text in recitative loses the irony by giving no weight to the word 'my', as shown in the lower vocal line of Ex. 1. Jennens's solution was to overwrite Handel's setting with the alternative vocal line shown in the example, which puts 'my' at the top of the musical phrase. This seems very sensible, and its acceptance by Handel is confirmed by the presence of an identical amendment in the conducting score.[26]

Jennens's second musical amendment occurs in the scene for David and the Amalekite and is much more startling. In recitative the Amalekite tells David that he has killed Saul at Saul's own request. David responds angrily in the vigorous air 'Impious wretch', condemning the Amalekite to death

---

[25] Plate V in Dean, *Handel's Dramatic Oratorios and Masques*, facing p. 306, shows the autograph of the sketch and the first page of the final version. Jennens's first annotation, heavily cancelled and illegible on the plate, appears between staves 5 and 6 of the sketch. A comparison of the plate with the transcription of the sketch in KB, p. 52, shows the latter to be highly misleading.

[26] HG, p. 198, and HHA, p. 250, give the amended reading, earlier editions the original. The original reading does not appear anywhere in HHA or KB – indeed KB makes no comment whatsoever on these bars.

Ex. 2
(a) Handel

(b) Jennens

for having slain the Lord's anointed. Jennens felt that the composer had not given enough dramatic impact to this moment, although by the time he came to consult the autograph Handel had already replaced the original 3/8 setting of 'Impious wretch'[27] with the much stronger common-time version printed in all editions. The relevant pages of the autograph are reproduced in Plates 5 and 6. Ex. 2(a) shows the final bars of the recitative and the opening of the air as written by Handel, and Ex. 2(b) shows Jennens's bold revision. He provided a new text for the last words of the Amalekite, replacing 'I am an Amalekite' with 'Of the race of Amalek–',

[27]   HG, pp. 284–6; KB, pp. 175–7.

Plate 5   Handel's autograph of the recitative 'Whence comest thou' in Act 3 of *Saul*, showing annotations by Charles Jennens. The scene heading 'Scen. 4. David, an Amalekite' is in Jennens's hand, and so are the alterations to the music and the added words 'Of the Race of Amalek –' at the bottom of the page. The other substantial alterations are in Handel's hand but were probably made to accommodate improvements to the words suggested by Jennens.

Plate 6 Handel's autograph of the start of the air 'Impious wretch' in its second, final version (intended to follow directly after the recitative shown in Plate 5), showing Jennens's insertion of an entry for the voice at the beginning of the air. The words 'Impious wretch' and the three notes in the first bar of the vocal line (stave 3) are in Jennens's hand.

and set it to a new musical phrase rising hysterically to a high F♯. He then
scratched out Handel's minim rest at the end of the recitative, changed the
bass semibreve to a minim and brought David in at the very start of the air
with another new musical phrase for the words 'Impious wretch!'.[28]

While one can sympathize with what Jennens was trying to do here, his
amendment does not quite work. The change at the end of the recitative is
surely too melodramatic, and the new vocal phrase at the start of the aria is
musically unsatisfactory, since the last word is covered by the entry of the
orchestra; the entry of the voice with the first continuo chord, rather than
after it, is also a shade clumsy. On the occasions when Handel himself
brings the voice in at the start of an aria he generally leaves the vocal line
entirely clear.[29] Perhaps this is why Handel seems to have rejected
Jennens's version (it does not appear in any source apart from the
autograph and the Aylesford material) – or perhaps, with the pardonable
pride of a professional, he felt that in this case Jennens had strayed too far
into territory that was strictly the composer's and therefore had to be
repulsed. Professionals naturally resent amateur criticism of their work,
especially when there is some justice in it.[30]

Jennens's criticisms were not directed only at Handel, however. Several
of his alterations were purely verbal and clearly intended as improvements
to his own text. In verse 6 of the Elegy (the air 'In sweetest harmony') the
text set by Handel reads:

> In sweetest Harmony they liv'd
> Nor Death their Union could dissolve:
> The pious Youth ne'er left his father's Side,
> But him defending bravely died:
> A Loss too great to be surviv'd.[31]

[28] In HHA, pp. 257–8, the end of the recitative is given in a version of the editor's own
invention, combining part of Jennens's musical amendment with the original verbal
text, and Jennens's version of the start of the air is printed without comment. In KB, p.
78, Jennens's changes at the end of the recitative are reported as readings of the
autograph without any hint that they are not in Handel's hand, and there is no
comment at all on the alteration of the start of the air.

[29] 'Flatt'ring tongue' in *Esther* provides an example to the contrary, but here Handel
does not have a continuo chord with the voice at the start, and the entry of the
orchestra over the voice is just as awkward as it is in Jennens's amendment of the *Saul*
air.

[30] The merits of Jennens's version *vis-à-vis* Handel's original may be judged from
recordings. The recording under Sir Charles Mackerras (first issued on DGG Archiv
2722 008) follows Jennens, while others – for example those under Mogens Wöldike
(Philips SAL 3508–10) and Philip Ledger (EMI SLS 5200) – follow Handel.

[31] The reading 'his father's side' is that of the autograph and the conducting score in bars
30–1 and 38–9 and is also that of the 1738 wordbook. HG and the old English editions
reproduce it correctly. HHA prints '*the* Father's Side' without explanation on both
appearances of the phrase in the full score, pp. 277–8, and repeats the error in KB, p.
30, in what purports to be a reprint of the wordbook text.

Jennens amends 'dissolve' and 'Youth' to the stronger readings 'divide' and 'Son'. These are the readings of the 1738 wordbook and were presumably accepted by Handel, though in the conducting score only the first alteration is made, 'Youth' remaining unaltered. In the next number, the chorus 'O fatal Day' (incorporating solos for David), Jennens changes all appearances of the phrase 'for thy King and Country slain' to read 'for thy King and People slain' – a technicality touching upon the still sensitive issue of the political status of Israel; here the wordbook retains the reading 'Country', as does the conducting score. Another of Jennens's verbal alterations occurs in the bass air 'Ye men of Judah',[32] where Handel actually writes 'Ye sons of Judah' but Jennens makes the change to 'Men', the reading of the wordbook. In this case Jennens is probably doing no more than correcting a slip of the composer's: 'Men' is the reading of the earlier recitative setting of the same text and Handel himself correspondingly amended the words of the air in the conducting score.

More substantial verbal amendments, visible in Plate 5, occur in the scene for the Amalekite and David; these, together with the appropriate musical adjustments, are in Handel's own hand, but the new words must surely have been supplied by Jennens. There is no doubt that Jennens himself produced a considerably improved text for the last lines of David's tribute to Jonathan. The text first set by Handel reads:

> Great was the Pleasure I enjoyed in thee,
> Great as thy wond'rous Love to me;
> Let the fondest Women own,
> Their Love by thine was far outdone.

Happily Jennens ditched the last three lines in favour of a single alexandrine: 'And more than Women's Love thy wondrous Love to me!',[33] which he wrote between some blank staves above Handel's setting of the original lines, as shown in Plate 7. Handel then adjusted the music, removing three bars to accommodate the shorter text; the result is the version of the printed scores.

The only remaining amendments by Jennens that are of any significance (we may note in passing his substitution of the name 'Doeg' for the 'Messenger' in Act 2 scene 7[34]) are those that solve problems in the textual history of *Saul* that Dean was unable to resolve. In view of his comments on

---

[32]   HG, pp. 232–6; KB, pp. 182–4. The air is not represented in HHA, though it clearly formed part of Handel's first performing version.

[33]   The 1738 wordbook reads 'Woman's', a further refinement by Jennens; he altered the Aylesford score correspondingly. The biblical source (Authorized Version, 2 Samuel 2: 26) reads 'thy love to me was wonderful, passing the love of women'.

[34]   This change was not made in the conducting score, but the name appears in the wordbook.

Plate 7   Handel's autograph of part of the solo and chorus 'O fatal day' in Act 3 of *Saul*, showing Jennens's suggestion of an improvement to the words and Handel's subsequent adaptation of the music to fit it. The words 'And more than Women's Love thy wondrous Love to me!' between staves 5 and 6 are in Jennens's hand. Handel has deleted three bars of music to accommodate the new text.

Handel's treatment of the 'Hallelujah', quoted earlier, it is not surprising that Jennens's first note in the autograph concerns this very matter. Handel's first setting of the opening 'Epinicion, or Song of Triumph' was as follows:

> I.   'How excellent thy name, O Lord . . . '
>   Chorus, as published, but including three passages later cancelled.[35]
> II. 'An infant rais'd by thy command . . . '
>   Chorus, the music as in verse IV as published, except that the second section ('Could fierce Goliah's dreadful hand') is in common time, with halved note-values.
> III. 'Along the monster atheist strode . . . '
>   Four-part chorus in E minor.[36]
> IV. 'The youth inspir'd by Thee, O Lord . . . '
>   As published, the second section ('Our fainting courage soon restor'd') in halved note-values.
> V.   'How excellent thy name, O Lord . . . '
>   As published, a shortened version of I.

Handel did not write out the music for verses IV and V but simply gave directions for the repetition of the earlier music: 'replicat[ur] sub litera A (an Infant raisd) With other words . . . after vers 4 the Youth inspir'd replicatur sub litera B vers. 5 with the same words How excellent'. To which Jennens adds 'Then the Hallelujah, at the End of the Oratorio'.

The Aylesford material duly reflects this arrangement, giving the original form of the Epinicion followed immediately by the 'Hallelujah'. It also contains further amendments by Jennens which resolve a contradiction between the autograph and the 1738 wordbook over the words of verse II. The autograph text is:

> An Infant rais'd by thy Command
>   To quell thy Rebel Foes,
> Could fierce Goliah's dreadful Hand
>   Superior in the Fight oppose.

And the text of verse IV, which goes to the same music, is:

> The Youth inspir'd by Thee, O Lord,
>   With Ease the Boaster slew,
> Our fainting Courage soon restor'd,
>   And headlong drove that impious Crew.

The wordbook, however, has an entirely different text for verse II:

---

[35]   Printed in KB, pp. 120–6; the unplayable b' ♮ for the second trumpet in bar 5 on page 120 should be g'.

[36]   KB, pp. 127–30.

When thou to quell the Rebel Host
  An Infant didst ordain,
Thy rebels to the Child oppos'd
  A Giant's dreadful Rage in vain.

Dean suggests that the latter 'is perhaps an uncancelled survival of Jennens' earliest text'. He continues:

It seems probable that when Handel planned to use the same music for 'An infant rais'd' and 'The youth inspir'd' he had in mind the librettos' text of the former [*ie* 'When thou to quell'], the last line of which, 'A giant's dreadful rage in vain', is much more apt for the striking musical phrase now associated with 'And headlong drove that impious crew' than the colourless 'Superior in the fight oppose'. But the fact remains that this last is the line to which the music is set, 'And headlong drove' being cued in underneath. Perhaps a still earlier state of the manuscript is missing.[37]

Ex. 3 shows the 'striking musical phrase' with its three possible texts.

Ex. 3

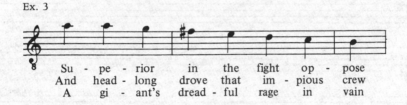

Jennens's amendments in the Aylesford score resolve the problem. In verse II he cancels the original autograph text as copied ('An Infant rais'd') and substitutes that of the wordbook. (His amendments at the start of the second section are illustrated in Plate 8.[38]) Thus the autograph does reflect the earliest version of the text, and it was indeed a happy chance that the line 'And headlong drove that impious crew' got so effective a setting in verse IV. Jennens himself must have been struck by the contrasting feebleness of the line 'Superior in the fight oppose' when sung to the same music and sought to improve matters by devising a new quatrain with a final line better fitted to the music. Meanwhile, however, Handel himself had dealt with the difficulty by resetting verses II and III to new music, thus creating the version now familiar, with 'An Infant rais'd' as a soprano solo and 'Along the Monster Atheist strode' as a three-part chorus in C

37   Op. cit., p. 306.
38   The heading 'in alla breve', taken from the autograph, is almost certainly an instruction to copy the music in doubled note-values, but S2 has misunderstood and copied the instruction instead.

Plate 8   A page of the score of *Saul* prepared for Jennens by the copyist S2, showing Jennens's alteration of the text of the second verse of the Epinicion in Act 1. The cancellations and new text ('Thy Rebels to the Child oppos'd . . .') are in Jennens's hand.

minor.[39] This is almost certainly the version of first performance.[40] Jennens must have sent the revised text of the Epinicion to the printer of the wordbook before he knew of Handel's own revision.

The other interesting textual problem, already mentioned, is to discover something about the arrangement of the beginning of Act 2 in Handel's first draft, a section now missing from the autograph. In the main Aylesford material the portion of the act up to the point where the autograph resumes exhibits two significant differences from the version of the printed scores. After Jonathan's recitative 'My father comes', there follows 'Author of peace', an air in C minor for alto. In the printed scores (representing the version of the first performances) this air appears later in the act, transposed to G minor and forming part of a solo scene for Merab which is not in the Aylesford material. The use of the alto voice clearly suggests that the air in its C minor version is for David, yet it is included in the Tenore I partbook as if it were for Jonathan. The other difference is the appearance of the air 'Love from such a parent sprung'[41] for Michal between the recitative 'A father's will has authoriz'd my love' and the duet 'O fairest of ten thousand fair'; the partbooks preserve the original ending of the recitative, with a final cadence in E♭.[42] This is presumably the original position of the air. The autograph of the rest of the act is extant, and so the main Aylesford material can offer no further information relevant to the version of the first draft.

We need to examine more closely the Aylesford version of the scene containing the C minor 'Author of peace'. It cannot represent Handel's first thoughts, because the autograph of the air, also in C minor, is not missing but is preserved on a loose sheet (now folio 77) bearing the 'NB' marking which Handel often used to indicate an insertion. No character name is now visible, though there may be one beneath a patch of impenetrable

---

[39] Not a Trio, as described in all editions. In the autograph the vocal parts are simply marked 'A', 'T' and 'B'; if Handel had intended solo voices he would have entered singers' names. This three-part texture seems to have been intended by Handel to indicate a 'soldier's chorus' from which the choral trebles and the female soloists (who normally sang with the chorus) would presumably have been excluded. Other examples are 'Bacchus' blessings are a treasure' in *Alexander's Feast*, 'Disdainful of danger' in *Judas Maccabaeus* and 'Venus laughing from the skies' in *Theodora*.

[40] In the conducting score the overture and the Epinicion appear in their revised forms, the overture featuring the organ solos in the third movement. Since the overture was printed in this form by Walsh shortly after the first performances, and the pagination of overture and Epinicion is continuous in the conducting score, the revisions to both must have been made before or during the first run. HHA prints the original version of the overture (with oboe solos in the third movement) but follows it with the revised version of the Epinicion. (The revised overture movement appears in KB, pp. 114–19.) No explanation for this arrangement is offered.

[41] See n. 8, above.

[42] Printed in KB, p. 67, from the Aylesford Canto I partbook. The presence of the same reading in the main Cembalo part is not mentioned.

obliteration at the top of the page. But since the air cannot be for anyone other than David, why should the character's name have been deleted, and why is the air apparently allocated to Jonathan in the Aylesford material? Part of the answer can be deduced from the text. What Handel set was as follows:

> Author of Peace, who canst controul
> Ev'ry passion of the Soul;
> To whose good spirit alone we owe
> Words that sweet as Honey flow:
> With thy dear influence his tongue be fill'd,
> And cruel wrath to soft persuasion yield.[43]

This makes sense as an air for David at the point where it appears in the main Aylesford material, after the recitative 'My father comes'. Jonathan has promised to try to intercede with the angry Saul on David's behalf, and in the air David prays that God, the 'Author of peace', will grant Jonathan the eloquence to fulfil his promise. This arrangement, however, would give David two airs in succession – he has just sung 'Such haughty beauties' – and that cannot have been Jennens's original plan. It would be more natural to have Jonathan's recitative followed by an air for Jonathan. There is evidence that this was indeed Jennens's first intention, which he attempted to reinstate. In the autograph Jennens has amended the fifth line of the air to read 'With thy dear influence *my* tongue be fill'd', so that the prayer becomes Jonathan's own; this is the text in the main Aylesford material and justifies its position in Jonathan's part.

The likelihood is, therefore, that 'Author of peace' was designed by Jennens as an air for Jonathan following the recitative 'My father comes'; that Handel at some point decided to transfer it to David; and that Handel wrote the C minor setting with this new arrangement in mind. What remains to be discovered is whether Handel had actually set the air for Jonathan as part of his first draft and, if so, whether the music survives in any form. The answer lies in the Aylesford material but not in the main group of scores and parts; we have to turn to the 'Additional Songs'. If we ignore the carillon part (bound with the additional Cembalo partbook but really belonging to the main material) the 'additions' are:

> (*i*)   Air 'Capricious man', F major version (as in the main text of all printed editions, but without the spurious da capo[44])

[43]   Handel first wrote 'all the passions' instead of 'ev'ry passion,' but this seems to have been a slip of no significance.

[44]   Chrysander in HG is the only editor to print this air correctly. The erroneous da capo did not originate with Walsh, as stated by Dean (*Handel's Dramatic Oratorios* p. 303 n. 2), but with the elder Smith's misunderstanding of the autograph. Instead of writing out the final ritornello Handel indicated with an incipit that bars 66–71 were to be repeated to close the air (hence the fermata on beat 3 of 71, which should be ignored in

    (*ii*) Air 'Author of peace' in an unpublished setting in G minor (quite different from the published G minor setting)

    (*iii*) Air 'Capricious man', C minor version[45]

    (*iv*) Air 'Impious wretch', 3/8 setting[46]

    (*v*) Accompanied recitative 'O Jonathan, thou wast slain in thy high places' and recitative 'Saul and Jonathan were lovely and pleasant in their lives'[47]

    (*vi*) Air 'Brave Jonathan his bow ne'er drew' in G major for soprano[48] – the first setting, leading directly into the chorus 'Eagles were not so swift as they' (which is also in the parts)

Presumably a score and vocal parts for these items were also prepared, but if so, they are lost. Comparison with the autograph indicates that items (*i*) and (*iii*) are late additions to the oratorio (i.e. added after the completion of the first draft but before the first performance), while (*iv*)–(*vi*) are discarded items from the first draft.

    This leaves (*ii*), the previously unknown setting of 'Author of peace'. It turns out that the music is by no means unknown: apart from a different text and consequential differences in the vocal line (included, as was customary, in the Cembalo part) it is the same as 'From this unhappy day', the third verse of the Elegy which, as previously noted, Handel cued into the autograph but did not write out.[49] (The vocal line is given complete in Ex. 4; this, taken with the orchestral accompaniment of 'From this unhappy day', allows the entire air to be reconstructed.) It will be observed that the words contain the reading '*my* tongue be fill'd', which I have already conjectured to be the text originally conceived by Jennens as an air for Jonathan. Unfortunately the air is not attributed to a character, and the voice part appears, as shown, in the treble clef, so we cannot immediately be certain that it was written for tenor rather than for the

---

    performance), but in copying the air into the conducting score Smith took this indication as a *dal segno* instruction. The repeat was cancelled by Handel in the conducting score with the note 'fine senza Da capo', as recorded in KB, p. 61; HHA nevertheless retains it.

[45]   Printed – unfortunately with several errors – in KB, pp. 149–53. The air is there shown with a full da capo, but both in the autograph and the Aylesford parts the voice re-enters with the syllable 'Cap-' in the final bar (bar 58) and the repeat is da capo *dal segno*, the sign being at the start of bar 12.

[46]   HG, pp. 284–6, and KB, pp. 175–7.

[47]   KB, p. 178.

[48]   Ibid., p. 179.

[49]   The description of the additional Cembalo part in KB, p. 10, mentions the presence of No. 64 in the edition (i.e. 'Author of peace' in its final version for Merab) without hinting that the music is quite different; the commentary on the air (ibid., p. 73) states that it appears in the Cembalo part 'in g-Moll' but again does not suggest that the music is anything other than the version printed. The other partbooks in this group were apparently not seen by the editor. No reference is made to the additional Cembalo part in the commentary on 'From this unhappy day' (ibid., pp. 80-1).

Ex. 4

Largo e piano

Au - thor of peace_____ who

canst con - troul ev' - ry pas - sion of the

Soul to whose good Spi - rit a - lone____ we

owe, a - lone we owe, words that sweet

as Ho - ney flow. With thy dear in - flu-ence

my tongue be fill'd, my tongue, my tongue be fill'd,

and cru - el wrath, and cru - el wrath to soft per -

- sua - - - - - - -

- - sion yield.

soprano voice used when it was transferred to the Elegy. (Soprano, alto and tenor parts, written by Handel in C clefs, are invariably transcribed in the treble clef in the Aylesford partbooks, though the C clefs are retained in the corresponding scores.) Confirmation that Ex. 4 was originally in the tenor clef can, however, be found in the Aylesford full score of Act 3. When transcribing the revised version of the air as 'From this unhappy day', S2 put a tenor clef in the empty voice part in the first system on the page (covering bars 1–4) and again in the second system (bars 5–9), though he noticed the error before copying the vocal entry in bar 9 and altered the clef in the second system to soprano, presumably picking up Handel's instruction for the change. (The rest of the vocal line has soprano clefs without alteration.) Thus there can be no doubt 'Author of peace' in the version of Ex. 4 is indeed the air for Jonathan which originally followed the recitative 'My father comes' in the lost section of Handel's draft of Act 2. Handel probably crossed out the original words and added the new ones *in situ*, making the appropriate adjustments to the vocal line. The original cadence of the recitative was probably in B♭, altered to the printed version in G minor when Handel replaced the air.

In his study of Handel's dramatic oratorios Winton Dean did much to demolish the image of Jennens as a pompous fool, placed beyond serious consideration as an author for having attempted to match Milton in *L'Allegro, il Penseroso ed il Moderato*, and as a critic for saying of *Messiah* that Handel 'had made a fine Entertainment of it, tho' not near so good as he might & ought to have done'.[50] Dean pointed out that Jennens's 'firm grasp of dramatic principles' is apparent throughout *Saul* and *Belshazzar* and that 'he understood the nature of Handel's genius a great deal better than his critics'.[51] Jennens's involvement in the creation of *Saul*, made visible in his amendments to Handel's score and in the score and parts copied for him while Handel was still composing the oratorio, amply justifies this view. Some of his suggestions were excellent, others were inconsequential, and a few were silly, but they never diminish the strengths of *Saul*. Every passage that Jennens sought to amend has a point of weakness; he was not always able to remove it but deserves no censure for that. His attention to his own literary lapses shows a degree of self-criticism that demands respect.

That Handel himself respected Jennens's views – which he was perfectly capable of accepting or rejecting as he thought fit – is shown not

50   Jennens's letter of 30 August 1745 to his friend Edward Holdsworth; see Deutsch, *Handel*, p. 622.
51   Dean, *Handel's Dramatic Oratorios*, p. 277.

only by his generosity in permitting Jennens to work over the autograph score of *Saul* but also by the fact that in 1744 Jennens was allowed the same liberty with the autograph of *Belshazzar*, the last work on which the two men collaborated. Examination of Jennens's few amendments in the latter manuscript does not, however, yield any significant new information; they concern only minor matters of verbal accentuation and underlay, and supply a few omitted stage directions. No sign of Jennens's hand appears in the autographs of *Messiah* and *L'Allegro*, but it seems to have been Jennens who made a couple of sensible adjustments to verbal underlay in the conducting score of *Messiah*, one in 'He shall feed his flock' and the other in 'If God be for us'.[52] The Aylesford score of *Messiah* bears more substantial amendments of verbal underlay in Jennens's hand, notably in 'I know that my Redeemer liveth',[53] and there are some minor ones in the two Aylesford scores of *L'Allegro*,[54] though to what extent these came to the composer's attention is not clear. Jennens's corrections of Handel's misaccentuation of the word 'Melancholy' in two places in *L'Allegro*[55] are certainly valid and are close to the readings adopted in modern editions.

At least one other Handel librettist was allowed access to the composer's autographs. The hand of Thomas Morell appears briefly in *Theodora*, making some verbal changes in the recitative 'Unhappy, happy crew' in Act 1, but here it appears that the librettist was responding to demands from the composer rather than the promptings of his own artistic conscience.[56] Morell's famous accounts of incidents during the composition of *Judas Maccabaeus* and *Alexander Balus* give the same impression.[57] The working relationship between Jennens and Handel thus seems to have been unique as far as English oratorio was concerned, though there may well have been parallels in the field of Italian opera. Certainly in the case of *Saul* it was a true collaboration, with each partner endeavouring to bring out the best in the other as the oratorio was pulled into shape during the

[52]   D. Burrows, 'The Autographs and Early Copies of "Messiah": Some Further Thoughts', *Music & Letters*, lxvi (1985), pp. 207–10. Burrows usefully discusses Jennens's possible influence on Handel's revisions of *Messiah*.

[53]   The score is in the Flower Collection at Manchester Central Library, MS 130 Hd4 v. 198–200. A facsimile of one of Jennens's amendments to 'I know that my Redeemer liveth' in this score is shown in J. Tobin, *Handel at Work* (London, 1964), p. 55, though Jennens's handwriting is not identified. A more general description of Jennens's annotations is given in W. Shaw, *A Textual and Historical Companion to Handel's 'Messiah'* (London, 1965), pp. 77–8.

[54]   One in Manchester Central Library (MS 130 Hd4 v. 189), the other in the Gerald Coke Handel Collection. Both scores have similar annotations by Jennens.

[55]   Handel placed the accent on the second syllable.

[56]   Handel seems to have refused to set the last three words of the phrase 'A Roman soldier led her to the Stews', not unreasonably. Morell replaced them by 'trembling hence' and made some other adjustments and additions.

[57]   See Deutsch, *Handel*, pp. 851–2.

last months of 1738. In composing his fourth English oratorio Handel found himself working for the first time with a librettist who had a clear vision of what such a work should be, and who stretched his limited talents to the utmost in his attempt to help the composer realize that vision. The consequences, both for *Saul* itself and for what was to follow, were magnificent.

'L'art dramatico-musical': an essay

DAVID CHARLTON

INTRODUCTION

The phrase 'L'art dramatico-musical' was used by Grétry in his self-anatomizing *Mémoires*, possibly in 1794.[1] Out of curiosity regarding what was meant (and implied) by it, I discuss in this paper the critical assumptions behind, and practice of, *opéra-comique* in its phase from 1759. I have been concerned to establish what librettists did and thought as much as what composers saw as their part of the musico-dramatic process. Limitations of space have obliged me to concentrate on two librettists, but they were the most important ones: Jean-François Marmontel (1723–99) and Michel-Jean Sedaine (1719–97).

There was no overriding consensus at the time in Paris about the path *opéra-comique* should tread. In effect, it was Grétry's art that was to prove the major synthesizing force in the genre up to the Revolution, partly by virtue of his musical superiority but partly because he relied on a strongly founded young tradition nurtured by many hands: the writers Charles-Simon Favart (1710–92), Antoine-François Quétant (1733–1823) and Antoine-Alexandre-Henri Poinsinet (1735–69) together with their musical collaborators Egidio Duni (1708–75), François-André Danican Philidor (1726–95) and Pierre-Alexandre Monsigny (1729–1817). It is probably not yet possible to discover all the assumptions made by makers of *opéra-comique*, particularly in this period of activity and change. Indeed, before 3 February 1762 such works might be seen in contrasting environments either at the Comédie-Italienne, the king's official comic troupe, or the

---

[1] A.-E.-M. Grétry, *Mémoires ou Essais sur la musique* (Paris, 1797), iii, Bk 6, chap. 9, p. 319. Although published early in 1797, the three-volume version was completed in August–September 1794: see *La Correspondance générale de Grétry*, ed. G. de Froidcourt (Brussels, 1962), pp. 166, 181. Vol. 1 had appeared alone in 1789 as *Mémoires ou Essai sur la musique*. Differences are listed in A. vander Linden, 'Réflexions bibliographiques sur les "Mémoires" de Grétry', *Revue belge de musicologie*, iii (1949), pp. 77–89.

private Opéra-Comique company, acting at one or other of the fairs, though within a solid structure.[2] A strong flavour of extempore practice was evident at both: semi-improvising Italian comedians were still employed at the Comédie-Italienne, and Sedaine reports that in 1759 *L'Huître et les plaideurs*, written for the close of the St-Laurent season, 'was written, words and music, learnt and acted in fourteen days'.[3] But *opéra-comique* came entirely under Crown influence in 1762, when the Italiens were ordered to absorb the best singers and repertory of the Opéra-Comique, which closed. In other words, it had attained a level of interest and bourgeois support sufficient to make even the Paris Opéra feel insecure and uncertain of its audience:

I: And you find beauty in these modern tunes? [i.e. by Duni etc.]
HE: Do I find beauty? Good Lord, you bet I do! How well it is suited to the words! what realism! what expressiveness! . . . The old wigs who have been going [to the Opéra] every Friday for the past thirty or forty years are getting bored . . . The reign of nature is quietly coming in.[4]

An anonymous observer likewise reported:

La bonne compagnie, qui ignoroit autrefois le langage trivial et grossier, est obligée de se transporter aujourd'hui, pour suivre le torrent qui l'entraîne, dans la boutique de Blaise le savetier [in Philidor's eponymous work], pour voir s'il a l'esprit, le jargon et le dégoûtant de son état.[5]

That is, *opéra-comique* had become a fashion in 'good company'; and once it was harnessed to the Comédie-Italienne it continued its inevitable transformation from 'low' towards 'high' culture. Sedaine explains certain effects lost in his *Le Jardinier et son seigneur* (1761), given originally at the St-Laurent fair:

Cet ouvrage eut sur le théâtre de la foire un succès qu'il n'a jamais eu et ne peut avoir sur le théâtre Italien [this is borne out statistically in its fifty-four performances

2   The St-Germain fair ran from 3 February until Palm Sunday, the St-Laurent fair usually from 9 August to the end of September. At the latter, works were seen in a fine small theatre decorated by Boucher: see J. G. Prod'homme and E. de Crauzat, *Les Menus Plaisirs du Roi, l'Ecole Royale et le Conservatoire de Musique* (Paris, 1929), p. 45. The Comédie-Italienne performed at the Hôtel de Bourgogne in rather cramped conditions that betrayed its sixteenth-century origins; in 1783 the company moved to a custom-built theatre.

3   'Quelques réflexions inédites de Sedaine sur l'opéra comique' (datable to early 1779 on internal evidence), in *Théâtre choisi de G. de Pixérécourt* (Paris and Nancy, 1841–3), iv, p. 505. This and subsequent translations are mine unless otherwise stated.

4   D. Diderot, *Rameau's Nephew*, trans. L. W. Tancock (Harmondsworth, 1966), pp. 97, 100–1.

5   'Mémoire pour le soutien des spectacles', Archives Nationales 0^1.851, f. 50, in E. Campardon, *Les Spectacles de la foire* (Paris, 1877), ii, p. 198; this document stressed the need to 'purify' public taste by amalgamating the Opéra-Comique and the Comédie-Italienne, and its position was the one borne out by events. See also G. Cucuel, 'Sources et documents pour servir à l'histoire de l'opéra-comique en France', *L'Année musicale*, iii (1913), p. 261.

between 1762 and 1771 and sixteen between 1772 and 1781]; la dignité des actrices ne
leur permettant pas de jouer comme il le faut les rôles des deux demoiselles qui y sont
en scène[6]

– the latter representing moral temptation in the shape of ladies-about-
town.

This point emphasizes not merely that the Comédie-Italienne enjoyed a
decorous tone but also an underlying factor of dramatic need: that of moral
purpose, a sense of moral relevance almost inversely proportional to the
generality of lyric tragedies then current at the Opéra. *Opéras-comiques*
reflected fashionable issues such as town life versus country life (Duni and
Favart's *Les Moissonneurs*, 1768) or sources such as English bourgeois
tragedy (Duni's *L'Ecole de la jeunesse*, 1765, after George Lillo's *The London
Merchant*) and the English novel (Philidor and Poinsinet's *Tom Jones*,
1765). The *Correspondance littéraire* accordingly approved the librettist
Louis Anseaume's ambitions in *L'Ecole de la jeunesse* in terms of a
heightening of, or a rise towards, 'true' dramatic experience: 'Il est l'auteur
du *Peintre amoureux de son modèle*, de *Mazet*, des *Deux chasseurs et la
laitière*, qui ont tous eu beaucoup de succès; mais ici il a pris un vol plus
haut, et il a voulu s'élever jusqu'à la véritable comédie.'[7]

The same review pointed to an aesthetic problem of the utmost
significance: there was no absolute merit in having just a libretto that a
Parisian of fashion could take somewhat seriously; there was a nebulous
yet imperative coincidence between a given tone or type of plot and the
tone or type of music proper to it. Duni's style of writing may, said
Friedrich Melchior Grimm, have suited Italian words, but it had become
dated, having grown out of the school of Vinci, Hasse and Pergolesi; it
lacked 'nerve' and vigour: 'Il est vrai que . . . son goût a un peu vieilli;
qu'il n'a pas ce nerf ni ce style vigoureux par lequel les compositeurs
modernes ont cherché à remplacer le génie des grands hommes que je viens
de nommer.'[8] The *Mercure de France* wondered whether this work were
better off without its music; and with the benefit of hindsight Pidansat de
Mairobert or his successor criticized the same score in 1779 for being in 'an
easy-going and gentle style hardly suited to the dark quality of this work'.[9]
If librettist–adapters like Anseaume, or Sedaine with *Le Roi et le fermier*
(1762, derived from Robert Dodsley's *The King and the Miller of Mansfield*),

6   'Quelques réflexions', p. 505. These and further performance statistics below have
     been compiled from the Registres de l'Opéra-Comique (Bibliothèque de l'Opéra).
7   *Correspondance littéraire, philosophique et critique de Grimm et de Diderot* (Paris, 1829–
     31), iv, p. 162 (1 February 1765).
8   Ibid. pp. 164–5. For an extract from Vinci, see p. 256, below.
9   *Mercure de France* (February 1765), pp. 195–6, and *Mémoires secrets* (12 October 1779)
     respectively, cited in K. M. Smith, *Egidio Duni and the Development of the 'Opéra-
     comique' from 1753 to 1770* (unpublished dissertation, Cornell University, 1980), p.
     262. But Smith finds, too, an 'unusual variety of musical material' in the score,
     especially at the close of Act 2.

made radical changes in material to suit French taste, their composers were seeking those styles – or even that Italian music – that they also could usefully import. It therefore proved difficult, in this period as in others, to achieve proper levels of aesthetic matching, and it was as likely that a work might fail because of its inadequate text though superior music as vice versa. This situation partly explains the success that would attend Grétry in Paris from 1768. And there could even be claimed a symbiosis between 'unhealthy' modern subjects and their music: a reactionary critic could argue in 1772 that it was now the attractiveness of musical scores that was supporting the toleration of 'monstrous' librettos. Bring back the old musico-dramatic values, he argued: 'Qu'on y rétablisse le vaudeville et la parodie qui l'occupoient . . . Ces Poëmes monstrueux se soutiennent à l'aide d'une Musique qui est au moins aussi révoltante.'[10] New musical and political values readily seemed subversive in those parts of the capital dominated by the Opéra and its power to command subvention, purloin, coerce and reward; to exert legal limitation on the work of other theatres; and to speak for the still-absolute hand of the monarchy.

At this point we must briefly address a related problem: the coexistence of speech (dialogue) and song in one work. Many argued against coexistence. Voltaire's view was noted by Chabanon, for example: 'If the music is fine, the ears of the audience revert painfully and with disgust from this harmony to simple recitation.'[11] Rousseau complained that 'the transition from speech to song and especially that from song to speech has an abruptness which the ear does not readily accept, and . . . destroys all the illusion . . .',[12] Chabanon, Goldoni (in 1762) and others felt the unpredictability of these transitions as a convention in itself,[13] something only justifiable on negative aesthetic grounds, for example superiority to 'boring recitative' (Goldoni) or popularity, variety or 'an operation of taste little susceptible to being reasoned out'.[14] The 'barbarous custom, in the new type of opéra-comique, of passing alternately from dialogue and declamation to song' and vice versa would 'hold up the progress of music in France for a long time'.[15] It probably did, in an indirect sense. But that

10   [V. de La Jonchère], 'Essai sur l'Opéra', in Théâtre lyrique (Paris, 1772), i, pp. 170–1.
11   M. P. G. de Chabanon, De la musique considérée en elle-même (Paris, 1785), p. 287 n., citing Voltaire's preface to Corneille's La Toison d'or.
12   J.-J. Rousseau, Lettre sur la musique française (Paris, 1753), trans. in O. Strunk, Source Readings in Music History (London, 1952), p. 651.
13   Mémoires de M. Goldoni, ed. P. de Roux (Paris, 1965), p. 293: 'et puisqu'on doit dans l'opéra-comique se passer de règles et de vraisemblance, il vaut mieux entendre un dialogue bien récité, que souffrir la monotonie d'un récitatif ennuyeux'.
14   Chabanon, De la musique, pp. 337–9.
15   Correspondance littéraire, iv, p. 166 (1 February 1765). Cf. Chastellux's view that it was an 'inherent defect' 'only to be ameliorated by an increase in the interest or emotion [in the spoken dialogue] which seems of itself to call for a new and exaggerated [type of] expression': [F.-J. de Chastellux], Essai sur l'union de la poésie et de la musique (The Hague and Paris, 1765), p. 84.

was inseparable from the primitive hierarchical organization of French theatre; in fact, spoken dialogue was imposed at the Comédie-Italienne by the legal force of the successive leases it had to negotiate with the Opéra: 'pieces in one or more acts forming sustained works of music, such as [Antoine Dauvergne's] *Les Troqueurs* and others similar', were banned.[16]

Not everybody shrugged their shoulders in critical despair. Diderot, with eyes fixed strongly on the necessity of integrating acting in the drive towards a naturalistic theatre, first implies approval in *Le Neveu de Rameau*: 'The simple language and normal expression of emotion are all the more essential because our language is more monotonous and less highly stressed . . . ', and then states it in the essay 'Pantomime dramatique', where the 'three tints of the musician's palette' are spoken dialogue, recitative and aria (*chant d'expression*); 'it seems to me that those who wrote our first opéras-comiques, and those writing tragédie lyrique today, have prefigured this form', i.e. of Diderot's proposed new theatrical genre.[17] A major apologist of *opéra-comique*, Barnabé Farmian de Rosoy, considered that dialogue opera did better then recitative opera in expressing the details of tenderness, fear or pride and the gradations of hate or of jealousy, and in comprising a multiplicity of incident which benefited both character depiction and plot.[18] Many Frenchmen would have agreed with this, simply because their taste so strongly valued propriety in drama, and verisimilitude in action and character. What neither Farmian de Rosoy nor his contemporaries argue, oddly enough, is that the loss of speech in *opéra-comique* would often mean the loss of rhymed poetry; in fact, with such capable poets as Favart and Marmontel verse provided an intrinsic heightening of tone which most valuably smoothed the transitions into music.

Farmian de Rosoy drew interesting conclusions from the speech–song alternation that can be mentioned only in passing here: 'Once it is agreed that it is no more singular to sing all the time than to interrupt oneself in order to sing, and speak after, one must decide whether the characters, situations, and variety of passions to be shown, do not of themselves dictate an intermediate genre between opera properly speaking, and *opéra-bouffon*.' Such a genre, he says, might be history, either of the human heart or of nations; fairy-tales; or ancient chivalry.[19] In the event none of these genres became the exclusive associate of *opéra-comique*.

What we do not read anywhere is the view that *opéra-comique* was to be construed as a play which happened to contain music. To begin with, the

[16]   See Cucuel, 'Sources et documents', p. 265, citing the lease of 1766.
[17]   *Rameau's Nephew*, trans. Tancock, p. 106; 'Pantomime dramatique, ou Essai sur un nouveau genre de Spectacle' (1769), *Oeuvres complètes*, ed. J. Assézat and M. Tourneux (Paris, 1875–7/R 1966), viii, pp. 459, 462.
[18]   *Dissertation sur le drame lyrique* (The Hague and Paris, 1775), pp. 11–13.
[19]   Ibid., p. 9.

range of invention was far too great, from *Blaise le savetier* at the musical end of the spectrum down to Favart's *Soliman II ou Les Trois Sultanes* at the spoken end. Critics do not prescribe ideal maxima or minima for any ratio of music to speech. Their criteria are instead integrative and empirical, centring on that difficult design problem of exactly where to site the music within the libretto; that is, they were interested by continuity and elementary musico-dramatic values.

En général, l'instant où le personnage peut s'arrêter quelque tems sur un sentiment qui le domine, est le plus convenable au développement d'un air: suspendre par un morceau de Musique complet, la situation qui demande à se précipiter vers sa conclusion, c'est substituer à contre-temps le repos au mouvement.[20]

Continuity and purpose as necessary to the music in all its respects was the idea developed by Grétry in the passage whence our opening phrase sprang. Here it is the orchestral ritornello that must perform a dramatic function or be excluded entirely. Elsewhere in his writing he describes, with examples, the almost note-by-note response of his music to its text, intended (as he said) to express 'the truth of moral details':

The ritornello is, in Italy, a returning musical phrase, an announcement of what the singer will perform, or a repetition of what he has uttered: it is a pause rather than a continuation of the speech. In France, where musico-dramatic art originated, the ritornello must have a dramatic character; it is excluded from the music whenever it is superfluous to the dramatic action; when it is included without necessary reason it is on the understanding that there is no urgent action, that the music is a concert and not the depiction of the feelings of the soul.[21]

It is no accident that Grétry repeatedly compared his art to that of Gluck; it was not through a misguided sense of his own achievements but because he saw that, with the help of his predecessors, he had prefigured the ideals and even the techniques observable in Gluck's Paris operas. This observation was widely accepted at the time.[22]

The establishment of such qualities in *opéra-comique* can best be discussed in two parts: first, collaboration in theory and practice, and dramaturgy; second, declamation and the design of texts.

COLLABORATION; DRAMATURGY

Aside from the undeniable greatness of Gluck's work from *Iphigénie en Aulide* to *Iphigénie en Tauride*, a further troubling concept acted as a

20   Chabanon, *De la musique*, p. 339.
21   *Mémoires*, iii, Bk 6, chap. 9, pp. 319f.
22   See, for example, the terms of the 1780 royal certificate granted to the Comédie-Italienne: 'It is works of this type that have formed taste in France, that have accustomed ears there to a more learned [sic] and expressive music and which finally have prepared for the revolution occurring even at our Academy of Music': *Les Spectacles de Paris . . . 1782* (Paris, n.d.), pp. 111–12.

background to the general development of *opéra-comique*. It effectively began in 1752 with Jean-Jacques Rousseau's *intermède Le Devin du village*, if not in 1757 with the French translation of Algarotti's *Saggio sopra l'opera in musica*, issued two years before: that if opera were to reach uncommon heights, as many acknowledged possible, it must attain unity, so 'it is therefore the poet's duty, as chief engineer of the undertaking, to give directions to the dancers, the machinists, the painters . . . The poet is to carry in his mind a comprehensive view of the *whole* of the drama.'[23] Within this model, the music was to act as a heightening, colouring or vivifying of the words. In 1772, however, the librettist of *Iphigénie en Aulide* (1774) advertised the work using a catch-phrase that was long to retain life: Gluck himself had 'become' the poet and, implicitly, usurped the unifying role – 'partout M. Gluck est Poëte et Musicien; partout on y reconnait l'homme de génie'.[24] Grétry himself was to accept such a concept. The librettists of *Orfeo* and *Alceste* were the true restorers of 'le drame lyrico-tragique', but one is tempted to believe that Gluck must have 'suggested the plan of which he made himself master'. 'Oui, l'on est poëte et musicien en opérant comme *Gluck*.'[25] This apparent necessary unity was of course later to inspire E. T. A. Hoffmann's eulogies of Gluck. The catch-phrase also prompted consideration of *Le Devin du village*, genuinely the product of one single human inspiration, in men's minds. So Sedaine, receiving his seat at the Académie Française in 1786, used this work to articulate the desire for the emergence of one highly and equally talented composer–poet, the super-Rousseau who was still awaited: 'L'auteur du Devin du Village, foible peut-être dans l'un et l'autre art, mais fort par leur réunion, nous a prouvé ce qu'ils peuvent lorsqu'un même génie les rassemble.'[26] Nothing, unfortunately, was then said about the precise kind of operatic work that such a being might create. At all events, the pursuit of unity presupposed intimate connections between poet and composer; but the presence of spoken dialogue was a unique obstacle preventing the *opéra-comique* composer from usurping the role of 'poet'. Music's sway held only so long as a librettist permitted music to sound.

We shall see later how one composer took the initiative and set to music words intended as spoken dialogue. But commoner presuppositions were represented by the ideas in a now little-known 'Essai sur l'opéra-comique'

23   Francesco Algarotti, *Saggio sopra l'opera in musica* (Bologna, 1755), trans. (1768) in Strunk, *Source Readings*, pp. 657–8.

24   F. L. Du Roullet, 'Lettre à M. D. un des Directeurs de l'Opéra de Paris' (originally published in *Mercure de France*), in [G. M. Leblond], *Mémoires pour servir à l'histoire de la révolution opérée dans la musique par M. le Chevalier Gluck* (Naples and Paris, 1781), p. 5.

25   *Mémoires*, i, pp. 345–6.

26   'Discours prononcé le 27 avril 1786 par M. Sédaine', in *Choix de discours de réception à l'Académie françoise* (Paris, 1808), ii, p. 341.

of 1765 by Quétant. Influenced by emergent values which granted that the musical side was now liable to be the more memorable,[27] it still gives the impression that only the hardships of the librettist are worth discussing, let alone liberating or even experimental aspects, such as mime. Quétant wrote texts for Philidor (*Le Maréchal ferrant*, 1761), Gossec (*Le Tonnelier*, 1765) and Josef Kohaut (*Le Serrurier*, 1764). Of these, *Le Tonnelier* had the most lasting success.[28]

The dialogue should be concise, agreeable, natural and without affectation or conceits. Gibes, placed with judgement and skilfully managed, have a good effect. Ever since the establishment of [composed] music, we no longer have the comic resource that the vaudevilles furnished. The ariettes [i.e. arias: see p. 252] have taken their place, and it is no easy matter to make them attractive and lively; it would be equally difficult to give definite rules for a method of using them and writing them; taste is the best master one may consult. However, one can observe that, in general, ariettes should only be situated in places where the stage scene is calm, or in monologues; for it is ridiculous that a character who has his own interests to sort out, or feelings to express, should stop uniquely to listen to music, and I cannot conceive how authors have been found so rash as to risk such a blunder, and audiences so patient as to tolerate them and get accustomed to them.

Since one has so few resources on the side of speech, one must throw quite a lively interest into the work in order to create room for tender feelings and amusing or pathetic situations; that depends upon the constitution of the subject.

One is advised in [spoken] comedy to spin out the scenes well. Quite the reverse happens in opéra-comique. The scenes should merely be outlined, one rapidly giving rise to the next, and proceed hurriedly; even a little disorder and carelessness can often make them more piquant and agreeable. The scenes should be varied as much as possible, and mixed, so that a happy one follows a tender conversation [or] a ridiculous detail follows a graceful situation, and so on. Passions operate more in opéra-comique than in comedy; but they should be much less detailed. They should be expressed in the commonest, liveliest phrases, avoiding paraphrase and poetic circumlocution . . . besides, music requires vigour, clarity and precision, and it is usually the melody which should paint the affections of the soul in the new type of opéra-comique . . .

The arrangement of the subject needs work and theatrical knowledge . . . [although] in these sorts of work, long study disgusts or makes one too serious; in this genre particularly, the art consists in concealing such things.[29]

Quétant's appreciation here of music's requirements is at one with his earlier observation that 'characters ought to be made known more by their

---

27   Cf. the oft-quoted extract from a review of *Le Jardinier et son seigneur*: 'La musique, qui est devenue la partie intéressante d'un opéra-comique, est de M. Philidor . . . il a rendu dans cette pièce des images que l'on n'avait pas encore osé risquer en musique': *Mercure de France* (March 1761), p. 198, cited from L. P. Arnoldson, *Sedaine et les musiciens de son temps* (Paris, 1934), p. 89 n.

28   See Charlton, *Grétry and the Growth of Opéra-comique* (Cambridge, 1986), chaps. 7, 26. Both *Le Tonnelier* and *Le Maréchal ferrant* held the stage until the Revolution.

29   A.-F. Quétant, 'Essai sur l'opéra-comique', in *Le Serrurier* (Paris, 1765), pp. 43–7.

actions than by their speeches'.[30] Yet there is no word about moulding a text to suit action in music or even expression in ensembles; and Quétant's remarks admit no room for his composer's own dramatic ideas. The whole aesthetic is dominated less by unity than diversity. This position would not have been unpopular, for assumptions that the genre must be 'light', impermanent and unpretentious were justified by tradition. Even in 1785 Chabanon, generalizing, decided that the genre was essentially a mixed collection of elements whose expression was 'only partial and of the moment'.[31] Moreover, in *opéra-comique* as in *tragédie-lyrique* the libretto was something to be assessed separately. In the hands of a Favart, literary interest could mean that to him and certain others there was a fear 'that the originality of music would harm their personal success'.[32]

Quite how different was the approach of, say, Marmontel is indeed striking. He was Grétry's first important librettist, furnishing him with six *opéra-comique* texts; none of the resulting works (1768–75) was a failure. Marmontel's unsuccessful first public *opéra-comique, La Bergère des alpes*, set by Kohaut, did not emerge until 1766; but earlier operatic collaboration with Rameau, Dauvergne and Jean-Benjamin de La Borde[33] was presumably reflected in this sensitive account published in 1763:[34]

So that understanding be more perfect, one will readily perceive that it is to be hoped that the poet himself be a musician. But if he does not unite the two talents, at least he should possess that of sensing the effects of music; of imagining which route it would like to follow, were it left to its own devices; at which moments it would quicken or hold back its movement; which syllabic structure[35] and inflexions it would use to express this feeling or that image; which inner emotion would provide it with the most beautiful modulation; which circle it may describe in the area of this or that mode; and at what moment it should change mode. This all demands a trained ear and, further, an intimate exchange, a habitual communication between poet and musician.

The almost sexual imagery of 'un commerce intime, une communication habituelle' is not unique in such contexts. It is echoed in 1771 by Diderot: 'le poète est fait pour le musicien; et . . . si le poète tire à lui toute la couverture, ils passeront tous les deux une mauvaise nuit'.[36] And Grétry, citing a friend, wrote to Beaumarchais in 1791: 'You are husband and wife

---

30   Ibid., p. 44.
31   *De la musique*, p. 340.
32   G. E. Bonnet, *Philidor et l'évolution de la musique française au XVIIIe siècle* (Paris, 1921), p. 94.
33   Four librettos for Rameau, 1751–3; *Hercule mourant*, a tragedy (1761), for Dauvergne, unperformed; *Annette et Lubin* for La Borde (1762), performed privately. See J. Rushton, 'Marmontel, Jean François', *The New Grove*, xi, p. 694.
34   *Poétique françoise* (Paris, 1763), ii, p. 352: article 'Opéra'.
35   Ibid., i, p. 261.
36   'Lettre au sujet des observations du chevalier de Chastellux sur le traité du mélodrame', *Oeuvres complètes*, viii, pp. 509–10.

when you join together in writing a work; you [i.e. Grétry] have helped show off the words just as the poet has led you to make fine music by preparing the place where one is to sing.'[37] Sedaine, in *Le Roi et le fermier* — set by Monsigny in 1762 — 'achieved what I had believed impossible: raising the tone of this genre, even placing a king on stage in a three-act work that occupied as long in the theatre as a five-act play at the Théâtre Français'.[38] Under its impact a contemporary critic enthused thus:

Where can one find a musician, a great artist who might dare to risk such a new genre in music? That is what M. de Monsigny has undertaken, and virtually uncontested success has rewarded these two friends. They have made known to their colleagues with what [sense of] union poets and musicians must go to each other's aid if they wish to obtain the approbation of connoisseurs and the multitude.[39]

These, then, were the newer strains of thought; Quétant's, typical of the older, may never have produced a work of 'musico-dramatic art' in Grétry's sense, but the values he represented never died out.

Grétry had the quiet stubbornness – and the sense of publicity – that he needed to realize what seems to have been a genuine vision of the potential of the genre. The basic trust implicitly required between partners had never to be compromised: when Marmontel (already famous and an Academician) became too patronizing towards him, so that even his servant referred to Grétry as 'Monsieur's musician', Grétry retorted by requesting the servant to 'go and say to my poet that I thank him for the changes he sends me'.[40]

The writings of both men are exceptionally illuminating about the practice of partnership. (Ironically, this is because Marmontel misrepresented Grétry's attitude to it in his posthumous *Mémoires*; Grétry made a detailed self-defence in his posthumous *Réflexions d'un solitaire*.) Although Marmontel 'was greatly occupied with the musical part' of a collaborative work,[41] it appears that he was not musically literate and was prone not to notice differences in a setting once it had been improved or elaborated.[42] Such a degree of musical myopia was, incidentally, not characteristic of other friends and advisers of Grétry, including D'Alembert, Jean-Baptiste Suard and François Arnaud. Marmontel would read sketches for a libretto to Grétry, obviously before the text had got to

37   *La Correspondance générale de Grétry*, pp. 158–9.
38   Sedaine, 'Quelques réflexions', p. 507.
39   [A. G.] Contant d'Orville, *Histoire de l'opéra bouffon* (Amsterdam and Paris, 1768), cited in A. Pougin, *Monsigny et son temps* (Paris, 1908), p. 92.
40   Grétry, *Réflexions d'un solitaire*, ed. L. Solvay and E. Closson (Brussels and Paris, 1919–24), ii, chap. 29, p. 98.
41   Ibid., iii, chap. 17, p. 97.
42   Ibid., ii, chap. 29, p. 101. All subsequent quotations in this context are taken from this chapter, entitled 'Appendice à mes Mémoires ou Essais sur la Musique'.

the 'official' stage of being read at (later, on behalf of) the general assembly of
the Comédie-Italienne for approval. Grétry's adverse reactions alerted the
poet to the need for changes: ' . . . avec quelle défiance hautaine il me lisoit
ses premières esquisses des pièces auxquelles je devois participer! Un de
ses yeux ne quittoit point ma physionomie; quand il me voyait inquiet,
souffrant: "C'est bon, c'est bon, disait-il, je sais ce qu'il faut changer." ' At
a more finished stage, but still before submission to the theatre, Grétry
would sometimes begin setting a text; the force of enthusiasm was enough,
without the necessary preliminary practical, let alone financial, backing.
In this way he set, to no immediate purpose, eight items for Marmontel's *Le
Connaisseur* and two whole acts of music for his *Les Statues*, both (*inter
alia*) turned down at the theatre. Either at this stage or a somewhat later one
the progress of a work would be influenced by various trials and opinions.
If Grétry was won over, perhaps inspired by Marmontel's language ('Son
style aimable m'entraînoit donc'), this did not prevent his requesting
literary changes; for example, in *Sylvain* Marmontel substituted shorter
lines ('Je tremble, j'espère / Qu'un juge, qu'un père . . .') for longer ones in
the duet 'Dans le sein d'un père' and acknowledged Grétry's correct
judgement. Furthermore, invention of music was not confined to the
study: the composer was asked to improvise settings for the poet before
working them out fully. Here, perhaps, the team most obviously
approached unity of creation: 'Pressé par lui, combien de fois ne lui ai-je
pas chanté et improvisé des morceaux de longue haleine, dont je ne m'étois
nullement occupé! J'y travaillois ensuite . . . ' Yet other sessions, whose
outcome determined musico-dramatic policy, took place in the presence of
third parties, such as Grétry's Swedish patron and friend Gustave-
Philippe de Creutz. The complete draft text of *Zémire et Azor* was read in
such circumstances. At the end of Act 3, Azor was to show Zémire her
family in Persia by supernatural means, but only in the audience's
imagination. Grétry and Creutz thought this would not work dramatically,
so Creutz suggested a 'magic picture' and Grétry the trio to be sung within
it by Zémire's father and sisters. This solution made the opera famous.

More extensive disclosures about *La Fausse Magie* (1775), the last, slow-
ripening *opéra-comique* of the collaboration between Marmontel and
Grétry, were recorded later: the first-act trio was converted from a solo; a
too obvious explanatory couplet was rejected; and Grétry made up a kind
of finale by purloining spoken dialogue which otherwise would have made
a cold conclusion to Act 1:

Enfin, le finale du premier acte n'étoit pas préparé pour la musique. Marmontel rit aux
éclats quand il m'entendit chanter le dialogue qui devoit être parlé. – 'Vous verrez, lui
dis-je, ce que les Italiens appellent un finale, il ne me faut que quelques vers de
remplissage pour les ensembles.'

It is symptomatic that by 1773, in his first collaboration with Sedaine (*Le Magnifique*), Grétry had already made important advances in adapting Italian finale styles to *opéra-comique*, which presumably gave him the confidence to take such an initiative with Marmontel.[43] The latter remained a formalist and became an anti-Gluckist. One can hear him scolding Sedaine together with Grétry as he penned part of an article on the aria during the early 1770s:

The one thing you [a composer] must not do is to say [to a poet] 'Write what you will: metre, rhythm, phrasing, concise or periodic style, all are the same to me; I shall always find the means of writing melody.' Yes, broken, mutilated, formless and inconsequential melody which will attempt to be expressive but which, being quite unmelodious, shall have neither the truth of nature not the attractiveness of art.[44]

In spite of their temperamental differences Grétry and Marmontel went a long way towards bridging the divided lands of music and drama. Poet tried to be musician; musician actively helped librettist. Karin Pendle observes that 'musician and poet matured together' in range and ambition.[45] The case they made for such reciprocal attitudes, and the care they evinced, are as undeniable as the success their work enjoyed.

Marmontel had been elected to the Académie Française in 1763 and become Perpetual Secretary in 1783. Given his presence there it seems appropriate that the official reply made to Sedaine on the latter's election three years later should have formulated not a divisive but an inclusive definition of modern collaboration in *opéra-comique*. The speaker, Sedaine's friend the playwright Antoine-Marin Lemierre, at first adopted a slightly disparaging simile: almost like a bauble, an impermanent piece of luminescence, an *opéra-comique* was likened to a coloured slide whose music was analogous to a light-source.[46] But, by the same token, the work of art was a joint production in which music had to be allowed parity of status: 'The two authors work together in order to excite the same sensations; they show each other off to advantage; they are the twin causes of a single effect; and these two movers of our pleasures hold us under a single charm, dividing the laurels between them.'[47]

---

43   The end of the collaboration is described in K. Pendle, 'The Opéras Comiques of Grétry and Marmontel', *The Musical Quarterly*, lxii (1976), pp. 433–4. But Grétry's own explanation is omitted: that refusals of Marmontel librettos by the Comédie-Italienne simply led to a shortage of available texts. See Grétry, *Réflexions*, ii, chap. 29, p. 104.

44   'Air', *Supplément à l'Encyclopédie ou Dictionnaire raisonné des sciences, des arts et des métiers* (Amsterdam, 1776), i, p. 238. Cf. his letter to Voltaire of 27 December 1771: 'This year I shall work on the Supplement of the Encyclopédie.'

45   'The Opéras Comiques', p. 427.

46   ' . . . des canevas remplis par la musique, et qui, hors de la scène, perdent tout leur éclat, comme des transparens dont on a retiré la lumière': 'Réponse de M. Le Mierre au discours de M. Sedaine', in *Choix de discours de réception*, ii, p. 357.

47   Ibid., p. 357.

I turn now to dramaturgy, taking a chronological approach. By this means I hope to expose some essentially operatic problems and their solutions in *opéra-comique* in the fifteen or so years from 1759.[48]

Sedaine, initially an unwilling dramatic author, lost no time in creating his own 'reforms' in *opéra-comique*. They were seen in *Blaise le savetier* (1759), a one-act farce, in particular; all Sedaine's pieces of 1759–61 (which he was persuaded to write by Jean Monnet) are 'full of life and spontaneity [and] had shown him to possess admirable dramatic sense, but they were written in a hasty, unpolished style'; yet this style intentionally depended on music for success.[49] The printed libretto of *Blaise le savetier* reveals much of interest, quite apart from the fact that Sedaine's preface to it (as well as his 'Réflexions') lauded Philidor's music. This 'avertissement' pinpointed failings in the then current musico-dramatic situation as he saw it: arias were not being conceived in terms that comprised stage action, through the fault either of the librettist or the musician, the latter not always providing 'true gestures [or actions] and feelings'. Sedaine's words are as follows:

Si quelqu'un me reproche l'attention avec laquelle j'ai écrit la Pantomime de cette farce, qu'il fasse réflexion que le grand défaut de la plûpart des Ariettes au théâtre, est de se voir dénuées d'action, soit que ce défaut vienne des paroles et de la situation théâtrale, soit que l'Auteur seulement musicien, ne sçache point les revêtir des gestes et du sentiment vrais.[50]

His idea was, on the contrary, to synthesize word, melody, musical 'gesture' and, not least, actions: 'Cependant, si quelque chose m'excitait, ce serait le plaisir d'essayer de mettre toute une scène en musique, scène qui serait composée de plusieurs interlocuteurs mis en actions.'[51] For the convenience particularly of those actors outside Paris, Sedaine printed acting instructions (quoted in part below). There is no doubt that *Blaise le savetier* achieved its aims and that Philidor seconded Sedaine's intentions completely. The amount of spoken dialogue between numbers is often very small, and the length of the seven solos and seven duets or ensembles

---

48 The standard bibliographical citation is C. E. Koch, Jr, 'The Dramatic Ensemble Finale in the Opéra Comique of the Eighteenth Century', *Acta musicologica*, xxxix (1967), pp. 72–83. But, as Smith has noted, this article 'deals only with finales to acts, which are often vaudevilles or simple choruses. It gives a poor idea of the importance of ensembles to an opera as a whole. This is especially true of Philidor, for whom Koch lists only two dramatic ensembles': *Egidio Duni*, p. 157 n. 7.

49 M. A. Rayner, *The Social and Literary Aspects of Sedaine's Dramatic Work* (unpublished dissertation, University of London, 1960), pp. 73ff.

50 'Avertissement de l'auteur', *Blaise le savetier* (Paris, 1759), p. [3].

51 'Quelques réflexions', p. 504, in the context of Monnet's initial efforts at persuading Sedaine to write for him.

as set to music can be considerable, not least by comparison with the restricted quantity of words provided.[52]

There are three interesting things about Sedaine's footnoted acting instructions. Firstly, they demand participation from both or all the actors on stage during the music; secondly, even in a solo an actor who is not required to sing may well be required to steal general attention by virtue of his mime; and thirdly, repeated sections of music (typically in an ABA aria form) are disguised or the effect of their repetition minimized by means of variety designated in the acting instructions. A concise illustration of this is Scene 5 No. 7. Blaise, penniless, is hidden in a cupboard; the old landlord Pince is entering preparatory to an attempt to evict him and his wife Blaisine; Blaisine sings an aria soliciting Pince's sympathy by claiming that Blaise maltreats her. Sedaine's instructions demand that, when the aria starts, Pince pay no special attention but continue compiling an inventory; and that Blaisine should create variety at the musical reprise by sitting down and putting one elbow on the cobbler's workbench, the better to view surreptitiously Pince's reaction to her. Realism, dramatic continuity, mobility, unity – all are assumed to be essential.

Pince: Il fait avec un crayon, une petite note des meubles: il examine l'armoire, et ne paroit faire qu'une médiocre attention au commencement de l'Ariette.

Blaisine: A la reprise de cette Ariette, Blaisine pour varier son jeu, peut s'asseoir sur l'escabeau, un coude sur l'établi, regarder pardessous son bras si M. Pince l'écoute.

To indicate that he was not interested in writing a 'play mixed with [Italianate] arias' (comédie mêlée d'ariettes: the frequent generic designation), Sedaine called this libretto 'Opéra-Comique'. He called Le Jardinier et son seigneur (1761), which also contains acting instructions, 'Opéra Comique . . . mêlé de morceaux de Musique'; Le Roi et le fermier (1762) 'Comédie . . . mêlée de morceaux de musique'; and Le Déserteur (1769), also composed by Monsigny, 'Drame . . . mêlé de musique'.[53] Philidor's collaboration with Sedaine ended when he gave back the text of Le Roi et le fermier, saying that it was 'impracticable' (infaisable),[54] a judgement that helps to explain the fulsome recognition in its eventual preface of

[52]   Blaise le savetier had 92 performances in the decade 1762–71, 25 in 1772–81 and 13 in 1782–5.

[53]   This kind of nicety deserves respect (cf. also n. 58, below). An interesting dissertation deals at length with material contiguous to mine: J. B. Kopp, The 'Drame lyrique': a Study in the Esthetics of Opéra-comique, 1762–1791 (unpublished dissertation, University of Pennsylvania, 1982). This is quite a wide survey, yet its use of theoretical evidence tends to overbalance its dramatic assessments of stage works. As a result, the term drame lyrique is too generously applied as a label. Kopp's many references to Nougaret's De l'art du théâtre (Paris, 1769) should be read alongside the valuable musical chapters in M. Hobson, The Object of Art (Cambridge, 1984), where Nougaret is interpreted as an ironist.

[54]   Sedaine, 'Quelques réflexions', p. 507. Sedaine added: 'Il y a tout lieu de croire que quelqu'un l'avait dissuadé de le mettre en musique.'

Monsigny – the musician and friend who had the confidence to risk failure in pursuit of a new ideal ('un ami qui voulût bien risquer un genre nouveau en musique').

Le Roi et le fermier and *Le Déserteur*, bestriding the 1760s in time, popularity and stature, were however preceded, in 1761, by *On ne s'avise jamais de tout*, a one-act comedy set by Monsigny and containing a pair of young lovers (who become free to marry) as well as strong elements of farce. This work achieved a definite ebb and flow of dramatic tension which was articulated by the placing of its music, comprising no fewer than seventeen vocal numbers. That is, the spoken word is more prominent during the exposition of the play; the various solo arias and a duet are drawn into much closer proximity at the heart of the work, giving expression to the personalities of the lovers in particular; and the main action is placed near the end, where it is made effective in two ensembles: the duet/quartet 'Ouvrez s'il vous plaît', where the old tutor and the duenna hammer on the lovers' door, embarrassingly watched and joined in music by a fishwife and a street-porter while yet other characters are attracted on to the stage; and the climactic quintet 'La voilà', where the lovers, the tutor, the duenna and the police commissioner work out their various reactions to the tutor's defeat by young Dorival. The comedy – which eschews precomposed vaudevilles – engages us more through situation, movement and music than through either the spoken word (taking the entertainment as a whole) or character. As it proceeds, and the linking dialogue tends to decrease, the spectator becomes attuned, during speech, to expect a new and contrasting piece of music of some sort rather than the development of that dialogue. It is interesting that just as in this, Sedaine's last purely comic text for music, the score comes to predominate, so also much later, in his last serious librettos, the same principle would be asserted, though organized by totally different internal means (*Richard Coeur-de-lion*, *Raoul Barbe-bleue*, *Guillaume Tell*).

With further advances there was a broadening of subject-matter in the way noted earlier, so that *Le Roi et le fermier* 'quickly became the model for a series of sentimental, moralizing opéras-comiques tinged with social satire'.[55] New musico-dramatic means appeared. While Act 3 presented the least original disposition of dialogue and aria, an ambitious royal hunt and storm was conceived in order to exploit both stage continuity and contrast of dramatic levels in the transition from Act 1 to Act 2. Here is Sedaine's continued joy in the naturalness that simultaneity afforded. The climax of Act 2 is a quartet, provided with a fugued opening. The innocent picture of Jenny, Betsy and their mother that opens Act 3 turned out to need the sophisticated juxtaposition and recombination of three different

[55]   Smith, *Egidio Duni*, p. 254.

songs, 'required' by their independent activities. Everything could not, of course, be achieved by ingenious scene-painting or other formal operations. Sedaine's gift for creating 'living' characters was inimitable in the 1760s. The ultimate seal of the partnership lay in Monsigny's ability to write arias whose music is not felt to mask or dominate one's perception of those characters as established in speech. Musical development is limited, and its style and tone are appropriate; there was thus a very satisfactory matching of aesthetic levels, to which public approbation unhesitatingly bore witness.[56]

To compensate for lack of correspondence showing something of these reforms in the making, I quote Grétry's recollections:

Sedaine, who had the most dramatic consciousness, was hardly a musician at all, sacrificing nothing to music; that is why his pieces have unity . . . Sedaine's replies to objections made to him at rehearsals were remarkable. 'Your ritornello is too long', he said to his composer (and, thank God, it was not me). 'I cannot make it shorter.' 'If anything kills me, it'll be a ritornello', said Sedaine, going out.
– 'You must cut half this scene', say the actors.
– 'Speak it more slowly, it will appear the shorter.'[57]

Sedaine's beliefs were sketched haphazardly in various of his prefaces. That to *Rose et Colas* (1764) described in particular the musico-dramatic precision and the simultaneous depiction of emotions proper to a new musical drama;[58] that to *Le Déserteur* picked on the very fact that he had wanted musical as well as dramatic solutions to be found for the crucial junctures of his work: 'Une de celles [critiques] qui m'ont été reprochées dans la Pièce du Déserteur, est d'avoir placé des morceaux de musique dans les instans où l'intérêt a de la chaleur, et ils l'éteignent: je ne l'ai pas fait sans y avoir réfléchi.'[59] In a sense, Sedaine was liberated as a dramatist by the apparent limitation of not being able to write music; when the latter flowed, his characters could take on mimetic life that would have seemed too ridiculous in a spoken play. Alternatively, music was used to dignify lower-class characters and their situations without the aesthetic effect of polished spoken verse forms that were even more seemingly unnatural to their station (French drama being dominated by figures from the leisured classes) and beyond his power to command.

Critics found it hard to discuss Sedaine's achievements because his

---

[56]   *Le Roi et le fermier* secured 206 performances in the decade 1763–72, the same authors' *Rose et Colas* 182 in 1764–73, Anseaume and Duni's *Les Deux Chasseurs et la laitière* 177 in 1763–72, *Tom Jones,* by Poinsinet (revised Sedaine) and Philidor, 149 in 1766–75 and the same authors' *Le Sorcier* 120 in 1764–73.

[57]   *Réflexions*, iii, chap. 17, p. 97.

[58]   Reprinted in Pougin, *Monsigny et son temps*, pp. 93–4. Sedaine here explicitly rejects the phrase 'pièces à ariettes'.

[59]   *Le Déserteur* (Paris, 1770), p. vii.

literary style when intended for musical setting was so unorthodox, and because the correct vocabulary for describing what they experienced was lacking. Perhaps his most familiar supporter to us today was Grimm (also, incidentally, one of the many anti-Marmontellians). For example, under the widely felt impact of *On ne s'avise jamais de tout* he found Sedaine 'the only poet who in sixty years recalls Molière's comedies', and continued:

It is a pity that M. Sedaine has not slightly more facility in his style. Often he is stiff and uneven. His verses above all are written to harm the ear when read. That all disappears in the theatre through the magic of acting and music . . . one cannot conceive of these pieces by reading them, and M. Sedaine is a man by whom I set infinite store.[60]

And he compared him favourably with Favart: 'M. Favart does not suspect any more than the public that the workings [*la marche*] of opéra-comique are quite different from those of a play. It is Sedaine who knows that secret, and that one does not march cavalry in the same way as infantry.'[61] One person, in this period, attempted to unite the roles of composer and librettist: Nicolas Etienne Framery (1745–1810) in the *opéra-comique La Sorcière par hazard* (shown privately in 1768 and at the Comédie-Italienne in 1783). It was condemned on the grounds of insufficient originality, its music apparently being too heterogeneous as well as ill-suited to the drama.[62]

Philidor's later 1760s works provide a fascinating contrast to Monsigny's. In *Le Sorcier* (1764) the librettist Poinsinet

adopts some of the features of continuity which had worked so well in Monsigny's *Le Roi et le fermier*. The first scene, for example, begins with two instrumental ideas, in G minor and G major respectively, which serve simultaneously as the second and third movements of the overture and as anticipations of the two themes of the first *ariette*.[63]

But it is an aria (which becomes a duet) that is far from dramatically straightforward: it resembles a musical scene-complex that throws us into action and a relationship. The idea of simultaneity is ingeniously exploited as Agathe's undesired fiancé Blaise comes in unnoticed and sings his own words against those of her third strophe. In this way, with music as the means, the true face of each character is revealed before his/her interaction shows us a different side. Later, in Act 2 scene 7, Julien's accompanied recitative 'Noirs habitants' is joined to a free-form duet, with Bastien,

60   *Correspondance littéraire* (December 1761), quoted in French in Smith, *Egidio Duni*, 182.

61   *Correspondance littéraire*, vi, p. 245 (1 October 1769), attacking Favart for making a former play into a libretto, *L'Amant déguisé*, for Philidor by 'stitching into all its scenes words intended for arias'.

62   *Correspondance littéraire*, ed. M. Tourneux (Paris, 1877–82), xiii, pp. 360–1 (September 1783).

63   Smith, *Egidio Duni*, pp. 258–9. Poinsinet includes many acting directions.

carrying forward the action significantly, as do other ensembles. Nevertheless, in the overall context these 'modern' and effective designs are less satisfactory than the apparently static ones of *On ne s'avise jamais de tout*. For works like *Le Sorcier* contain an amalgam of stylistically mixed and formally varied numbers whose dramatic placing has an arbitrary, bumpy feel and in which sophisticated Italianate pieces imply but do not receive sophistication of dramatic content.

Similar characteristics affected *L'Ecole de la jeunesse*: Anseaume 'undermined the unconventional, serious plot with conventional, predictable *ariettes*', while Duni too often 'responded with overblown, Italianate numbers', [64] even though Sedaine-like technical advances in continuity were deployed in the Act 2 septet and in the climactic scene in Act 3, including an accompanied recitative, arioso and aria. More successful was Philidor's *Tom Jones* (Sedaine had to rework Poinsinet's libretto), which rejected formal musical complexes yet created a notable climax in the second-act septet. And the suavity of much of the score forms an apt analogue to the gentility of the social world portrayed.

It is worth briefly considering duets as such, almost as an indicator of basic belief in the ensemble as a modern resource, promoting musico-dramatic realism. We saw above the prophetic opening scene of *Le Sorcier*. In Act 2 of that work there are equally curious duets – Nos. 13, 'Mais buvons', and 15, 'Que vois-je?' – whose eccentricities are brought about when the protagonist, Julien, is disguised and expressing two levels of emotion, while the other character expresses a yet further one. In *Tom Jones* Sophie has four duets: with Honora, her own mother, her father and her lover. Only the last-mentioned conforms to the orthodoxy of the 'dialogue duet' described below. The others express stubborn disagreement in music and drama; on a primary level this is perceived through the opposition of musical motifs (see Ex. 1). Years later a critic made Ex. 1a something of a *locus classicus*: 'When in a duet characters are in different situations, they should not be made to sing to the same motif; the opposition of their music can even produce a piquant effect, as in the so happily contrasted duet in *Tom Jones*, "Que les devoirs".'[65] The *Tom Jones* duets, however, expressed fixed differences. It was in this sort of light that the *Mercure de France* wrote in June 1772 (p. 173): 'Music cannot and should not convey a long conversation. It excels at seizing and conveying a rapid moment where the passions of the interlocutors form a contrast and a tableau.'

Readers of the *Supplément à l'Encyclopédie* (1776) were faced with a confusing pair of entries. Marmontel's 'Duo (*Poësie lyrique*)' gave the

64   Ibid., p. 261.
65   [J. D.] Martine, *De la musique dramatique en France* (Paris, 1813), pp. 42–3.

Ex. 1 *Tom Jones*

(*a*) No. 1

Allegro moderato

Que les— de - voirs que tu— m'im -

Soir et ma - tin la jeune I -

- po - ses

- set - te, triste et seu - let - te cède au cha - grin

(*b*) No. 7

Allegro assai

Dai - gnez cal - mer

Je veux bien cal - mer ma co - lè - re, je— veux—

bien— cal - mer ma co - lè - re

(c) No. 13

classical musico-dramatic justification for the modern (Italianate) duet form as opposed to the old French type wherein the characters sang more or less the same thing at the same time:

> On the contrary the Italian *duo* is a concise, rapid, symmetrically constructed dialogue and, like the aria, susceptible of regular, simple design. In this dialogue, the voices are first heard separately, each saying what it must say; the characters reply, the various feelings thwart each other and conflict; up to then, all passes as in nature. But there comes a moment when the dialogue is so urgent that there is no further alternative, and from each side the impulses of the soul escape at the same time: then the two voices join.[66]

That Marmontel here regarded *opéra-comique* on an equal footing with recitative opera is shown by the paragraph appended to the foregoing at the time of its republication in 1787: 'Since this article was first published the Italian form of the Duo, Trio, Quartet etc. has been received with greatest applause at our two lyric theatres. I have myself had thirty pieces of this sort produced at both the Opéra-Comique and the Opéra.'[67] The second entry offered a bizarre verbal duet headed 'Duo, (*Musiq.*)',

66   *Supplément à l'Encyclopédie*, ii, p. 743.
67   'Duo', *Elémens de littérature*: *Oeuvres complettes de M. Marmontel* (Paris, 1787), vii, p. 51. Piccinni and Grétry are named shortly after as his collaborators.

consisting of exchanges between 'S' (Rousseau) and 'F.D.C.' (Castillon *fils*).[68] Responding to the cautions of Rousseau – whose views dated back to the fifth volume of the *Encyclopédie* issued in 1755 – concerning the necessary unity of melody in duets and also the viability of duets expressing anger or fury, Castillon asserted that any difficulties encountered in these areas were soluble by composer and singer and that moreover Carl Heinrich Graun had already shown the way forward by 1750.[69] Theory was yet again lagging behind practice. Indeed, Sedaine and Monsigny had in 1769 presented a remarkable development of the modern trio (*Le Déserteur* No. 15) that included perhaps the most surprising change of emotional direction of any *opéra-comique* ensemble before the establishment of the Italianate finale in France. Alexis's lover and his father here react to the revelation that Alexis has deserted and will therefore be executed. But the sheer despair resolves into a Lento amoroso expressing mutual consolation and resignation. The musical weight of development in each section would justify the view that the piece comprises two distinct dialogue trios; but in context the emotional impact is clearly more than twice the sum of its parts.

In his work with Grétry, Marmontel found limited occasion to write larger ensembles, but, especially after *Le Huron* (1768, their honeymoon work), poet and composer constructed duets of great formal and dramatic diversity. In several we see notions of opposition developed at length, and it is interesting how often the dramatic resolution involves a change of emotional direction. By insisting on these qualities we are bound to reject the assertions that 'the eleven musical numbers [in *Lucile*] are non-dramatic'[70] and that 'most of Marmontel's ensembles are written to be set in a rather free rondo form . . . Contrasts of sentiment or personality seldom occur in the text, hence are not required in the music.'[71] A virtually opposite case could be made by considering examples such as *Lucile* No. 8, 'Ah! ma belle maîtresse'; *Silvain* No. 9, 'Dans le sein d'un père'; *L'Ami de la maison* No. 13, 'Tout ce qu'il vous plaira'; and *Zémire et Azor* Nos. 4, 'Le tems est beau', and 12, 'Je veux le voir'. The flavour of these is quite unlike that of earlier ensembles, often owing to Grétry's subtlety of thematic working, which suggests an inner arrangement of relations between the characters as well as a satisfying musical architecture. The most 'modern'

---

68 Identified in A. R. Oliver, *The Encyclopedists as Critics of Music* (New York, 1947), p. 179.

69 He cites, from Graun's *Ifigenia in Aulide* (1748), 'Segui per giovane audace' and, from *Fetonte* (1750), 'Tralascia un vano amore'.

70 Pendle, '*Les philosophes* and *opéra comique*: the Case of Grétry's *Lucile*', *The Music Review*, xxxviii (1977), p. 185.

71 Idem, 'The Opéras Comiques', p. 424. See pp. 424–7 for brief discussion of two ensembles, each selected to show least contrast: *Silvain* No. 9; and *Lucile* No. 4, the tableau-like 'Où peut-on être mieux'.

of them are *Lucile* No. 8 and *Zémire et Azor* No. 12, both in the minor mode, and it is symptomatic that they betray strong sonata tendencies, though never the stylistic formalism that would be inimical to 'l'art dramatico-musical'. 'Ah! ma belle maîtresse' also shows the tendency to aggregation typical of the 1760s: Lucile's melancholy aria No. 7 runs into it, whereupon it begins as a duet for Lucile and her maid Julie but then turns into a trio – at the 'development' section – with the surprise entrance of the bridegroom, Dorval. For the first time, he is in a position to observe that something untoward has occurred. He questions, converses and finally kneels, thinking he can repair a wrong; but matters are too fundamentally serious. He is asked to leave and is led to believe he is no longer loved. The ensemble ends in the tonic, C minor, in complete perplexity. One striking detail is that, although the original text contains rondo-like returns of the opening five lines, Grétry ignored them in favour of a dynamic approach.

Dorval enters *in medias res*; in *Zémire et Azor* Nos. 4 and 12, one character is trying to persuade another to leave the stage; in *L'Ami de la maison* No. 13, Agathe teaches her lover to be more trusting before she shows him a letter she has received. This duet, like some others, ends with a new metre and tempo in order to express the change of heart and seal it in the audience's mind. If Grétry merely took the idea from Italy, where he had been studying,[72] that did not lessen the myriad dramatic possibilities additionally offered by 'two-tempo' form. Since he commanded a sure technique Grétry willingly designed music around the shortest, the longest or the most scenically complicated pieces of text that a dramatist might provide. This inevitably led to exploration of the Italianate finale.

Sedaine had demanded a substantial sequence to end *Le Déserteur*: aria–obbligato recitative–choral link–scene change–ensemble–resolution. His first text to be set by Grétry (though it was certainly not designed specially for him[73]) was the Florentine tale *Le Magnifique*, after Boccaccio and La Fontaine, given in 1773. If *Le Déserteur* offered a 'French' solution to the musical finale, dictated by a tense and realistic order of events as seen on stage, then *Le Magnifique*'s Italian setting and domestic denouement afforded the excuse to adapt the Italian 'chain' finale technique. Care had to be taken because Parisian taste, even a generation later, rejected poor verisimilitude and character motivation in *opera buffa*, especially when these qualities were perjured for the sake of a finale.[74] Thus *Le Magnifique*

---

[72]   'Two-tempo' forms have been traced back in particular to Galuppi's *opere buffe* as well as those of Piccinni; the evidence is summarized in E. O. D. Downes, *The Operas of Johann Christian Bach as a Reflection of the Dominant Trends in Opera Seria, 1750–1780* (unpublished dissertation, Harvard University, 1958), i, pp. 417ff, 435ff.

[73]   Sedaine, 'Quelques réflexions', p. 513: 'Quelque sujet que j'eusse d'être content de mon association avec M. Monsigny, comme il avait entre ses mains deux opéras de moi, qu'il ne finissait pas, je crus pouvoir prier M. Grétry de faire cette pièce.'

[74]   See Charlton, *Grétry and the Growth of Opéra-comique*, chap. 22.

concludes with a dramatically truthful Andante, not an Allegro, although it forms the last of a set of seven musical sections in varying keys and metres. Grétry later bestowed on *opéra-comique* a number of distinguished Italianate finales – in *Le Jugement de Midas*, *Les Evénements imprévus*, *L'Epreuve villageoise*, *Les Méprises par ressemblance* and *Le Rival confident*. None of these, however, is to a text by Sedaine, who instead sought fables whose intrinsic disposition made them suitable for music. We can see this tendency in Act 2 of *Le Magnifique*, that part of the tale which, he tells us, inspired him in this manner. Clémentine, the heroine, is not permitted to address the Magnifique, while he formally declares his love to her. Meanwhile her guardian and his servant are watching and timing the interview and interpolate occasional comments in music. Clémentine's aria 'Quelle contrainte' runs into the main scene, itself formed as an aggregation of sections that Grétry subsequently boasted of in terms of its unprec edented length.[75] Simultaneous action and mimetic play are resultingly fused, but the crux of the mime (Clémentine's silent indication of assent to the Magnifique by letting fall a rose) also becomes the very heart of the *opéra-comique*. It is the moment of truth from which all the remaining dramatic threads must stem. (Making them stem naturally caused, I think, partly unresolved problems.) And the pattern of a second-act musico-dramatic sequence that held a work together from within was to bear fruit in *Richard Coeur-de-lion*, *Le Comte d'Albert* and *Raoul Barbe-bleue*. There are only three short spoken episodes in the entire second act of *Richard* and two spoken episodes in its third. In speaking of the later Sedaine we are speaking of a special type of opera in which every musical item potentially occupies a dramatically necessary position.

Grétry himself articulated an objection to stock *opera buffa* finales: 'you commonly see very long finales where, against a minimal accompaniment, a young girl of fifteen and an old man of eighty sing the same thing'.[76] At the same time *opéra-comique* – which, socially speaking, acted as surrogate for *opera buffa* up to 1789 – was gradually involving more performers, especially after the new theatre opened in 1783, and making heavy technical demands on leading singers.[77] We noted earlier how Grétry took over dialogue text for the close of Act 1 of *La Fausse Magie*. The extent to which he and, presumably, Marmontel were prepared to expand what is after all labelled 'Quatuor' may be judged from its twenty-seven pages of score and some 375 bars of music. Its action proceeds from the exposition

---

[75]   *Mémoires*, i, p. 247. Sedaine's evidence is found in the 'avertissement' to *Le Magnifique* (Paris, 1773): the subject 'promettoit des situations sur lesquelles la Musique pût s'arrêter, et j'ai cherché à en profiter'.

[76]   *Mémoires*, i, p. 334.

[77]   See Charlton, 'Orchestra and Chorus at the Comédie-Italienne (Opéra-Comique), 1755–1799', *Slavonic and Western Music: Essays for Gerald Abraham*, ed. M. H. Brown and R. J. Wiley (Ann Arbor and Oxford, 1985), pp. 87–108.

of the main dilemma through some initial reactions to the imagining of a solution, and ends with a *buffo* coda section of over a hundred bars. In 'l'art dramatico-musical' the musical treatment, even at its most Italianate, was a consequence of the inherent dramatic situation, not vice versa.

DECLAMATION AND TEXTS

I am discussing declamation and the text in the context of the solo aria. Three main points seem to be at issue: the declamatory approach to word-setting, the problems created by the language, and the problem of the length of texts.

At the outset we should divest ourselves of any false notions perpetuated by the term *'ariette'*. Linguistically, it is a diminutive ('little aria') and was retained merely through popular usage and convenience long after the historical circumstances giving rise to its application had changed. Marmontel explains the matter thus:

> . . . It was when some notion of Italian music was obtained, and when the imitation of its brilliant passages was tried, that the word *ariette* was made from that of *aria* . . . This light melody, the least estimable part of Italian music and the easiest to imitate, was introduced into opéra-comique and had much success . . . But the opéra-comique subsequently having adopted a more elevated character, and the emotions animating it having made it susceptible of a more varied, expressive music . . . melodies [or songs: *chants*] were composed that had intrinsic character and expression . . . [However, in spite of the need to distinguish these from more rudimentary styles], usage prevailed, and retained the noun *ariette* for all sung arias at the theatre where the *ariette* had shone.[78]

Grétry, as is well known, placed his accomplishment of a declamatory melodic style at the centre of his achievement, and the tradition he always acknowledged was the Italian one: 'I analysed Pergolesi's music when I sought to develop my musical faculties; may I not, I wondered (having his music before me), declaim in singing with as much truth and charm?'[79] The kind of naturalism engendered by such a style had often been fought over in Paris. It is nevertheless interesting that Grimm in 1761 connected the declamatory concept of word-setting that obtained in the best *opéras-comiques* with that of 'musical drama', notably of a kind not then seen at the Opéra. The former was to be a precondition of the latter:

> [From Duni] les musiciens français peuvent apprendre ce que c'est que de mettre des paroles en musique, art absolument ignoré en France malgré le grand nombre d'opéras dont le magasin de l'Académie royale fourmille, et qu'il faudrait d'abord jeter au feu si l'on voulait représenter des drames en musique sur le théâtre de l'Opéra.[80]

78   'Ariette', *Elémens de littérature*, v, p. 260.
79   *Réflexions*, i, chap. 60, p. 229.
80   *Correspondance littéraire* (15 August 1761), cited in Smith, *Egidio Duni*, p. 207.

From 'le grand Rameau' to 'le petit Boismortier' French prosody had been 'crippled' in music. Diderot inevitably puts it more vividly, if impractically:

What is the model for a musician or a tune [*chant*]? Speech, if the model is alive and thinking; noise, if the model is inanimate. Speech should be thought of as a line, and the tune as another line winding in and out of the first. The more vigorous and true the speech, which is the basis of the tune, and the more closely the tune fits it and the more points of contact it has with it, the truer that tune will be and the more beautiful.

The text itself also needs complete revision: 'Lyric poetry has yet to be born.'

It is the animal cry of passion that should dictate the melodic line, and these moments should tumble out quickly one after the other, phrases must be short and the meaning self-contained, so that the musician can utilize the whole and each part, omitting one word or repeating it, adding a missing word, turning it all ways like a polyp, without destroying it. All this makes lyric poetry in French a much more difficult problem than in languages with inversions.[81]

An analytical eye has been cast over Diderot's prescriptions by Daniel Heartz, who concluded that the writer 'was thinking less in terms of opéras-comiques such as they existed already around 1760, than the revival of the *tragédie lyrique*, of which nobody had a very precise notion before Philidor wrote his *Ernelinde, princesse de Norvège* in 1766'.[82] However, one should not minimize the 'new' aspects of Duni's and others' declamation, even in Diderot's terms, for Diderot wanted not simply expressive or analogical verity but repetition of words and short phrases. Now, repetition of words could never be arbitrary, but it was, I suspect, already more practised in Duni than in, say, Boismortier's *ballet comique Don Quichotte chez la duchesse* (1743). Repetitions here, if occurring at all, are based on the poetic line or phrase rather than the word (permitted ones like 'règne', 'vole' etc. excepted). The principle was that of verse symmetry in tandem with musical periodicity, and the nearest one gets to any word-repetition is the Italianate *ariette* style traditionally kept for divertissements (as in the Air de la japonaise, 'Vole amour').

Opéra-comique, on the other hand, had the task of forging a new unity between three demands of a verbal–musical kind: intelligibility on the grammatical level, especially when threatened by unexpected word-repetition; fidelity of declamation, that is to the rise and fall as determined by the meaning of the poetic line; and interesting manipulation of the

---

[81]   *Rameau's Nephew*, pp. 98, 105. Compare Chabanon, *De la musique*, p. 209: 'Songez qu'entendre de la Musique avec des paroles, c'est entendre parler deux langues à la fois, c'est commenter l'une par l'autre.'

[82]   'Diderot et le théâtre lyrique: "le nouveau stile" proposé par *Le Neveu de Rameau*', *Revue de musicologie*, lxiv (1978), pp. 244–5.

Ex. 2   Duni, *La Clochette*, No. 2

Ex. 3   Duni, *La Clochette*, No. 2

available mid-century musical idioms, particularly in view of the rise of the sonata. Assimilation not surprisingly took time, and, because musical styles were developing quickly, progress was often uneven throughout a given work. As a random example, Ex. 2 shows Colin lamenting his own love for a temporarily ungrateful Colinette in Duni's *La Clochette* (1766). It has a variety of motivic rhythm, repetition of words, accentual fidelity to the words, and analogical fidelity to the meaning. Up to a point there is a synthesis between the demands of declamation, language and music. On either side of this supposed median, however, a work might contain both more and less declamatory music. Comic and quick pieces formed the readiest model for repetition and verbal–musical matching (see Ex. 3), while on the other hand more subtle dramatic demands easily swung the balance towards purely musical values or, in some cases by Duni, adaptation of old music to new words, which obviously cast doubt on higher ideals of declamation. When Colinette first appears in *La Clochette*, complete with flock of sheep, she has what sounds in context like a concert aria.

As Diderot perceived, the problems required joint solution by poet and composer. It is easy to accuse a composer of doing something, while forgetting the part played by his poet. In a farce like *Blaise le savetier* the discrepancy between brevity of text and length of setting was bridged by the histrionic dimension. Its quintet No. 5, with thirty short lines of text, some two words long, gave rise to 246 bars of music. Four bare lines of text were provided for the duet No. 8; nine lines of text in the final duet produced 268 bars of music. In fact, ensemble texts of the period were already very irregular in rhyme, line-length and syllabic construction, providing obvious opportunities for freer musical treatment (*Le Sorcier*, a case in point, has been mentioned). But solo aria texts seem generally to have been more constrained by the inheritance of two four-line stanzas, the first of which was traditionally repeated. The octosyllabic line was common and is seen in *Blaise le savetier* in Pince's aria No. 9: 'L'argent seul fixe le caprice; / L'argent seul sçait donner la loi. / Ah! quels momens! ah! quel délice! / Ah! que de plaisir j'entrevois!' Where there was action rather than moralizing, Sedaine and others used irregularity of syllabic form. Blaisine's No. 7, seen below, still adheres nevertheless to the double-stanza scheme:

	No. of syllables
Ah! le scélérat!	5
Il me frape [sic]	3
Et s'échape.	3
Ah! le scélérat	5
Il me bat.	3
La colère	3
Me suggère	3
De me venger	4
D'un mari qui sçait m'outrager.	8

The first five lines are then repeated.

The pursuit of a modern declamatory style did not follow a single direction; Heartz traces it to obbligato recitative such as is seen in Philidor's *Ernelinde*[83] (and also in *Tom Jones* Act 3). In these, though, it should be noted that repetition of word or phrase was actually inappropriate, even though passion, disjunction and immediacy of dramatic impact were of the essence. Their effect is rather of a unidirectional 'stream of consciousness', taken up later by Marmontel and Grétry in *Le Huron*, *Silvain* and *Zémire et Azor*.

[83]   Ibid., pp. 248–9.

Certain types of text probably made it easier to create variety while satisfying our three demands. One was the strophic song form, but this was little used; another was the narrative–descriptive text: the tale of a voyage, the conditions of one's work, the imitation of sounds and actions. By definition, this type was non-symmetrical, used repetition of words to facilitate word-painting in the score, and formed a musico-dramatic whole on a simple level. Philidor made good use of it, but by Grétry's time it had almost outlived its usefulness. A third and quite ubiquitous form was the rondo text, especially to open a work. Such texts obviously embodied diversity within unity but with ample scope for overplaying musical values at the expense of those of the text. Grimm couched a critical response to them in these terms, when reviewing Grétry's *Lucile*:

> He could be reproached for writing most of his arias in rondo form, wherein the first and principal couplet returns twice or three times [actually, most are in ABA' form], but I think that this type of solo, symmetrical and circular, is inevitable when one sets French words, whose idiom never allows the composer to phrase [*phraser*] or elaborate at length [*s'étendre*].[84]

French linguistic 'stiffness' impels the composer to 'cut himself short' and return to an all-enveloping idea.

If however the musical form were the commonplace ABA or ABA', and an aria's emotional temperature were calm, repetition could overstretch syntactical connections or produce that commitment to pure music (cf. *La Clochette*) which was the very thing the French despised in Italian opera. A trenchant illustration of such anti-dramatic art was adduced by Grétry:

> Si nous passons au siècle dernier, c'est chez les Romains modernes qu'il faut voir combien la mélodie avoit encore peu de rapport avec la déclamation.
>
> Voyez cet air de *Vinci* (*Artaserse di Metastasio, scena XIII, atto primo*):

Ex. 4   Vinci, *Artaserse* (Act 1; as printed by Grétry)

Correspondance littéraire (Paris, 1829–31), vi, p. 122 (15 January 1769).

Que veulent dire ces *Torna, torna* répétés, sans dire *innocente*? Dans la bouche de la princesse, soeur d'*Arsace*, cet air de gigue devoit être ce que nous appelons *air de fureur* . . . L'opposition la plus triviale étoit donc de faire un air de danse gai, pour exprimer la fureur; c'est, si l'on veut, la colère de *Polichinel*.[85]

If, then, what was needed was a dramatically intelligent way of allowing modern music to expand itself stylistically, the dilemma can be pinned down on the textual side of the monologue or aria. We can perhaps see this already in *Le Sorcier*, for when Poinsinet provided the young daughter Justine with the following words in Act 1, he may well have envisaged a fairly simple song. Philidor clearly decided that he wished to paint a rather more penetrating picture of adolescent sensibility, and adopted sonata form.

	No. of Syllables	
Jeune fillette	4	Opening subject
Sans trembler, n'ose faire un pas	8	
Les mamans, les papas,	6	Second subject
Chacun la guette;	4	
Tout l'inquiète.	4	
C'est une gêne, un martire.	7	Development
Danses, chansons, petits jeux,	7	
Regards, sourire,	4	
Tout pour elle est un crime affreux.	8	
Jeune fillette . . .		Recapitulation

Certainly these syllabic changes may have assisted the invention of contrasting musical ideas; nonetheless there is an aesthetic discrepancy between the restricted scope of this text and the increased emotional scope suggested by the musical style and form.

It must be said here that this view is not necessarily representative of 1760s criticism. Chastellux in 1765 pushed for the modern Italianate aria style at all costs, since he believed that the principal pleasure resides in the music, not the text, of pieces like Philidor's 'Reviens, reviens, ma voix t'appelle' from *Le Sorcier*. To this lyrical feast in sonata style (though da capo form) he contrasts the 'sham arias': the narrative–descriptive 'Dès le matin' from Philidor's *Le Bûcheron* and the hunting aria 'D'un cerf dix cors' from *Tom Jones*; and this in spite of the fact that they use long texts. The reason is that he finds their music motivically disparate and 'unperiodic': 'Either you will use many words and ideas in your arias, and then your music will be vague and incoherent; or you will use few words and ideas, and then your music will be simple and beautiful, but you will have to repeat yourself.'[86]

[85]   *Mémoires*, i, pp. 422–3 (final 'Récapitulation'). Leonardo Vinci's *Artaserse* actually dates from 1730.

[86]   *Essai sur l'union de la poésie et de la musique*, pp. 43–7. Chastellux's view of periodicity involves 'a certain unity, a proportion in the component members, a roundness of melody which suspends the attention and sustains it to the end': p. 18 n. 7.

Philidor's other methods of musical expansion involved a propensity for contrasting sections of music using different metres and tempos. These could either form a traditional ABA pattern or become parts of the sonata. In this tendency Philidor stands apart from his French contemporaries and from Grétry later.[87] He appears to want to increase the 'emotional space' of the arias within the confines of existing text patterns. Ultimately the aesthetic value of this approach proved limited, but the composer at least attempted thereby a new manipulation of modern styles in music, and also attained greater fidelity to contrasts in the text. It was the balancing of all elements that was elusive.

The significance of a modern sonata style in the aria cannot be overstated in terms of detailed musico-dramatic relationships. This can be suggested on the level of declamation, quite apart from implied emotional scope. For this style permitted subtle changes in the interaction between text and music, such as (a) verbal repetition coming about thanks to musical prolongation of the cadence; (b) the use of opposing rhythmic cells, perhaps accommodating antithetical verbal phrases; (c) yet permitting these cells to be satisfactorily developed side by side; (d) the employment of irregularly barred musical phrases that 'obeyed' the demands of declamation in the short term but could 'obey' musical logic over the long term; or (e), for poetic purpose, giving room to a short minor-mode episode within a major-mode piece (and vice versa). Sophie in *Tom Jones* (see Ex. 5) is trying to persuade her father away from his plan for her marriage to Blifil. The diverse rhythms and contours match the declamation of verbal phrases, and even short phrases ('Que votre âme') are repeated. As the dominant cadence is attained, a yet new area of text and music is exposed. Nevertheless the text for the main exposition section is only six lines long (five of them octosyllabic), so the composer has to use the first of them no fewer than five times: 'C'est à vous que je dois la vie, / Vos bontés me la font chérir. / A la voix de votre Sophie / Que votre âme daigne s'ouvrir. / Ecoutez son coeur qui vous crie, / Me voulez-vous contraindre d'en gémir.'

It was Marmontel who realized the need that had been demonstrated for a greater quantity of words in the aria, which would solve such difficulties and give music 'more space to run through'; he was of course committed to the importation of modern musical styles in opera, having become opposed to French styles even during his collaboration with Rameau:

. . . words repeated too much tire us, whatever the facility they afford to musical modulation. From this it follows that the French aria, within a small circle of words, can only with difficulty have the same freedom, variety and extent as the Italian aria.

---

[87]   Smith points to the generally greater quantity of sonata-form elements in Philidor compared with Monsigny: *Egidio Duni*, pp. 163–5, 176–7.

Ex. 5   Philidor, *Tom Jones*, No. 12

The real way to make up for the freedom that the Italians grant melody to make light of the words is thus to give [the aria] varied designs to follow within the words themselves, and detours through which to run.[88]

Marmontel's first libretto for Grétry (*Le Huron*, 1768), while not rejecting the rondo or the double quatrain for aria texts (e.g. Nos. 1, 8 and 13), certainly tested out longer texts, whether in their orthodox position in narrative–descriptive arias (Nos. 2 and 10) or for a declaration of affection (No. 5, with seventeen lines). It is noteworthy that he intended there to be three obbligato recitatives, which would have been an impressive feature even in a *tragédie lyrique* of this period; Grétry set only two of them as such.

[88]   'Air', *Supplément à l'Encyclopédie*, i, p. 239. Last phrase: 'des desseins variés à suivre, et des détours à parcourir'. Variant reading from *Elémens de littérature*, v, pp. 110–11: 'des desseins plus développés, et plus d'espace à parcourir', i.e. 'more space to run through'.

Later librettos show that Marmontel used varied designs and greater text-lengths as appropriate, without ousting the double quatrain (e.g. Azor's 'Ah! quel tourment d'être sensible'). Taken in order and not counting repeated lines, the arias in *Lucile* have sixteen, eleven, twenty-four, thirty-four (Blaise's rondo-form monologue), eight and eleven lines. These facts did not pass unnoticed: 'la plupart des airs ont trop de paroles, qui n'ont fait qu'embarrasser le musicien'.[89] But time vindicated Grétry's handling, since this work became one of the most popular of all *opéras-comiques* in Paris (it was given 172 performances in the decade 1769–78).

The declamatory ingredient in Grétry's work thus did not exist in a vacuum but in partnership with sympathetic thinking in text composition and with the sonata style in music. The vocal line came into equilibrium, as needed, with musical expansion or verbal repetition. But it had in Grétry's hands special qualities: he had a genius for fine melody that fused, as if inevitably, with accurate declamatory principles. Because it respected the vocal undulations suggested by the poetry, it even fulfilled Diderot's formulation (and here we may note that the two were acquainted): 'Speech should be thought of as a line, and the tune as another line winding in and out of the first.'[90] This partly boiled down in practice to an appreciation of the key words and syllables: 'The expressive note very frequently wants to be on the verb, quite frequently on the noun, sometimes on the adjective. That is not all: this good note must be situated on the good syllable of the word.'[91] However, poetic sensitivity was also paramount: an appreciation of the rhythms that the verse would demand in a reader, as well as the rise and fall of the voice. It was surely this principle that gave Grétry's melodic line its happy irregularity.

I have said that music is a discourse; therefore it has, like verse and prose, pauses and inflections of the comma, the colon, the exclamation and question marks and the full stop . . .

One can express [something] legitimately by making much use of harmony, much orchestral working and an often accessory vocal line, or minimally song-like declamation; that is in general what Gluck did.

One can express [something] legitimately by making a pure and easy melody spring from the declamation, with an orchestral accompaniment that shall only be accessory: that is in general what I have sought to do.[92]

---

89   *Correspondance littéraire* (Paris, 1829–31), vi, p. 122 (15 January 1769).

90   See above, p. 253.

91   Grétry, *Réflexions*, i, chap. 62, p. 236.

92   Idem, *Mémoires*, i, pp. 240–3. Elsewhere, Grétry counselled that only composers with Gluck's conceptual powers of unity should attempt that composer's path: ibid., ii, p. 48. Lully, on the other hand, was found wanting: he 'had some presentiments of declamatory music; his recitative proves it; but he knew only how to note declamation, not be melodic while being declamatory': ibid., i, p. 426.

Ex. 6   Grétry, *Lucile*, No. 1

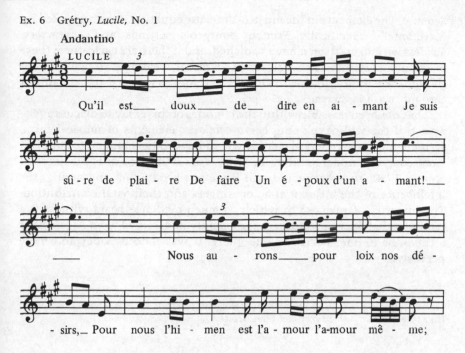

In Ex. 5 it will be observed that Philidor created 'classical' musical symmetry in his twinned opening phrases. In Grétry this commonplace Italianate feature, so common that we hardly register its symmetry as such, is not part of the melodic style. In so far as his music has balancing or reflecting phrases, these are subtly woven into a line whose primary melodic inflexions are governed by the response to the principal words and syllables of the poetry, which become its high points. In Ex. 6 a single (and, in context, beautiful) excerpt shows roughly how this works; the fluid text by Marmontel is the opening of the first monologue in *Lucile*:

> Qu'il est doux de dire en aimant
>   Je suis sûre de plaire
>   De faire
>   Un Epoux d'un Amant!

The music describes a ten-bar sentence prior to a balancing repetition of the music of bars 1–4.

Grétry's musical range took him into widely differing dramatic worlds, but it was particularly fortunate that he began collaborating with Marmontel (quite how he came to do so remains disputed). An equilibrium was set up whose aesthetic credibility was quite distinct from that of

Sedaine. The elements in the musico-dramatic equation were harnessed by Marmontel's specifically French bourgeois settings and characters. Tradesmen and craftsmen have vanished, and if there are caricatures these exemplify stupidity (not vulgarity) or moral weakness. It was reform through sensibility, just as in Gluck the reform happened to be manifest through neo-Classicism.

It has not been possible within the confines of this essay to discuss every aspect of the still-developing *opéra-comique*: elements of musical form, accompaniment, even local colour, would have to be included to supply a more complete understanding of what 'l'art dramatico-musical' implied around 1790; and that would still leave out production and acting, the intelligence of the influential actor–singers and their vital contribution. The integrity of purpose to which so much evidence bears witness is a reminder that operatic reform cannot simply be ascribed to an Algarotti or a Gluck or to one theatre or one genre: it was indeed wider and more pervasive.

I should like to express my thanks to the following for their assistance: M. Elizabeth C. Bartlet, Daniel Heartz, Margaret Rayner and Clive Scott.

Mendelssohn's operas

JOHN WARRACK

From his earliest years, Mendelssohn took the keenest interest in dramatic music as well as in the more naturally domestic media of chamber music, piano music and songs. By the time he achieved the first public production of one of his operas, with *Die Hochzeit des Camacho* in Berlin in 1827, he had four comic operas and fragments of other dramatic works behind him and had reached the age of only eighteen. The failure of *Camacho* was clearly a shock to the gifted, favoured boy, who had had no experience of worldly set-backs. When a contretemps developed over the availability of Eduard Devrient to take part in the private first performance of *Die Heimkehr aus der Fremde*, he threw a fit of hysterical rage and had to be put to bed;[1] and he was reluctant to allow the work on to the public stage in 1829. This time the opera was a success; but, despite the urgings of friends and his own wish to write more operas, nothing else was to ensue until the fragments of *Loreley* which were all he left of the work on his death in 1847. Two years after *Die Heimkehr* he was lamenting to Devrient, 'Put a real opera [text] in my hands and in a couple of moments it'll be composed, for every day I long afresh to write an opera . . . A text that doesn't really suit me I won't set. If you know a man who's in a position to write an opera, for God's sake tell me about him: I look for nothing else.'[2] In Dresden in 1842, Wagner, fresh from the triumph of *Rienzi*, found Mendelssohn ruefully admiring: 'Mendelssohn himself had long wanted nothing more ardently than to write a successful opera.'[3] Librettists with whom he entered into discussion ranged from Scribe to Helmina von Chezy and James Robinson Planché – about as far as it is possible to range in professional competence. There were well-advanced plans for a treatment of Edward III's siege of Calais by Planché,[4] for a libretto based on Wieland's *Pervonte* by Karl

---

[1]   See E. Devrient, *Meine Erinnerungen an Felix Mendelssohn-Bartholdy* (Leipzig, 1891), p. 91.

[2]   Ibid., p. 114.

[3]   *Mein Leben*, ed. M. Gregor-Dellin (Munich, 1963), p. 250.

[4]   For a full account of the project and the exchange of correspondence on the subject, see J. Planché, *Recollections and Reflections* (London, 1872), ii, chap. xxi.

263

Klingemann and for a version of *The Tempest* by Benjamin Lumley; and at least a dozen other writers and subjects were considered.[5] Yet none proved suitable, and time and again Mendelssohn entered into a project with enthusiasm only to find it rapidly waning. He was never to follow up the promise of the early operas.

Mendelssohn's earliest surviving work is dramatic by intention, if not in fulfilment. The first volume of his manuscripts[6] opens with a piece of quasi-operatic music in piano score, beginning with a *recitativo*[7] leading to other movements in various tempos. No words appear until the music reaches a G major 3/8 aria for Vermeille, beginning 'Quel bonheur pour mon coeur de toujours aimer de toujours charmer' and continuing in sentimental vein to extol the delights of living for ever in a state of amorous dalliance. At this point Vermeille is joined by Lubin, and the sentiments are reiterated; the words then vanish, though there follow a number of short movements in a dramatic style with some instrumental indications. The volume continues with scraps of sonatas (including a somewhat Weberian one in F for violin and piano) and the Allegro of a piano trio (not the published Op. 1). There is a piano piece ending with a crossed-out passage of recitative; then a turn of the page brings a firm new heading, *Singspiel in 3 Szenen*.

Scarcely more than a single scene survives of this little domestic drama, entered in catalogues of Mendelssohn's music, from its opening words, as *Ich, J. Mendelssohn*.[8] Onkel (tenor) and Vater (bass) begin by congratulating themselves on their kinship in self-satisfied tones (see Ex. 1).[9] Uncle Joseph Mendelssohn (1770–1848) was the oldest of Moses Mendelssohn's children and together with the next son, Felix's father Abraham (1776–1835), had originally established the family banking and import business in Hamburg as J. und A. Mendelssohn in 1803, moving it to Berlin by 1813; it prospered and remained a leading German bank until its liquidation by the Nazis, as part of their policy of 'Aryanizing' German banks, at the end

---

5   For a summary of Mendelssohn's operatic plans, see W. Kunold, *Felix Mendelssohn-Bartholdy und seine Zeit* (Regensburg, 1984), pp. 225–48.

6   Berlin, Deutsche Staatsbibliothek, Mendelssohn MSS, i (1820).

7   Illustrated in *The New Grove*, xii, p. 135. It is not really 'entitled "Recitativo" ' as the caption suggests: it is simply a recitative passage.

8   This, together with *Die Soldatenliebschaft*, *Die wandernden Komödianten* and *Der Onkel aus Boston*, remains in manuscript, though all are to be published in the *Neue Mendelssohn Ausgabe*. I am grateful to Wolfgang Goldhan and the staff of the Musikabteilung of the Deutsche Staatsbibliothek for allowing me to examine these manuscripts and other material, and for their help with some points of difficulty.

9   This passage and others are quoted (though sometimes incompletely or otherwise inaccurately) in the most thorough account of Mendelssohn's operas yet to appear, G. Schünemann, 'Mendelssohns Jugendopern', *Zeitschrift für Musikwissenschaft*, v (1923), pp. 506–45. Schünemann deals only with the works mentioned in n. 8, including *Ich, J. Mendelssohn*, together with *Die beiden Pädagogen*: he regards Mendelssohn's so-called *Studienopern* to have ended with *Der Onkel aus Boston*.

Ex. 1

of 1938.[10] Little is known about Joseph, but he maintained his artistic and intellectual interests throughout his life. Abraham had with good-humoured pride observed, in a famous remark, 'Früher war ich der Sohn meines Vaters, jetzt bin ich der Vater meines Sohnes.'[11] Wilhelm Hensel's portrait shows a strong, resolute profile, with the arms severely folded; and though an affectionate as well as a proud father, he was capable of formidable rages. One of these breaks out, after a D major Adagio in which the two brothers swear 'Süsse Freundschaft' in honeyed thirds and sixths, over an artistic matter. For though united in their professional resolve to deal only in 'bares Geld und Tresorschein', Abraham's assertion that Joseph understands nothing of music, since he admires *Olympie*, brings about a vehement Presto altercation. The eleven-year-old Felix, author of text as well as of music, must have witnessed many such arguments in the home (even though Spontini's opera was not to reach Berlin until the following year); he must also have felt secure in his elders' affection to be able to offer this candid piece of portraiture as a birthday surprise for domestic performance. The row brings in the cashier Emden, who complains that he can't get on with the accounts if they persist in making such a noise; but it is not until a singer appears, and in relentless coloratura demands an engagement, that the brothers recover their unanimity and send him packing. His answer is a spirited vengeance aria in the manner the young Mendelssohn could have encountered in many a contemporary opera, though the melodic line suggests that if the singer could really manage it the older men's judgement was at fault (see Ex. 2). The second scene is set in the counting-house and includes music for the factotum Herr Jordan and a chorus of bank clerks; but with a brief intervention by Emden into the disturbance they are making, the manuscript breaks off. Mendelssohn deleted this scene, though he allowed the first one to stand.

In the same year, 1820, Mendelssohn completed his first work with possibilities for a wider stage, *Die Soldatenliebschaft*. The text is by a family friend, the young doctor Johann Ludwig Casper. Born in Berlin in 1796, Casper had qualified in Halle in 1819. He was to make a distinguished reputation as a pathologist and for his work in forensic medicine, but though he published many learned articles and was a prominent editor in the field of medical journalism, his literary talents also took the form at this stage of his career of writing four librettos for Mendelssohn. His travels in France, which led him to publish a study of French medicine, had also familiarized him with French vaudevilles and light stage pieces. The

---

[10]   See W. Treue, 'Das Bankhaus Mendelssohn als Beispiel einer Privatbank im 19. und 20. Jahrhundert', *Mendelssohn-Studien*, ed. C. Löwenthal-Hensel (Berlin, 1972), pp. 29–80.

[11]   Quoted in S. Hensel, *Die Familie Mendelssohn* (Leipzig, 1880), p. 89.

Ex. 2

source of *Die Soldatenliebschaft* has not come to light, but from its atmosphere it is likely to be a minor French comedy.[12]

The scene is set in the castle of the widowed Spanish Countess Elvire (sop.), during the French occupation of Spain at the beginning of the century. A mysterious suitor has been leaving flowers on the balcony by her rooms. As much concerned about security as his mistress's honour, the overseer Tonio (bar.) complains to Felix (ten.), the French colonel of hussars, that one of his men must be responsible. Tonio also hopes to win Elvire's maid Zerbine (sop.), unaware that she is in love with the colonel's sergeant, Victor (ten.). However, permission for them to marry is refused. Night falls, and Tonio lies in wait for the intruder. Victor appears and consoles Zerbine. Climbing a tree that gives access to the balcony, he sets off alarm bells placed there by Tonio; however, Tonio siezes a passing sentry, Ernst (bar.), by mistake and is knocked flying. Victor, caught up the tree, now observes to his surprise a rendezvous between the countess and the colonel. When he inadvertently makes a noise, they flee leaving their headgear behind. Victor uses this to exact permission for his marriage, and in the end both couples are happily united.

12   Devrient, *Meine Erinnerungen*, pp. 12–13, refers to the three works *Die Soldatenliebschaft*, *Die beiden Pädagogen* and *Die wandernden Virtuosen* (sic) as being 'aus französischen Vaudevilles vom jungen Doctor Caspar [sic] ... zusammengestellt'.

Ex. 3

This plot is aptly matched to the boy Mendelssohn's talents not only in its neatness and simplicity but in its lack of serious musical demands. The score is laid out, with the instinct for elegant proportion that he seemed to possess even at the age of eleven, into an overture and eleven numbers (though the finale really divides up into three numbers); and the childishness of the musical script belies the skill of the music. The overture begins with a nimble theme that is no discredit to the composer of later and more brilliant scherzos (see Ex. 3), and the working-out of this in the middle section would have earned nods of approval from Mendelssohn's counterpoint teacher Zelter while also keeping the wit of the music alive (see Ex. 4). For the rest, the numbers are very much in the Singspiel vein

Ex. 4

that Mendelssohn would have known from contemporary examples, and they are often worked with real skill. He can do little to characterize Elvire, settling in the E♭ Terzett for flights of coloratura that he no doubt thought proper to operatic sopranos; and Victor is simply characterized, with a cheery horn theme providing the tune for his 'So leben wir Soldaten'. For the most part, the characters are little more than conventional figures expressed in some deft music – Tonio a German buffo bass in the Osmin manner, Zerbine not for nothing a near-namesake of Zerlina, Victor a fairly routine tenor à la Pedrillo, Felix and Elvire a pair of sentimental lovers. It is in some skilful touches of working-out, as with the excellent Rondo for Tonio and with the opening duet between Felix and Tonio in which the declamation cleverly follows the instrumental development, that Mendelssohn's natural gifts show at their best. He also reveals signs of the born opera composer's gift for instrumental colour in some of the later numbers, such as the cello obbligato for Zerbine's G minor aria (No. 6, the first minor-key aria in the work) and the lightly scored succeeding duet (composed later). Elvire's Cavatine 'Still und freundlich ist die Nacht' has some charming echo effects on woodwind, and the finale includes an admirable passage when woodwind gradually join in over a soft, slow series of chords on strings.

It is almost as if Mendelssohn's skills were developing as fast as he wrote; for the next work, the one-act Singspiel *Die beiden Pädagogen*, is the first that can well stand revival (it has had a few stagings in modern times and has been recorded). Casper took as his source Scribe's comedy *Les Deux Précepteurs, ou Asinus asinam fricat*, first performed at the Théâtre des Variétés in Paris on 19 June 1817, and adapted it with some skill for German taste. The eponymous pedagogues Cinglant ('Flogger') and Ledru ('Sprightly') become Kinderschreck ('Scarechild') and Luftig ('Flighty'), and the subjects of their dispute not Rousseau and Voltaire but the respective educational methods of Pestalozzi and Basedow. It was an argument currently rending German scholastic circles, the adherents of Johann Bernhard Basedow holding that the child should be given a practical upbringing and a disciplined instruction in the realities of living, while Pestalozzian theory suggested that the child's individual genius should be discovered and encouraged. Such discussions were no doubt only too familiar to a brilliant child of solicitous parents. For many years the text, like that of *Die Soldatenliebschaft*, was lost, though the Scribe original enabled the plot to be followed; but in 1960 the Mendelssohn scholar Karl-Heinz Köhler discovered both texts in the Bodleian Library, Oxford.[13]

The wealthy Robert (bass), hoping to give his son Carl (ten.) the education he himself lacks, requires him to live and study in a secluded garret. Carl is less than enthusiastic, being in any case in love with his cousin Elise (sop.). Together with the gardener's girl Hannchen (sop.), who has suffered a disappointment in love in Vienna, they agree to resist these restraints. Robert appears with Hannchen's uncle, the village schoolmaster Kinderschreck (bass), who emphasizes the virtues of strictness and that sparing the rod will spoil the child. He recommends the engagement of just such a pedagogue as himself and is put out to find that Robert has hired someone else, from Vienna. When this new pedagogue arrives, Hannchen thinks she recognizes him as her former lover Luftig but cannot be sure and conceals her identity; he for his part is resolved to stick to his imposture, assumed in place of his indisposed master. He is startled to find that his new pupil is not a child but a young man better educated than himself. Hannchen tricks him into revealing his true identity and threatens exposure if he deserts her again. They are interrupted by Robert and Kinderschreck, with whom Luftig is obliged to engage in bluff and counter-bluff on the theories of Pestalozzi and Basedow. Meanwhile Carl has learnt the truth about Luftig from Hannchen and proposes a party after his father has left on a forthcoming journey. But Robert returns suddenly to find his 'teacher' leading the dancing with a violin, and at the same time Kinderschreck

---

13   See K.-H. Köhler, 'Zwei rekonstruierbare Singspiele von Felix Mendelssohn-Bartholdy', *Beiträge zur Musikwissenschaft*, ii/3–4 (1960), pp. 86–93. See also idem, 'Das dramatische Jugendwerk Felix Mendelssohn-Bartholdys – Basis seiner Stil- und Persönlichkeitsentwicklung', *International Musicological Society: Report of the Eleventh Congress, Copenhagen 1972*, ed. H. Glahn *et al.* (Copenhagen, 1974), pp. 495–9. The texts, in Casper's hand, were passed to the Bodleian Library by Paul Benecke (son of Mendelssohn's sister Marie), who had been a Fellow of Magdalen College. See Oxford, Bodleian Library, MSS M. Deneke, Mendelssohn e. 12 and e. 13. The former is a fair copy by Casper; the latter consists of six separately stitched booklets containing sections of the work in the hand of Fanny Hensel.

Ex. 5

discovers evidence of a man having been in Hannchen's room – a brief-case. Out of this falls a letter exposing Luftig as only the servant of the Viennese professor; but when he agrees to marry Hannchen, Kinderschreck is mollified. Robert in turn is forced to admit the mistake of his whole enterprise and to give his blessing to Carl and Elise.

Though the form and manner of *Die beiden Pädagogen* remain that of Singspiel as closely as before, the skill of the handling has advanced considerably. The overture is at once nimbler and more economical, understanding the point, for a comedy, of spinning a rapid and witty series of musical events out of virtually nothing, in this case the little figure shown in Ex. 5. As before, the characters hardly move beyond the confines of Singspiel, with Elise now the sentimental heroine, Hannchen the *Zofe* or soubrette role, Kinderschreck the blustering bass, and so forth. But

Hannchen has some individuality, and personal feeling clearly shows through the handling of Elise, who declares early on that one cannot always be practising music and who suffers from an uncle who once was always fussing over his accounts and now can't let his son's education alone for a minute. The A major Terzetto has a skill beyond anything in *Die Soldatenliebschaft*, as the lovers take off in elaborately decorative melodic lines, while on the same word, 'küssen', Hannchen is chattily remarking that kisses are for a brunette today, a blonde tomorrow. The situation is the conventional one of the amorous heroine and the flighty soubrette, but it is handled with a quick ear for novel effect. Inventiveness with familiar conventions is the hallmark of the work, as when the three seal their bond of resistance in the brotherly tones of the Berlin Liedertafel. But if Mendelssohn could only have experienced all these emotions at second hand through his knowledge of Singspiel, he had had first-hand experience of pedagogues. He was spared anything as grim as Kinderschreck, but he knew the type; and Kinderschreck is his first real portrait in music. Though the expressive background is that of Singspiel, and the voice of Osmin makes more than one appearance, Kinderschreck is a vivid pedant, stuffy, absurd, more backward and stupid than actually cruel, for all his relish of the cane in the aria where he jovially describes its 'klipp und klapp und schwipp und schwapp', to music that good-humouredly removes at any rate some of its sting. Much the most original number is the disputation with Luftig, who is trying to get the subject away from Pestalozzi (of whose works, one fictitious chapter in particular, he has rashly pretended knowledge) on to that of Basedow. With Carl and Robert standing amazed at the heat generated by this *odium scholasticum*, the argument, based on total ignorance, takes refuge in irritated shouts of 'Pestalozzi! Pestalozzi!' from Kinderschreck to Luftig's sonorous answering booms of 'Basedow!' Luftig has the last word, but only just (see Ex. 6). Not surprisingly, this number, which constructs a clever piece of music out of no more than a hint in the text, made the greatest effect when the little opera was given to a gathering in the Mendelssohn family house, with Eduard Devrient and Dr Casper himself taking the parts of the two schoolmasters.

The text of Casper's third opera for Mendelssohn, *Die wandernden Komödianten* (sometimes *Die wandernden Virtuosen*), is said by all writers, including Köhler in *The New Grove*, to be lost, but it can actually be found among the large collection of manuscripts relating to Mendelssohn in the Bodleian Library, Oxford. It too is in Casper's hand, copied in neat *Schrift* and clearly laid out.[14]

Three strolling players are sitting in the Goldene Esel in Schilda, the town where they are due to perform. They are the convivial Fröhlich ('Cheerful') (ten.), the timorous Hasenfuss ('Coward') (ten.) and the poet Fixfinger (perhaps 'Scribbler') (bass), author of some dark and sinister verses. They are planning their performance and awaiting the arrival of their director, Flink ('Crafty'), who is however in danger of arrest for having lampooned the judge, Schwarzauge ('One-eye'), in the last town in which they played, Krähwinkel.[15] They are in the process of devising excuses to avoid paying the bill of the hostess, Mme Germain (sop.), rhapsodizing on the beauty of its script and refusing to allow one another to pay, when Flink arrives. Mme Germain recognizes him as a former lover, 'Rosenburg', and warns him about Schwarzauge, to whom she has become engaged and towards whom she is also under an obligation because of a lawsuit against her former husband. Flink offers to marry her and is told that the vengeful Schwarzauge has teamed up with the local judge, Holzbein ('Pegleg'). After they have gone, Schwarzauge arrives and is irritated to find his advances to Mme Germain repulsed; her attempted defence of Flink is met with the response that the miscreant's sentence will be six months' imprisonment and thirty lashes. Flink now appears dressed as a judge and is mistaken by Schwarzauge for Holzbein, whom he has not met; whereupon Flink offers help ('Amicitia amicorum amicaliter existiert', he declares in mock-legal Latin). After Schwarzauge has gone, Holzbein appears; so Flink now presents himself as the visiting Schwarzauge. There ensues a scene when, in the growing dark, the two judges, one half-blind, the other lame, blunder about in the

14   MSS M. Deneke, Mendelssohn e. 14. iii.
15   'Krähwinkel' was a fictitious little town that had passed into common parlance as epitomizing the so-called *Kleinstadterei* of parts of Germany, with its backwardness and complacency.

Ex. 6

- dow

Pest - a - loz - zi, Pest - a - loz - zi, Pest - a - loz - zi, Pest - a - loz - zi

ending as:

murk and each succeeds in arresting the other in the conviction that he has secured Flink. Trumpets sound for the play to begin: Mme Germain is persuaded to play a role she once took with the company, and they lay plans to make their getaway during the performance. As the curtain is about to rise, Fixfinger bursts in with the news that he has persuaded the local prince to attend. The play concerns an interrupted wedding, but the interruptions come from the two judges trying to make their arrest on stage, to the bemused delight of the audience. A description of the wanted man is read out, and first Fröhlich offers himself as the culprit, as Hasenfuss's nerves will not stand the strain of the deception. Just as Flink feels that he must reveal himself, Fixfinger returns with the news that the prince has made them all Hofkomödianten. The judges are confounded, and all ends happily.

Though in some ways *Die wandernden Komödianten* is an advance on its predecessors, chiefly in that the numbers are musically more extended, more widely varied and ambitiously constructed, it lacks the sharpness of *Die beiden Pädagogen* and is moreover awkwardly proportioned as a libretto and hence musically. There is only one female character, Mme Germain, who is not very sympathetic or clearly characterized: Mendelssohn hardly gives her a chance to reveal herself, since she has neither of the only two solo numbers in the entire score. Only one number, the mock-overture for the play, is in triple time, and no number is basically in a minor key. The indecision in such a plot as to where sympathies should lie is behind this lack of variety and uncertainty of proportion, and it is not really surprising that the best of the work is in its incidental felicities. But these are not negligible. The overture is an excellent piece of work, swift and well scored: it could stand concert revival. In the mock-overture for the play there is a neat parody of the fairly threadbare musical manner that must have characterized most Wandertruppen; and the finale is cleverly put together, as one after another the fictive Flinks are presented for arrest while the judge laboriously reads out the description on the warrant (oddly anticipating the Inn Scene in *Boris Godunov*) and the music neatly varies the repetitions for each character. Mendelssohn also makes much of the scene in which the two wretched judges blunder about in the dark, clutching hopefully at what they believe to be the elusive Flink and only succeeding in arresting each other. He also shows a developing operatic gift in his initial characterization of the three friends as they sit down in the tavern, Fröhlich cheerfully hailing wine, women and gambling and Fixfinger trying out some of his grimmest verses, while Hasenfuss wishes they would shut up and let him get on with learning his part (see Ex. 7).

The fourth and last of the Casper opera texts written for Mendelssohn is *Der Onkel aus Boston, oder Die beiden Neffen*: the former title heads the overture, the latter is on the cover of the manuscript and volume. Again, the libretto has long been presumed lost, but a manuscript copy of Act 1 is

Ex. 7

nie dein Wü - then en - den, willst du denn
- der Ver - rück-ter Mör-der, fahr zur
Es le-ben die Mäd-chen, die Wür-fel, der Wein!
nie   etc.
Höl - - - - le!'

to be found among Mendelssohn's manuscripts in the Bodleian Library; a
separate copy of Act 2 is in the same library; Act 3 has not yet come to
light.[16] The plot concerns, roughly, the return from America of Carl and
Theodor (both tenors), whither they had been taken by their father; he is
killed in the War of Independence, and the brothers return to their old
home where they find Fanny and Lisette (both sopranos). The complications of this intricate arrangement have to be set out in a lengthy, not to say
interminable stretch of dialogue, after which the very artificial ins and
outs of the plot have more or less run their course by the end of the first act;
Act 2 and, as far as one can make out, Act 3 are chiefly occupied with

[16]   MSS M. Deneke, Mendelssohn e. 15/1. iv: copy of Act 1, with some corrections by
        Casper and others, by Lea Mendelssohn-Bartholdy. Acquired from Miss Wach,
        daughter of Mendelssohn's youngest daughter Lili, between 1950 and 1960. MSS M.
        Deneke, Mendelssohn e. 15/2: copy of Act 2, with some corrections by Casper.

festivities and congratulations. These include a patch of quite attractive ballet music. The lack of dramatic effectiveness in the text is the more regrettable as Mendelssohn is here showing some signs of increased interest in continuous music for situations: he is some way off writing a continuously composed opera, but there is evidence that his study of Mozart's finales was bearing riper fruit, and by 1822 he had had time to absorb the lessons of the Berlin sensation of the previous year, *Der Freischütz*, especially when he came to write the Act 1 finale. The first orchestral rehearsal of the work in the Mendelssohns' house on 3 February 1824 coincided with Felix's fifteenth birthday: his health was drunk, and Zelter took him by the hand and declared before the company, 'My dear son, from today you are no longer an apprentice, from today you are a journeyman. I make you a journeyman in the name of Mozart, in the name of Haydn and in the name of old Bach.'[17]

Devrient, who helped to prepare *Der Onkel aus Boston* for two domestic performances, describes the work as representing 'an obvious step forward in melodic writing and in the handling of the voices'; and he dismisses as 'unacceptable' the comparison made by some of the guests between one of the choruses and the Bridesmaids' Chorus in *Der Freischütz*.[18] Mendelssohn made a considerably greater step forward, however, with his next opera, the most ambitious in scale that he was to attempt; and in it he seems to have been able to absorb for his purposes the lessons not only of *Der Freischütz* but of *Euryanthe*. This was *Die Hochzeit des Camacho*.

The story on which this is based is one of the most celebrated episodes in *Don Quixote*, and it has provided librettos for several operas, among them one contemporary with Mendelssohn's by Mercadante. Its plot is substantially the same in essence as that of Schenk's popular *Der Dorfbarbier* (1796). In Cervantes, Quiteria is forced by her father Carrasco to abandon her lover Basilio in order to marry the rich Camacho. Distraught, Basilio pines away, and his morbid pallor leads everyone to suppose him at the point of death. When the local doctor certifies that he is indeed about to expire, he is permitted as his last wish to go through a form of marriage with Quiteria so that he may die consoled. As soon as the ceremony is concluded, he leaps to his feet, fit and well. In the general consternation, Camacho decides to accept the inevitable with a good grace and allows his wedding feast to proceed with these new arrangements. Don Quixote and Sancho Panza play only a peripheral role.

Uncertainty exists as to who was the author of Mendelssohn's libretto, which has also hitherto been supposed lost. Some sources give the author

---

[17]   Quoted in Hensel, *Die Familie Mendelssohn* p. 161.
[18]   *Meine Erinnerungen*, p. 13.

as Carl von Lichtenstein.[19] Devrient refers to Klingemann, probably
meaning not Mendelssohn's friend Karl but the elder August Klingemann,
whose *Don Quixote und Sancho Panza, oder Die Hochzeit des Gamacho* was
performed in Berlin in 1811 and published four years later;[20] however,
Klingemann's play, though cast as a Singspiel with suggestions for
interpolated songs with named tunes, bears virtually no resemblance to
the manuscript libretto. Others, most recently Rudolf Elvers, have argued
that a large part, at any rate, of the text was the work of the Hanover writer
Friedrich Voigts.[21] No clue is given to the authorship in the manuscript
copy in the Bodleian Library: this is in an unidentified hand, with many
deletions, corrections, substitutions and insertions, suggesting a working
draft. Despite this, and though the first eight pages are missing, enough is
available taken in conjunction with the opening musical numbers for
reconstruction to be possible in this case also, though the two manuscript
full scores and the printed vocal and full scores all show many
differences.[22]

The idyllic love of Quiteria (sop.) and Basilio (ten.) is interrupted by her father Carrasco
(bass) insisting that she must marry the rich Camacho (bass). Basilio is supported in his
despair by Vivaldo (ten.), a light-hearted poet who is in love with Lucinda (sop.). The
wedding celebrations begin, but the unhappy Quiteria turns again to the place where
she last sat holding hands with Basilio, who now appears distraught. The noise arouses
Sancho Panza (bass), who halts them with admonitions and a farrago of proverbs; he
declares that Don Quixote (bass), the Knight of the Sorrowful Countenance, defender
of all fair ladies, is at hand. As the chorus renews the celebrations, Basilio appears in
travelling clothes; Vivaldo draws off Camacho and deludes Carrasco into thinking
Quiteria has been sold off elsewhere by her father, gaining time for Quiteria to escape.
Carrasco and Camacho reappear with their relations and retainers and try to organize
an attack on the house where Basilio is believed to be hiding. But they fail to find him in
the darkened house, and believing Don Quixote responsible they pour out into the
surrounding woods. Meanwhile, in the woods Basilio pretends that he must leave
Quiteria, wishing to test her loyalty to him; her distress convinces him that she is true
and persuades him to see if he can deceive Camacho and Carrasco. However, the
situation is further confused by Don Quixote mistaking her for his imagined love
Dulcinea del Toboso; and when Basilio intervenes, he is in turn mistaken for the giant
Montesinos. When Carrasco and Camacho arrive with torches and their supporters,
Don Quixote is still further confused. Quiteria is produced, and as efforts to hold the
wedding are renewed, Basilio's voice is heard pronouncing death to Quiteria's
bridegroom in ghostly tones; Camacho's enthusiasm for marriage begins to wane, and

19   E.g. A. Loewenberg, *Annals of Opera, 1597–1940*, (London, rev. 3/1978 by H.
       Rosenthal).
20   Op. cit., p. 28.
21   R. Elvers, ' "Nichts ist so schwer gut zu componieren also Strophen". Zur
       Entstehungsgeschichte des Librettos von Felix Mendelssohn-Bartholdys Oper *Die
       Hochzeit des Camacho*', *Veröffentlichung der Mendelssohn-Gesellschaft*, iv (Berlin and
       Basle, 1976).
22   MSS M. Deneke, Mendelssohn, e. 16, as *Die Hochzeit des Gamacho* (sic).

when Basilio, who Vivaldo says is wandering insane in the region, appears with his head wrapped in a mysterious cloth, they all flee.

In Act 2, Sancho is discovered enjoying the culinary preparations for the wedding feast. All gather, and there ensues a ballet of Love and Wealth, with a contest between Cupid, who shoots arrows, and Wealth, who hurls golden balls, for possession of a girl contained in the castle. Don Quixote intervenes, knocks down the castle and prostrates himself in wonder before the girl inside. Quiteria is now finally brought forward for marriage, miserably refusing to believe Vivaldo's whispered encouragements that Basilio is alive and at hand. She sees a glimmer of hope when Don Quixote also joins the gathering; but now the Alcade arrives to celebrate the marriage. Carrasco refuses to listen to Quiteria's pleas, when suddenly Basilio's voice is heard. Camacho orders him to be seized if he comes near. Ashen and with a cypress wreath on his brow, he approaches and renounces Quiteria to Camacho; suddenly he produces a stiletto and stabs himself. As his strength ebbs, he asks to be allowed to marry Quiteria as his dying wish; when this is granted, and having carefully assured himself of the union's legal validity and indissolubility, he leaps up and embraces her. Don Quixote steps forward to defend what they have done and threatens any objector with his lance. Camacho accepts the situation and allows the feast to proceed.

Though the style of the music remains rooted in Mendelssohn's earlier Singspiel manner, he has expanded it as much as Weber expanded the techniques of *Der Freischütz* when he came to write *Euryanthe* – with the difference that *Der Freischütz* is a far more assured piece of theatre than anything that Mendelssohn had written (as is only to be expected given their different ages and stations) and that *Euryanthe* dispenses with spoken dialogue while Mendelssohn in *Camacho* does so only in the ensemble scenes. These are skilfully composed, though the sixteen-year-old's dexterity constantly shows over his actual experience. A Septet with Chorus (No. 7) and the succeeding chorus build up a multiple movement with much ingenuity and show a good deal of interest in letting dramatic contrasts of tempo and texture respond to the implications of the text (it is the scene in which Basilio and Quiteria are being parted). Yet Mendelssohn's tendency to regularity constantly takes over, so that the dramatic movement halts while the music continues energetically enough but with somewhat bland harmonies and with too well-proportioned entries from the voices in concert, while in the orchestra there is still a tendency to suggest busy activity on stage with passages of fugato. These whiffs of oratorio constantly blow across the scene. When they are dispersed, Mendelssohn is more than capable of showing dramatic awareness. The end of No. 8, as Basilio turns his back on his home and his hopes, is beautifully managed. Orchestra, stage band and chorus conclude their foursquare celebration of the union of Camacho and Quiteria, and all depart, leaving Basilio alone. He is ready to leave, and it is evening. Soft clarinet and bassoon phrases accompany his leave-taking as he turns from the bluntness of the stage band's phrases to the softer lines and textures that, swelling and growing richer, surround him like the woods into which his voice slowly vanishes. Not everything in the score matches this kind of felicity; some of the other ensembles are what might be called self-continuous, in that their progress is motivated by efficient musical development more than by dramatic necessity; and even the overture, splendidly vigorous piece that it is, seems somewhat protracted for its sentimental–comic purpose. Yet Mendelssohn shows more of the skill he had displayed to comic ends in *Die wandernden Komödianten* for writing contrasting characterizations into a single ensemble, as when Carrasco is furiously denouncing Basilio and Quiteria in the time-honoured manner of a vengeance aria while they cling together musically against this onslaught (see Ex. 8).

Basilio is characterized in his first solo aria with the mixture of heroic ardour and troubadourish lyricism that Weber had put into operatic currency with Adolar (as in his No. 3, 'Noch tröstet mich das Vorgefühl'); later his character is at once more subtly but less lucidly defined. He cannot be said to emerge at the end of the opera with the composer, and hence the audience, clear as to whether he is to be regarded as heroic or as a sympathetic young village lad who has outwitted them all with a little help from his friend Vivaldo. Quiteria, too, is for much of the time a lovelorn village maiden, as in the charming if conventional opening duet with Basilio, all honeyed phrases with string zephyrs and woodwind billings and cooings (No. 1, 'Beglücktes Jugendleben'). Her finest hour is that of her madness, when Mendelssohn, taking his cue from the text, calls upon his Shakespearian memories of Ophelia to write her a Mad Aria that is far more tender and more touching than the Italian convention that was to become an operatic standard fitting (No. 9, 'Wer klopft so leise an die Thur?'). After a deceptively gentle opening, with Quiteria posing and answering her own questions, Mendelssohn takes her off into a contrasted set of tempos, with a recitative suddenly precipitating an Allegro molto before a desperate Agitato e presto that effectively portrays her disintegrating reason; and there is a masterly touch at the end when the tempo is pulled back to Andante, and a *pianissimo* cadenza before the soft cadential bars suggests her parting from normality and measure.

Carrasco and Camacho are less vividly portrayed, and the secondary lovers Vivaldo and Lucinda are given some charming music appropriate to their operatic social class; while Sancho Panza is the familiar greedy braggart whose characteristics are glimpsed from time to time in Leporello and Papageno (though he has few of their sympathetic qualities) and were the staple stuff of Singspiel buffoonery. Don Quixote's position in the drama is anomalous. As a slightly unhinged *deus ex machina*, he defies characterization; and Mendelssohn does well to give him a certain

Ex. 8

CARRASCO

O ver - derb - niss uns - rer Zeit!   Un - er -

Str

- hör - te Drei - stig - keit,   un - er - hör - te, un - er -

Ob

awkward dignity and authority, which he achieves by solemn melodic lines and some portentous brass to introduce him on his appearances. The reiteration of these has led to claims that here is a pioneering use of Leitmotif; but the figure can scarcely be described as more than a Reminiscence Motif, of which French opera shows many examples before Weber and Spohr made more sophisticated use of it ahead of Mendelssohn.

Nevertheless, its faults notwithstanding, *Die Hochzeit des Camacho* is an impressive enough work to earn revival (only a few attempts at performing the music, usually in concert, seem to have been made since Mendelssohn's day); and the belief that the composer was indeed now out of his apprenticeship led to approaches being made to Count Brühl, Intendant of the Berlin Royal Theatre, who liked what he saw. Spontini did not. Summoning Mendelssohn, he went through the score, then led the composer to the window and, with a gesture at the French church lying at their feet, declared, 'Mon ami, il vous faut des idées grandes – grandes comme cette coupole'. Nevertheless, the opera was performed, on 29 April 1827, according to the *Allgemeine musikalische Zeitung* 'with tumultuous applause, later with some opposition to the exaggerated displays of repeated clappings and calls for the composer'.[23] The writer went on to suggest that there was in the work a striving for effect that the young composer could not quite bring off, and pointed to its modelling on Beethoven, Mozart and Weber. There was also a warning against too much flattery and protectiveness for the boy composer from his rich parents. The performance was in fact hemmed with difficulties, not the least of which was a postponement because the famous baritone singing Don Quixote, Heinrich Blume, contracted jaundice. Despite this, the chorus appear not to have known their parts, and though the house was full the evening was not a success. Mendelssohn himself left before the end.[24]

The equivocal success achieved by *Camacho* does not seem to have deterred Mendelssohn in his search for a good libretto, though for the occasion of his parents' silver wedding in 1829 he was perhaps relieved to fall back on the tradition of Liederspiel of which he had already become an accomplished practitioner. The libretto of *Die Heimkehr aus der Fremde* was the work of Karl Klingemann, now established as counsellor to the German Legation in London; and Mendelssohn, appropriately, brought the score home with him on his return from his first English visit. The plot is neatly contrived in the manner of Casper's French-inspired vaudevilles.

Hermann (ten.) has been away in the army for six years, leaving his mother (con.) still sorrowing for him despite the attentions of her foster-daughter Lisbeth (sop.).

23   xxix (1827), p. 373.
24   Despite this fiasco, a beautifully printed vocal score of the opera's musical numbers, made by Mendelssohn, was printed in 1828. Perhaps Mendelssohn's parents helped over this.

Tomorrow, recruiting officers are again expected, and it is moreover the fiftieth anniversary of the Magistrate's entry upon office and hence the occasion for great celebrations. There now appears Kauz (bar.), a travelling pedlar and confidence trickster; he allows Lisbeth to mistake him for the recruiting officer and offers his services as master of ceremonies for the festivities. Another stranger appears, and from his singing Lisbeth recognizes him as the long-lost Hermann. Kauz, who only knows that the Magistrate's son has been away a long time, now decides to pass himself off as the prodigal and begins by warning the Magistrate (bass) against the young man who has just turned up and who seems to be paying unwelcome attentions to Lisbeth. When Kauz disguises himself as the nightwatchman and tries to chase Hermann away from serenading Lisbeth, Hermann in turn borrows the real nightwatchman's cloak and horn and interrupts Kauz's serenading with the nightwatchman's song. Eventually the Magistrate calms matters down, and night falls. Next morning, as the festivities begin, Kauz steps forward to announce himself as the Magistrate's son. But Hermann now reveals himself: the discomfited Kauz retreats in disarray, Hermann and Lisbeth are united, and the festivities are renewed.

Five out of the opera's thirteen vocal numbers are entitled 'Lied', and the work is constructed with a simplicity that does not exclude great craft; indeed, released from the ambitions of *Camacho*, Mendelssohn rediscovers his most delightful dramatic vein. Kauz is at least as skilfully characterized as the bumbling braggarts Lortzing was putting into operatic convention in these years with Van Bett, Baculus and others; and his introductory song (No. 7, 'Ich bin ein vielgereister Mann') has at once a boastfulness and a nimbler wit that make his pretensions seem harmless. There is a curious anticipation of Wagner in the scene where Kauz pretends to be the nightwatchman; he sings a romantically serenading adaptation of the traditional words also used by Wagner in Act 2 of *Die Meistersinger* (the melody is modified), and at the end Hermann cuts across him with a discordant flattened supertonic in identical manner to Wagner's Nightwatchman blowing his horn.

One of the opera's most attractive characteristics is its deft and eloquent scoring. Hermann's contrasting of the song about the village bells, which he used to sing, with the military life to which he has grown accustomed gives an obvious opportunity for such scoring; but Mendelssohn seizes it delightfully, the evening bells being hinted at in the pizzicato violins over held horn and cello notes, the military life in a little trumpet figure that is softened by clarinet and bassoons (No. 5, 'Wenn die Abendglocken lauten'). There is poetic suggestion where before Mendelssohn might have fallen back on more imitative conventions. The nocturnal encounter (No. 8, 'Es steigt das Geisterreich herrauf') has a marvellous delicacy tinged with apprehension, in the scoring almost entirely for two flutes in *pianissimo* detached quavers with violins and violas pizzicato *pianissimo* on the off-beats. Mendelssohn has clearly learnt still more from Weber in the matter of the subtle use of individual instruments or of a few instruments in novel combinations, such as his use of cello obbligato with answering flutes in sixths in Lisbeth's first Lied (No. 3, 'So mancher zog in's Weite') and still more in the divided violas in the middle of the soft string texture at the end of the previous duet (No. 2, 'Man geht und kommt'); while the transformation from night to a radiant dawn in the Zwischenmusik owes everything to the sunrise in *Oberon*. The overture includes a song tune from Klingemann's collection, used near the end of the opera: Mendelssohn intended it as his introductory bow to his parents, he told Devrient.[25] The overture was much admired by the young Richard Strauss, perhaps not least for its splendid horn entry near the end. It has enjoyed some success as a concert piece, with good reason; and the entire opera once had a modest career on English stages as *Son and Stranger*. The first, private, performance seems to have been a convivial family occasion, with Felix's brother Paul playing the cello obbligato, his sisters Fanny and Rebekka singing the Mother and Lisbeth and with Devrient as Kauz and a student friend named Mantius as Hermann. Even Mendelssohn's brother-in-law Wilhelm Hensel was pressed into service, though he could not sing a note; or rather, he was given a single note, an F, to repeat in the Terzett, No. 7. To the general delight, he failed to manage even that.[26]

The domestic success of *Die Heimkehr* led to renewed pressure on Mendelssohn to write more operas; and he was not reluctant to seek out subjects and potential librettists. Yet nothing else ever came to fruition. In some cases an exchange of letters with a librettist swiftly came to nothing; in others, a draft scenario was agreed upon, only for Mendelssohn to back off. His doubts found an echo with some of his friends, who appear to have sensed a larger difficulty. Karl Holtei, a librettist with whom he had discussions, is quoted as saying, 'Mendelssohn will never find an opera subject that pleases him: he's too clever for that'.[27] Heinrich Heine, who was properly dubious about Mendelssohn's capacity to compose a projected grand opera for Paris, thought that he would be 'alt und murrisch' before he did anything good in that field.[28]

The nearest he came to setting another text was with *Die Loreley* in 1847; but this project, with Eduard Geibel, never proceeded further than a somewhat bland prayer based on the Ave Maria (interestingly scored and with intoning horns on a persistent dominant pedal) and a few other pieces including a lively wine-growers' chorus and a first-act finale in which the betrayed Leonore is consoled by water spirits. Yet even if this scene, when she throws her ring back to the Rhinemaidens, did not now conjure up overwhelming comparisons, it would remain a somewhat inert piece of

25   Devrient, *Meine Erinnerungen*, p. 95.
26   Ibid., p. 91.
27   Ibid., p. 96.
28   *Augsburger Zeitung*, 25 April 1844.

music. The Rhinemaidens and their delight in their element have none of Wagner's magic; and their opening exchanges as they ask one another where they have come from ('Vom Drachenfels, vom Wolkenstein; und ihr, woher?' 'Vom Bodensee') suggest not so much the gathering of a host of spirits as girls joining a new school. Despite some agreeable textures in the orchestra, the music remains static, the manner closer to Mendelssohn's own cantata *Die erste Walpurgisnacht* than to anything dynamically dramatic.

It is tempting to feel that Mendelssohn's heart was not really committed to this project and that possibly his head also told him that it was unlikely to result in the operatic masterpiece he continued to assure his friends and himself he was capable of writing. By the mid-1840s, the Singspiel manner in which he had been educated was virtually an anachronism, with Lortzing the only composer of any stature continuing to explore its possibilities. German opera had progressed a long way since Mendelssohn had been struck by the example of *Der Freischütz*, whose implications he perhaps only partly understood. Spohr and, more significantly, Marschner had produced several Romantic operas, and Wagner had written *The Flying Dutchman* and *Tannhäuser*. To attempt to use the Loreley theme, which belonged to an earlier phase of Romanticism, with an obsolescent musical genre was surely a lost cause. Yet Mendelssohn could scarcely have adapted his idiom to Romantic opera: he was too ordered and elegant a composer, essentially a classicist working in Romantic times. In childhood and youth, his astonishing gifts enabled him to make brilliant use of the Singspiel genre he found to hand; but those gifts were formed and matured too early for him then to find it easy to adapt them to novel forms and ideas. Yet it is an oversight of posterity to have therefore relegated his youthful operatic works to the shelf. They belong, some occasionally and a few more regularly, on the stage.

Wagnerian tendencies in Italian opera

JULIAN BUDDEN

Reviewing a book on Wagner that appeared in the year of the composer's death, Filippo Filippi, critic of *La perseveranza*, wrote: 'Wagnerian opera, says Signor Marsillach, certainly does not represent the last word in lyric drama, and he is perfectly right; but it does represent a trend which none of today's composers has been able to escape, and it aims at a progress, a perfectibility, from which the art itself may expect new horizons and new manifestations of genius.'[1] Which is as much as to say that we are all Wagnerians nowadays. This, from an Italian, suggests a remarkable feat of conversion on Wagner's part; for him, generally speaking, Italian opera was the enemy, the prostitute from whose embrace the German music-lover needed to be rescued.

True, this had not always been the case. In an essay of 1837 he had held up Bellini as a model for all German composers and a sovereign cure for their intellectual abstruseness ('we could wish that their tangled skeins could be unravelled within the fixed forms of the Italians').[2] But once his theories of music drama began to be formulated, all approval of those 'fixed forms' ceased. Italian opera, he maintained, had failed to evolve from primitive dance music; its ready-made designs were strung together without coherence and allowed no dramatic development since each number expressed an unchanging state of mind. Rossini's operas aimed merely to gratify the senses; but they were more durable than the 'consumptive variations that Bellini and Donizetti devised on those very themes that he himself had fed to the public'.[3] Later, as the dogma of *Oper und Drama* gradually relaxed, and even changed, under the influence of Schopenhauer, something of Wagner's benevolence towards Italian opera returned. A visit to Rossini in 1860 left him with considerable respect for

[1] Cited in F. D'Arcais, 'Riccardo Wagner, poeta, musicista, uomo politico', *Nuova antologia*, xxxviii (1883), p. 30.
[2] 'Bellini: ein Wort zu seiner Zeit', R. Wagner, *Sämtliche Schriften und Dichtungen* (Leipzig, 5/1911), xii, pp. 19–21.
[3] 'Erinnerungen an Spontini', ibid., v, p. 87.

the man and the musician, and disposed to attribute any shortcomings in the opera composer to the age for which he wrote. His old enthusiasm for Bellini reawoke. 'They think me an ogre in all that concerns the musical school of Italy, and they set me up in especial opposition to Bellini. No, no, a thousand times no. Bellini is one of my favourites, because his music is all heart, deeply felt, closely and intimately bound up with the words.'[4] This to Francesco Florimo in 1880; and to the conductor Anton Seidl after playing him various melodies from *Norma*, *La straniera* and *I Capuleti e i Montecchi*: 'Despite a certain poverty there's real passion and feeling here; it only needs to be sung by the right singer to make a deeply moving effect . . . I've learnt from such things as regards my own melodies all those lessons that Messrs Brahms and Co. have never learnt.'[5] In his 'Letter to an Italian friend' (Boito) on the occasion of the Italian première of *Lohengrin* he talked vaguely of a wedding between the Italian and the German genius for which 'my poor *Lohengrin*' might be the marriage-broker.[6] Clearly Wagner was not immune from that northern longing for 'the land where the lemon trees bloom' (not for nothing did he spend more and more of his last years in various parts of Italy). The possibility of a fruitful relationship between his own and the Italian muse was therefore not so remote as some of his writings would imply.

Unfortunately such a relationship was bedevilled from the start by the fact that Wagner's theories were known and discussed in Italy before a note of his music had been heard. In 1856 Abramo Basevi, a leading light in the musical life of Florence, wrote approvingly of operatic reforms that were taking place in Germany under the stimulus of Wagner. Apprised of Basevi's article Wagner replied to it urging him to read *Oper und Drama*. But if he imagined he had found a supporter in that quarter he was mistaken. A year later Basevi pronounced in favour of Meyerbeer for having avoided the tortuous methods of Wagner with their sacrifice of melody to declamation; and in 1859 he reproached Verdi for having seemed in *Simon Boccanegra* to wish to follow in Wagner's footsteps 'if at a distance'.[7] By 1861, the year of the Parisian *Tannhäuser*, the anti-Wagnerians had taken up an entrenched position, summed up in a letter from Rossini to Lauro Rossi, director of the Milan Conservatory, attacking the 'new principles that would make the Art of Music a literary or representational art'. Music, he maintained, was by its nature 'ideal and expressive'. Its purpose should be to give pleasure: 'simple melody – clear

4   F. Florimo, *Bellini: memorie e lettere* (Florence, 1882), p. 40.
5   C. F. Glasenapp, *Das Leben Richard Wagners* (Leipzig, 1911), p. 65.
6   Wagner, op. cit., ix, pp. 287–91.
7   A. Basevi, *Studio sulle opere di Giuseppe Verdi* (Florence, 1859), p. 264. See also L. Pinzauti, 'Prospettive per uno studio sulla musica a Firenze nell'Ottocento', *Nuova rivista musicale italiana*, ii (1968), pp. 265–73.

rhythm'.[8] A preconceived system, it was felt, could only kill spontaneity.

Among the 'scapigliatura' – a radical avant-garde movement in the arts – on the other hand, Wagnerian theory fell on more fertile ground. Its iconoclasm, its emphasis on the role of the orchestra, its notion of a fusion of the arts, all touched a sympathetic chord in young firebrands such as Boito. Indeed Wagner's dismissal of those 'ready-made forms' that preclude psychological or dramatic development finds a parallel in Boito's denunciation of the traditional 'formula' that had limited the horizons of Italian opera for so long.[9] And had not Wagner won the admiration of that idol of the 'scapigliati', Baudelaire? But the affinity went no further. Boito's alternative to the formulas of Italian opera was a cloudy conception of the 'grand', the 'spherical' form.[10] That he saw *Tannhäuser* at the Opéra in the course of his travelling scholarship is more than likely; what he would not have realized is that it was mostly written before Wagner's theories were formulated. He could therefore write three years later about

one of those . . . spoilers of theories by their practice and of practice by their theories; talents more swollen with vanity than nourished by knowledge: Richard Wagner . . . the Bar Jesus of art in his day. But his day, by great good fortune, is over. The confiding crowd of young men who followed him closely in Germany and from afar in Italy is today falling away, with disillusion in their faces and indifference in their hearts.[11]

True, he soon changed his opinion, and during the 1870s did much to promote Wagner's works in Italy, translating several of the texts himself. Yet even in 1893 he could still describe *Die Walküre* as having a 'silly plot that moves more slowly than a stopping train . . . passing through a succession of duets during which the stage remains miserably empty and the characters ridiculously immobilized'.[12] For all that, his own *Mefistofele* of 1868 procured him the reputation of being a thoroughgoing Wagnerian among a public that had never heard a single opera by Wagner performed. Giulio Ricordi, sympathetic as he was to the 'scapigliatura' and to the revival of the Italian instrumental tradition, detected here the presence of a 'preconceived' (for which read 'Wagnerian') theory of opera, and he predicted that if he persisted in this direction Boito would never achieve greatness as a composer. Given the simple-minded antithesis – voice

8   Letter to L. Rossi, 28 June 1868: G. Mazzatinti, *Lettere di Gioacchino Rossini* (Florence, 3/1902, with F. and G. Manis), pp. 326–7.

9   From *La perseveranza* (13 September 1863): *Arrigo Boito: Tutti gli scritti*, ed. P. Nardi (Milan, 1942), pp. 1079–82.

10   From *Giornale della Società del Quartetto* (7 May 1865): ibid., pp. 1169–72.

11   'Mendelssohn in Italia', *Giornale della Società del Quartetto* (29 June 1864): ibid., p. 1257.

12   Letter to G. Verdi (31 December 1893): *Carteggio Verdi–Boito*, ed. M. Medici and M. Conati (Parma, 1978), i, p. 221.

(Italian) versus orchestra (German) – that prevailed in people's minds it was enough that an opera should give a certain prominence to the instrumental side for it to be automatically dubbed Wagnerian. The 'Wagnerisms' that Filippi claimed to detect in Verdi's *Don Carlos* and *Aida* are mostly the stylistic elements that both composers derived from the Paris Opéra.

The first work of Wagner's to be performed in Italy was *Lohengrin*, given at the Teatro Comunale, Bologna, in the Italian translation of Salvatore Marchesi in November 1871. Opera, year and venue were well chosen. The outcome of the Franco-Prussian War had resulted in an increased interest in all things German. Imperial Germany was viewed as a northern counterpart to the recently united Italy. Both were young nations with a glorious future before them. Liszt in Rome and Bülow in Florence had already begun to spread the Wagnerian gospel. Under the leadership of Camillo Cesarini, who was both mayor and artistic director of its principal theatre, Bologna was challenging the artistic pre-eminence of Milan. Ever since 1860 it had had a permanent call on the services of Italy's leading conductor, Angelo Mariani, resident at Genoa. He it was who gave the much acclaimed Italian première of *Don Carlos* in the Teatro Comunale in 1867; and he would do the same for *Lohengrin*. With La Scala, Milan, under the sway of the hostile house of Ricordi, Bologna had no difficulty in securing from the rival firm of Lucca the privilege of a Wagnerian 'first' in Italy. Finally the 1870s was the decade *par excellence* of Italian grand opera, or 'opera ballo' as it was called; and, despite its lack of a central ballet, *Lohengrin*, with its imposing spectacle and its massive choral scenes, is ineffably 'grand'. At the same time it carries many of those seeds of reform that were to bear fruit in the mature operas. Although it remains a singer's opera, the vocal line carrying the main burden of the musical argument, everything in *Lohengrin* is concentrated on the drama; there is no concession to hedonism, to variety for variety's sake in Meyerbeer's manner. Above all there is a sense of artistic commitment not to be found in the average Italian product of the mid-century. Many of the professed anti-Wagnerians were won over. To G. A. Biaggi, critic of the Florentine *La nazione*, the prelude provided 'one of the most valuable experiences the art of music has to offer: that of removing the listener from all material things to the life of the spirit'; Elsa's song to the night was a jewel, the Act 3 duet a 'model of declamation rich in the most beautiful melodies'.[13] It took a composer, admittedly a minor one, Stefano Golinelli, to state in so many words that he was relieved to find in *Lohengrin* no trace of the 'music of the future'. Verdi at the time was prepared to praise only isolated moments in a

[13]   For these and subsequent quotations from leading Italian critics of the day, see A. Ziino, 'Aspetti della critica wagneriana in Italia', *Wagner in Italia*, ed. G. Rostirolla (Turin, 1982), pp. 329–60.

score which as a whole he found slow and uneventful. But in the end he too would come round.

Among the Wagnerians, Filippi drew attention to the 'newness' of the melody – as did the conservative Francesco D'Arcais after a later performance in Rome. This may seem a surprising comment on a work written as early as 1848. Yet in the context of an operatic tradition in which for years fioritura had been almost its life-blood, conditioning the structure of the melodies, it makes sense. In the music of Verdi's contemporaries the withering away of this element caused the melodies themselves to languish like the gods of Valhalla when deprived of Freia's golden apples. To Wagner, as to Berlioz, coloratura was abhorrent; the melodic style of *Lohengrin*, limited in range as it may be and much of it based on the same metrical system that obtained in Italy, had evolved quite independently of display and could thus be seen as pointing the way forward for Italian opera of the 1870s and '80s. So it is no treason to see in the rhythmic design of the love duet from *Otello* traces of the Act 3 duet between Elsa and Lohengrin.

The introduction of the early Wagner canon into Italy might have proceeded smoothly enough but for the war of the publishers; and that same *Lohengrin* that pleased Bologna had a much rougher passage two years later at the Ricordi stronghold of La Scala, Milan. Conducted by Franco Faccio and with Italo Campanini in the title role, it filled the theatre for seven nights. The first performance was relatively successful, disturbed only here and there by a hostile claque. But the opposition gathered strength during the course of the season. By the third performance pro- and anti-Wagnerians were coming to blows in the stalls; after the fifth several arrests were made. At the seventh a chorus of howling and whistling brought down the curtain in the middle of the second act; all further performances were suspended. Fifteen years would pass before another Wagner opera was heard in Milan.

In all this the press had sided mostly against the composer. Articles appeared denouncing his supporters as worshippers of the Calf of Gold, traitors to native art. A journalist in Ricordi's house magazine hopefully predicted another revolution that would drive the Germans out of Italian theatres and concert-halls as they had already been driven out of Italian barracks and fortresses. But the Wagnerian tide was not so easily held back. Elsewhere in the peninsula the early operas won a cautious acceptance throughout the 1870s, *Lohengrin* being the invariable favourite.

Meanwhile the Bayreuth festivals of 1876 and 1882, to which many leading Italian critics were invited, together with Angelo Neumann's touring production of *The Ring*, which he took to four of the leading cities of Italy (sung, however, in German), at least made it possible to bring

Wagnerian theory and practice into proper focus. Across the spectrum from left to right there was less disagreement than might be supposed. For Filippi, Wagner was glorious when he gave free rein to his imagination but tortuous and over-elaborate when he involved himself too consciously in his system. The love duet in *Die Walküre* was 'the language of the heart that carries all before it . . . Here are no gods that argue and tell stories and pester one another, but a man and a woman in love.' *Götterdämmerung* seemed to him 'a night of polyphony', here and there irradiated by flashes of inspiration. Enrico Panzacchi too found it obscure and prolix; and, while praising the composer for his serious approach to the problem of modern opera, he regretted the absence of vocal melody and *pezzi concertati* – in a word, everything that he enjoyed in *Lohengrin*. To Biaggi it was necessary to separate Wagner the theorist from Wagner the musician, to forget such notions as 'endless melody' and 'the music of the future', and to see in the composer merely a reformer following in the steps of Gluck and the Florentine camerata. D'Arcais found the ideas of *Parsifal* 'as clear as those of *Lohengrin*' but thought the method of entrusting the principal thread of the music to the orchestra rather than the voice distinctly untheatrical. Even the aged Florimo, who in 1876 had thundered against Wagner in the columns of the *Gazzetta musicale di Milano*, in a publication of 1883 – doubtless mollified by the composer's praise of Bellini – urged young Italian composers to absorb those elements in Wagner's music that they found congenial, while remaining purely Italian. All appeared to agree that the whole intricate apparatus of Wagner's theory, far from threatening to impose a preconceived system, was not essential to the enjoyment of Wagner's music and therefore need frighten no one.

The final and most important stage in Wagner's penetration of Italy was the performance of *Tristan und Isolde* at Bologna in 1888 under the baton of Giuseppe Martucci in an Italian translation by Boito. By now the tumult and the shouting had died; and the performance was generally hailed as a major cultural event. *Die Meistersinger* followed in Milan in 1889; and after that *Die Walküre* (1893), *Götterdämmerung* (1896), *Siegfried* (1899) and *Das Rheingold* (1903). (*Parsifal*, of course, had to await the lifting of Cosima Wagner's embargo in 1914.) Meanwhile in 1890 Luigi Torchi published a critical study of Wagner's work viewed essentially as a German phenomenon, a moment in the evolution of the nation's culture, coloured by the nature of its people and therefore unsuitable for imitation by Italians. Four years later he brought out an Italian translation of *Oper und Drama*; and throughout the next two decades he would attack Mascagni and others for wishing to apply methods of which they had no real understanding. The Wagnerian die-hards were by now very few; but it is surprising to find as late as 1902 in the *Rivista musicale italiana* a series of articles by Vincenzo Tommasini (remembered mainly as the orchestrator of Domenico

Scarlatti's music for the ballet *Le donne di buon umore*) endorsing Wagner's theories *in toto*, including his historicist approach, his belief in a fusion of the arts and the conviction that absolute music had been superseded. Such, then, was the general critical view of Wagner in late-nineteenth-century Italy; and so, broadly speaking, it would remain until the rediscovery of Italy's Baroque heritage – begun by Torchi himself – and the coming of age of the 'generazione dell'ottanta' brought a reaction against the values of German Romanticism.

Meanwhile for the Italian composers born during the 1850s and '60s and destined to enter the reformed conservatories with their enlarged European outlook, Wagner was the major prophet of the age – the Dalai Lama, as Busoni derisively put it.[14] To the young Mascagni he was 'the Pope of all musicians, present and future'.[15] His operas represented 'the highest pleasure that the soul of an artist could desire' (Catalani).[16] Puccini was involved in the Italian première of *Die Meistersinger*, having travelled to Bayreuth with Giulio Ricordi and the conductor Franco Faccio to advise on cuts; he was delighted with the result and only regretted that the public stayed away. A later visit to Bayreuth he described as 'three days of pure magic. Divine, lofty, sublime music.'[17] Antonio Smareglia physically assaulted an anti-Wagnerian at the notorious Milan *Lohengrin* of 1873. But apart from Smareglia himself, who had been educated in Austria, how much of Wagner's music could these composers have experienced at first hand before the Bologna *Tristan* of 1888? They could have attended occasional performances of the pre-*Rheingold* canon; they could have studied such operas as had been published in vocal score; and they could have heard excerpts performed at concerts under conductors such as Pedrotti or Mancinelli. But the chief obstacle to the application of Wagnerian principles was the prevailing fashion for grand opera on the Meyerbeerian model. *Les Huguenots*, as one writer put it, remained 'the Pillars of Hercules of dramatic music';[18] and the closed form still obtained, though its boundaries were crumbling. A fondness for northern subjects, the occasional echo of a rhythm from *Lohengrin* or *Tannhäuser* – these are the limits of Wagnerian influence during that period. It was inevitable that Catalani's *La falce* (1876) and Puccini's *Le villi* (1884) – the first with its symphonic prologue depicting the Battle of Breda, the second with its

14   Cited in S. Sablich, *Busoni* (Turin, 1982), p. 135.
15   Letter to V. Gianfranceschi, 8 April 1887: *Pietro Mascagni*, ed. M. Morini (Milan, 1964), i, p. 273.
16   Letter to G. Depanis, 20 August 1889: A. Catalani, *Lettere*, ed. C. Gatti (Milan, 1946), pp. 100–1.
17   Letters to M. Puccini, 5 January 1890, and L. Pieri, 11 August 1912: *Carteggi pucciniani*, ed. E. Gara (Milan, 1958), pp. 35, 401.
18   G. Pozza, cited in M. Smareglia, *Antonio Smareglia nella storia del melodramma italiano* (Pola, 1934), p. 20.

'mourning' intermezzo and its 'tregenda' (a kind of Italian 'Walkürenritt') – should have been called Wagnerian; in fact the early music of both composers owes much more to Massenet.

An exception should be made, however, for *Isora di Provenza* (Bologna, 1884) by Luigi Mancinelli. Today he is a name from the music criticisms of Bernard Shaw – the conductor of *Lohengrin* at Covent Garden whose 'Italian temperament frequently came into conflict with the German temperament of the composer'.[19] In fact Wagner himself thought very highly of his interpretations. He wanted him to conduct the London premières of both *Tristan und Isolde* and *Die Meistersinger*; and it was to Mancinelli that he turned for the conductor in Venice of a concert in honour of Cosima's birthday that would include a performance of his own early Symphony in C (in the end, pressure of work prevented Mancinelli from accepting and Wagner conducted the concert himself). Certainly no one did more for the Wagnerian cause in Italy in the early 1880s than Mancinelli; he even wrote to the composer himself for advice on how to perform the 'Walkürenritt' and the prelude to *Tristan*. Clearly his knowledge of the operas extended well beyond the early canon; and this the score of *Isora di Provenza* amply confirms.

Reviewing the first performance D'Arcais drew attention to the 'Wagnerian' use of Leitmotif. Nor was he far wrong. But a few distinctions should be made. In a century which saw a steady progress towards the concept of an opera as an organic unity, the use of thematic recurrence inevitably plays an increasing role in the general structure. The recurrences may be of two kinds. The more common is the orchestral recall of a phrase that has already been sung and whose repetition is associated with memories of the accompanying words ('Quel vecchio maledivami' from *Rigoletto* or 'Di quell'amor' from *La traviata*). The second kind is what might be called the 'labelling' theme. This will appear in the orchestra from the start accompanying either a character at his or her first entrance or a concept when it is first mentioned; and from then on the two will be firmly linked in the listener's mind (e.g. the 'star' theme in Meyerbeer's *L'Etoile du nord*). Wagner uses both types – the first for Alberich's curse, the second for the Rhine – but, as is already clear, neither is specifically Wagnerian. For that term to be applied legitimately, two conditions must be fulfilled: the motifs must seem to amplify and complement in music what the text articulates in words; and more important still they should be the generating force in the music's continuity. In other words, a motif stuck up at wide intervals like a placard, as in Verdi's *I due Foscari*, has nothing whatsoever to do with

19   G. B. Shaw, 'A Butchered *Lohengrin*', *The Star* (31 May 1889): *Shaw's Music*, ed. D. H. Laurence (London, 1981), i, pp. 647–8.

Ex. 1   Mancinelli, *Isora di Provenza*

[Allegro brillante]

Wagner's method. That each motif should have a precise significance is not important – indeed the habit of naming every motif in *The Ring* did not arise until after Wagner's death and is now discredited. It is sufficient that at every appearance a motif should 'project' the dramatic situation.

All this Mancinelli seems to have understood, however difficult he found it to put into practice. The story of *Isora di Provenza* is based on the legend described by Victor Hugo according to which every ruler of medieval Provence was required to spend the night before his coronation in a gallery peopled by the statues of his ancestors. If anyone should attack him during his vigil the statues would come to his aid. All this is outlined in a Symphonic Prologue, the score of which is sprinkled with quotations from Hugo's *La Légende des siècles* and whose principal subject (Ex. 1) will recur throughout the opera whenever danger threatens, usually in the form of the villains Folco and Berardo. Not much Wagnerian psychological resonance here; nevertheless Mancinelli shows a certain skill in adapting the theme to its various contexts and even linking it to other motifs. Where Rolando, the hero, enters to announce sadly that his father's death has required him to enlist as a Crusader and thus postpone his wedding to Isora, this same motto theme, now in a minor key, forms a consequent to another motif (x) which had connoted the court of Provence *en fête* (Ex. 2). The long-drawn-out postlude during which the characters merely ruminate is another Wagnerian trait, evident as early as *Die fliegende Holländer*. Elsewhere we find Ex. 1 developed in sequences with or without other themes. It has a 'feminine' counterpart connoting Isora's love for Rolando (Ex. 3a), a more expressive theme and capable in true Wagnerian fashion of yielding more than one variant and even generating a kindred idea (Ex. 3b). It ends the opera in much the same way as the so-called 'redemption-by-love' theme ends *Götterdämmerung* and on a similar note of consolation for loss. For the Rolando who has come to Isora's rescue in the gallery is only a ghost.

So much, then, intimates mature Wagner; yet the opera as a whole remains inescapably 'grand', with dances and spectacular choruses and ensembles, and therefore susceptible mostly to the influence of Wagner's early works. The first act contains a song contest, the second a scene in which the heroine is falsely arraigned, prays for a champion to come to her aid and is duly granted her wish – two eminently Wagnerian situations, from *Tannhäuser* and *Lohengrin* respectively. So there is no lack of massive periodic melodies with *Tannhäuser*-like triplets in the accompaniment. If they are mostly entrusted to the orchestra, one reason is that so many of their phrases have blunt, masculine endings on which the Italian language sits awkwardly (see Ex. 4). *Isora di Provenza* succeeded at Bologna but nowhere else; and after two more essays in the genre, Mancinelli, like Faccio before him, gave up composition to devote himself entirely to conducting.

1888, the year of Italy's first *Tristan und Isolde*, saw the first opera by another Wagnerian enthusiast: *Asrael* by Alberto Franchetti. The libretto by Ferdinando Fontana is typical of the wilder extravagances of the 'scapigliatura'. Asrael, a fallen angel turned demon, longs to return to earth for just one year to taste again the 'delights of love'. Lucifer grants his request on condition that he bring with him on his return a 'spotless white dove' (i.e. the soul of an innocent maiden). Otherwise he will forfeit his privileges as a member of staff. The bizarre events that enable him to get the best of all three worlds required a wealth of musical vocabulary such as could only be supplied with the help of the late Wagnerian idiom. There are only two recurring themes throughout the opera: one chromatic, tonally unstable, with whirling 3/4 rhythm, which denotes Lucifer and thus the negative side of Asrael; the other bland and lyrical, for the redeeming Sister Clothilde. For once again we are in the realm of grand opera with its crowded stage and its variety of 'genre' pieces. However, in the love duet between Asrael and the gypsy girl Loretta, 'Quando lo

Ex. 2 Mancinelli, *Isora di Provenza*

Moderato maestoso

viene lacri - mando?

pp dolciss. e legatissimo

AHMED & CHORUS

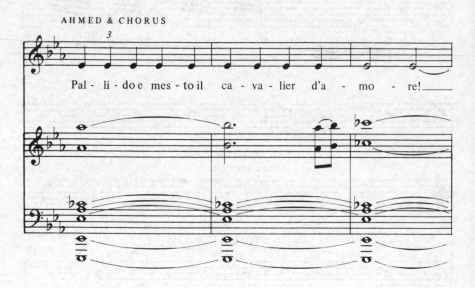

Pal - li - do e mes - to il ca - va - lier d'a - mo - re!

Ex. 3   Mancinelli, *Isora di Provenza*

(*a*)

(*b*)

Ex. 4   Mancinelli, *Isora di Provenza*

'sguardo mio', it is not hard to see a conscious tribute to 'O sink' hernieder, Nacht der Liebe' (see Ex. 5). Wagnerian too is Franchetti's habit of constantly side-stepping a full close by means of an interrupted cadence. But he is a cautious composer whose boldest effects are so carefully prepared as to lose all sense of spontaneity. His experiments, as Luigi Torchi put it, are those of a Kapellmeister.[20]

He was, however, sufficiently well thought of at the time to be commissioned by the city of Genoa to write an opera that would commemorate the 400th anniversary of the discovery of America by its most illustrious citizen. Written to an anonymous libretto (in fact by Luigi Illica), *Cristoforo Colombo* (1892) is the *ne plus ultra* of grand opera, with a cast of thousands, several *émeutes* (one of them aboard the *Santa Maria*), exotic, modally flavoured Indian dances and a love duet that, characteristically, develops as a concertato (no one here is allowed the privacy of Tristan and Isolde). Once again it is the sound and the vocabulary rather than the method that recall Wagner. There are recurring themes for the Council of Genoa, for the three Romei who foretell the discovery of a new world across the sea, for the villain, Roldano (Ex. 6a), who is clearly first cousin to Lucifer, and for the sighting of America (Ex. 6b). This last is twisted into 4/4 for a hymn of triumph for the end of Act 2, to appear subsequently in its original rhythm but with appropriately altered harmonies and mode whenever the Indians allude with rancour to the conquistadors. Several of the themes are resumed in the epilogue, where Columbus, deprived of his honours and rejected by the court of Ferdinand, loses his reason. But what remains most in the mind are the moments of grand theatre – especially the one where a desperate mutiny is suddenly quelled by the sighting of land. Indeed, over the whole opera looms the shade of *L'Africaine*. Roldano is closer to Nelusko even than to Lucifer; while the motif of the three Romei, with its veneer of counterpoint and its restless bass in the manner of a chorale prelude, recalls all too clearly the Anabaptists from *Le Prophète*. 'The need to understand Wagner à la Meyerbeer' (Torchi again) '– that was the gift of Franchetti's fairy godmother.'[21]

[20]   'Germania', *Rivista musicale italiana*, ix (1902), p. 418.
[21]   Ibid., p. 387.

Ex. 5   Franchetti, *Asrael*

Ex. 6 Franchetti, *Cristoforo Colombo*
(*a*)

Allegro moderato

Dor - mon l'a - gi - li pro - - re nel lac - cio d'un ab - brac-cio d'a - li-ghe im - mon - de; e a

(*b*)

Andante maestoso ♩ = 69

E là la nuo-va ter - ra che fre - me al - l'o-riz -

- zon - te.

After two excursions into a more intimate style – *Fior d'Alpe* (1894) and *Monsieur de Pourceaugnac* (1897) – Franchetti returned to the grand scale with *Germania* (1902), which concerns the *Tugendbund* and the resistance of young patriots to Napoleon. Here, if anywhere, one would expect a closer adherence to the Wagnerian method; and indeed there is both a wealth of recurring themes and a serious attempt to extend and combine them as Mancinelli had done but within a far richer orchestral texture. Moreover, several have a genuine suggestive power. In Ex. 7 the motif associated with Worms's guilt and remorse (x) is effectively dovetailed into that of the heroine, Ricke (y), whom he has seduced (as in Verdi's *La battaglia di Legnano*, there is a triangular situation among the patriots). In order to evoke a German ambience Franchetti infuses an element of German popular music of the time. Sometimes he quotes well-known melodies: 'Gaudeamus igitur' (used ironically, as a symbol of thoughtless youth, with altered harmonies), the folksong 'Da unten im Tale', and 'Lützows wilde Jagd' by Weber. Elsewhere he aims at a plain, rather symmetrical style of melody that matches that of his quotations but which resists motivic technique. The result is that the motifs are worked in only in the formal interstices of the score; the duets, solos and ensembles remain square and dull, sometimes varied by restless modulation (it is remarkable how often in ternary structures the reprise is in a different key from the opening). Once again Franchetti has failed to free himself from the conception of Meyerbeerian grand opera; as a result, *Germania* is Wagnerian only by fits and starts. 'Adulterated Wagner', Torchi called it, and rightly.[22]

The *verismo* movement which came into being with *Cavalleria rusticana* and which left Franchetti untouched represents, if anything, a turning away from Wagner inasmuch as it restored the unchallenged supremacy of the voice. True, the 'veristic' orchestra can make as much noise as Wagner's, but the singer, with his exasperated 'vocalità', can always beat it. The vocal climaxes of a Wotan, Brünnhilde or Isolde seem to be generated from the orchestral pit; those of a Chénier or a Santuzza are the culmination of an emphatic cantilena that the instruments merely reinforce. Then, too, *verismo* aims as far as possible at a naturalistic pace such as precludes the long Wagnerian rumination. Certainly orchestral motifs are plentiful, if only to carry the action forward; but, apart from those of the statutory intermezzos, they are rarely very memorable. There is a certain kinship with Wagner in the flights of emotional rhetoric in which the operas of the 'giovane scuola' abound, since, paradoxically, 'realism' in Italian opera coincided with a late inundation of musical Romanticism which the formal nature of the post-Rossinian tradition had

[22]   Ibid., p. 417.

Ex. 7 Franchetti, *Germania*

Worms cogitabondo guarda Ricke allontanarsi;
un profondo abbattimento s'impossessa di lui

held in check. But too often the rhetoric degenerates into formless rhapsodizing of which very little stays in the listener's mind, however much he might enjoy being swept off his feet at the time. Otherwise all that remains of Wagner in the *verismo* score is the occasional sonority or thematic echo (the 'dawn' motif from Mascagni's *Iris* is clearly from the same stable as the arpeggio-born melodies from which so much of *The Ring* is built).

However, if Giordano and Cilea remain confined within the same veristic idiom whether their subjects were taken from low life or not, Mascagni and Leoncavallo made several attempts to escape from it that sometimes took them in Wagner's direction. One such is Mascagni's 'lyric tragedy' *Parisina* (Milan, 1913), his only collaboration with Gabriele D'Annunzio. Here everything seems to point to an Italian *Tristan*, not least certain of D'Annunzio's lines:

> Take me to the forest. Carry me afar, like Isolde of the fair tresses:
> You with your bow and sword, I with only my love.
> . . . Perhaps in the land of Forgetfulness I shall again find my harp
> Hung upon the bough of a hazel tree entwined with flowering honeysuckle.[23]

'It is very free in form', Mascagni wrote to a friend,

except for certain pieces which are bound together by a rhythm, a type of bar, or a key. The opera is essentially thematic with continual reminiscences and re-statements and repercussions of ideas; but these reminiscences are inspired by a concept that is profound and at times philosophical, and which reflects the inner spirit of the characters rather than their outward appearance and their words.[24]

In a newspaper article he insisted on the need to give melodic form to the declamation, admitting that to 'set in relief every element of the poetic discourse and at the same time allow the human voice – that most perfect of instruments – to expand in waves of melody is a fearsome problem and one to frighten the most hardened and experienced composer. Perhaps only Wagner has solved it in his marvellous *Mastersingers*.'[25] Elsewhere he specifically repudiated the 'orchestral polyphony' – or 'phonism', as he called it – of Richard Strauss in *Salome* and *Elektra*.[26]

Among Mascagni's special gifts was the ability to set verse of whatever metre freely and flexibly without ever falling into fixed patterns, yet giving each word its appropriate accent. As early as *Guglielmo Ratcliff* (Milan, 1892) he had accomplished the feat of setting the whole of Heine's play in Andrea Maffei's translation – all blank verse save for the occasional

23   Vocal score (Milan, 1913), pp. 264–5.
24   Letter to V. Gianfranceschi, 10 December 1912: *Pietro Mascagni*, i, pp. 374–5.
25   *La tribuna* (18 December 1912): ibid., i, p. 376.
26   *Orfeo* (15 March 1913).

ballad – in a basically homophonic style without lapsing into rhythmic monotony. There, however, he had been sustained by a youthful melodic fertility on which by 1913 he could no longer count. *Parisina* is tricked out with all manner of artifices – liturgical modality, pentatonic and whole-tone scales, heavy chromatic harmony, passages of 5/4 metre – which never yield a bar of memorable melody, let alone coalesce into a unified style, such as keeps Zandonai's *Francesca da Rimini* (Milan, 1914) – also D'Annunzio-based, no less homophonic in conception and free in form – alive and in the repertory to this day. *Parisina* has Wagnerian length (three and a half hours of music) without Wagnerian significance. 'There are some very beautiful things in *Parisina*', was Puccini's verdict, 'but Mascagni has made the mistake of being over-deferential to D'Annunzio.'[27]

Among Leoncavallo's earliest operatic projects was a trilogy to be entitled *Crepusculum* (tell-tale word!), to a text written by himself. The operas were to be called *I Medici, Girolamo Savonarola* and *Cesare Borgia*, but only the first was completed. Like Mascagni twenty years later, the composer saw fit to precede the première with a public explanation of his aims and intentions.

I wished to prove myself in a genre that has not yet been exploited on stage: by which I mean the *epic poem*. And why should music not have its own *epic*, possessing as it does the language which is best suited to that genre and is, I would say, more poetic than poetry itself? Therefore, in order to arrive at *epic music* I have aimed at *epopea* . . . while remaining true to my convictions as a realist ['verista'] in literature and art. Because, I must confess, for me music is simply the *most poetic and perfect expression of the human spirit*. I will merely say that following the precepts of the great master of Bayreuth I have tried to make a *national poem* and hence I wanted a great feeling of *'italianità'* to fan the musical breeze of the poem.[28]

Fine words! But how to convert them into practice? Certainly the text, which concerns the love of Giuliano de' Medici for Simonetta Cattaneo, and the conspiracy of the Pazzi whose defeat brought Lorenzo de' Medici into absolute power, shows every sign of painstaking research. The style of the verse is modelled on the poetry of Poliziano, to whom there are constant footnoted references, as also to Carducci, Gregorovius, Roscoe and even Shakespeare; for of all Italian composers of the time, Boito apart, Leoncavallo was the most profoundly lettered. And with him, as with Boito, the musician is mostly at the mercy of the poet, if for a different reason. Boito's failing is the inability to think continuously in music – something which barred him from Wagnerian influence from the start. His ideas are often striking and refined, but they never proceed very far;

27   Interviewed by E. Cavicchioli, *Il secolo* (25 December 1914): *Pietro Mascagni*, i, p. 380.
28   Letter to F. Tonolla, cited in R. Giani and A. Engelfred, '*I Medici* di R. Leoncavallo', *Rivista musicale italiana*, i (1894), pp. 95–6.

this is why his *Mefistofele* remains basically a string of attractive miniatures, sometimes breaking down into incoherence, as in the Brocken scene. Leoncavallo's ideas are more prolific, if less distinguished. His melodies, mostly vocal, are short, regular in construction and heavily conditioned by the metre of his verse; and his attempts to extend those swirling tunes in 6/4 or 6/8 by clever harmonic twists or to vary the rhythmic symmetry tend to sound artificial. His gift for elegant pastiche, exemplified by the Harlequinade in *Pagliacci* and here by Lorenzo's gavotte-like serenade and Simonetta's Tuscan stornello, yields no more than a decorative tinsel. There is no place for that kaleidoscopic succession of short movements that makes the final scene of *Pagliacci* so theatrically effective. Despite moments of orchestral busyness *I Medici* remains mostly an opera of vocal tune and accompaniment. For the 'Allocution' of Lorenzo that turns the fury of the crowd on to the murderers of his brother, Leoncavallo clearly had in mind Mark Antony's speech from Shakespeare's *Julius Caesar* but failed to find the musical ideas to match.

All the grand opera apparatus is here, including the big static concertato. More damaging are those uncertainties of taste that permeate all Leoncavallo's works from *Chatterton* to the posthumous *Edipo Re*. The grandiose jostles the trivial, sometimes in the same melody; an unconscious quotation from a Schumann Novellette will be followed by a strain of café music. Given an idiom so eclectic it is not surprising that Wagner likewise is broadly hinted at (see Ex. 8). The première of *I Medici*, given at the Teatro Dal Verme, Milan, in 1893 was treated mercilessly. However, its performance in Berlin the following year so impressed Kaiser Wilhelm that he commissioned from Leoncavallo a historical opera on a German subject to be given in Berlin's leading opera-house. *Rolando*, performed in German as *Roland von Berlin* in 1904, no more concerns the Frankish knight than Mascagni's *Piccolo Marat* concerns the famous Jacobin murdered in his bath. It is a comedy from the period of *Die Meistersinger* with would-be heroic overtones and a tragic ending, which a wise, beneficent Elector (*verb. sap.*!) tries vainly to avert. An appendix tells us that the composer used five German melodies dating from between 1500 and 1700. Orchestral motifs are more plentiful than in *I Medici*, some of them remarkably graphic. But the uncertainty of direction that marks the original play by Willibald Alexis is all too faithfully reflected in the music, with its jumble of styles and its moments of irretrievable bathos. Echoes of Chabrier alternate with veristic ranting. The second act opens with a pretentious variant of the famous 'Jealousy' tango (Ex. 9a); and when Henning, the hero, proclaims that he has a sword to place at the emperor's service, it is clear that he has Nothung in mind (Ex. 9b).

Grand opera *à la française* and *verismo* both resisted Wagnerian influence beyond a certain point. Two composers, however, both

Ex. 8   Leoncavallo, *I Medici*

(*a*)

Andante sostenuto ♩.= 48

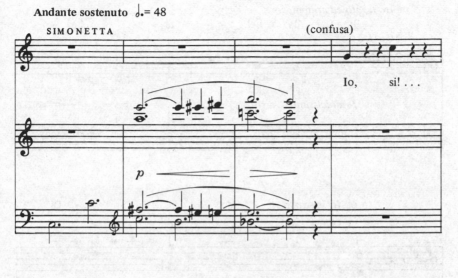

(b)

Ex. 9   Leoncavallo, *Rolando*

(*a*)

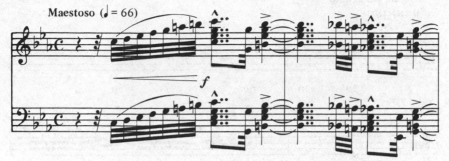

(b)

Wagnerphiles and both born in 1854, succeeded in freeing themselves from the first while remaining virtually untouched by the second. Alfredo Catalani was launched on an operatic career by the success of his one-act eclogue *La falce*. Then he plunged into the world of grand opera, from which he finally emerged with *La Wally* (1892). The subject, taken from a novel by the Austrian writer Wilhelmine von Hillern and set among the dour peasants of the Tyrol, has affinities with *verismo*; but Catalani's treatment remains on the level of picturesque Romanticism. The first act is a remarkable instance of tight − almost symphonic − thematic working in which the only closed forms are Walter's Song of the Edelweiss and

Wally's 'Ebben ne andrò lontano'. Yet once his dramatic exposition is over
and he starts to concentrate on the feelings of his characters, Catalani
abandons the use of developing motifs for a looser discourse, with much
use of tremolando strings, orchestral gestures and even the occasional
vocal period. Much of Act 2 is spun over the strains of a waltz. Motivic
working of a sort accompanies the ensemble at the end of Act 3 where
Wally directs the rescue of the man she has tried to have killed; but it
amounts to little more than sophisticated 'hurry' music. The orchestra
comes into its own at the start of Act 4 with a magnificent evocation of the
lonely heights of the Murzoll; and it effects a powerful cataclysm in the
opera's final pages. The rest of the act is all straightforward songs and
duets. *La Wally* remains an ambivalent work, in which the penetration of
the Italian tradition by Wagnerian and other German elements achieves
only a partial synthesis. Where it stands out from its predecessors is in its
absorption of post-*Tristan* chromaticism (see Ex. 10).

An even more isolated figure in the Italian tradition was Antonio
Smareglia. Born in Pola in the Istrian peninsula, he was educated in Vienna
and Graz before returning to Italy to devote himself to composition under
Faccio at Milan Conservatory. His earliest operas are written in the
fashionable manner of the time, though on a smaller scale than most, and
show an unusually refined craftsmanship. In 1889 he won fame in Vienna
with *Il vassallo di Szigeth*, a powerful drama of fratricidal jealousy and
vengeance produced at the Kärntnertortheater under Hans Richter. Even
Brahms was impressed ('At last an Italian opera worthy of the Viennese
shrine!').[29] This he followed up with *Cornil Schut* (Vienna, 1893),
concerning a Flemish painter torn between love and devotion to his art.
Here it is hard to discern a trace of Italian melody. Much of it could be said
to be in Humperdinck's manner, with a well-nourished orchestral texture
and a number of folk-like choruses that recall Smetana. Yet there is also
more than a hint of Smareglia's beloved *Mastersingers* – note the kinship of
Gertrude's melody in Ex. 11a with that of Eva; and also how close
Smareglia comes to that labile melodic style so characteristic of Wagner's
comedy (Ex. 11b). In *Nozze istriane* (Trieste, 1896), the composer's one
enduring success, he touches hands with *verismo* in both the subject-matter
and some of the vocal writing; indeed he might well have joined the ranks
of Mascagni's followers had he not in the meantime met the poet Silvio
Benco, who became the librettist of his last three operas. All three, but
especially *Oceàna* (Milan, 1903), betray the 'aestheticizing' influence of
D'Annunzio. Indeed it is not so much an opera as a symphonic legend with
voices and stage action. The story is set in ancient, pagan Syria. The orphan
Nersa is loved passionately by Vadar, the elderly head of the tribe among

29   Smareglia, *Antonio Smareglia*, p. 140.

Ex. 10   Catalani, *La Wally*

(*a*)

(*b*)

Ex. 11 Smareglia, *Cornil Schut*

(*a*) **Allegro con fuoco**

whom she has been brought up, and hated by everyone else as an interloper. She herself feels vague inexpressible longings for a more adventurous love. The sea-god Ers appears with a message summoning her to the court of Init, King of the Sea, who wishes to make her his bride. In the tug-of-war which follows, partly among the cornfields, partly by the sea-shore amid a chorus of tritons, nereids and undines, Init is finally successful; while Vadar prays for, and receives, the affliction of madness to take away all memory of the girl he has lost. Nersa has all the inarticulacy of Mélisande; but unlike her she is unable to create any kind of tension between her two lovers since both Vadar and Init inhabit two different planes of existence – which is why Maeterlinck's poem, for all its understatement, is a genuine drama while Benco's remains a mere fable of fantastic events.

Musically, however, the result seems to have been to set the composer's imagination free. Here the leading-themes – for Init, Ers, Nersa's longing, Vadar's loss, and Hareb, his envious brother – are used on a broader scale than in any of Smareglia's previous operas. These and others of less specific nature merge and proliferate in a flow of sweet orchestral polyphony. The nereids and undines – indeed, one might say the whole opera – take their starting-point from the Rhinemaidens of *Götterdämmerung* Act 3, with their diaphanous chromatic harmonies – so different from their robustly diatonic strains in *Das Rheingold*. But, whatever its lineage, Smareglia's style in this opera is entirely integrated and individual. In the balancing of vocal and orchestral melody in the ensembles he often seems to anticipate the solutions of Richard Strauss. Yet the opera as a whole remains basically untheatrical – dreamily impressionistic rather than dramatic. It survives mostly in the form of a suite arranged by the composer himself.

By now a few tentative conclusions may be drawn. Wagner aroused huge interest among Italian music-lovers and critics and a fanatical admiration in a generation of composers born in the mid-nineteenth century. But the principles of *Oper und Drama*, even in the modified form in which they are applied in the later works, never took root in Italy, if only because they prescribe a relationship of voice to orchestra completely alien to the Italian tradition. Secondly, different operas in the Wagner canon appealed in different degrees. Until 1890 the favourite, as well as the most influential was *Lohengrin*; from 1890 onwards it was *Die Meistersinger*. *Tristan und Isolde* was much admired (by, among others, the aged Verdi), but its slow pace and inward character precluded it from anything like imitation by Italians ('Enough of this music', Puccini remarked after a performance, 'We're mandolinists, amateurs . . . This terrible music destroys one . . . !'[30]). Yet it remained to be drawn upon for its harmonic vocabulary.

30   G. Marotti, *Giacomo Puccini intimo* (Florence, 2/1942), p. 203.

The Ring was the least liked: its subject-matter and philosophical content held no attraction for a nation that had never regarded the theatre as a place of instruction or a school of morals as the Germans had done from Gottsched through Goethe and Schiller to Wagner himself.

The predilection for *Die Meistersinger* is not hard to understand. Of all Wagner's late works it is the freest in its application of Wagnerian principles; it is saturated from first to last with extrovert melody; and in general shape it is not unlike an Italian opera. The finales to Acts 1 and 2 have the same architectural function as the typical Italian *finali concertati* but with an important difference. They are essentially action pieces,[31] as distinct from those massive, static ensembles to which many Italian composers continued to cling. Among the first to understand this and to exploit its implications was Giacomo Puccini. Beginning with the embarcation scene in *Manon Lescaut*, all his grand finales follow the example of *Die Meistersinger*. Manon and Des Grieux, absorbed in their poignant lyrical flights, may seem to have lost count of time; but the relentless roll-call of the Sergeant-at-Arms reminds us of the passing moment, as does the quarrelling of Marcello and Musetta in the no less lyrical finale to Act 3 of *La bohème*. To claim Puccini as an Italian Wagnerian may seem rather odd. His idiom is basically that of the *veristi*, though more powerfully individual and better integrated. Not a single bar of his recalls the Master of Bayreuth; yet of all Italian composers of the time he was the one who learnt best the Wagnerian lesson. He too organizes his acts motivically; but unlike those of his fellow *veristi* his motifs are incisive and theatrical. He can arrest the attention with a figure of three descending notes as at the beginning of *Tosca* Act 2. What is more, such motifs generate the musical argument. Like Wagner, Puccini will make the orchestra tell us things that are not in the text, as when in Act 1 of the same opera Cavaradossi's tender duet with Tosca is interrupted by a brief burst of the Angelotti motif, thus explaining his absent-mindedness to the audience if not to Tosca herself. As in Wagner, coming events sometimes cast their shadows before. So while Scarpia is writing out a safe-conduct a minatory theme takes shape *pianissimo* on the strings – the idea of murder slowly insinuating itself into Tosca's mind. The ability to integrate the finite solo or duet into an act thus organized is likewise something learnt from *Die Meistersinger*. In one respect Puccini's motifs differ from Wagner's: their semantic content is far vaguer. Puccini uses them partly as a principle of construction and partly for their emotional charge, which may vary according to dynamics and scoring. The same theme may express wistful affection when played softly by the strings (e.g. 'Sono andati? Fingevo di dormire' from *La bohème*) and tragic despair when thundered out by the full orchestra at the final curtain, which makes nonsense of Joseph

[31]   An exception is the quintet from Act 3, a piece which violates every rule in the Wagnerian book.

Kerman's gibe that at the end of *Tosca* 'the orchestra screams the first thing that comes into its head'.[32] On the contrary, its reprise of 'E lucevan le stelle' expresses the situation perfectly, as well as rounding off the act in a musically logical manner. Wholly Wagnerian, on the other hand, is the painstaking calculation of notes in relation to words and gesture, which, combined with the brisk pace typical of the *veristi*, makes Puccini's operas among the most stageable in the repertory. Indeed his very accessibility has done him harm in critical and academic circles, from Fausto Torrefranca in Puccini's own day to Kerman in ours. Yet whatever his spiritual limitations – which are undeniable – his integrity as an artist was total. He was neither boastful nor insincere when he wrote to a friend, 'I write music as I feel it, not as others want me to. This grave fault of mine is that of all the great composers from Bellini to Wagner, so I shan't make an effort to change my ways even if I could.'[33]

In a word, Wagner's best Italian pupil was Puccini.

[32]   *Opera as Drama* (New York, 1956), p. 19.
[33]   Letter to A. Creschi, 8 October 1902: *Carteggi pucciniani*, p. 224.

The cathartic slow waltz and other finale conventions in Janáček's operas

JOHN TYRRELL

In Act 1 of Janáček's *Jenůfa*,[1] at the height of the festivities with which Števa celebrates his escape from conscription, the Kostelnička stops the dancing. She forbids her foster-daughter Jenůfa to marry Števa until a trial period of a year has elapsed, thereby destroying Jenůfa's hopes of the early marriage which she desperately needs – she is already three months pregnant with Števa's child. After the Kostelnička has left, Jenůfa's Grandmother tries to console her: 'Every young couple must get over its problems.' In Gabriela Preissová's play, on which Janáček based his libretto, the scene continues immediately with mutual recriminations between Števa and Jenůfa. In the opera, however, Janáček expands this single line into a substantial 'ensemble' – so designated in the earliest copy of the vocal score[2] – in which the Grandmother's words, 'Každý párek si musí svoje trápení přestát', are taken up successively by the mill Foreman, Laca, a four-part chorus and finally Jenůfa herself. Its climax is an *a cappella* section in which Jenůfa, and then Laca in imitation, soar up to a top C♭ before the orchestra returns and provides a short postlude.

The mere presence of a formal concertato for soloists and chorus is surprising in a work vaunted by its composer for its naturalism, and he felt it necessary, soon after its première, to defend the fact that everyone sang the same words and to the same tunc:

Why is it only these few words that are repeated so often? *Because I had no more to hand* [Janáček's emphases] and yet I felt I had to linger here to allow the closely matched musical motif to be taken up by all eight parts naturally, but also naturally to swell and then to die away into the faintest pianissimo, as a thought fades into oblivion . . .

Why should the Grandmother, the Foreman, Laca, Jenůfa and the four-part chorus begin with the self-same motif? Surely that goes against the principle of distinguishing each individual with his own, natural melody?

---

[1]   *Její pastorkyňa* ('Her Foster-Daughter', 1904). Dates given in parentheses after opera titles are of first performances unless otherwise stated.

[2]   Brno, Moravian Museum, Music History Division: Janáček Archive, A 7426.

Firstly, in the interests of effectively developing the musical motif I made a slight concession that I would scarcely have made today . . . [3]

Janáček's claim that were he writing 'today', i.e. in 1904, he would have done differently, reinforces Bohumír Štědroň's theory that the composition of the first act of the opera considerably antedated that of the other two.[4] After Janáček completed the first act there seems to have been a thoughtful pause in which he reconsidered many aspects of opera writing, particularly his approach to ensembles. Even his revisions before the publication of the vocal score in 1908, in which he shortened many duet and ensemble passages (and incidentally cut fifteen bars from the 67-bar 'Každý párek' concertato), could not disguise the fact that Act 1 broke down rather more easily into set numbers than did the other acts. Nor did his revisions alter the fact that the first dramatic event in the opera – the Kostelnička's stopping of the dancing – generates a slow 'ensemble of perplexity' that looks back to a tradition common in the operas of Rossini and his successors.[5] Such an ensemble is usually placed towards the end of an act, where it can be followed at once by a stretta to provide an effective curtain. Despite his many changes to the play, Janáček left alone its dramatic shape and act endings so that the act concludes, like the play, with two further scenes: one between Jenůfa and Števa, ending with a short 'trio' with the Grandmother, and the crucial scene in which Laca slashes Jenůfa's cheek with a knife. Laca's stunned remorse is captured in his long-held notes, set in relief against the faster, more chattery reactions of the other three characters. The voices are accompanied by an orchestral *moto perpetuo* of sextuplet quavers that in its 1904 version would have had an even greater cumulative effect, given that Janáček reduced it by a third in his 1908 revisions. Just as traces of a number opera can be detected in the original first act of *Jenůfa*, so the slow concertato and the stretta conclusion to the act can equally well be seen as vestiges of nineteenth-century finale conventions.

The object of this study is to examine the finales or act-endings in Janáček's operas and to see what traditions, if any, shaped his approach. I am here concerned only with the ends of acts, not the ends of scenes. Though the ends of internal scenes in some of Janáček operas may involve both a curtain and a double bar, these internal scenes – for instance in *Kát'a*

---

[3]   *Jeviště*, i (1904), p. 103; reprinted in B. Štědroň, 'Ke zrodu Janáčkovy opery Její pastorkyňa II' ('On the origin of Janáček's opera *Jenůfa* II'), *Slezský sborník*, lxiv (1966), p. 519.

[4]   See, for instance, Štědroň, *Zur Genesis von Leoš Janáčeks Oper Jenůfa* (Brno, rev. 2/ 1972), p. 63.

[5]   See W. Dean, 'Italian Opera', *The New Oxford History of Music*, viii: *The Age of Beethoven 1790–1830*, ed. G. Abraham (London, 1982), pp. 422–5; see also J. Budden, *The Operas of Verdi*, i (London, 1973), pp. 18–19.

Kabanová (1921) – are joined by the direction 'attacca' and by a clear musical link such as the lingering F♭ at the end of Act 1 scene 1, which passes enharmonically to the E♮ pedal on which the second scene opens. A few years later Janáček was to consolidate the scene-links of Acts 1 and 2 by more extended interludes to cover scene changes.[6] In his next opera, *Příhody Lišky Bystroušky* ('The Cunning Little Vixen', 1924), there are similar changes of scene which break up each of the outer acts into discrete halves, though, as in *Kát'a*, ones which are linked musically by key. Within each of these half acts there are further scene changes bridged by interludes, some of them quite extensive. In Act 2 there is a similar interlude link between the first two scenes, but between the second and third there is an abrupt shift (and a pause) from the final chord of A major to the A♭ opening of the final scene. This can be explained by Janáček's original plan, realized in his early sketches, for a four-act opera, with these two halves of Act 2 forming separate acts.[7] In Janáček's final two operas, *Věc Makropulos* ('The Makropulos Affair', 1926) and *Z mrtvého domu* ('From the House of the Dead', 1930), there are no scene changes within the acts, except in the third act of the latter opera, which is accompanied by an interlude.

Seven of Janáček's nine operas are in three acts. In the cases of *Šárka*, *Jenůfa* and *The Makropulos Affair*, the composer inherited this structure from the materials which served as his librettos. In the four other cases, including the final version of *The Cunning Little Vixen*, Janáček himself was responsible for the act divisions. This includes his operas based on novels, such as *From the House of the Dead*, as well as *Kát'a Kabanová*, whose three acts were carved out of the five acts of Ostrovsky's play *The Thunderstorm*. Only two of his operas, both earlier works, were not in three acts. *Počátek románu* ('The Beginning of a Romance', 1894), is in one act, perhaps after the model of Dvořák's *Tvrdé palice* ('The Stubborn Lovers', 1881) or Vilém Blodek's popular *V studni* ('In the Well', 1867). The two *Výlety páně Broučkovy* ('Excursions of Mr Brouček', 1920) are in two acts each. The first, *Výlet pana Broučka do měsíce* ('Mr Brouček's Excursion to the Moon', composed 1908–17) was originally planned in four acts, but the fourth fell away when the second excursion was added, and its first two acts were joined by an interlude.

In all Janáček's earlier operas, up to and including his fourth opera *Osud* ('Fate', composed 1903–5), the acts are divided in the score into 'scenes' in the classical manner according to the entrances and exits of individual characters. Act 3 of *Jenůfa*, for instance, has twelve 'scenes', though there

---

6   See T. Straková, 'Mezihry v Káti Kabanové' ('The interludes in *Kát'a Kabanová*'), *Časopis Moravského musea: vědy společenské*, xlix (1964), pp. 229–36; abridged Eng. trans. in *Leoš Janáček: 'Kát'a Kabanová'*, ed. J. Tyrrell (Cambridge, 1982), pp. 134–43.

7   Brno, Moravian Museum . . . , A 7455 c.

is no curtain between any of them, and musically the act is so continuous that these divisions would seldom be felt as articulating points by any listener. In his sixth opera, *Kát'a Kabanová*, Janáček dispensed with such divisions (still printed in the Czech translation of Ostrovsky's play which served as his libretto), just as a little earlier, in his 1918 revisions of *Šárka*, he removed all the 'scenes' that he had taken over from the play into the first two versions of this opera.

There is a case for taking *The Beginning of a Romance* out of sequence. It was Janáček's first opera to be staged, in Brno in 1894, though his second to be written, in 1891, three years after he had abandoned *Šárka* (composed 1887–8) with its orchestration incomplete. While *Šárka* was eventually performed in 1925, as a delayed tribute to the composer's seventieth birthday, Janáček had no wish to revise his other early opera. He had in fact destroyed sections of the score (they were reconstructed from the parts after his death),[8] and in one of his few later references to it he dismissed it as 'an empty comedy'.[9] The opera is a rarity among his works in being one of his two comic operas – *Brouček* is the other – and, uniquely, in being planned as a number opera with spoken dialogue. Its most singular feature, however, is its use of recycled material. This is particularly evident in its clear-cut finale, the most elaborate ensemble number in the opera, with a final section combining five solo voices and a four-part chorus and concluding with a brief chorus. It began life as a ternary-form piece for chorus and orchestra completed in 1890 to words by Svatopluk Čech, *Naše píseň* ('Our Song'). Before its transformation into an operatic finale Janáček had made a second version a month later for unaccompanied chorus, and then adapted the original score (with orchestra) to fit entirely new words, a Silesian folk-ballad whose eleven verses suggest a strophic or through-composed setting rather than the ternary strait-jacket that Janáček imposed. Realizing perhaps that this version was unsatisfactory, Janáček then adapted the same material again, to a third set of words, to form the final number of *The Beginning of a Romance*. Here the ternary form worked better: the slower middle section provided a contrasting setting for the entries of the two aristocrats Adolf and Irma, who otherwise take no part in the ensemble. Apart from omissions or repetitions in the first section and alterations to the coda, Janáček took over the original chorus intact, with few changes even to the orchestration. The chief difference between the opera finale and the earlier

---

8   See O. Fiala, 'Libreto k Janáčkově opeře Počátek romanu' ('The libretto to Janáček's opera *The Beginning of a Romance*'), *Časopis Moravského musea*, xlix (1964), pp. 211–12.

9   *Leoš Janáček: Pohled do života i díla* ('A view of the life and works'), ed. A. Veselý (Prague, 1924), p. 93.

material lies in the new distribution of the original SATB chorus parts among a varying texture of one to five solo parts.[10]

If the musical material of Janáček's finale to *The Beginning of a Romance* originates from an earlier work of his, its texture and conventions have affinities with earlier Czech comic operas. Act 3 of Smetana's *Prodaná nevěsta* ('The Bartered Bride', 1866) has a denouement finale which develops into an ensemble mixing seven solo voices with a four-part chorus. *Šelma sedlák* ('The Cunning Peasant', 1877), Dvořák's only opera to be performed in Brno before the composition of *The Beginning of a Romance*,[11] concludes its first act with an ensemble for four solo voices and its second and final act with an ensemble for eight solo voices followed, after various denouements, by a brisk four-part chorus. Two other Czech comic operas staged in Brno before *The Beginning of a Romance*, Karel Bendl's *Starý ženich* (composed 1871) and Blodek's *In the Well*, take a similar approach to the finale. Janáček knew all these operas and in his capacity as chief critic of the periodical he founded, *Hudební listy*, reviewed them several times.

There were fewer native models at hand when Janáček began writing his first, tragic opera *Šárka* in 1887, nor did he know many foreign operas. During his studies in Prague (1874–5) and Leipzig (1879–80) he had been too poor to attend the opera. He made this point in a letter to his fiancée when, having moved from Leipzig to Vienna, he wrote that he was going to the opera that night for the first time.[12] The next day, however, he wrote that he had been too engrossed in his work to go out.[13] When he did go, the next evening (14 April 1880), to Weber's *Der Freischütz*, he did not care for it.[14] His only other visit to the opera in Vienna was seven weeks later, to see Cherubini's *Les Deux Journées*, which he found even less interesting ('I wasn't taken by it at all, except for one single place'); he was much more enthusiastic about his first encounter, the same evening, with ballet ('*Dayla*' – no composer is mentioned).[15] It would appear from the tone of his comments that Janáček, now twenty-six, was little acquainted with the standard operatic repertory of the time.

Janáček's fervently nationalistic stance meant that he never went near the German opera-house in Brno, but with the opening of a Czech one in

10   See Tyrrell, 'The Musical Prehistory of Janáček's Počátek románu and its Importance in Shaping the Composer's Dramatic Style', *Časopis Moravského musea*, lii (1967), pp. 247–51.

11   Information on the performances of opera in Brno is derived from J. and V. Telcovi, 'Přehled repertoáru v období 1884–1960' ('Survey of repertory 1884–1960'), *Almanach Státního divadla v Brně* (Brno, 1974).

12   L. Janáček, *'Intime Briefe' 1879/80 aus Leipzig und Wien*, ed. J. Knaus (Zurich, 1985), p. 208.

13   Ibid., p. 209.

14   Ibid., p. 210.

15   Ibid., p. 241.

1884 he began following opera avidly, and his earliest, unrealized, plans for operas date from this year.[16] Several Czech comic operas were given in Brno in these early years: in addition to the four mentioned above, Smetana's *Hubička* ('The Kiss', Prague 1876, Brno 1884) and *Dvě vdovy* ('The Two Widows', Prague 1874, Brno 1887), Vojtěch Hřímalý's *Zakletý princ* ('The Enchanted Prince', Prague 1872, Brno 1886), J. R. Rozkošný's *Mikuláš* (Prague 1870, Brno 1888), Karel Šebor's *Zmařená svatba* ('The Frustrated Wedding', Prague 1879, Brno 1885) and Karel Kovařovic's *Ženichové* ('Bridegrooms', Prague 1884, Brno 1887). But Janáček would have had little opportunity of seeing Czech serious operas in Brno. Smetana's *Dalibor*, a failure in Prague until its 1886 revival, was not staged in Brno until January 1888, after Janáček had completed one version of *Šárka* and was in the middle of a second, while Smetana's other serious operas *Braniboři v Čechách* ('The Brandenburgers in Bohemia', 1866) and *Libuše* (1881) were given in Brno only in 1889 and 1899 respectively. It was not until the new century that any of Fibich's operas were played in Brno or any more of Dvořák's other than *The Cunning Peasant*. Janáček would have had access to the vocal scores of Smetana's *Libuše* and *Dalibor* (published in 1882 and 1884 respectively), Fibich's *Nevěsta messinská* ('The Bride of Messina', published 1884) and Dvořák's *Dimitrij* (published 1886) and through his friendship with Dvořák may have learnt something about the unpublished *Vanda* (premièred in 1876 and restaged in revised form in 1880). Other serious Czech operas performed in Prague in the 1880s, but not published, included Šebor's *Nevěsta husitská* ('The Hussite Bride', 1868), Fibich's *Blaník* (1881) and Bendl's *Černohorci* ('The Montenegrins', 1881).

How many of these works Janáček might have seen in Prague is difficult to say. From the early 1880s, when he settled down in Brno with posts at the Teachers' Institute and later at the Organ School that he founded, he could allow himself the occasional trip to Prague. His growing friendship with Dvořák and the definitive opening, in November 1883, of the Czech National Theatre in Prague provided further incentives. However, there is only sparse documentation from this period and it is possible that his heavy workload in Brno restricted his visits to Prague to the handful recorded by Jan Racek in his study of Janáček's contacts with Prague. Some of these trips, moreover, were occasioned by performances of Dvořák's oratorios, not operas (1884 and 1885), or by Tchaikovsky's visit to Prague in 1888. In fact the only operas that Janáček is known to have seen in Prague before he began writing his first operas are Meyerbeer's *Le Prophète*, Smetana's *Tajemství* ('The Secret'), Halévy's *La Juive* and Verdi's *Il trovatore* and *Un ballo in maschera*.[17]

[16]   See T. Straková, 'Janáčkovy hudebně dramatické náměty a torsa' ('Janáček's musico-dramatic projects and fragments'), *Musikologie*, iii (1955), pp. 417–19.

[17]   J. Racek, 'Leoš Janáček a Praha', *Musikologie*, iii (1955), pp. 18–19.

The only serious Czech opera that we can say with certainty that Janáček saw before he composed Šárka is one that is scarcely known today, Rozkošný's *Svatojanské proudy* ('The St John's Rapids'). This work, first performed in Prague in 1871, was still playing there in the 1880s. A vocal score, published in 1882, allowed Janáček to study the work and write a detailed review of it when it was given in Brno on 13 March 1887.[18] Janáček's extended notice is uncharacteristic of his reviews in *Hudební listy* in that it deals more with the work itself than with its performance. Since he was at work on Šárka at the time (his first version of the opera was written some time between February and August 1887), his comments on Rozkošný's opera are probably less the reactions of a critic than the polemical musings of a creative artist in the midst of grappling with a similar task. Many of his criticisms, for instance of the rhythmic monotony of the piece, need not concern us here, but it is pertinent that he complained about Rozkošný's use of older, standard forms ('starší užité formy'). This stricture would seem to refer to the presence of self-contained arias, duets and choruses, rather than to the finales, which are not particularly developed. Act 1 concludes with a short trio in which a male chorus is added for the final six bars; Act 2 ends with a declamatory solo; Act 3 with a short duet to which a female chorus is added at the end; the first scene of Act 4 concludes with a duet, its second with a trio.

Janáček concluded the first two acts of Šárka with even simpler means: Act 1 ends with a short Adagio lament by Ctirad, Act 2 with a gloomy orchestral postlude. Act 3, however, is a different matter. It is so short that all of it could be taken together as the 'finale' to the whole work. In its style it is markedly different from the other two acts: static, and oratorio-like in its frequent use of male, female and mixed choruses and in combining these choral forces with the three remaining soloists in extended concerted sections. The nearest parallels in contemporary Czech opera are the spacious concertato textures in some of the act-endings in Smetana's festival opera *Libuše*, a work in which stylistic affinities with Šárka have long been noted;[19] the plot of Šárka is itself a continuation of that of *Libuše*.

In establishing the finale conventions of Šárka there is no need to differentiate between the three very different versions of the opera. Janáček's first version, sent to Dvořák in August 1887, was succeeded by a second version written soon after and completed on 18 June 1888. Dvořák allegedly advised 'more melody',[20] which perhaps explains the 'second verses', often untexted, to several arias or the expansion of the central Act 2 love duet.[21] But the conventions remained much the same – both versions

18   Reprinted in L. Firkušný, *Leoš Janáček: kritikem brněnské opery* ('Leoš Janáček as critic of the Brno opera') (Brno, 1935), pp. 69–70.
19   See V. Helfert, *Leoš Janáček*, i (Brno, 1939), p. 373, and J. Racek, 'Leoš Janáček a Bedřich Smetana', *Slezský sborník*, xlix (1951), pp. 469–73.
20   See J. Vogel, *Leoš Janáček* (London, rev. 2/1981), p. 88.
21   Brno, Moravian Museum . . . , A 23.522.

Ex. 1   *Šárka*

[How her sunny eyes . . .]

retained choruses, duet texture and combinations of solos and chorus –
and, though the act conclusions of Acts 1 and 2 were tightened up, there is
no evidence of change in Janáček's attitude towards them. Janáček's later
revisions, carried out mostly in 1918, were written into the 1888 vocal
score. Their main object was to bring the voice parts into line with
Janáček's current practice. Most of the Act 2 simultaneous duet
disappeared, but the act-endings and the concertato textures of Act 3 (the
least revised act) remained.

The conclusions to the first two acts of *Šárka* provided Janáček with
strikingly similar ingredients. Both involved the male and female warriors
Ctirad and Šárka, and Šárka's band of women soldiers. Both end after
confrontations between the adversaries, leaving them shattered and
confused (or dead). In the final section of Act 1 a bemused Ctirad extols
Šárka's beauty. In Act 2, after her plans to disarm and then to kill Ctirad
have succeeded, Šárka is filled with remorse in the realization, now too
late, that she loves him. Janáček emphasized the parallels by building the
final music to both acts from the same thematic material. In Act 1 it is
presented in a warmly harmonized 3/2 Adagio (Ex. 1).[22] Ctirad sings his
thoughts against this, and his voice part, even in Janáček's final revision,
frequently mirrors the orchestral tune. Its descending theme (*a*) is
curiously prophetic of the descending theme at the end of *Jenůfa* (Ex. 2):
stepwise motion down (*Šárka* has three notes, *Jenůfa* four), then a jump

22   Reproduced by permission of the Moravian Museum, Music History Division, Brno.

Ex. 2 *Jenůfa*

down of a fourth (*Šárka*) or a fifth (*Jenůfa*), with a dotted rhythm between
the third and fourth notes. In both cases the theme generates a slow waltz
which makes up the final section of the piece. In Act 1 of *Šárka* it provides a
mood of dreamlike intoxication in which Ctirad reveals that his simple
view of the world is shattered: he is in love with his enemy. In Act 3 of
Jenůfa the slow waltz provides the background against which Jenůfa, at
last overcome by Laca's warmth of heart, signals with her great cry 'O
Laco, duša moja!' ('O Laca, my soul!') that she loves him. It is at this point
that Janáček removes the stubborn pedal C that has hitherto clouded the
B♭ tonality. From then on the slow waltz, with its descending theme,
becomes increasingly triumphant.

The Act 2 conclusion of *Šárka* has none of this warmth. It is instead a
deliberately bitter, angular reminiscence of Act 1, its hopefulness drained
away by Ctirad's death. Act 3 of *Šárka* is notable for having little music in it
that is not moderate in pace (if not downright slow, as in the concluding
Adagio) or in triple time. It is, admittedly, rather earthbound, with none of
the radiance of the slow-waltz ending of *Jenůfa* – Šárka's remorseful self-
immolation is hardly as uplifting as the healing love that Jenůfa and Laca
achieve.

At first sight, Act 2 of *Jenůfa* seems to have the same type of ending that
we will encounter in several later Janáček operas: a dramatic event
followed by a few tense bars in the orchestra to bring down the curtain.
Here, the dramatic event is the gradual disintegration of the Kostelnička's
mind as she begins to bless the young couple and then to curse Jenůfa's
former lover Števa, a disintegration exacerbated by a window suddenly
blowing open, which the Kostelnička takes as an ill omen: 'As if death were
peering in here!' Janáček set these final words, 'Jako by sem smrt
načuhovala!', with the greatest dramatic emphasis – a jump down almost
two octaves to middle C for the final word – and then created a short
orchestral postlude based on the rhythm (five equal notes) of the last word
(see Ex. 3). In the context of this highly dramatic ending, the eight bars
shortly before the Kostelnička's blessing in which the three voices on stage
combine, Laca singing at first with Jenůfa and then with the Kostelnička as
well, present an odd anomaly in the score today, overshadowed by the
realistic declamation of the final section. But it seems that Janáček
originally saw the end of the act differently. The eight-bar duet-and-trio is

Ex. 3   *Jenůfa*

[As if death were peering in here! (quick curtain)]

all that remains of a 62-bar 'number' in the 1904 score.[23] It began with a rather conventional lyrical solo for Laca (the continuation of 'Jenůfka, chci, Jenůfka' – 'I want you, Jenůfa') with Jenůfa joining in for a sixteen-bar duet before a trio version of the final eight bars, which, adapted, survived Janáček's 1908 revisions. If this is not quite the 'trio' that Janáček noted in his copy of the play at this point,[24] it is clear that he felt the need to include a formal set-piece towards the end of Act 2, just as he had engineered a concertato ensemble near the end of Act 1. Perhaps the powerful stage effect of the Kostelnička's derangement persuaded the composer at early performances of the opera that the act ending was dramatically compelling on its own, without the added weight of combined voices shortly before this. By the time he composed Act 3 Janáček's finale conventions had become even more naturalistic. The final scene between Jenůfa and Laca could easily have been made into a simultaneous duet instead of the present dialogue. The dialogue itself follows a number of dramatic events – the discovery of the corpse of Jenůfa's baby, the threatening reactions of the villagers, and then the confession, by the Kostelnička, that she was the murderess – which all provided promising material for a traditional concertato response. Instead Janáček presented the reactions to the discovery of the corpse as 'realistic' hubbub, while the only choral reactions to the Kostelnička's confession are the occasional interruptions of 'Ježíši Kriste!' or 'Kostelnička!' by the chorus.

The change of attitude towards concerted and solo ensemble conventions that one sees progressively through the composition and then revision of *Jenůfa* (from about 1894 to 1908) seems to follow Dvořák's practice at the time – not surprisingly, considering the close personal ties between the two men. Hitherto Dvořák had been considered a conservative in such matters. In *Dalibor* (1868) Smetana abandoned the conventional concerted finales of his earlier serious opera *The Brandenburgers in Bohemia* (composed 1862–3, performed 1866) and concluded the acts with duets or even, in Act 3, just a declamatory solo. But Dvořák's serious operas in the next decade, *Vanda* (1876) and *Dimitrij* (1882), both retained the elaborate double choruses and full-blown concertatos that, together with their original five-act plans, looked more towards French grand opera than to Smetana.

In the 1890s, however, Dvořák's attitudes to opera changed. This was first manifest in his radical revisions to *Dimitrij* (1894), in which he shortened the long Act 3 concertato and completely excised the magnificent one in Act 4. In his next opera, *Čert a Káča* ('The Devil and Kate',

---

23   A facsimile of four pages from the deleted number is printed in Štědroň, 'Ke zrodu . . . '.

24   Brno, Moravian Museum . . . , L 6.

1899), he took an even harsher line, restricting duet writing to a couple of short passages and avoiding concertato completely. Only choruses abound, concluding two of the three acts, but even this feature became noticeably sparser in his next opera, *Rusalka* (1901), which has solo ends to two acts and a duet in the other.

Following Dvořák, Janáček found himself taking a more radical line on finale conventions than many of his Czech contemporaries. Fibich, often seen as Smetana's heir, was surprisingly conservative in such matters. His *Bride of Messina* (1885) abounds in elaborate concertatos growing out of his treatment of Schiller's 'Greek' choruses. In the 1890s, Fibich could still write a formal, multi-tempo concerted finale for double chorus and soloists to end the third act of *Hedy* (1896), and even his final opera, *Pád Arkuna* ('The Fall of Arkona', 1900), has choral weight at the ends of all its acts except for the chamber-like prologue.

Among the younger generation Kovařovic, in his very popular *Psohlavci* ('The Dogheads', 1898), retained a choral end to the second act, preceded by a slow unaccompanied ensemble for seven soloists. Otakar Ostrčil's first opera, *Vlasty skon* ('The Death of Vlasta', 1904), concludes the first act with a male chorus and the second with a full concertato. The nearest to Janáček among the leading Czech opera composers of this generation was Foerster, whose *Eva* (1899) was based on a play from the same school of village realism as *Jenůfa* and by the same playwright, Gabriela Preissová. While Janáček worked straight from Preissová's prose, Foerster first put it into verse. Consequently it is not surprising that some numbers, such as choruses (as in *Jenůfa* confined to the outer acts) and duets (more extensive than those in *Jenůfa*), have a rather more conventional cut than Janáček's. On the other hand there is no concertato, and all three acts have solo endings.

Janáček's operas after *Jenůfa* by no means bid farewell to duets and choruses. The new patterns of act-endings which Janáček developed after his encounters with contemporary European operas such as Charpentier's *Louise* (a great favourite in Prague, where Janáček saw it in 1903),[25] or those of Puccini, specifically rely on solo and choral ensembles in some of their finales. In *Jenůfa* Janáček had avoided a duet ending to the third act, and cut out most of the duet texture with which he had originally weighted the end of Act 2, but *Mr Brouček's Excursion to the Moon* ends with a *pianissimo* duet for soprano and tenor in octaves. The parallel to the end of Act 1 of *La bohème* (first staged at the Czech opera-house in Brno in 1905) is so striking that it seems possible that Janáček wished his audience to sense a connection between Puccini's Parisian Bohemian lovers and his own

[25]   See Racek, 'Leoš Janáček a Praha', p. 21.

Prague lovers – Bohemian in both senses of the word. This model, too, may lie behind the major-key ending of Act 2 of *Kát'a Kabanová*, among Janáček's last four operas the only quiet ending to an act. The lovers' octaves, however, come somewhat earlier in the scene.

The first-act finale of *The Excursion of Mr Brouček to the Fifteenth Century* provides another new pattern of act-ending in Janáček's operas. The combination and alternation of on-stage solos and an off- or backstage ecclesiastical chorus recalls the Te Deum finale of Act 1 of *Tosca*, an opera that Janáček first encountered in Prague in 1903.[26] In *Brouček* Janáček has the male-voice chorus gradually approach; its closing *fortissimo* version of the Hussite chorale, with chorus tenors up to top C against the full force of the orchestra (to which Janáček, like Puccini, added an organ), provides one of the most resplendent moments in any Janáček opera. The nearest parallel in the later operas is the choral finale to Act 2 of *The Cunning Little Vixen*, an exuberant, wordless celebration of the wedding of the Vixen and the Fox. Like the *Brouček* chorale ending, it is well prepared musically; in this case it is a speeded-up version of the off-stage wordless melisma with which the scene (originally act) opened.

It is interesting to see how strongly the choral aspect asserted itself in the final acts of the four last Janáček operas. In *Kát'a Kabanová* the heroine's soliloquy in the final scene is cut through by the voices that, in the play, Kát'a says she hears and that in Janáček's opera are heard by the audience as well, sung by an off-stage chorus. The voices become increasingly insistent during Káťa's farewell to her lover, and their absence in her brief monologue before her suicide contributes to its atmosphere of uncanny calm. In the final Maestoso bars of the opera the voices, now in a triumphant *fortissimo*, are heard for the last time. In this case Janáček picked up a reference in the play and dramatized it musically. His model may well have been the off-stage voices, 'the voice of Paris', that lure Louise away from her family in the last act of Charpentier's opera, or, in another favourite opera of Janáček's, the wordless off-stage voices which, in unison with the viola d'amore, accompany Butterfly's vigil. But what other composer would have added an off-stage symbolic chorus to a conversational 'comedy' such as Čapek's *Makropulos Affair*? The effect of the off-stage male-voice chorus echoing some of Marty's phrases (the four males on stage are similarly drilled into a bizarre semichorus) suggests, together with the stately music Janáček provided, that a strange, other-wordly dimension has invaded the matter-of-fact original and changed its meaning.

There is no need for an off-stage chorus in Janáček's last opera, *From the House of the Dead*, since the prison-camp setting provides a ready-made

26   Ibid.

chorus of prisoners, of which Janáček took full advantage. The final part of Act 3 is no exception. The chorus based laconically on the words 'Orel car! Svoboda! Svobodička!' ('Eagle tsar! Freedom!'), sung as Petrovič leaves the prison and the prisoners symbolically release their caged eagle, could easily have provided a triumphant choral end to the opera – as it did at its première in 1930. This, however, was the work of Janáček's pupil Osvald Chlubna, who revised the opera after Janáček's death under the misapprehension that it was incomplete. Janáček's own ending is quite different. The final 'freedom' music is interrupted by the guard's 'Marrrš!', and the opera ends grimly with the automaton-like march for the prisoners as they are forced back to work.

Janáček's version of the concertato stretta at the end of *Jenůfa* Act 1 – an action finale with plenty of commotion on stage, a *moto perpetuo* in the orchestra and above it a number of fast-moving and sometimes simultaneous voices – recurs in some of his later works, for instance at the end of Act 1 of *Mr Brouček's Excursion to the Moon*. Etherea's love-song to Brouček goes straight into a Presto section in which the various elements – Etherea's love-song, Brouček's aghast reaction, the despairing cries of Etherea's jealous lover – are compacted into short vocal or orchestral units to form a rapid and continuous mosaic. Above the orchestral continuum the voice parts begin to overlap, moving into a trio texture in the following Moderato. In the following Presto, Etherea and Brouček fly away on the winged horse Pegasus, urged on by Etherea's female retainers, who add their voices to the ensemble. The act ends with a short comic coda.

Much the same ingredients go into the finale of the first act of *The Cunning Little Vixen*. This is an action ensemble based this time on the commotion in the farmyard caused by the Vixen's despatch of the Cock. The death shriek sets into motion a Più mosso in just the same way as Jenůfa's cry of 'Ježíš, Maria!', as her cheek is slashed, launches the action finale of *Jenůfa* Act 1. As in the *Brouček* Act 1 finale an orchestral *moto perpetuo* is made up of a mosaic of small orchestral motifs, Janáček's characteristic *sčasovky* (short, repeated rhythmic figures) providing the equivalent of Rossinian ostinatos. Against this the distinctive cries of the Hen ('Kokokodák!'), the Gamekeeper's Wife ('Ou [a long melisma] bestio!') and the Vixen's laugh ('Cha cha cha cha') are juxtaposed, occasionally colliding, though without the continuous overlapping of the *Brouček* Moderato section. As the vixen escapes, the orchestra concludes with a brief Presto.

There are two recurring patterns of act-endings in Janáček operas provided by an orchestral epilogue – short and long. The assignation between Emilia Marty and Baron Prus at the end of Čapek's second act of *Makropulos* ('Bring it to me!', 'And when?', 'Tonight!', 'Agreed!') is faithfully transmitted into the second-act ending of Janáček's opera. After these words twelve bars, merely an extended, wonderfully suggestive, cadence formula crowned by a deafening cymbal roll, is all Janáček needs to conclude the act. *From the House of the Dead* Act 2 ends with another dramatic incident: the assault on Aljeja by the Small Prisoner. A short choral reaction is followed, as the guards rush on, by an even briefer orchestral conclusion of six bars with a prominent side-drum roll. In both cases Janáček seems to have been content to let the dramatic events speak for themselves without more than a striking cadential formula to follow. In both cases this music is emphatic and slow-paced: Adagio in *From the House of the Dead*, Maestoso in *Makropulos*.

The precedent for this 'short ending' in Janáček's operas is the Act 2 ending of *Jenůfa* discussed earlier, with the Kostelnička's dramatic cry followed by a brief orchestral Maestoso consisting entirely of juxtaposed chords animated by the ominous five-note hammerings on the timpani (Ex. 3). In his 1908 revision Janáček jettisoned the duet weight that he had provided just before, and in his next opera *Fate* (to his own scenario – the libretto was written up by a young helper) he attempted much the same thing at the end of the first act. Here, however, it is less effective. For a start the situation is less striking: the reaction of Míla's mother when she hears that Míla has eloped with her former lover Živný. Her voice part is less dramatic, and the hammered chords, groups of four this time, less emphatic (Ex. 4).

From the House of the Dead follows the pattern of its predecessor not just in the brief orchestral conclusion to its second act but also in the long orchestral ending to the first. In *Makropulos* Kolenatý returns excitedly with the will exactly where Emilia Marty said it would be. The prospects for him and his client are now much rosier, except that, as their rival Baron Prus points out, one detail is missing. Marty undertakes to supply yet another document, and Kolenatý collapses in wonder and incomprehension. This is how Čapek ended his Act 1, as did Janáček, given a few cut lines. But while Janáček writes 'curtain' six bars after Kolenatý's last word, the music continues for another fifty. In Act 1 of *From the House of the Dead* Petrovič, beaten almost to death, returns at the end of Luka's story, which has described a similar incident. This juxtaposition generates a sufficient *frisson* to end the act, but Janáček's orchestral postlude continues for 74 bars after the last voice has sounded. That the scene was something of a problem for its first producer is evidenced by the elaborate stage directions for further 'business', all unauthentic, added by him and still printed in the vocal score. The parallels between the two operas are particularly interesting in view of their different origins – one a play with Janáček taking over existing act-endings and doing little more than cutting, the second an opera carved out of incidents from Dostoyevsky's novelized

Ex. 4   *Fate*

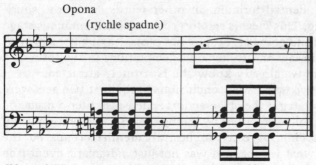

[No, no! What utter misfortune! (quick curtain)]

prison reminiscences, rearranged and restructured by Janáček himself.

Why are Janáček's Act 1 endings so long? Is there a reason for having a short second-act conclusion (*Jenůfa*, *Makropulos*, *From the House of the Dead*; *Fate* Act 1 is the odd one out) but a long orchestral conclusion to the first acts? There is evidence in his sketch material that Janáček considered a short conclusion to *From the House of the Dead* Act 1, a cadence formula based appropriately on the motto theme that dominates this act.[27] But something compelled him to discard this and instead take up a theme heard during the earlier episode devoted to Skuratov – a character now absent from the stage action – and expand it into the substantial orchestral postlude. Maybe Janáček felt the Act 2 situations in his last two operas were so clear-cut dramatically that they could be left to speak for themselves without further musical comment while those in Act 1 were more ambiguous, needing to be stoked up musically by progressive accelerations into presto or prestissimo conclusions (both are also broadened at the very end, either by an 'a tempo' or by thematic augmentation). Or maybe Janáček had in mind a three-act plan whereby tension is increased at the ends of acts by progressively terser orchestral commentaries until the third-act catharsis.

The orchestral conclusion to Act 1 of *Kát'a Kabanová* lies somewhere between the short and the long act-ending. It looks short, being only twelve bars long, but these are 3/2 bars (with quaver movement within them), not the 3/4 or 3/8 bars of the Act 1 endings of the two later operas. Furthermore these twelve long bars take even longer as they remain in a stately Maestoso throughout, rather than being hurried along by increasingly faster tempos. The tension of the passage derives not from the tempo increases but from the clash arising from a theme with a prominent F♮ presented several times against the E♭ pedal, a clash emphasized by the orchestration of the passage. But since all this amounts to is a strong dominant preparation for the hammering home of the 'fate' theme in A♭ minor in the final bar, it could be argued that the passage is nothing more than a prolonged cadential formula, in other words Janáček's 'short' orchestral act-ending. This view is reinforced by a clearly ominous stage action – Kát'a's husband going off despite her pleas, leaving her a prey to her jealous mother-in-law and to her own temptations in the form of a young man to whom we already know she is strongly attracted.

In Janáček's last two operas the conclusions to the first two acts were based on a simple strategy: the stage action ended just after a dramatic event or revelation, followed either by a long orchestra peroration or by little more than a short but suggestive orchestral cadential formula. For the final act, however, what was needed was not just a dramatic event (the

27   Brno, Moravian Museum . . . , A 33.746.

release of Petrovič, or the burning of the Makropulos elixir formula) but an interpretational frame in which to view it. In *Makropulos* Janáček took great liberties with Čapek's text in order to achieve a cathartic slant. He suppressed the ironical speeches of the other characters and concentrated instead on Marty's rather more lofty-sounding reflections. The other characters' interruptions are also reduced so that what we are left with is a great solo for Marty, a *scena* supported by the off-stage chorus and the on-stage semichorus and in which Marty's part, abounding in high and sustained notes and even the occasional melisma, is lifted quite out of the ordinary conversational style of most of the opera. The section moves from an Adagio or Maestoso 6/4 to an even more stately 3/2 – one of Janáček's most haunting slow waltzes. We are back in the world of the end of Act 3 of *Jenůfa*, with the 'positive' interpretation that this implies.

The slow-waltz cathartic finale to Act 3, in which a principal character becomes reconciled to his fate, has a parallel in *Makropulos*'s immediate predecessor, *The Cunning Little Vixen*. As in *From the House of the Dead*, Janáček was wholly responsible for the dramatic structure. The original novel ends where Janáček's second act ends. Janáček constructed the third act out of earlier incidents in the novel and concluded, after the death of the Vixen (Janáček's invention) and the second inn scene, with some wise words for the Gamekeeper, set to another slow waltz. That Janáček felt he was dealing with solemn things is underlined by the request he made that this scene should be played at his funeral. But, with the originality that makes him so unique, he added the delightfully unexpected incident with the frog at the end. This has the effect of placing the catharsis of the previous scene in a larger, forward-looking perspective, just as, in a rather harsher fashion, the prisoners' march at the end of *From the House of the Dead* cuts into the optimistic freedom-chorus of the prisoners and provides a new focus on it in the concluding bars of the opera.

Some of the intentions behind Janáček's act-endings are more ambiguous. *Fate* Act 2 ends with a particularly dramatic situation – the deaths of both Míla and her mother. One might have felt that this was the appropriate signal for one of Janáček's terse Act 2 endings. Instead there follows a long orchestral postlude (Živný's voice part is so fragmented and incidental, mostly fitted in between the 'cracks' of the tune, that it can be discounted). It is an impressive and exciting piece of music, and something of this nature might have helped to give the more dramatically ambiguous Act 1 a stronger finish. Another possible area of confusion is that much of it comes in a slow three-in-a-bar – a premature catharsis pre-empting that of the following act.

Act 3 itself concludes with Živný's long narration. The concentration on a single character foreshadows the Act 3 finales of *Vixen* and *Makropulos*, and the slow waltz of the penultimate section seems to signal a 'reconciled' catharsis. As in *Makropulos*, there is even a supporting chorus. While the music is some of Janáček's most opulent and compelling, the stage action that follows (Živný's collapse and especially his rather odd revival) is so unclear – unlike the Frog incident in *Vixen* – that the twist at the end, if it is a twist that was intended, misfires. Janáček was more successful in his next opera, where Brouček's final moments in the fifteenth century are drawn to an exciting close as he is bundled into a barrel to be burnt, hounded by the cries of the chorus and the vengeful threats of the irate Kedruta. Janáček skilfully dissolves the climax orchestrally and winds down into the ironical anticlimax as Brouček relates his adventures to a sceptical landlord. A brief orchestral epilogue – five bars of pathos howled down by nine scherzando bars – puts the final ironical seal on the piece.

Fate and to a lesser extent the four-act *Brouček* represent a departure from the finale patterns that Janáček established so successfully with *Jenůfa* and took up again in his final operas. In Act 1 these consist of a 'long' ending – either an action ensemble showing vestiges of the concertato stretta (*Jenůfa, Brouček, Vixen*) or its orchestral equivalent (*Makropulos, From the House of the Dead*, possibly *Kát'a*). The endings to the middle acts show rather more variety. Some are brief orchestral cadential formulas after particularly dramatic events on stage (*Jenůfa, Makropulos, From the House of the Dead*). Others are more spacious, generally slow endings: the love scenes in *Kát'a Kabanová* and *Mr Brouček's Excursion to the Moon* or the choral conclusions to *Mr Brouček's Excursion to the Fifteenth Century* Act 1 or *Vixen* Act 2.

In Act 3 Janáček was not concerned with articulating a moment in the drama but with concluding it and providing an interpretation. As early as *Šárka* he started experimenting with slow-waltz cathartic finales. He made further attempts in *Jenůfa* and *Fate* (now taking the form of a monologue) and perfected the genre in *Vixen* and *Makropulos*. Most of these are penultimate movements – the long slow waltz followed by an almost throwaway ending which shifts the meaning either to a more positive view, as in *Vixen*, or to a gloomier one, as in *From the House of the Dead*, where the relentless prisoners' march succeeds the freedom chorus (another stately 3/2 movement). *Kát'a Kabanová*, uniquely among Janáček's mature operas, ends after the last words (Kabanicha's grim thanks to those who have brought Kát'a's corpse from the river) with an orchestral winding-up more reminiscent of Janáček's Act 1 endings to which a *fortissimo* off-stage wordless chorus – Kát'a's 'voices' – provides a surrealist gloss.

Grimes and Lucretia

PHILIP BRETT

One of the sure tests of a composer's stature is how he reacts to success. The furore over *Peter Grimes* both at home and abroad after its première in 1945 was possibly more remarkable than that accorded any opera this century. In the first few years of its existence *Grimes* was produced almost everywhere, even at La Scala, Milan, and at the hidebound Metropolitan Opera, New York. In connection with the Met production (a severe test of the work by all accounts), Britten's face appeared against a background of fishing-nets on the cover of *Time* magazine, which ran a lengthy and informative article on him in its inimitable house style (16 February 1948). Not all the attention was adulatory, of course. As the anonymous reporter of *Time* put it, 'English critics, having adopted Benjy Britten as a national hero, now insist on talking like Dutch uncles to him.' When one examines the London reviews of the first run of performances at Sadler's Wells one cannot help being appalled by their superficiality and patronizing tone. Dyneley Hussey's in *The Spectator* (15 June 1945) may be taken as an example: 'There is no limit to what such a talent may accomplish, if the composer will aim at bold and simple effects, avoid excess of clever devices and subtle points that fail to make their effect in the theatre, and above all, concentrate on the broad vocal melody as the central feature of his music.' Another striking thing about these reviews is their tendency to begin enthusiastically and gradually to exert control, as though it would somehow threaten the critic's masculinity if he – and they were all men – were to write in response to his spontaneous feelings. Nevertheless, what journalists actually write is never so important as the amount of attention they show: it was clear to everyone that *Grimes* was a success from the start, and the sort of success that might have tempted a lesser composer to continue in the same vein. *The Rape of Lucretia*, first performed a little more than a year after *Grimes*, represents a radical departure from the earlier work in more ways than one.

The chamber proportions and scoring of *Lucretia* can of course be explained by practical considerations, which were always a challenge to creativity for Britten. The path to further grand opera had been closed off for the moment as a result of a row between the Sadler's Wells company on the one hand and those associated with Britten (including Joan Cross, Eric Crozier and Peter Pears) on the other. Indeed, it led to the withdrawal of *Peter Grimes* from the repertory after surprisingly few performances. Moreover, Covent Garden's new operatic venture, which was to include *Peter Grimes* in its very first year, did not get under way until 1947.[1]

The idea of chamber opera must long have been fermenting in Britten's mind, and with the encouragement of Crozier and Ronald Duncan, whom he chose as his librettist for the new work, he apparently went ahead before there was any question of commitment from John Christie at Glyndebourne, where *Lucretia* was first performed.[2] The change in timbre that resulted from the new medium naturally enough involved a change in musical style. And with *Lucretia* Britten's distinctive *secco* recitative first comes into its own. *Grimes* is not without good recitative, of course, most notably in the pub scene. But the sheer bulk of information in the *Lucretia* libretto was a challenge to Britten to develop a characterful approach. Take, for instance, the opening of the opera, where the treacherous climb to power of the elder Tarquinius, who never appears in the opera, is marvellously set out in a declamatory manner that can make vital music out of such leaden mouthfuls of syllables as these:

> and always he'd pay his way
> With the prodigious liberality
> Of self-coin'd obsequious flattery.

The chief accompanying instrument is the piano, used in almost exactly the same way as it was used during this post-war period to accompany recitative in works of the seventeenth and eighteenth centuries. The punctuating ritornello from the full chamber band of single woodwind, horn, harp, percussion, string quartet and double bass hints by means of its reiterated chords at some of the tonal areas that will be important in the development of the musical argument, most notably C minor and E minor. With the entry of the Female Chorus, the background to the ensuing scene of an army encampment and its mood of frustration is suggested by an accompaniment seemingly locked to a chord constructed over B♭. The mention of Christ and redemption causes a shift to a unison G, the dominant of the whole work, over which Male and Female Chorus sing their expressive C major arioso. This is all done deftly and with an economy of means all the more striking after the expansiveness of *Grimes*.

[1]   See E. Crozier, '"Peter Grimes": an Unpublished Article of 1946', *Opera*, xvi (1965), pp. 412–16, and P. Brett, 'Breaking the Ice for British Opera: "Peter Grimes" on Stage', *Benjamin Britten: 'Peter Grimes'*, ed. Brett (Cambridge, 1983), pp. 90–1.

[2]   See R. Duncan, *How to Make Enemies* (London, 1968), pp. 54–5.

Another distinct development in *Lucretia* is the characterization of arias and scenes by means of particular instrumental combinations – the instrumentation of *Grimes* is by comparison fairly standard. Take, for example, the opening aria for the Male Chorus, in which the see-sawing soft string chords, double-bass punctuations (glissandi and pizzicati) and short falling *pianissimo* scales on the harp create the atmosphere of an oppressive summer night, complete with crickets and bull-frogs – tone painting every bit as fine as, and rather more subtle than, anything in the Sea Interludes. The lullaby that portrays the sleeping Lucretia at the beginning of Act 2 is also worthy of attention. This is an early example of Britten's favourite combination of bass (or alto) flute and bass clarinet, here combined with the muted horn; the harp harmonics that articulate the notes of the Female Chorus are a special touch. The passage is cast in an 'innocent' C major, which provides the maximum contrast to the troubled C♯ minor with which the act begins and also serves as a foil to the E major in which Tarquinius begins his ensuing aria, 'Within this frail crucible of light', a more Grimes-like moment.

Even more notable than the development of musical style in *Lucretia*, however, is the radical change of subject-matter and dramatic attitude. It was a change that most critics at the time deplored. Joseph Kerman, writing after the New York performance of 1949, contrasted the two works in this way:

Grimes is straight melodrama, set in the early nineteenth century, written in *verismo* style; for all its faults it tells a story and tries to tell it dramatically. *Lucretia*, on the other hand, is a moral discussion, based on a classical legend elevated to a myth, and operates by means of narrative and contemplative choruses to such an extent that the tenor and soprano singing these choruses have the largest roles in the opera. There is no plot, properly speaking; the story, pared to a bare minimum, simply serves as a series of logical examples with the help of which Chorus and characters conspire to project a turgid metaphysic.[3]

After examining the effect on Britten of turning to the then self-consciously modern verse drama for a libretto, and quoting Duncan's lines for Lucretia at the climax of the drama with disapproval, Kerman concludes that 'if there were not the example of *Grimes*, Britten's willingness to set this book would seem to convict him of complete inadequacy for dramatic composition'.[4]

Finely composed though the score is, as Kerman gruffly acknowledges, its odd dramaturgy puts *Lucretia* among the most problematical of Britten's stage works. But this oddness can, I believe, be illuminated, if not entirely explained, by further comparison with the earlier, more traditional and

3   'Grimes and Lucretia', *The Hudson Review*, ii (1949), pp. 281–2.
4   Ibid., p. 283.

more successful work. *Grimes* dramatizes with extraordinary power the conflict between the individual and society. Britten regarded it as 'a subject very close to my heart – the struggle of the individual against the masses. The more vicious the society, the more vicious the individual' (*Time*, 16 February 1948). The extended poem on which Britten and Pears based the scenario they drafted before returning to England was 'The Borough' by the eighteenth-century poet George Crabbe. Crabbe's Grimes is an out-and-out villain, the grim representative of a morally enfeebled society who merely takes advantage of the licence allowed him under the Poor Laws of the time to brutalize the boys whom he buys from the work-house. Britten changed Grimes, not, as had been claimed (even by the librettist Montagu Slater himself[5]), into a Byronic hero, but into a victim of that society who at the same time reflects its values.

The crux of the dramatic thrust of the opera occurs at the climax of Act 2 scene 1. The passage begins (seven bars after fig. 15) with Ellen's challenge to Peter's compulsive desire to work and to succeed in worldly terms: 'What aim, what future, what peace will your hard profits buy?' The F major chord on 'peace', sounding forced as though Ellen is engineering the drift of the conversation towards a showdown, becomes the F pedal over which Peter sings, to an earlier melody signifying his stubborn pride, 'Buy us a home, buy us respect . . . ' But his determined D Major is constantly undermined by the relentless thrust of the bass from A♭ to the pedal F. On this note the chorus then begin to recite the Creed – a 'symbolum' indeed, not of spirituality but of the mob instinct 'sanctified' by ritual. Though they fade out, a persistent repeated F on the horns reminds us of their continuing recitation. Staccato G♭ triads, suggestive in their relationship to the F of the minor ninth and second that characterize Peter's isolation, punctuate the conversation as Ellen first presses with seemingly genuine questions, then asks – in what David Matthews aptly calls 'her sweetest even-note manner'[6] – 'Were we mistaken when we planned to solve your life in lonely toil?' Peter answers in leaping intervals supported by an even weaker set of D major fragments in the bass. But Ellen can hear nothing, and, lost to him, she changes her rhetorical question into a statement: 'We *were* mistaken', the word 'mistaken' sung here as elsewhere to a B♭ triad that hints at the devastation to follow. The saccharine sound of a solo violin underlines her falseness. Then, as she sings 'Peter, we've failed, we've failed' to a rising octave on F, Peter strikes her, and the orchestra breaks loose in a mêlée created from the ironic superposition of Ellen's and Peter's melodies, only to be cut short by the chorus, who sing a loud 'Amen' to

---

[5]   'The Story of the Opera', *Benjamin Britten: Peter Grimes*, ed. Crozier (London, 1945), pp. 15–16.

[6]   'Act II Scene 1: an Examination of the Music', *Benjamin Britten: 'Peter Grimes'*, ed. Brett, p. 133.

their unholy creed. Peter literally and psychologically takes his note from them to sing, on a massive B♭ cadence and to a downward-plunging Lydian motif that informs most of the rest of the opera, 'So be it then, and God have mercy upon me', a motif that the orchestra takes up in a rough canon as Peter stumbles off with the boy.

The passage is more than a brilliant musical illustration of cruelty masquerading as concern and of the way in which society inculcates what it sometimes eases its conscience by, by labelling paranoia. Grimes at this moment not only succumbs to the Borough but also in his own mind becomes the monster he perceives they think him to be. After the enormously long dominant pedal, the cataclysmic cadence on B♮ – the key used to characterize the Borough right from the beginning of the opera – signifies as clearly as any musical gesture could the process in Grimes of what sociologists call 'internalization' – the acceptance of society's values and judgement by the victim.

The opera argues, moreover, that the psychological process of internalization (and that of the 'paranoia' that contributes to it) is a simple one resulting directly from social pressure and not from some subtle Freudian operation of the subconscious. While writing the work, the composer gradually jettisoned any matter that might be seized upon to manufacture psychological or pathological explanations for the central character. All mention was expunged of the father whose ineffectual attempts to control Peter the boy, Crabbe obliquely suggests, may partly be responsible for the villainy of Grimes the man. Britten's Grimes does not see the ghostly father and dead apprentices rebuking him – as was originally intended in the hut scene. Nor did the librettist's insistent development of emotional ties between Grimes and his apprentice survive the composer's intelligent scrutiny: it is with some surprise that we learn that Peter's soliloquy before the Storm Interlude, as well as the aria, 'And she will soon forget her school-house ways', in the hut scene were both originally addressed to the boy. All this had to go. By eliminating what might have been interpreted as pathological elements, the composer insisted on the social message of the drama. (The critics who nevertheless discerned psychopathy were for the composer part of the problem the opera addressed.)

A crucial moment in the scheme is the posse's arrival at the hut towards the end of Act 2 scene 2, an episode that is not in Crabbe, of course. The loud knock which distracts Peter at the moment the boy falls symbolizes society's implication in the death. We hear the posse approaching, its rising pitch suggesting the increasing suspicion and panic arising in its victim's breast. The cadence that heralds the knock signifies a kind of resolution, with the ensuing string and celesta tremolo suggesting the suspension of time in a moment that is to prove fateful. As I have argued at length, *Grimes* is a powerful dramatization of the view that crime is the result of the workings of society at large and that the individual reflects society however hard he tries to remain distinct.[7]

A dramatic argument that places all the blame on society, reducing individual responsibility to such a degree, proved too much for most music critics at the time and still causes problems now. Whether or not Grimes is technically guilty of his boys' deaths, a certain moral ambiguity has always been discerned in his portrayal. And as a visionary with no real emotional ties (his Ellen is part of his fantasy, the real one deserts him at the moment of truth) he is so dissociated from the realism of his surroundings that in his alienation he becomes a truly existential figure. Britten, however, was not by nature an existentialist. He later related this powerful drama of the outsider to his own predicament as a pacifist, and it hardly needs now to be argued that it involved his sexuality as well. Conceived at the very moment when he decided to return to Britain after an abortive attempt to emigrate to the United States, the opera served as a catharsis, purging the darker side of his feelings towards the repressive and embattled society he had fled. Hence its intensity. Yet it was born not so much out of alienation as from an intense desire to be accepted and to play a part in society.

Perhaps even deeper issues were at stake. It is notable that the composer replaced Slater's original text for the great soliloquy in the storm (it recurs at the end of the opera) with a verse beginning 'What harbour shelters peace,/Away from tidal waves, away from storms?/What harbour can embrace/Terrors and tragedies?' This passage is one of the most powerfully symbolic in the work, because it juxtaposes Grimes's grandest sweep of melody, signifying his visionary side, with an inversion of a motif associated with the Borough in the inquest scene at the beginning, hinting again at the process of 'internalization' and the seeds of destruction that it inevitably sows. The longing for peace, for resolution, is a theme that returns often in Britten's works. In *Grimes* it is not available. The protagonist goes silently to his death, a death, moreover, with no resonance, since society ignores the suicide of its victim as the daily round is resumed at the end of the opera.

Lucretia also involves death, a death that has political consequences in the myth, for it triggers the downfall of Tarquinius and Etruscan rule at the hands of Brutus Junius, who thus becomes the focus in some accounts. It is not surprising that Britten showed no interest in this aspect of the story. The source of the opera is a play, *Le Viol de Lucrèce*, written by André Obey in the early 1930s for the Compagnie de Quinze, an idealistic group founded by Jacques Copeau to purify and revivify the French theatre. Crozier mentions this company as an inspiration for the idea of the English Opera Group, and, much impressed by the play and its performance, he

[7]   See 'Postscript', ibid., pp. 193–6.

suggested it to Britten as a possible subject.[8] Obey takes over from Shakespeare the element of what Ian Donaldson calls 'magical thinking' about Lucretia's death. 'Like a religious sacrifice, the suicide seems to cleanse the effects of pollution, and to restore innocence and purity.'[9] To the notion of sacrifice in the play, the opera adds the theology of redemption. Critics were happy to assign this interpretation to the almost universally reviled librettist. Ronald Duncan later claimed[10] that it was the composer's idea, and in view of the preoccupation with redemption in Britten's later works, this rings true.

In *Lucretia* the heroine is of course also, like Grimes, a victim. The society in which she exists is also portrayed as corrupt and oppressive, and she is raped by an Etruscan prince who embodies its worst features. But there is nothing the least alienated about her. In place of the broad cross-section against which Grimes is thrown into relief, *Lucretia* presents a tightly knit and balanced group of which the heroine is a fully integrated member. The allegory here is clearly not that of the *out*cast oppressed. Duncan saw it, in typically high-flown terms, as 'fertility or life devoured by death' and 'spirit defiled by fate', with Lucretia symbolizing the former and Tarquinius the latter.[11] But the musical opposition of motifs built on adjacent notes symbolizing men and on thirds symbolizing women, outlined in some detail by White,[12] suggests rather that Britten was making a point about the male and female principles in conflict. Furthermore, whereas Britten allowed Grimes's tragedy to speak for itself, he decided to present Lucretia's demise within a frame, to enhance its personal meaning with a universal message. Obey's play already contained the two choruses who weave in and out of the action, taking on some of the functions carried over from the Shakespearian soliloquy and also commenting on the tragedy from a contemporary point of view. It was Britten and his librettist, however, who made them specifically Christian.

Historically, Christianity has had some difficulty with the Lucretia myth, as Donaldson demonstrates.[13] Though to most of the early Fathers she seemed a natural proto-martyr, her example was eventually rejected because of the sin of suicide, which is clearly a stumbling-block to any

---

[8]   See 'Staging First Productions 1', *The Operas of Benjamin Britten*, ed. D. Herbert (London, 1979), p. 27.

[9]   *The Rapes of Lucretia: a Myth and its Transformations* (Oxford, 1982), p. 25.

[10] *Working with Britten* (Welcombe, Devon, 1981), p. 85. Much of the material in this book comes directly (but sometimes with missing details) from Duncan, *How to Make Enemies*. I cite the original 'unedited' version in all cases.

[11] 'The Libretto', B. Britten et al., *The Rape of Lucretia: a Symposium* (London, 1948), p. 62.

[12] See E. W. White, *Benjamin Britten: his Life and Operas* (London, rev. 2/1983 by J. Evans), pp. 148–54.

[13] See *The Rapes of Lucretia*, pp. 25–8.

orthodox Christian interpretation. For Augustine, Lucretia's was not a heroic but a murderous act: failing to appreciate the Roman code of honour, he asks, reasonably enough, 'If she is adulterous, why is she praised? If chaste, why was she put to death?'[14] Shakespeare, allowing his Lucrece to debate the Christian point of view for three stanzas (ll. 1156–76), copes with the paradox by invoking the body/soul distinction:

> 'Ay me! the bark pilled from the lofty pine,
>   His leaves will wither and his sap decay:
>   So must my soul, her bark being pilled away.
>
> 'Her house is sacked, her quiet interrupted,
> Her mansion battered by the enemy;
> Her sacred temple spotted, spoiled, corrupted,
> Grossly engirt with daring infamy.
> Then let it not be called impiety,
>   If in this blemished fort I make some hole
>   Through which I may convey this troubled soul.'   (1167–76)

But the metaphor and conclusion sound archaic and forced, as though rehearsed from some mid-century anthology of sententious verse, and Lucrece is immediately diverted by the contemplation of revenge in the following stanzas.

Despite these difficulties, however, and quite apart from the question of the composer's personal belief, there is a strong case for the introduction of Christianity in connection with this tale. A religion which celebrates the victim and therefore the very concept of victimization, Christianity offers a universally understood context for the Lucretia story as well as a personal and spiritual way of interpreting it. In *Grimes*, Britten had of course represented religion only in its guise as a social institution, offering the basis in its hollow observance for hypocritical judgement and ruthless persecution. In *Lucretia* we are asked to divorce the moral and spiritual values of Christianity from their institutional connotations as a means not only of seeing the universal significance of the tragedy but also of finding a path out of the dilemma with which the opera ends:

> How is it possible that she
> Being so pure should die!
> How is it possible that we
> Grieving for her should live?

Not quite articulated, but clearly underlying the work, is also the question of the ambiguous nature of beauty, one that exercised Britten a good deal and came to occupy a central position in his last opera, *Death in Venice*. The

[14]   *Concerning the City of God against the Pagans*, trans. H. Bettenson (Harmondsworth, 1972/R 1984), p. 30.

pessimism of the later work had no place in *Lucretia*, however. The librettist reports that on reaching what was to have been the end – 'So brief is beauty. / Is this it all? It is all! It is all!' – the composer begged for more words. That is, he demanded from Duncan a different poetic resolution because he did not or could not allow the musical argument to end: 'from your point of view the opera is dramatically complete with Lucretia's death and the finale of epitaphs sung over her body, but I've just discovered that musically it's not finished. I want to write a final piece beyond the curtain as it were to frame the entire work.'[15]

Tonally, the work revolves around, and builds tension from, an opposition of keys centred on C and E♭ and keys centred on C♯ and E. Peter Evans goes so far as to see C♯ minor as a symbol of sin and shame in Act 2, and C as one of innocence and purity, and his reasoning is fairly convincing.[16] C is very definitely heard as the key of untroubled innocent beauty when we find Lucretia sleeping in the passage already referred to above, and after that the E major in which Tarquinius sings seems another world of experience. As a result of this, the E that is a melodic pole of attraction for her is reharmonized when she awakes, and her C becomes C♯ minor, the minor third of the melodic figure here being symbolically pierced by the horns' brassy D♯ (fig. 27) (a gesture repeated more violently in E♭ minor at fig. 41).

When Lucretia appears next morning her first arioso consists of chromatic confused utterances over a G pedal (fig. 71). The reference is to Tarquinius's music when he first wakes her (fig. 28), but in this context the pedal remains stationary so that Lucretia's C can be reinterpreted as C minor at the moment she sings her own name. At the appearance of Collatinus and Junius the insecure C slips to an unambiguous B minor for the denouement. As the heroine dies to a series of falling womanly thirds, the rhythm ♩. ♫ ♪ is heard and is tried out on a number of pitches before the ground of the ensuing passacaglia emerges in E as unambiguously as Tarquinius's aria to her beauty earlier on. First Collatinus, then Junius, then the two maidservants, echoing Lucretia's falling thirds, sing over it. When the Female Chorus enters with a particularly far-fetched Duncanian metaphor, the ground migrates to the treble and the tonal complication grows. At the entry of the Male Chorus, the C♯ minor interpretation of the ground, latent in Junius's first statement, grows in strength, and it returns after the whole cast have tried to force a unison melody based on C against the ground to the crucial words quoted above, 'How is it possible that she / Being so good should die! . . .'

[15]   See Duncan, *How to Make Enemies*, pp. 134–6.
[16]   See *The Music of Benjamin Britten* (London, 1979), p. 138.

A stalemate has been reached at this point. Lucretia's tragedy is being viewed through eyes, the music seems to suggest, as human and sinful as Tarquinius's, and the burden of guilt cannot be lifted so easily. The music 'is swept back into limp reiterations of its final thirds, "It is all"'.[17] In an ensuing transformation and reconciliation as remarkable in its own way as the great B♭ chord in the epilogue of *Billy Budd* we are presented with a gradual resolution of the key conflict into a pure C major underpinning the correspondingly pure glimpse of the theology of Christian redemption. First of all the Female Chorus asks questions each of which seeks to escape from, but is brought firmly back to, what is now a burdensome C♯ minor chord. When she finally reiterates the 'Is this it all?' after mentioning the Crucifixion, a G major dominant chord placed high on the strings, which have been silent since the end of the passacaglia, heralds the appearance of the Male Chorus, who gently takes up her note. Singing a melody in contrary motion to a bass that actually contains statements of the Tarquinius motif, he resolves everything on to a B major which, as it were, purifies the B of Lucretia's shame in the simplest and largest arpeggio of the opera (beginning three bars before fig. 106). But even this is not all, for suddenly the fragmentary 'it is all' rhythm appears all over the score like a galaxy of twinkling stars, and before we have time to assimilate it aurally, the bass gives way to G, a C pedal creeps in on a weak beat, and the Chorus sing their great melody, even-handed in its distribution of 'male' tones and 'female' thirds, for the last time.

This conclusion is irresistible and sure from a musical point of view. And, as in so many cases in the history of opera, the music transforms the words. Here, as in the extraordinary prayer after the rape itself (reminiscent of the chorale in the trial scene of *The Magic Flute*, perhaps) we are helped over the perfumed High Church diction of a libretto written under the shadow of Eliot towards a vision of forgiveness and compassion that for Britten was evidently simple and real. Nonetheless, the Christian frame has raised serious problems for the opera, even among those most sympathetic to the composer. As Evans (most recently) has pointed out, 'the tragedy could have been played out entirely in its own terms and the universal resonances would have been sensed'.[18] More important still, once Christianity is invoked, it is no longer merely a question of 'Great Love . . . defiled by Fate or Man': the sacrificial element of the religion comes into play ('But here/Other wounds are made, yet still His blood is shed'), and the question of sin supersedes that of Fate.

The problem with sacrifice and sin in this context is that they are both made to devolve upon Lucretia. A careful reading of the libretto scarcely disturbs the notion that Tarquinius remains simply an agent of Fate – the

17   Ibid., p. 140.
18   Ibid., p. 141.

cruel, degenerate, but inevitably attractive male whose phallic aspects Duncan is at pains to emphasize. Since the act of rape (after which he does not appear) is his chief purpose in the action, we cannot observe his subsequent feelings. His one great moment, the exquisite aria 'Within this frail crucible of light', possibly written in response to the phrase 'the pity is that sin has so much grace' that precedes it, indeed gives some musical validity to the odd transference that occurs.

For Lucretia shoulders both. She is sacrificial lamb and at the same time the sinner begging forgiveness. Evans claims that the only view of her that makes any sense in the dramatic context is one in which she is both 'revolted by Tarquinius' assault and horrifyingly attracted towards the realization of a nightmare . . . Her mental torture after the event suggests a recognition that revulsion and attraction can co-exist, that some part of her has shared the guilt';[19] and he quotes several aspects of both music and words that support this notion.

It is difficult to overcome revulsion at the view of rape which shifts the onus of responsibility on to the victim in this fashion. At first sight it may seem all too characteristic of that identifiable male approach which typically minimizes female rape either by denying its enormity or by throwing the responsibility for it back on to the woman. In his book on Richardson's novel, Terry Eagleton quotes V. S. Pritchett's extraordinary statement (in *The Living Novel*) that 'Clarissa represents the extreme of puritanism which desires to be raped' and shows Ian Watt turning the ambiguous nature of Clarissa's feelings about Lovelace into her 'unconscious love' for him.[20] Similarly, Ernest Newman in his first review of Britten's opera undercuts the work by referring to its central action as 'the rather conventional mishap of Lucretia' and by finding the climactic point 'too commonplace for stage representation' (*The Sunday Times*, 28 July 1946). It would be disturbing indeed to find Britten in this company.

In fact, an examination of *Grimes* in the terms I have suggested clarifies the matter and shows why Britten countenanced this approach to Lucretia. As I argued earlier, what lies behind the exploration of the outsider's condition in the earlier opera – and what has been so misunderstood about it – is Britten's realization, no doubt gained from a cool assessment of his own predicament and perhaps some prompting from Auden and Isherwood, that those who are oppressed in one way or another tend to internalize their oppression. Grimes is a classic case, an unclubbable man who can think of nothing better than joining the club while doing everything to ensure that he could never be accepted. Similarly, Lucretia in the second scene of Act 2 dramatizes the shame and guilt involuntarily

19   Ibid.
20   *The Rape of Clarissa: Writing, Sexuality and Class Struggle in Samuel Richardson* (Oxford, 1982), pp. 65, 68.

experienced by rape victims even though they are totally innocent and have been wronged in a particularly horrible manner. Not sharing the attitudes of male heterosexual orthodoxy, Britten may well have been specially alive to this aspect of the tragedy.

And so, if we accept at face value the speech Duncan gives Lucretia at her moment of decision in Act 2 (just before fig. 94) – 'Even great love's too frail to bear the weight of shadows' – then she stands convicted of lack of faith, and her suicide is a gesture of despair. If, however, the insistent B minor of her guilt is seen as symbolic of an involuntary, conditioned response – of internalization – and her words, her doubt, her guilt, even the whole panoply of Tarquinius's attractiveness, are seen as the projection of an internalized role, then first her hysteria, and later her self-destruction, like Grimes's, begin to make sense. Her story becomes an equally modern tragedy.

But Britten is not even-handed with his victims. The fisherman whom we suspect to be at least partly guilty of the deaths of his apprentices is musically represented as a slightly tarnished yet still innocent victim of society. Lucretia, who on the other hand is the truly innocent victim of a ludicrous patriarchal order, is represented as at least partly guilty. Grimes's dreams give him an almost heroic stature and set him apart from society and the world of the audience, whereas Lucretia's dreams only betray her by turning natural desire into the material out of which her guilt is fabricated ('In the forest of my dreams/You have always been the Tiger'). By raping her, in other words, Tarquinius manages to make his desire her crime. And musically, the transference is accomplished quite literally by the recall of his 'Yet the linnet in your eyes/Lifts with desire' (Act 2, fig. 32) during Lucretia's 'confession' (fig. 88); also, on a symbolic plane his E major rubs off on her in the form of its dominant, B, which also represents the fall from grace from her own limpid C major. In classical terms this tragic paradox must result in her death, but it becomes here in addition the very basis of the opera's Christian vision and the larger paradox that that implies: 'Though our nature's still as frail/And we still fall/ . . . yet now/He bears our sin and does not fall/And He carrying all/ turns round/Stoned with our doubt and then forgives us all.'

In musical terms, as we have seen, there is every reason to make the leap of faith this assertion requires; but it is an odd sleight of hand from an emotional or dramatic point of view, and one that may cause doubt or disquiet as we leave the theatre. To make sense of it I think it must be seen in relation to Britten's lifelong preoccupation with the senseless violence of man and the attendant guilt by implication that he seems to have felt so strongly. In turning to Christian doctrine for relief and resolution in this opera he was attempting to answer the question that he had posed and left unanswered in *Grimes*:

What harbour shelters peace,
Away from tidal waves, away from storms?
What harbour can embrace
Terrors and tragedies?

Britten could not end yet again in the terrifying decrescendo to non-musical speech which, as Kerman put it, 'is a powerful evocation of the dead hopelessness, past tragedy, of Grimes's ultimate predicament'.[21] It is perhaps no accident that in *Lucretia*, written after the crisis of career and roots had taken place, Britten began the search for a more consoling and positive solution.

[21]   'Grimes and Lucretia', p. 279.

A bibliography of the writings of Winton Dean

COMPILED BY STEPHEN DEAN

This bibliography brings together almost all Winton Dean's writings on music to the end of 1985. It omits unpublished lectures and a few minor articles (in particular for *Radio Times*); programme notes, broadcast talks and letters to the press appear in selection only. Works cut or bowdlerized by editors are marked with an asterisk.

BOOKS

1 *Bizet* (The Master Musicians), London, Dent, 1948; New York, Collier Books, 1962 (Great Composers Series); rev. and enlarged as *Georges Bizet: his Life and Work*, 1965; rev. (The Master Musicians) 1975, 1978; Italian trans., Turin, EDT/Musica, 1980
2 *Carmen*, London, The Folio Society, 1949 (with Mérimée's novel, trans. Lady Mary Loyd)
3 *Introduction to the Music of Bizet*, London, Dennis Dobson, 1950
4 *Franck* (Novello's Biographies of Great Musicians), London, Novello, [1950]
5 *Handel's Dramatic Oratorios and Masques*, London, Oxford University Press, 1959
6 *Handel and the Opera Seria*, Berkeley and Los Angeles, University of California Press, 1969; London, Oxford University Press, 1970
7 *The New Grove Handel*, London, Macmillan, 1982; New York, Norton, 1982; French trans., Monaco, Editions du Rocher, 1985
8 *Handel's Operas 1704–1726* (with John Merrill Knapp), Oxford, Clarendon Press, 1987

WORK EDITED

9 Edward J. Dent, *The Rise of Romantic Opera*, Cambridge, Cambridge University Press, 1976

CONTRIBUTIONS TO COMPOSITE WORKS

10 'Giacomo Puccini, 1858–1924' in *The Heritage of Music*, vol. 3, ed. H. Foss (London, 1951), 153–71
11 'Bizet's *Ivan IV*' in *Fanfare for Ernest Newman*, ed. H. Van Thal (London, 1955), 58–85

12 'Handel's Dramatic Works' in *Purcell–Handel Festival* (London, 1959), 24–9
13 'Shakespeare and Opera' in *Shakespeare in Music*, ed. P. Hartnoll (London, 1964), 89–175
14 'Shakespeare in the Opera House' in *Shakespeare Survey*, xviii, ed. A. Nicoll (Cambridge, 1965), 75–93
15 'Verdi's *Otello*: a Shakespearian Masterpiece' in *Shakespeare Survey*, xxi, ed. K. Muir (Cambridge, 1968), 87–96
16 'Vocal Embellishment in a Handel Aria' in *Studies in Eighteenth-Century Music: a Tribute to Karl Geiringer on his Seventieth Birthday*, ed. H. C. R. Landon with R. E. Chapman (New York and London, 1970), 151–9
17 'Beethoven and Opera' in *The Beethoven Companion*, ed. D. Arnold and N. Fortune (London and New York [as *The Beethoven Reader*], 1971), 331–86
18 'Handel Today' in *Handel and the Fitzwilliam* (Cambridge, 1974), 18–21
19 'Some Echoes of Donizetti in Verdi's Operas' in *Atti del III° congresso internazionale di studi verdiani* (Parma, 1974), 122–47
20 'Handel's *Sosarme*, a Puzzle Opera' in *Essays on Opera and English Music in Honour of Sir Jack Westrup*, ed. F. W. Sternfeld *et al.* (Oxford, 1975), 115–47
21 'Die Ausführung des Rezitativs in den Opern der Händel-Zeit' in *G. F. Händel und seine italienischen Zeitgenossen*, ed. W. Siegmund-Schultze (Halle, 1979), 94–105
22 'Die Aufführung von heroischen männlichen Rollen in Händels Opern' in *G. F. Händel – Aufführungspraxis und Interpretation*, ed. W. Siegmund-Schultze (Halle, 1980), 32–7
23 'Meyerbeer's Italian Operas' in *Music and Bibliography: Essays in Honour of Alec Hyatt King*, ed. O. Neighbour (London, 1980), 170–83
24 '*Otello*: the Background' in *Otello* (English National Opera Guide 7) (London, 1981), 7–12
25 'French Opera', 'Italian Opera', 'German Opera' in *The New Oxford History of Music*, vol. 8, *The Age of Beethoven 1790–1830*, ed. G. Abraham (London, 1982), ch. II: 26–119, ch. IX: 376–451, ch. X: 452–522
26 'The Recovery of Handel's Operas' in *Music in Eighteenth-Century England: Essays in Memory of Charles Cudworth*, ed. C. Hogwood and R. Luckett (Cambridge, 1983), 103–13
27 'Mattheson's Arrangement of Handel's *Radamisto* for the Hamburg Opera' in *New Mattheson Studies*, ed. G. J. Buelow and H. J. Marx (Cambridge, 1983), 169–78
28 'The Musical Sources for Handel's *Teseo* and *Amadigi*' in *Slavonic and Western Music: Essays for Gerald Abraham*, ed. M. H. Brown and R. J. Wiley (Ann Arbor and Oxford, 1985), 63–80
29 'Handel's Early London Copyists' in *Bach, Handel, Scarlatti: Tercentenary Essays*, ed. P. Williams (Cambridge, 1985), 75–97
30 Unpublished: 'Handel's Operas 1720–1741' (contribution to abortive symposium on Baroque opera). Written 1972

FOREWORD

31 A. D. Walker, *George Frideric Handel: the Newman Flower Collection in the Henry Watson Library: a Catalogue* (Manchester, 1972), ix

ARTICLES IN DICTIONARIES

32 *Grove's Dictionary of Music and Musicians*, 5th edition, ed. E. Blom (London, 1954): 'Bizet', 'Criticism', 'Postage Stamps' (addendum), 'Turina' (work-list); Supplementary Volume (London, 1961): 'Postage Stamps' (addendum)

33 *Encyclopaedia Britannica* (London, Chicago): 'Bizet' (1955, rev. 1963), 'Oratorio' (1966)

34 *New Catholic Encyclopaedia* (New York, 1967): 'Handel'

35 *Encyclopedia Americana* (New York): 'Bizet', 'Carmen', 'Cherubini' (1968), 'Handel' (1970)

36 *Dictionnaire de la musique*, ed. M. Honegger (Paris, 1970, rev. 2/1986): 'Bizet', 'Handel'

37 *Enciclopedia della musica*, ed. C. Sartori (Milan, 1972–4): 'Bizet'

38 *Sohlmans musiklexikon* (Stockholm, 1975–9): 'Bizet'

39 *The New Grove Dictionary of Music and Musicians*, ed. S. Sadie (London, 1980): 'Bizet', 'Criticism', 'Gluck' ix–x, 'Newburgh Hamilton', 'Handel' (see no. 7), 'Nicola Haym', 'Johann Jakob Heidegger', 'Samuel Humphreys', 'Charles Jennens', 'Thomas Morell', 'Opéra Comique' vi–ix, 'Rescue Opera', 'Paolo Rolli', 'Giacomo Rossi', and the following singers: Albertini, Andreoni, Annibali, Antinori, Avoglio, Bagnolesi, Baldassari, Baldi, Beard, Bendler, Berenstadt, Bernacchi, Berselli, Bertolli, Bigonzi, Faustina Bordoni, A. Borosini, F. Borosini, R. Borosini, Boschi, Caffarelli, Calori, Campioli, Carestini, Carli, Casarini, Cassani, Champness, Chimenti, Mrs Clive, Conti, Costantini, Croce, Curioni, Cuzzoni, Dotti, Duparc ['La Francesina'], Durastanti, Miss Edwards, Fabri, Frasi, Frederick, Galerati, Galli, Gallia, Gambarini, Girardeau, Gismondi, Gordon, L'Epine, Lindelheim, Lottini, Lowe, Manina, Marchesini, Merighi, Montagnana, Monza, M. C. Negri, M. R. Negri, Nicolini, Pacini, Palmerini, Passerini, Pellegrini, Pilotti-Schiavonetti, Pinacci, Powell, F. C. Reinhold, H. T. Reinhold, Riemschneider, Anastasia Robinson, Ann T. Robinson, Miss Robinson, Rochetti, Russell, Salvai, Scalzi, Scarabelli, Senesino, Sibilla, Sorosina, Strada, Sullivan, Urbani, Vico, Waltz, Wass, Zannoni

40 Unpublished: 'Bizet', 'Handel' (commissioned by Alfred A. Knopf, New York, for *Encyclopedia of Music and Musicians*, ed. W. Brockway; project abandoned on the editor's death). Written 1967

ARTICLES IN PERIODICALS

About the House
41 *'Orfeo ed Euridice'*, iii/2 (May 1969), 9–10
Adelphi
42 'Massenet', second quarter 1953, 228–34
The Amor Artis Bulletin (New York)
43 'On Handel's *Susanna*', v/1 (October 1965), 1–2, 7–8
44 'On Handel's *Semele*', v/2 (November 1965), 1–2, 8–9
45 'On Handel's *Esther*', v/3 (April 1966), 1–2, 5–6
The Chesterian
46 'Joaquin Turina', xxiii (1949), 92–8

47 'Verdi's Transitional Operas', xxvii (1952), 8–13
   Concerto (Cologne)
48 '*Alessandro*. Zur Oper *Alessandro* von Georg Friedrich Händel', ii/3 (1985), 47–51
   Current Musicology
49 'Handel and Keiser: Further Borrowings', ix (1969), 73–80
   Englische Rundschau (Bonn)
50 'Ein Gedenkjahr als historische Aufgabe', 10 April 1959
51 'Händels erste Londoner Oper', 6 October 1961 (see no. 85)
   Händel-Jahrbuch, 2nd ser.
52 'Händels kompositorische Entwicklung in den Opern der Jahre 1724/25', xxviii
   (1982), 23–34
53 'Some Aspects of Handel Scholarship Today', xxxi (1985), 131–7
   High Fidelity
54 'Four Thousand Choristers Can't Be Right', ix/4 (April 1959), 46–8, 130–2
   The Listener
55 'Handel's Operas', 16 December 1948
56 'Weber and the Opera', 24 March 1949
57 'Handel and the English Oratorio', 4 May 1950
58 'Handel and the "Secular Oratorio"', 17 May 1951
59 'Handel's *Giulio Cesare*', 13 September 1951
60 'Berlioz and *Faust*', 7 February 1952
61 'Unfamiliar Bizet', 8 January 1953 (see letters, 15, 22 January)
62 'A Composer of the French Revolution [Méhul]', 19 February 1953
63 'The Choice of Hercules', 11 June 1953
64 'Bizet's First Full-Length Opera [*Les Pêcheurs de perles*]', 25 March 1954
65 'Janáček and *Katya Kabanova*', 27 May 1954 (reprinted in *Leoš Janáček: Kát'a
   Kabanová*, ed. J. Tyrrell, Cambridge, 1982)
66 'Gasparo Spontini: a Neglected Opera Composer', 5 August 1954
67 'Lennox Berkeley and *Nelson*', 16 September 1954
68 'Handel's Italian Cantatas', 6 January 1955
69 'Lennox Berkeley's Orchestral Music', 7 April 1955
70 'Rossini in Paris', 16 June 1955
71 'A Lost Bizet Opera [*La Coupe du roi de Thulé*]', 7 July 1955
72 'Weber and *Euryanthe*', 22 September 1955
73 'The Dilemma of Radio Opera', 12 April 1956
74 'Cornelius and *The Barber of Bagdad*', 16 August 1956
75 'Bizet in Scotland', 4 October 1956
76 'Berlioz and *The Trojans*', 13 June 1957
77 'Cimarosa and *Il matrimonio segreto*', 15 August 1957
78 'Handel's *Theodora*', 6 February 1958
79 'Verdi and *Don Carlos*', 8 May 1958
80 'Two Aspects of Handel', 19 March 1959
81 'Cherubini and the Opera', 25 June 1959
82 'Berlioz and the Comic Muse', 17 March 1960
83 'Bellini and *I puritani*', 9 June 1960
84 'Gluck and the Reform of Opera', 12 January 1961
85 'Handel's First London Opera', 18 May 1961 (see no. 51)

86 'Weber and Romantic Opera', 26 October 1961
87 'Handel's Oxford Oratorio [*Athalia*]', 25 June 1964
88 'Gluck and Operatic Tradition', 15 October 1964
89 'Handel's Operas', 31 December 1970 (see no. 214)
90 *'Handel's First Oratorio [*Esther*]', 28 February 1974
91 'Heroic Stature [Lennox Berkeley's operas]', 20 October 1983
   The Monthly Musical Record
92 'What is a Leitmotive?', lxxix (1949), 4–8
93 'The Abridgement of Handel', lxxx (1950), 178–82
   Music & Letters
94 'An Unfinished Opera by Bizet [*La Coupe du roi de Thulé*]', xxviii (1947), 347–63
95 'Music – and Letters? An Impertinent Enquiry', xxx (1949), 376–80
96 'Schoenberg's Ideas', xxxi (1950), 295–304
97 'Arnold Schönberg 1874–1951' [contribution to symposium], xxxii (1951) 309–10
98 'Barzun's Life of Berlioz', xxxiii (1952), 119–31
99 'Handel's Dramatic Music on Records', xxxix (1958), 57–65
100 'Bizet's Self-Borrowings', xli (1960), 238–44
101 'Charles Jennens's Marginalia to Mainwaring's Life of Handel', liii (1972), 160–4
102 'A French Traveller's View of Handel's Operas', lv (1974), 172–8
103 'Edward J. Dent: a Centenary Tribute', lvii (1976), 353–61
104 'The Performance of Recitative in Late Baroque Opera', lviii (1977), 389–402
   The Music Review
105 '*Carmen*: an Attempt at a True Evaluation', vii (1946), 209–20
   Music Survey
106 'The Libretto of *The Secret Marriage*', iii (1950), 33–8 (reprinted in *Music Survey*: Collected Edition, London, 1981)
   Musica (Kassel)
107 'Händel heute', xxxviii (1984), 522–6
   Musical America
108 'George Frederick Handel (1685–1759): a View of the So-Called "Non-Dramatic" Works', lxxviv/3 (February 1959), 3, 159, 188
   Musical Newsletter
109 'How Should Handel's Oratorios Be Staged?', i/4 (October 1971), 11–15 (see no. 194)
110 'The Corruption of *Carmen*: the Perils of Pseudo-Musicology', iii/4 (October 1973), 7–12, 20
   The Musical Times
111 'Handel's *Alexander Balus*', xciii (1952), 351–3
112 'The Essential Handel', c (1959), 192–4 (see letters, 335, 428, 536, 666; ci, 166, 310)
113 'Beethoven in his Letters', ciii (1962), 156–9
114 'The Letters of Gluck', ciii (1962), 230–1
115 'The Man Verdi – a Review', civ (1963), 26–9
116 'Handel's *Giulio Cesare*', civ (1963), 402–4
117 'Handel's *Riccardo Primo*', cv (1964), 498–500
118 'Operas on *The Tempest*', cv (1964), 810–14 (excerpts from 'Shakespeare and Opera' in *Shakespeare in Music*: see no. 13)

119 'The True *Carmen*?' cvi (1965), 846–55
120 '*Athalia* Comes to London', cviii (1967), 226–7
121 'Masque into Opera [*Acis and Galatea*]', cviii (1967), 605–6
122 'Handel's *Scipione*', cviii (1967), 902–4
123 'Handel's *Amadigi*', cix (1968), 324–7
124 'A Handel Tragicomedy [*Flavio*]', cx (1969), 819–22
125 'Handel's Wedding Opera [*Atalanta*]', cxi (1970), 705–7
126 'Handel's *Ottone*', cxii (1971), 955–8
127 'A Note on Opera', cxv (1974), 34–5
128 'Bizet after 100 Years', cxvi (1975), 525–7
129 'An Unrecognised Handel Singer: Carlo Arrigoni', cxviii (1977), 556–8 (see letter, 725)
130 'Opera and the Literary Approach', cxix (1978), 854–8
131 'Handel on the Stage: the Tercentenary in London', cxxvi (1985), 221–3
    Opera
132 'Critic and Composer', iii (1952), 154–61 (reprinted in *The Opera Bedside Book*, ed. H. Rosenthal, London, 1965)
133 'Further Thoughts on Operatic Criticism', iii (1952), 655–9 (reprinted in *The Opera Bedside Book*; trans. in *Musik der Zeit* (Bonn), iv, 1953)
134 'Gluck's *Orpheus*', iv (1953), 13–17
135 'Donizetti and Queen Elizabeth [*Roberto Devereux*]', iv (1953), 333–6 (reprinted with additional note in *The Opera Bedside Book*)
136 'An Introduction to *The Pearl Fishers*', v (1954), 145–8
137 'Verdi and Shakespeare', vi (1955), 480–4
138 '*The Trojans*', viii (1957), 339–44 (reprinted in *The Opera Bedside Book*)
139 'A Reply to Arthur Jacobs [on the staging of Handel's oratorios]', x (1959), 369–71
140 '*Iphigénie en Tauride*', xii (1961), 505–10
141 'Shakespeare and Italian Opera – without the Prince', xv (1964), 225–32
142 'The Riddle of Meyerbeer', xv (1964), 297–302
143 'Twenty Years of Handel Opera', xxvi (1975), 924–30
144 'Handel and *Rodelinda*', xxxii (1981), 233–8
    Opera Cues (Houston, Texas)
145 '*Rinaldo*', October 1975, 4–6
    Opera Jaarboek
146 'De twee vormen van Händel's muziekdrama', 1983–4 [unpaginated]
    Proceedings of the Royal Musical Association
147 'The Dramatic Element in Handel's Oratorios', lxxix (1952–3), 33–49
148 'Opera under the French Revolution', xciv (1967–8), 77–96
149 'Donizetti's Serious Operas', c (1973–4), 123–41 (see also *Royal Musical Association Centenary Essays*, ed. E. Olleson, London, 1975)
    Radio Times
150 'A Wild Success . . . and then Forgotten [*Les Huguenots*]', 25 April 1952
    The Score
151 *'English Music Today', xviii (September 1953), 5–10
152 'Handel Reconsidered', ix (September 1954), 49–53

The Times Literary Supplement
153 *'English Musical Growth', 24 August 1951
154 'Advances in British Music', 29 August 1952
155 *'Whose *Carmen*?', 24 August 1973
156 'When the Gods Descend', 21 June 1974

GRAMOPHONE-RECORD NOTES

157 Handel, *Arias and Choruses*, HMV DLP 1200, 1959
158 Handel, *Acis and Galatea*, L'Oiseau-Lyre SOL 60011–12, 1960; Harmonia Mundi, DR 216–17, 1970 (French trans.)
159 Handel, *L'Allegro ed il Penseroso*, L'Oiseau-Lyre SOL 60025–6, 1960
160 Handel, *Coronation Anthems*, Argo ZRG 5369, 1963
161 Handel, *Julius Caesar Arias*, Decca SDD 574, 1964
162 Handel, *Rodelinda*, Westminster WST 320, 1964
163 Handel, *Serse*, Westminster WST 321, 1965
164 Handel, *Hercules*, RCA SER 5569–71, 1967
165 Handel, *Solomon*, RCA SER 5579–81, 1968; Philips 412 612-1, 1985 (rev.) (see no. 201)
166 Handel, *Jephtha*, Vanguard VSL 11089–91, 1970
167 Handel, *Giulio Cesare*, DG 2720 023, 1970
168 Handel, *Orlando*, RCA SRS 3006, 1971
169 Handel, *Ariodante*, RCA LSC 6200, 1971
170 Handel, *Agrippina*: cantata and opera title-role arias, Cambridge CC 2771, 1972
171 Bizet, *Carmen*, Decca D11D 3, 1976
172 Handel, *Admeto*, EMI IC 163 30808–12, 1978
173 Handel, *Alexander's Feast*, EMI SLS 5168, 1979
174 Handel, *Xerxes* (*Serse*), CBS 79325, 1979
175 Bizet, *L'Arlésienne* Suites 1 and 2, *Carmen* Suite, DG 2531 329, 1981
176 Handel, *Hercules*, Archiv 2742 004, 1983
177 Handel, *Alessandro* (commissioned for Deutsche Harmonia Mundi but not printed. See no. 48)

SELECTED PROGRAMME NOTES

178 Schumann, Quintet in E flat for piano and strings, Op. 44; Fauré, Quintet No. 2 in C minor for piano and strings, Op. 115, Freemasons' Hall, Edinburgh, 18 Aug. 1952
179 Dvořák, Quintet in A major for piano and strings, Op. 81; Franck, Quintet in F minor for piano and strings, Freemasons' Hall, Edinburgh, 20 Aug. 1952
180 Mozart, Piano Quartet in G minor, K.478; Fauré, Piano Quartet No. 1 in C minor, Op. 15; Brahms, Piano Quartet No. 2 in A major, Op. 26, Usher Hall, Edinburgh, 24 Aug. 1952
181 'French Opera', Aldeburgh Festival, 1954 (reprinted in *Aldeburgh Anthology*, ed. R. Blythe, Aldeburgh, 1972)
182 'Handel and the Theatre [*Samson*]', Leeds Festival, 1958
183 Beethoven, *Missa solemnis*, Royal Festival Hall, 4 Oct. 1959

184 *Belshazzar*, Royal Festival Hall, 5 Oct. 1959
185 Beethoven, Piano Sonata in C major, Op. 53, Usher Hall, Edinburgh, 29 Aug. 1961
186 Bizet, Symphony in C major, Leith Town Hall, Edinburgh, 6 Sept. 1961
187 *Idomeneo*, Royal Albert Hall, 17 Aug. 1964
188 *Alessandro*, English Bach Festival, 1966
189 *Julius Caesar*, New York City Opera, 1966
190 'The Drama of *Macbeth*', San Francisco Opera, 1967
191 *Leonore* (1805), Royal Festival Hall, 22 June 1969
192 *Saul*, Leeds Festival, 1972
193 'Handel and his *Imeneo*', Royal Academy of Music 150th Anniversary, 1972
194 'Wie sollten Händels Oratorien auf die Bühne gebracht werden?', Göttinger Händel-Fest 1975 (see no. 109)
195 *Julius Caesar*, Barber Institute, Birmingham, 1977
196 *Samson*, English Bach Festival, 1977
197 *Rinaldo*, *Terpsicore*, English Bach Festival, 1978
198 *Rodelinda*, Welsh National Opera, 1981
199 *Solomon*, Leeds Festival, 1981
200 *Agrippina*, Kent Opera, 1982
201 *Solomon*, *Textbuch*, Göttingen, 1984 (German trans.: see no. 165)
202 *L'Allegro, il Penseroso ed il Moderato*, St John's, Smith Square, 7 Jan. 1985
203 *Teseo*, Boston Early Music Festival, 1985
204 'Handel and the Theatre', Handel Tercentenary Festival, London, 1985
205 *Deborah*, St Giles's, Cripplegate, 16 Nov. 1985

SELECTED BROADCAST TALKS

All broadcast on BBC Third Programme (later Radio 3) unless otherwise stated.
206 'French Music' (review of M. Cooper, *French Music from the Death of Berlioz to the Death of Fauré*), 24 July 1951
207 'Bizet and the Stage', 30 Aug. 1951
208 'Bizet' (Composer of the Week), BBC General Overseas Service, 1 March 1953
209 'Handel's *Samson*', 2 Jan. 1959
210 'Berlioz's *Te Deum*', Music Magazine, BBC Home Service, 18 Jan. 1959
211 'Bizet and his World' (review of M. Curtiss, *Bizet and his World*), Music Magazine, BBC Home Service, 21 June 1959
212 'Handel's Secular Oratorios', Music Magazine, 3 Nov. 1968
213 'Handel's *Solomon*', Music Magazine, 19 Oct. 1969
214 'Handel's Operas Today', 1 Aug. 1970 (a shortened version was published in *The Listener*: see no. 89)
215 'Handel's *Semele* as Music-Drama', 18 March 1971
216 *Acis and Galatea*, 29 Jan. 1972
217 'Handel's *Saul* as Music-Drama', 20 May 1972
218 'Bajazet' (Great Characters from Opera), 22 Nov. 1972
219 '*Esther* and the Birth of English Oratorio', 9 Dec. 1972
220 'Opera of the French Revolution' (The French Opera), 4 March 1973
221 'Handel the Magician', 31 May 1973
222 *La Jolie Fille de Perth*, 1 July 1973

223 'Early English Opera and Masque', Music Weekly, 5 May 1974
224 'Twenty-One Years of Opera at the Camden Festival', Music Weekly, 16 Feb. 1975
225 *Ivan IV* (The Operas of Bizet): introduction and three interval talks on the three versions of Ivan's war song, the strange history of the opera, and Büsser's alterations to the score, 5 Oct. 1975
226 'New Light on Donizetti and Verdi', 7 Feb. 1976
227 'Donizetti and *Opera Seria*', 4 Sept. 1976
228 'Another Fidelio': Paer's *Leonora*, Music Weekly, 7 Nov. 1976
229 '*Carmen* in Performance', Music Weekly, 13 Feb. 1977
230 'The Caesar Manuscript' (Discoveries), BBC 2 television, 25 Sept. 1978
231 *L'Allegro, il Penseroso ed il Moderato*, Early Music Forum, 17 May 1980
232 *La Resurrezione*, Music Weekly, 19 April 1981
233 'Edward J. Dent' (Makers of Musical Taste), BBC World Service, 19 Dec. 1982

REVIEWS

From this point onwards page references are to initial pages only.

Abbreviations

BBC	BBC Third Programme (later Radio 3)
BT	Bloomsbury Theatre
Camden	Camden Town Hall
CG	Royal Opera House, Covent Garden
Col.	London Coliseum
CT	Collegiate Theatre (later Bloomsbury Theatre)
E	Edinburgh
f.s.	full score
Fulham	Old Town Hall, Fulham
G	Glyndebourne
HHA	*Hallische Händel-Ausgabe*
JC	Jeannetta Cochrane Theatre
JL	John Lewis, Oxford Street
NOHM	*New Oxford History of Music*
QEH	Queen Elizabeth Hall
RAM	Royal Academy of Music
RCM	Royal College of Music
RFH	Royal Festival Hall
St P	St Pancras [later Camden] Town Hall
SW	Sadler's Wells Theatre
UC	University College, London
v.s.	vocal score

234 *The Cambridge Review*
E. Anderson, trans. and ed., *Letters of Mozart and his Family*, vol. 1, 28 Oct. 1938
235 *The Cranleighan*
Belshazzar, May 1951
236 *The Daily Telegraph*
M. Cooper, *Beethoven: the Last Decade*, 17 Jan. 1970
237 *The Financial Times*
'Collingwood's Macbeth', Fulham, 26 May 1970; *Julius Caesar*, *Semele*, Cambridge, 1 Aug. 1972; *The Judgment of Paris* (D. Purcell), Abingdon, 9 Nov. 1972; 'Handel and Rameau': *Judas Maccabaeus*, Somary, Vanguard, *Castor et Pollux*, Harnoncourt, Telefunken (records), 23 Nov. 1972
238 *Haydn Yearbook*
Haydn, *L'anima del filosofo ossia Orfeo ed Euridice*, ed H. Wirth, Henle, f.s., xii (1981), 203; Haydn, *L'infedeltà delusa*, Dorati, Philips (records), xiii (1982), 257
239 *The Listener*
'The Bloch Concerto', 15 Sept. 1949; 'Ancient and Modern', 22 Sept. 1949; M. Curtiss, *Bizet and his World*, 26 Feb. 1959
240 *The Monthly Musical Record*
'Handel's *Susanna* at Cambridge', Dec. 1937
241 *Music & Letters*
(a) Books
    1948 (xxix): Roland-Manuel, *Maurice Ravel*, 86; E. M. and S. Grew, *Bach*, 175; N. Flower, *George Frideric Handel*, 177; A. Hutchings, *Delius: a Critical Biography*, 276
    1949 (xxx): W. L. Crosten, *French Grand Opera: an Art and a Business*, 74; G. Abraham, ed., *Grieg: a Symposium*, 154; M. Carner, *The Waltz*, 175; N. Demuth, *César Franck*, 263; J. Culshaw, *Sergei Rachmaninov*, 381; A. Werth, *Musical Uproar in Moscow*, R. Moisenko, *Realist Music: 25 Soviet Composers*, 384
    1950 (xxxi): P. M. Young, *The Oratorios of Handel*, 63; G. Abraham, *Design in Music*, 66; S. Northcote, *The Songs of Henri Duparc*, 164; A. Schoenberg, *Style and Idea*, 295 (see no. 96); W. R. Anderson, *Introduction to the Music of Brahms* and *Introduction to the Music of Elgar*; P. M. Young, *Introduction to the Music of Mendelssohn*, 357
    1951 (xxxii): M. Flothuis, *Modern British Composers*; E. W. Schallenberg, *Tchaikovsky*, 75; A. W. Ganz, *Berlioz in London*, 165; J. Horton, *Some Nineteenth-Century Composers*, 166; P. R. Farnsworth, *Musical Taste: its Measurement and Cultural Nature*, 169; R. Illing, *A Dictionary of Music*, 171; R. W. S. Mendl, *The Soul of Music*, 172; M. Cooper, *French Music from the Death of Berlioz to the Death of Fauré*, 366; E. W. White, *The Rise of English Opera*, 373
    1952 (xxxiii): E. Lockspeiser, *Debussy*, 68; J. Barzun, *Berlioz and the Romantic Century*, 119 (see no. 98)
    1954 (xxxv): A. Copland, *Music and Imagination*, 50; A. Yorke-Long, *Music at Court*, 374; P. M. Young, *A Critical Dictionary of Composers and their Music*, 384
    1955 (xxxvi): E. Newman, *More Opera Nights*, 167; O. E. Deutsch, *Handel: a Documentary Biography*, 269
    1956 (xxxvii): D. McVeagh, *Edward Elgar: his Life and Music*, 71; W. C. Smith, *The Italian Opera and Contemporary Ballet in London 1789–1820*, 81
    1957 (xxxviii): R. M. Myers, *Handel, Dryden and Milton*, 76; A. Heriot, *The*

Castrati in Opera, 82

1958 (xxxix): D. Arundell, *The Critic at the Opera*, 286

1960 (xli): K. Ameln, *Das Alexander-Fest . . . Kritischer Bericht*, 86; W. Serauky, *Georg Friedrich Händel*, vol. 5, 261

1971 (lii): W. Meyerhoff, ed., *50 Jahre Göttinger Händel-Festspiele*, 186

1973 (liv): J. Budden, *The Operas of Verdi*, vol. 1, 341

1978 (lix): W. Mann, *The Operas of Mozart*, 334; J. A. Hiller, *Anweisung zum musikalisch-zierlichen Gesange* [facsimile], 353; J. Mitchell, *The Walter Scott Operas*, 460

1979 (lx): H. E. Smither, *A History of the Oratorio*, vols. 1 & 2, 341

1980 (lxi): W. Weaver and M. Chusid, eds., *The Verdi Companion*, 391; C. Floros *et al.*, eds., *Hamburger Jahrbuch für Musikwissenschaft*, vol. 3, 403; E. J. Dent, ed. H. Taylor, *Selected Essays*, H. Carey, *Duet for Two Voices*, 406

1981 (lxii): R. L. and N. W. Weaver, *A Chronology of Music in the Florentine Theater 1590–1750*, 84; H. Bushnell, *Maria Malibran*, 206

1982 (lxiii): J. Budden, *The Operas of Verdi*, vol. 3, 91; D. R. B. Kimbell, *Verdi in the Age of Italian Romanticism*, 281

1983 (lxiv): *Händel-Handbuch*, vol. 1: S. Flesch, *Lebens- und Schaffensdaten*, B. Baselt, *Thematisch-systematisches Verzeichnis: Bühnenwerke*, 232; J. Milhous and R. D. Hume, eds., *Vice Chamberlain Coke's Theatrical Papers 1706–1715*, 269

1985 (lxvi): W. C. Holmes, '*La Statira' by Pietro Ottoboni and Alessandro Scarlatti: the Textual Sources, with a Documentary Postscript*, 165; M. Conati, ed., *Interviews and Encounters with Verdi*, 178; E. W. White, *A History of English Opera*, 181; W. Ashbrook, *Donizetti and his Operas*, 272

(b) Music

1959 (xl): Handel, *Das Alexander-Fest*, ed. K. Ameln, HHA, f.s., 299

1974 (lv): Handel, *Radamisto*, ed. H. Rückert, Deutscher Verlag, v.s., 367

1976 (lvii): E. Maconchy, *The Birds*, Boosey and Hawkes, v.s., 79; J. Mattheson, *Cleopatra*, ed. G. J. Buelow, Schott, f.s., 212

1977 (lviii): J. J. Fux, *La donna forte nella madre de' sette Maccabei*, ed. O. Wessely, Bärenreiter, f.s., 355; Haydn, *La vera costanza*, ed. H. Walter, Henle, f.s., 486

1978 (lix): A. Scarlatti, *The Faithful Princess*, ed. D. J. Grout, Harvard, f.s., 373

1979 (lx): F. J. Habermann, *Missa Sancti Wenceslai, Martyris*, ed. W. D. Gudger, A–R Editions, f.s., 106; A. Salieri, *Tarare*, ed. R. Angermüller, Henle, f.s., 479

1982 (lxiii): J. E. Hartmann, *Balders død*, ed. J. Mulvad, Egtved, f.s., 149; A. Scarlatti, *La caduta de' Decemviri*, ed. H. W. Williams, Harvard, f.s., 156

1983 (lxiv): A. Scarlatti, *Gli equivoci nel sembiante*, ed. F. A. D'Accone, Harvard, f.s., 301

1985 (lxvi): Haydn, *Il mondo della luna*, ed. G. Thomas, Henle, f.s., 67; A. Scarlatti, *Tigrane*, ed. M. Collins, Harvard, f.s., 297

242 *The Music Review*

D. C. Parker, *Bizet*, xii (1951), 236; R. Vaughan Williams, *The Sons of Light*, Oxford, v.s., D. ApIvor, *The Hollow Men*, Oxford, v.s., H. Murrill, 'Sonata for treble recorder and harpsichord', Oxford, E. J. Moeran, 'Songs from County Kerry', Augener, xiii (1952), 74; W. Serauky, *Georg Friedrich Händel*, vol. 3, xix (1958), 234

243 *The Musical Quarterly*
     'England': *Orlando, Theodora,* SW, *Jephtha,* G, liii (1967), 87
244 *The Musical Times*
     (a) Performances of operas (and other works)
        1953 (xciv): *Ino* & *Pimpinone* (Telemann), Mary Ward Hall, 274; *Armide* (Gluck), Toynbee Hall, 326
        1954 (xcv): 'Radio Music', 133; 'Radio Music', 193; 'Radio Music', 257
        1957 (xcviii): *The Secret,* Oxford, 94; 'Broadcast Music', 260; 'Broadcast Music', 319
        1959 (c): *Samson,* CG, 26
        1960 (ci): *Alcina,* CG, 710
        1961 (cii): *Imeneo,* Birmingham, 303; *Semele, Rinaldo,* SW, 427; *Iphigénie en Tauride,* E, 635; *Carmen,* SW, 706
        1962 (ciii): *Alcina,* CG, 320; *Artaxerxes* (Arne), St P, 321; *I masnadieri,* St P, 322; *The Three Pintos,* JL, 409; *William Tell,* SW, 476; *Euryanthe,* St P, 477; *Floridante,* Abingdon, 479; *Jephtha, Radamisto,* SW, 616
        1963 (civ): *Count Ory,* SW, 267; *I due Foscari,* UC, *Ernani,* St P, 267; *The Peasant Rogue* (Dvořák), JL, 346; *La pietra del paragone* (Rossini), St P, 346; *Ulysses* (J. C. Smith), St P, 347; *Fra Diavolo,* Morley College, 423; *Linda di Chamounix,* St P, 490; *Julius Caesar, Xerxes, Jephtha,* SW, *Agrippina,* Abingdon, 564; *Doktor und Apotheker* (Dittersdorf), Orpington, 644
        1964 (cv): *Attila,* SW, 39; *Aroldo,* St P, 280; *The Makropulos Case,* SW, 281; *Iphigenia in Aulis,* St P, 366; *Pygmalion* (Cherubini), St P, 366; *L'infedeltà delusa* (Haydn), St P, 366; *Otello, A Midsummer Night's Dream, Falstaff,* CG, 441; *L'Arlésienne* (Daudet/Bizet), JL, 442; *Ariodante,* Birmingham, *Admeto,* Abingdon, 518; *Macbeth,* G, 523; *Semele* (Eccles), Oxford, 524; *Athalia,* Oxford, 591; *La pietra del paragone,* G, 594; *The Gipsy Baron* (J. Strauss), SW, 597; *Our Man in Havana* (Williamson), SW, 597; *Riccardo Primo, Semele,* SW, 670; *The Magic Flute,* G, 671; *Idomeneo,* G, 671
        1965 (cvi): *Il trovatore,* CG, 41; *One Man Show* (Maw), JC, 42; *Tartuffe* (Benjamin), SW, 43; *Das Liebesverbot,* UC, 280; *The Mines of Sulphur* (Bennett), SW, 281; *L'Enfant et les sortilèges* & *L'Heure espagnole,* SW, 363; *The Lodger* (Tate), St P, 364; *Il ritorno d'Ulisse in patria,* St P, 364; *The Marriage of Figaro,* SW, 449; *Bluebeard* (Offenbach), JL, 450; *Boccaccio* (Suppé), Guildhall School, 451; *Moses* (Rossini), SW, 526; *Mignon,* Fulham, 526; *Hippolyte et Aricie,* Birmingham, 529; *Il matrimonio segreto,* G, 531; *Moses and Aaron,* CG, 612; *Saul,* SW, 613; *Rinaldo,* SW, 614; *Anna Bolena,* G, 617; *The Fiery Angel,* SW, 693
        1966 (cvii): *L'incoronazione di Poppea,* Berkeley, 700; *Orlando, Theodora,* SW, 788; *Jephtha,* G, 790; *Agrippina,* Eltham Palace, 976; *Poro,* Abingdon, 978; *Gloriana,* SW, 1072
        1967 (cviii): *The Violins of Saint-Jacques* (Williamson), SW, 53; *The Thieving Magpie,* SW, 53; *Benvenuto Cellini,* CG, 149; 'Two Donizetti Revivals': *Poliuto,* UC, *Marino Faliero,* Camden, 343; *The Wandering Scholar* (Holst), *There and Back* (Hindemith) & *The Sofa* (Maconchy), Camden, 345; *Athalia,* QEH, 439; *Lucio Silla* (Mozart), Camden, 439; *Sapho* (Massenet), Camden 439; *Edgar* (Puccini), Fulham, 526; *The Grand Duchess of Gérolstein* (Offenbach), City Temple Hall, 531; *Tiefland* (d'Albert), Camden, 531; *The Travelling Companion* (Stanford), JL, 532; *Giustino,*

Abingdon, 536; *Orfeo* (Haydn), Camden, 627; *Iris* (Mascagni), Fulham, 628; *Carmen*, CG, 628; *L'Elisir d'amore*, G, 630; *Erismena* (Cavalli), BBC, 636; *Die Frau ohne Schatten*, CG, 719; **La Fille du régiment*, CG, 720; *Livietta e Tracollo* (Pergolesi), *The Tide* (Blacher) & *The Cadi Outwitted* (Gluck), UC, 720; *Don Giovanni*, G, 727; *Ormindo* (Cavalli), G, 727; *Il maestro di cappella* (Cimarosa) & *L'inganno felice* (Rossini), Oxford, 729; *Castaway* (Berkeley) & *The Bear* (Walton), SW, 821; *Acis and Galatea* & *The Impresario*, SW, 822; *Johnson Preserv'd* (Stoker), Camden, 822; *L'Ivrogne corrigé* (Gluck) & *Thomas and Sally*, Commonwealth Institute, 823; *Orfeo* (Haydn), *I Capuleti e i Montecchi*, E, 923; *A Penny for a Song* (Bennett), SW, 1127; *Orpheus* (Gluck), SW, 1127; *Scipione*, QEH, 1129

1968 (cix): *Hercules*, Victoria & Albert Museum, 251; *The Mastersingers*, SW, 352; *Bánk Bán* (Erkel), CT, 353; *Elisabetta, regina d'Inghilterra*, Camden, 353; *Mozart and Salieri* (Rimsky-Korsakov), *Iolanta* (Tchaikovsky), Camden, 451; *The First Commandment* & *Scipio's Dream* (Mozart), Camden, 451; *The Midsummer Marriage*, CG, 554; *Amadigi*, Abingdon, 558; *Fennimore and Gerda* (Delius) & *Sāvitri* (Holst), Fulham, 647; *L'Arlesiana* (Cilea), International Students' House, 647; *Eugene Onegin*, G, 649; *Admeto*, Birmingham, 651; *Deidamia, Saul*, SW, 740; *Adina* (Rossini), Oxford, 748; *Die Entführung aus dem Serail, Anna Bolena*, G, 749; *Griselda* (A. Scarlatti), BBC, 752; *Una cosa rara* (Martín y Soler), JC, *The Prodigal Son*, St Paul's, 828; *Peter Grimes, Elektra, Die fliegende Holländer*, E, 942

1969 (cx): *Manon Lescaut*, CG, 53; *The Wreckers*, Fulham, 53; *Susanna, La Resurrezione*, Victoria & Albert Museum, 399; *Leonore*, CT, 403; *L'incoronazione di Poppea*, RAM, 403; *The Opera Rehearsal* (Lortzing) & *Gianni Schicchi*, SW, 510; *The Little Barber of Lavapies* (Barbieri), Commonwealth Institute, 510; *Julius Caesar Jones* (Williamson), JC, 651; *Under Western Eyes* (Joubert), Camden, 760; *La donna del lago*, Camden 761; *Beatrice and Benedict*, Camden, 761; *Agar et Ismaele esiliati* (A. Scarlatti), JC, 761; *Così fan tutte*, G, 764; *Werther*, G, 764; *Hamlet* (Thomas), CT, 849; *La rondine*, RAM, 850; *Xerxes, Susanna*, SW, 952; *La Rencontre imprévue* (Gluck), Hintlesham, 960; *Flavio*, Abingdon, 1058; *Maria Stuarda, Rigoletto, Il Signor Bruschino* (Rossini) & *Gianni Schicchi, Sette canzoni* (Malipiero) & *Il prigioniero* (Dallapiccola), *The Undertaker* (Purser) & *Full Circle* (Orr), E, 1059; *Les Troyens*, CG, 1151; *The Rape of Lucretia, Purgatory* & *The Grace of Todd* (Crosse), SW, 1151

1970 (cxi): *Pelléas et Mélisande*, CG, 59; *The Valkyrie*, Col., 289; *Alzira*, CT, 406; *The Condemnation of Lucullus* (Dessau), Cambridge, 412; *A Life for the Tsar*, Reading, 413; *Leonora*, Col., 514; *Cardillac*, SW, 514; *Victory* (Bennett), CG, 622; *L'Etoile* (Chabrier), JL, 623; *Carmen*, Col., 725; *The Fair Maid of Perth*, Birmingham, 729; *Statira* (A. Scarlatti), JC, 732; *Fennimore and Gerda* & *The Donkey's Shadow* (R. Strauss), Camden, 732; *La Voix humaine* & *Les Mamelles de Tirésias*, Camden, 733; *La bohème* (Leoncavallo), Camden 733; *Calisto*, G, 733; *Salome*, CG, 817; *Il turco in Italia*, G, 821; *The Rising of the Moon* (Maw), G, 913; *Atalanta*, Hintlesham, 914; *The Fiery Angel*, E, 1017; *Elegy for Young Lovers*, E, 1018; *The Cunning Little Vixen, The Makropoulos Affair, The Excursions of Mr Brouček*, E, 1018; *Sosarme*, Abingdon, 1127; *Semele*, Col., 1241

1971 (cxii): *The Knot Garden*, CG, 47; *Ariodante*, Cambridge, 61; *Armide* (Gluck), CT, 363; *Secular Masque* (Boyce) & *Pyramus and Thisbe* (Lampe), St John's, Smith Sq., 459; *Adriana Lecouvreur*, CT, 576; *Tancredi*, CT, 576; *La fedeltà premiata*

(Haydn), CT, 577; *Shamus O'Brien* (Stanford), JL, 578; *Fierrabras* (Schubert), BBC, 588; *Zazà* (Leoncavallo), Fulham, 683; *Paris and Helen*, Birmingham, 684; *Rodelinda*, Brighton, 687; *The Queen of Spades*, G, 688; *The Rising of the Moon*, G, 688; *The Clandestine Marriage* (Wishart), Guildhall School, 771; *The Padlock* (Dibdin) & *Gianni Schicchi*, CT, 884; *La Cenerentola*, E, 988; *Die Entführung aus dem Serail*, E, 988; *Melusine* (Reimann), E, 989; 'Cav and Pag', Col., 1084; *Il pastor fido*, Abingdon, 1092; *Ottone*, SW, 1183; *Susanna*, SW, 1185

1972 (cxiii): *The Coronation of Poppaea*, Col., 59; *Il crociato in Egitto* (Meyerbeer), QEH, 284; *The Scene-Machine* (Gilbert) & *Time Off? Not a Ghost of a Chance!* (Lutyens), SW, 376; *Hans Heiling*, CT, 376; *Ivan IV* (Bizet), Bristol, 386; *Belisario* (Donizetti), SW, 472; *Nabucco*, CG, 473; Bach-Handel concert, St John's, Smith Sq., 581; *Semele* (Eccles), St John's, Smith Sq., 584; *La Fille de Madame Angot* (Lecocq), JL, 584; *The Secret*, CT, 677; *Koanga*, SW, 677; *Aleko* (Rakhmaninov) & *La Navarraise* (Massenet), CT, 677; *Le convenienze teatrali* (Donizetti), CT, 678; *La clemenza di Scipione* (J. C. Bach), QEH, 679; *Rodelinda*, Birmingham, 687; *Il ritorna d'Ulisse in patria*, G, 691; *Macbeth*, G, 797; *Sosarme*, Wye, 798; *Taverner* (Maxwell Davies), CG, 879; *L'arbore di Diana* (Martín y Soler), CT, 881; *Caterina Cornaro* (Donizetti), RFH, 881; *Semele, Julius Caesar*, Cambridge, 889; *Die Soldaten* (Zimmermann), E, 995; *Rappresentazione di Anima e di Corpo* (Cavalieri), E, 996; *Attila*, E, 997; *La straniera*, E, 998; *Arminio*, Abingdon, 1106; *Elisabetta, regina d'Inghilterra*, E, 1110; *The Trojans*, E, 1111

1973 (cxiv): *Esther, Athalia*, BBC, 176; 'Alceste in triplicate' (Lully, Gluck), BBC, 296; *Don Pasquale*, CG, 392; *The Indian Queen*, CT, 397; *Stiffelio*, CT, 398; *L'amor coniugale* (Mayr), St John's, Smith Sq., 399; *Der Vampyr*, Nottingham, 410; *Rienzi*, Reading, 411; *Robinson Crusoe* (Offenbach), CT, 508; *Don Giovanni*, CG, 617; *The Nose* (Shostakovich), SW, 618; *Infidelio* (Lutyens) & *Time Off? Not a Ghost of a Chance!*, SW, 618; *Undine* (Lortzing), JL, 618; *Maria Padilla* (Donizetti), QEH, 619; *Owen Wingrave*, CG, 719; *The Trial* (Einem), CT, 720; *Die Feen*, Fulham, 721; *Ivanhoe*, Fulham, 722; *The Visit of the Old Lady* (Einem), G, 731; *The Daughter of St Mark* (Balfe), College of St Mark & St John, Chelsea, 816; *Death in Venice*, Aldeburgh, 819; *Carmen*, CG, 925; *Capriccio*, G, 930; *Don Giovanni*, E, 1037; *Bluebeard's Castle* & *The Miraculous Mandarin*, E, 1037; *Blood Wedding* (Szokolay), E, 1038; *Tolomeo*, Abingdon, 1154; *The Devils of Loudun* (Penderecki), Col., 1251

1974 (cxv): *Atalanta, Ottone*, SW, 53; *Florimel* (Greene), St John's, Smith Sq., 54; *Masaniello furioso* (Keiser), Sheffield, 61; *Mistaken Identities* (Grétry), Birmingham, 243; *Gli equivoci* (Storace), CT, 318; *Torquato Tasso* (Donizetti), CT, 319; *Clytemnaestra* (Wishart), CT, 321; *The Story of Vasco* (Crosse), Col., 403; *The Patience of Socrates* (Telemann), Croydon, 405; *La canterina* (Haydn) & *Le Portrait de Manon* (Massenet), Guildhall School, 406: *Arden Must Die* (Goehr), SW, 492; *The Tenor* (Dohnányi), Morley College, 590; *Calisto*, G, 593; *Wat Tyler* (Bush), SW, 677; *The Voice of Ariadne* (Musgrave), Aldeburgh, 678; *L'incoronazione di Poppea*, Goldsmiths' Hall, 765; *Tolomeo*, Drapers' Hall, 766; *Idomeneo*, G, 773; *Jephtha*, Göttingen, 775; *Alceste* (Gluck), E, 866; *Il pastor fido*, E, 866; *The Vision of Thérèse* (Werle), E, 867; *Arianna in Creta*, Abingdon, 966; *The Bassarids*, Col., 1057; *Ariodante*, SW, 1059; *Jephtha*, SW, 1060; *Maria di Rudenz* (Donizetti), QEH, 1061

1975 (cxvi): *Faust*, CG, 64; *Potter Thompson* (Crosse), St Mary Magdalene, Munster Sq., 260; *The Pirates* (Storace), Birmingham, 265; *L'Etoile du nord*, CT, 352; *Torquato Tasso*, CT, 352; *Euryanthe*, CT, 354; *Orfeo* (Monteverdi), Oxford, 361; *Gli Orazi ed i Curiazi* (Mercadante), QEH, 555; *King Roger*, SW, 641; *Cendrillon* (Massenet), SW, 641; *Beatrice di Tenda*, Birmingham, 648; Handel Opera Society concert, RFH, 723; *The Rake's Progress*, G, 724; *Utopia Limited*, RFH, 811; *The Magic Flute*, Col., 897; *Le nozze di Figaro, Hermiston* (Orr), E, 899; *Lotario*, Henley, 993; *Lulu*, E, 997; *Alcina, Semele*, SW, 1081

1976 (cxvii): *La vestale*, Nottingham, 248; *Macbeth* [1847], CT, 328; *Suor Angelica* & *Die Kluge* (Orff), RAM, 329; *La vera costanza* (Haydn), Curtain, Whitechapel, 329; *Paul Bunyan*, BBC, 338; *Simon Boccanegra*, CG, 416; *Il campanello* (Donizetti) & *Das Pensionat* (Suppé), Guildhall School, 417; *Maria Golovin* (Menotti), CT, 419; *Le muse de l'opéra* (Clérambault), *L'Amour fléchy par la constance* (Lalande) & *Pygmalion* (Rameau), Banqueting House, Whitehall, 504; *The King of the Golden River* (Maconchy), BBC, 512; *I lombardi*, CG, 585; *El retablo de Maese Pedro* & *El amor brujo* (Falla), QEH, 590; *Tom Jones* (Oliver), Brighton, 592; *Faramondo, Imeneo, Deidamia, Acis and Galatea, Samson, Solomon*, Halle, 678; *We Come to the River* (Henze), CG, 752; *Macbeth*, E, 844; *Paul Bunyan*, SW, 925; *Dalibor*, Col., 925; *Jephtha*, E, 927; *Moses und Aron*, E, 927

1977 (cxviii): *Troilus and Cressida*, CG, 55; *Bomarzo* (Ginastera), Col., 56; *The Royal Hunt of the Sun* (Hamilton), Col., 321; *Giovanna d'Arco*, Oxford, 323; *Masaniello* (Auber), Nottingham, 323; *Saul og David* (Nielsen), CT, 324; *Alfonso und Estrella* (Schubert), Reading, 324; *The Abbot of Drimock* (Musgrave) & *Daphnis and Chloe* (Offenbach), Guildhall School, 408; *Alceste* (Lully), SW, 408; *Tamburlaine* (Hamilton), BBC, 415; *Elisabetta al Castello di Kenilworth* (Donizetti), CT, *Orfeo* (Monteverdi), CT, 495; *Tintomara* (Werle), SW, 576; *Le Jardinier et son seigneur* (Philidor), French Institute, 576; *A Gentle Spirit* (Tavener) & *The Soldier's Tale*, CT, 657; *The Fairy Queen*, SW, 657; *La Voix humaine* & *The Cunning Little Vixen*, G, 662; *The Ice Break*, CG, 747; *The Rake's Progress*, G, 753; *Carmen*, E, 847; *Mary, Queen of Scots* (Musgrave), E, 941

1978 (cxix): *Euryanthe*, Col., 59; *Ezio*, SW, 60; *Acis and Galatea*, SW, 61; *The Marriage of Figaro*, Cardiff, 66; *The Maid of Orleans*, CT, 343; *Richard Coeur de Lion* (Grétry), Nottingham, 348; *The Lambton Worm* (Sherlaw Johnson), Oxford, 348; *La Spinalba* (Almeida), CT, 431; *Tom Jones* (Philidor), French Institute, 432; *Pia de' Tolomei* (Donizetti), QEH, 433; *Hulda* (Franck), Reading, 437; *Julietta* (Martinů), Col., 531; *Tamerlano, Lo speziale* (Haydn), Riverside Studios, 531; *Les Cloches de Corneville* (Planquette), JL, 532; *The Brandenburgers in Bohemia* (Smetana), Hurlingham School, 532; *The Two Foscari*, Col., 609; *Terpsicore* (Handel), Guildhall, *Rinaldo*, QEH, *Griselda* (Vivaldi), QEH, 613; *Luisa Miller*, CG, 698; *Radamisto, Teseo, La verità in cimento* (Vivaldi), *The Miser* (Pashkevich), *Alexander Balus, The Choice of Hercules*, Halle, 707; *Orfeo* (Monteverdi), *Il ritorno d'Ulisse in patria, L'incoronazione di Poppea*, E, 982; *Kát'a Kabanová*, E, 983

1979 (cxx): *L'Africaine*, CG, 55; *Rinaldo*, SW, 57; *Dimitrij* (Dvořák), Nottingham, 330; *L'Etoile*, RAM, 423; *Don Quixote* (Henze/Paisiello), Round House, 506; *Le Domino noir* (Auber), King's College, Strand, 507; *Arianna in Creta*, Reading, *Sosarme*, Birmingham, 595; *The Martyrdom of St Magnus* (Maxwell Davies),

Aldeburgh, 674; *Radamisto, Ezio, Alexander's Feast, Esther,* Halle, 680; *Così fan tutte,* G, 756; *La traviata,* E, 845; *Iphigénie en Tauride,* E, 846; *Thérèse* (Tavener), CG, 932; *The Turn of the Screw,* E, 936

1980 (cxxi): *The Duenna* (Prokofiev), CT, 262; *Jessonda* (Spohr), Oxford, 266; *The Italian Straw Hat* (Rota), CT, 332; *A Midsummer Night's Dream,* RAM, 333; *Lucrezia Borgia,* CG, 389; *Der Rosenkavalier,* G, 577; *Wozzeck, The Lighthouse* (Maxwell Davies), E, 719

1981 (cxxii): *Romeo and Juliet* (Gounod), Col., 190; *Robert le diable,* Nottingham, 193; *Lulu,* CG, 254; *Hérodiade* (Massenet), CT, 254; *Belisario,* RAM, 255; *Crispino e la comare* (L. and F. Ricci), CT, *Renaud* (Sacchini), BBC, *Gli Orazi e i Curiazi* (Cimarosa), CT, 323; *Bianca e Fernando* (Bellini), QEH, 325; *Si j'étais roi* (Adam), JL, 404; *Anna Karenina* (Hamilton), Col., 487; *Armide* (Lully), Birmingham, 491; *Faramondo,* Reading, 494; *A Midsummer Night's Dream,* G, 550; *Le nozze di Figaro,* G, 619; *Alessandro,* Chichester, 621; *The Voice of Ariadne* (Musgrave), *La clemenza di Tito,* E, 691

1982 (cxxiii): *Oberto,* CT, 275; *The Queen of Golconda* (Berwald), Nottingham, 280; *Francesca di Foix* & *La romanziera* (Donizetti), CT, *Adriano in Siria* (J. C. Bach), BBC, *Eritrea* (Cavalli), CT, 346; *Egisto* (Cavalli), Dominion, 348; *Agrippina,* SW, 424; *I puritani,* Dominion, 424; *Tamerlano,* BT, 425; *The Gypsy Princess* (Kálmán), SW, 425; *The Love of Three Oranges,* G, 492; *L'esule di Roma* (Donizetti), QEH, 626; *Manon Lescaut,* E, 709; *Tamerlano,* E, 773; *The Marriage* (Musorgsky/ Ustinov), E, 774; *La pietra del paragone, Ariodante,* E, 774

1983 (cxxiv): *Semele,* CG, 44; *Hercules, Xerxes,* SW, 44; *Roland* (Lully), Charing Cross Hospital, 180; *Gwendoline* (Chabrier), BT, 311; *Maria Tudor* (Pacini), BT, 312; *Metamorphoses* (Blackford), RCM, 313; *The Haunted Manor* (Moniuszko), JL, 376; *Thomas and Sally* & *Rosina* (Shield), Regent's Park, 497; *The Perfect Fool* (Holst) & *The Island of Tulipatan* (Offenbach), Baden-Powell House, 498; *Street Scene* (Weill), RAM, 498; *Idomeneo,* G, 500; *La Dori* (Cesti), Christ Church, Spitalfields, 562; *The Lady of the Inn* (Wishart), Reading, 565; *Toussaint* (Blake), Col., 694; *Eine florentinische Tragödie* & *Der Zwerg* (Zemlinsky), E, 700; *Death in Venice,* E, 700; *The Postman Always Rings Twice* (Paulus), E, 700; *Platée* (Rameau), SW, 758

1984 (cxxv): *Partenope, Giustino,* SW, 36; *Where the Wild Things Are* (Knussen), Lyttelton, 164; *Countess Maritza* (Kálmán), SW, 219; *Juditha triumphans* (Vivaldi), BT, 280; *Joseph and his Brethren,* St George's, Hanover Sq., 280; *I Capuleti e i Montecchi,* CG, 281; *Faust* (Spohr), BT, 281; *The Sicilian Vespers,* Col., 341; *Le Docteur Miracle* (Lecocq) & *Margot la Rouge* (Delius), BT, 343; *Guillaume Tell* (Grétry), JL, 400; *L'incoronazione di Poppea,* G, 454; *Solomon,* Göttingen, *Alessandro, Floridante, Saul,* Halle, 457; *Giustino* (Legrenzi), Chichester, 519; *Orion* (Cavalli), E, 586; *Osud* (Janáček), Col., 654

1985 (cxxvi): *Johnny Strikes Up* (Krenek), SW, 37; *Radamisto, Imeneo,* SW, 38; *Risurrezione* (Alfano), Polish Centre, Hammersmith, 106; *Samson,* CG, *Xerxes,* Col., *Rinaldo,* RCM, 221 (see no. 131); *Le villi* & *Edgar,* BT, 232; *Flavio,* St John's, Smith Sq., 419; *Carmen,* G, 420; *Berenice,* Keele, *Poro,* Birmingham, 421; *Beauty and the Beast* (Oliver), St John's, Smith Sq., 475; *Teseo,* Boston, 483; *Alcina,* Christ Church, Spitalfields, *Rodrigo,* SW, 544; *Teseo,* CG, 612; *L'Etoile, Anacréon*

(Rameau) & *Actéon* (M.-A. Charpentier), *The Death of Dido* (Pepusch), E, 683
(b) Books

1953 (xciv): J. Culshaw, *A Century of Music*, N. Demuth, *Musical Trends in the Twentieth Century*, 67; D. Mitchell and H. Keller, eds., *Benjamin Britten*, 165; L. Biancolli, *The Flagstad Manuscript*, 509

1954 (xcv): W. Furtwängler, *Concerning Music*, 77; A. L. Bacharach, ed., *The Music Masters*, vol. 4, 420 (see letters, 551, 663)

1955 (xcvi): the Earl of Harewood, ed. and rev., *Kobbé's Complete Opera Book*, 22; B. Grun, *Private Lives of the Great Composers*, 137; J. A. Westrup, *An Introduction to Musical History*, 421

1956 (xcvii): A. Silbermann, *Introduction à une sociologie de la musique*, 193; W. Beckett, *Liszt*, 468

1957 (xcviii): S. Hughes, *Great Opera Houses*, 135

1958 (xcix): J. P. Larsen, *Handel's Messiah: Origins, Composition, Sources*, 316

1959 (c): H. C. Wolff, *Die Händel-Oper auf der modernen Bühne*, W. Siegmund-Schultze, ed., *Händel-Jahrbuch*, 2nd ser., iii, 1957, 200

1961 (cii): W. C. Smith, *Handel, a Descriptive Catalogue of the Early Editions*, 158; J. S. Hall, *Handel*, 363

1962 (ciii): E. Anderson, trans. and ed., *The Letters of Beethoven*, 3 vols., 156 (see no. 113); H. and E. H. Mueller von Asow, eds., *The Collected Correspondence and Papers of Christoph Willibald Gluck*, 230 (see no. 114); S. Sadie, *Handel*, 607

1963 (civ): F. Walker, *The Man Verdi*, 26 (see no. 115); H. Berlioz, *Evenings in the Orchestra*, trans. C. R. Fortescue, 794; P. Howard, *Gluck and the Birth of Modern Opera*, 869

1964 (cv): W. Shaw, *The Story of Handel's 'Messiah'*, 195; K. Sasse, *Händel Bibliographie*, 432; J. Tobin, *Handel at Work*, 433

1965 (cvi): M. and E. Radford, *Musical Adventures in Cornwall*, 429; W. Ashbrook, *Donizetti*, 438; W. C. Smith, *A Handelian's Notebook*, 604; P. Prelleur, *The Modern Musick-Master or the Universal Musician* [facsimile], 681

1966 (cvii): B. Deane, *Cherubini*, 871

1967 (cviii): W. Shaw, *A Textual and Historical Companion to Handel's Messiah*, J. Tobin, *Der Messias, Kritischer Bericht*, 157 (see letter, 427); P. H. Lang, *George Frideric Handel*, 512; A. H. King, *Handel and his Autographs*, 514 (see letter, 618)

1968 (cix): J. Warrack, *Carl Maria von Weber*, 433; S. Hughes, *Famous Verdi Operas*, 633; D. Arnold and N. Fortune, eds., *The Monteverdi Companion*, 815 (see letter, 1118); H. Weinstock, *Rossini*, 1023

1969 (cx): L. Orrey, *Bellini*, 377; W. Ashbrook, *The Operas of Puccini*, 742; P. Howard, *The Operas of Benjamin Britten*, 834; H. Powers, ed., *Studies in Music History: Essays for Oliver Strunk*, 938; G. E. Dorris, *Paolo Rolli and the Italian Circle in London, 1715–1744*, 939

1970 (cxi): J. Tobin, *Handel's Messiah*, 161; L. Davies, *César Franck and his Circle*, 1109

1971 (cxii): E. W. White, *Benjamin Britten, his Life and Operas*, 32; E. H. Bleiler, trans. and intro., *Carmen by Georges Bizet*, 246; P. J. Smith, *The Tenth Muse*, 859

1972 (cxiii): E. Padmore, *Wagner*, J. Harding, *Rossini*, 269; E. Chisholm, *The Operas of Leoš Janáček*, 460; H. Weinstock, *Vincenzo Bellini: his Life and Operas*, 772

1973 (cxiv); M. F. Robinson, *Naples and Neapolitan Opera*, 261; R. Fiske, *English Theatre Music in the Eighteenth Century*, 1120

1975 (cxvi): H. D. Clausen, *Händels Direktionspartituren ('Handexemplare')*, 45; A. Porter, *A Musical Season*, 145; G. Adami, ed., *Letters of Giacomo Puccini*, 239; T. J. Walsh, *Opera in Dublin 1705–1797*, 793

1976 (cxvii): A. C. Bell, *Handel before England*, 136

1977 (cxviii): the Earl of Harewood, ed. and rev., *Kobbé's Complete Opera Book*, 9th edition, 477 (see letter, 819); J. Warrack, *Carl Maria von Weber*, 2nd edition, 562

1978 (cxix): G. Schmidgall, *Literature as Opera*, H. F. G. Swanston, *In Defence of Opera*, P. Conrad, *Romantic Opera and Literary Form*, 854 (see no. 130)

1979 (cxx): R. Donington, *The Opera*, 129 (see letter, 273); A. Porter, *Music of Three Seasons*, 1004

1980 (cxxi): *Phaidon Book of the Opera*, 31

1981 (cxxii): M. Carner, *Major and Minor*, 537

1982 (cxxiii): J. D. Drummond, *Opera in Perspective*, 259; J. Warrack, ed., *Carl Maria von Weber: Writings on Music*, 842

1985 (cxxvi): D. Rosen and A. Porter, eds., *Verdi's Macbeth: a Sourcebook*, 284

(c) Music

1954 (xcv): Delius, *Irmelin*, Boosey & Hawkes, v.s., 27

1961 (cii): Handel, *Ariodante*, HHA, v.s., 784

1962 (ciii): Handel, *Dixit Dominus*, ed. E. Wenzel, HHA, f.s., 110

1963 (civ): Handel, *Giulio Cesare*, HHA, v.s., 403 (see no. 116); Handel, *Dettingen Te Deum*, ed. W. Emery, Novello, v.s., 427

1965 (cvi): Handel, *The Choice of Hercules*, ed. W. Siegmund-Schultze, HHA, v.s., 212; Handel, *Messiah*, ed. W. Shaw, Novello, f.s., 701; Bizet, *Carmen*, ed. F. Oeser, Alkor Edition, f.s., 846 (see no. 119)

1967 (cviii): Handel, *Messiah*, ed. W. Shaw, Novello, f.s., *The Messiah*, ed. J. Tobin, HHA, f.s., 157

1969 (cx): Handel, *Utrecht Te Deum*, ed. W. Shaw, Novello, v.s., 'Music from Semele', ed. M. Blower, Novello, 966

1971 (cxii): Berlioz, *Les Troyens*, ed. H. Macdonald, Bärenreiter, f.s., 1098

1973 (cxiv): Bizet, *Te Deum*, ed. J. Wojciechowski, Simrock, v.s., 281

1975 (cxvi): Bizet, *Les Pêcheurs de perles*, Choudens, v.s., 982 (see letters, cxvii, 34, 228, 403, 825)

1976 (cxvii): Keiser, *Die grossmütige Tomyris*, ed. K. Zelm, Henle, f.s., 667

1985 (cxxvi): Bizet, 'Les Inédits et trois pièces du magasin des familles', Mario Bois, 737

(d) Records

1967 (cviii): Handel, Organ Concertos, Müller, Wenzinger, Archiv, 620

1968 (cix): Handel, *Ode for St Cecilia's Day*, Willcocks, Argo, 345; Handel, *Giulio Cesare*, Rudel, RCA, 345; Handel, *Brockes Passion*, Wenzinger, Archiv, 442; Mozart, *Il rè pastore*, Vaughan, RCA, 548; Gluck, *Orfeo ed Euridice*, Mackerras, Vanguard, 733; Bononcini, *Griselda* (excerpts), Bonynge, Decca, 821; Handel, Sonatas for violin and continuo, Menuhin, HMV, 822; Handel, *Chandos Anthems*, Willcocks, Argo, 822; Balfe, Wallace, Benedict, *The Bohemian Girl, Maritana, The Lily of Killarney* (excerpts), Nelson, HMV, 929

1969 (cx): Handel, 12 Grand Concertos, Marriner, Decca, 42; Eighteenth-Century Overtures, Leppard, Philips, 45; Berlioz, *Irlande*, etc., Gardiner, L'Oiseau-Lyre, 273; Berlioz, *La Mort de Cléopâtre*, etc., Davis, L'Oiseau-Lyre, 274; Cherubini, *Médée*, Gardelli, Decca, 638; Flotow, *Martha*, Heger, HMV Angel, 843; Handel, Two Italian Cantatas, Baker, Leppard, HMV, 843; Handel, *Solomon*, Simon, RCA, 1045

1970 (cxi): Handel, *Samson*, Richter, Archiv, *Theodora*, Somary, Philips Vanguard, 51; Beethoven, *Christ on the Mount of Olives*, Ormandy, CBS, 611; Donizetti, *Roberto Devereux*, Mackerras, HMV, 614; Handel, *Jephtha*, Somary, Philips Vanguard, 903

1971 (cxii): Bizet, *Carmen*, Frühbeck de Burgos, HMV, 37; 'Donizetti Rarities': scenes from *Torquato Tasso, Gemma di Vergy, Belisario, Parisina*, Caballé, Cillario, RCA, 348; Donizetti, *Anna Bolena*, Varviso, Decca, 349; Handel, *Giulio Cesare*, Richter, DG, 349; 'Great Operatic Duets', Caballé, Verrett, Guadagno, RCA, 353; Donizetti, *Lucia di Lammermoor*, Schippers, HMV, 450; Handel, Overtures, vol 2; Bonynge, Decca, 765

1972 (cxiii): Bizet, *Carmen*, Karajan, RCA, 273; Handel, *Orlando*, Simon, RCA, 370; Verdi, *I lombardi*, Gardelli, Philips, 470; Rossini, *La Cenerentola*, Abbado, DG, 782; Mayr, *Medea in Corinto*, Jenkins, Vanguard, 1195

1973 (cxiv): Handel, Overtures, Leppard, Philips, 269; Berlioz, *Benvenuto Cellini*, Davis, Philips, 801; Bizet, *Carmen*, Bernstein, DG, 905; Verdi, *Giovanna d'Arco*, Levine, HMV, 1019; Verdi, *Attila*, Gardelli, Philips, 1020

1974 (cxv): Donizetti, *Maria Stuarda*, Ceccato, HMV, 136; Rossini, *Guillaume Tell*, Gardelli, HMV, 483; Boito, *Mefistofele*, Rudel, HMV, 663; Donizetti, *Anna Bolena*, Rudel, HMV, 851

1975 (cxvi): Verdi, *Un giorno di regno*, Gardelli, Philips, 51

1976 (cxvii): Handel, *The Choice of Hercules*, Ledger, HMV, 576; Mozart, *Lucio Silla*, Hager, BASF, 577; Massenet, *La Navarraise*, Lewis, RCA, 661; Donizetti, *Maria Stuarda*, Bonynge, Decca, 913; Verdi, *Luisa Miller*, Maag, Decca, 916; Bellini, *I Capuleti e i Montecchi*, Patané, EMI, 1003; Verdi, *Il corsaro*, Gardelli, Philips, 1007

1977 (cxviii): Weber, *Abu Hassan*, Rögner, RCA, 135; Moore, *The Ballad of Baby Doe*, Buckley, DG, 402; Rossini, Ballet Music, Almeida, Philips, 403; Massenet, *Esclarmonde*, Bonynge, Decca, 487; Wolf-Ferrari, *Il segreto di Susanna*, Gardelli, Decca, 566; Walton, *Troilus and Cressida*, Foster, HMV, 827; Donizetti, *Gemma di Vergy*, Queler, CBS, 921; Handel, *Belshazzar*, Harnoncourt, Telefunken, 923

1978 (cxix): Handel, *Judas Maccabaeus*, Mackerras, Archiv, 243; Janáček, *Kát'a Kabanová*, Mackerras, Decca, 335; Beethoven, *Leonore* [1805], Blomstedt, HMV, 425; Cimarosa, *Il matrimonio segreto*, Barenboim, DG, 426; Handel, *Rinaldo*, Malgoire, CBS, 515; Meyerbeer, *Le Prophète*, Lewis, CBS, 603; Verdi, *I due Foscari*, Gardelli, Philips, 604; Nielsen, *Maskarade*, Frandsen, Unicorn, 770; Bizet, *Les Pêcheurs de perles*, Prêtre, HMV, 960; Falla, *Atlántida*, Frühbeck de Burgos, HMV, 963; Donizetti, *Ugo, conte di Parigi*, Francis, Opera Rara, 1051

1979 (cxx): Donizetti, *La favorita*, Bonynge, Decca, 41; Handel, *Acis and Galatea*, Gardiner, Archiv/Marriner, Argo, 313; Verdi, *La battaglia di Legnano*, Gardelli, Philips, 660; Donizetti, *Gabriella di Vergy*, Francis, Opera Rara, 745

1980 (cxxi): Paer, *Leonora*, Maag, Decca, 35; Handel, *Serse*, Malgoire, CBS, 180; Donizetti, *Lucrezia Borgia*, Bonynge, Decca, 249; Handel, *Partenope*, Kuijken, Harmonia Mundi, 251; Janáček, *Věc Makropulos*, Mackerras, Decca, 252; Rossini, *Otello*, López Cobos, Philips, 323; Verdi, *Un ballo in maschera*, Davis, Philips, 788

1981 (cxxii): Handel, *Ariodante*, Leppard, Philips, 33; Verdi, *Don Carlos*, Karajan, EMI, 113; Beethoven, Scottish, English, Irish & Welsh Songs, White, RCA, 181; Meyerbeer, *Dinorah*, Judd, Opera Rara, 390; Puccini, *Le villi*, Fredman, Chandos, 481; Donizetti, *Maria Padilla*, Francis, Opera Rara, 607; Handel, *Alceste*, Hogwood, L'Oiseau-Lyre, 607; Janáček, *From the House of the Dead*, Mackerras, Decca, 607

1982 (cxxiii): Donizetti, *Maria di Rudenz*, Inbal, CBS, 550; Handel, *Saul*, Ledger, EMI, 551; Ponchielli, *La Gioconda*, Bartoletti, Decca, 619; Handel, *La Resurrezione*, Hogwood, L'Oiseau-Lyre, 766; Bellini, *La sonnambula*, Bonynge, Decca, 845

1983 (cxxiv): Janáček, *The Cunning Little Vixen*, Mackerras, Decca/Neumann, Supraphon, 37; Donizetti, *Mary Stuart*, Mackerras, HMV, 364; Handel, *Semele*, Gardiner, Erato, 365; Rossini, *Il turco in Italia*, Chailly, CBS, 489; Handel, *The Triumph of Time and Truth*, Darlow, Hyperion, 687; Handel, *Hercules*, Gardiner, Archiv, 687

245 *The New Statesman*

C. P. E. Bach, *Essay on the True Art of Playing Keyboard Instruments*, G. S. Bedbrook, *Keyboard Music from the Middle Ages to the Beginnings of the Baroque*, R. Donington, *The Instruments of Music*, 26 Nov. 1949; 'Friedrich Gulda, at the Wigmore Hall', 17 Dec. 1949; *Falstaff*, SW, *Lohengrin*, CG, 24 Dec. 1949; F. Howes, *The Music of Ralph Vaughan Williams*, 9 Oct. 1954; M. Carner, *Puccini: a Critical Biography*, E. Greenfield, *Puccini: Keeper of the Seal*, 14 Feb. 1959; H. Weinstock, *Donizetti*, 7 Aug. 1964

246 *The New York Review of Books*

C. Hogwood, *Handel*, H. C. R. Landon, *Handel and his World*, J. Keates, *Handel: the Man and his Music*, R. Strohm, *Essays on Handel and Italian Opera*, xxxii/20 (19 Dec. 1985), 44

247 *19th-Century Music*

F. Noske, *The Signifier and the Signified: Studies in the Operas of Mozart and Verdi*, ii (1978), 173

248 *Opera*

(a) Performances of operas (and other works)

1951 (ii): *Belshazzar*, Cranleigh School, 319; *Parsifal*, CG, 484; *The Fairy Queen*, CG, 544; *Aida*, CG, 721

1952 (iii): *Billy Budd*, CG, 7; *Life on the Moon* (Haydn), Scala, 52; *The Magic Flute*, CG, 54; *Wozzeck*, CG, 181; *Tristan und Isolde*, CG, 432; *Love in a Village*, Aldeburgh, 466; *A Masked Ball*, CG, 756, 759

1953 (iv): *Orpheus* (Gluck), CG, 179

1954 (v): *Athalia*, Cambridge, 305; *Nelson* (Berkeley), SW, 692

1957 (viii): *Paride ed Elena*, BBC, 323

1958 (ix): *Le Roi d'Ys* (Lalo), BBC, 744

1959 (x): *Julius Caesar*, BBC, 331; *Xerxes*, Birmingham, 332; *Orlando*, Abingdon, 551

1960 (xi): *Alcina*, BBC, 513; *Anna Bolena*, BBC, 584; *Alcina*, CG, 713
1961 (xii): *Billy Budd*, BBC, 135; *Partenope*, Abingdon, 486
1962 (xiii): *Tamerlano*, Birmingham, 348
1963 (xiv): *Orlando*, BBC, 277 [misattrib. S. Sadie]; *Oberon*, BBC, 357
1964 (xv): *L'Africaine*, BBC, 502; *Paris and Helen*, BBC, 571
1965 (xvi): *Castor et Pollux*, BBC, 68; *Die Gezeichneten* (Schreker), BBC, 306
1968 (xvii): *Peter Schmoll*, Hintlesham, 916
1973 (xxiv): *Rosinda* (Cavalli), Oxford, 472
1976 (xxvii): *The Duenna* (Linley pasticcio), CT, 478; *Astarto* (Bononcini), JC, 570; *Faramondo, Imeneo, Deidamia*, Halle, Festival Issue, 100
1977 (xxviii): *Belshazzar*, SW, 94; *Ariodante*, SW, 96
1980 (xxxi): *The Jacobin* (Dvořák), Cardiff, 726; *Xerxes*, Cardiff, 829; *Rinaldo*, Cambridge, 839
1981 (xxxii): *Ezio*, SW, 79; *Esther*, SW, 80; *Rodelinda*, Dominion, 529; *Julius Caesar*, Col., 642 (see letters, 686, 804, 894); *The Greek Passion* (Martinů), Cardiff, 744

(b) Books
1952 (iii): M. Hamburger, ed. and trans., *Beethoven: Letters, Journals and Conversations*, 366
1955 (vi): H. Rosenthal, ed., *Opera Annual 1954–1955*, 123
1958 (ix): H. Rosenthal, *Two Centuries of Opera at Covent Garden*, 529

249 *The Score*
G. Abraham, ed., *Handel: a Symposium*, ix, 9 Sept. 1954 (see no. 152), 49
250 *The Spectator*
The Marriage of Figaro, Don Giovanni, Così fan tutte, RFH, 24 Sept. 1954; *Nelson*, SW, 1 Oct. 1954; K. Geiringer, *The Bach Family: Seven Generations of Creative Genius*, 29 Oct. 1954; P. A. Scholes, *The Oxford Junior Companion to Music*, 19 Nov. 1954
251 *The Sunday Telegraph*
Imeneo, Birmingham, 26 March 1961; *Tamerlano*, Birmingham, 25 March 1962; *Floridante*, Abingdon, 13 May 1962; *Riccardo Primo, Semele*, SW, 12 July 1964; *Saul*, SW, 27 June 1965; *Alceste* (Gluck), E, 25 Aug. 1974
252 *The Sunday Times*
P. H. Lang, *George Frideric Handel*, 30 April 1967
253 *Tempo*
W. Mellers, *François Couperin and the French Classical Tradition*, xix, spring 1951, 33; A. Einstein, *Schubert*, xxii, winter 1951–2, 36; G. Abraham, ed., *Schumann: a Symposium*, xxiii, spring 1952, 28; P. M. Young, *J. S. Bach*, J. S. Hall, *G. F. Handel*, lix, autumn 1961, 27
254 *The Times*
Giustino, Abingdon, 24 April 1967; 'Sixteen Organ Concertos by Handel': Müller, Wenzinger, Archiv (records), Rameau, Complete Harpsichord Works, Malcolm, Argo (records), 22 July 1967; *La Rencontre imprévue*, Hintlesham, 21 July 1969
255 *The Times Literary Supplement*
A. Carse, *The Life of Jullien*, 30 Nov. 1951; E. Lockspeiser, *Debussy*, 14 Dec. 1951; G. Abraham, ed., *Schumann: a Symposium*, 11 April 1952; A. L. Bacharach, ed.,

The Music Masters, vol. 3, 21 Nov. 1952; S. Moreux, *Béla Bartók*, 29 Jan. 1954; A. Schoenberg, *Structural Functions of Harmony*, 10 Sept. 1954; J. Rufer, *Composition with Twelve Notes*, 10 Dec. 1954; W. Mellers, *The Sonata Principle*, 7 March 1958; J. Russell, *Erich Kleiber*, 2 May 1958; M. Pincherle, *Vivaldi: Genius of the Baroque*, 1 Aug. 1958; A. Einstein, *Essays on Music*, 23 Jan. 1959; J. V. Cockshoot, *The Fugue in Beethoven's Piano Music*, E. Fischer, *Beethoven's Pianoforte Sonatas*, 20 Feb. 1959; S. Hughes, *The Toscanini Legacy*, 3 July 1959; M. Tippett, *Moving into Aquarius*, 9 Oct. 1959; L. Davies, *Franck*, 20 July 1973; G. Abraham, *The Tradition of Western Music*, 24 Jan. 1975: P. Cook, *Hugo Wolf's Corregidor*, 28 May 1976; A. Lewis and N. Fortune, eds., *Opera and Church Music 1630–1750* (NOHM 5), 16 July 1976; E. T. Harris, *Handel and the Pastoral Tradition*, 21 Nov. 1980; C. A. Price, *Henry Purcell and the London Stage*, 12 Oct. 1984; M. Collins and E. K. Kirk, eds., *Opera and Vivaldi*, 1 March 1985; *Samson*, CG, *Xerxes*, Col., 8 March 1985

MUSIC EDITED

256 Georges Bizet, suite: *La Coupe du roi de Thulé*, broadcast BBC Third Programme, 12 & 13 July 1955. Unpublished
257 G. F. Handel, *Three Ornamented Arias*, London, Oxford University Press, 1976
258 G. F. Handel, *Giulio Cesare in Egitto* (with Sarah Fuller), Oxford, Oxford University Press, f.s. & v.s., forthcoming

TRANSLATIONS

259 *The Frogs of Aristophanes* [the choruses], music by Walter Leigh, London, Oxford University Press, 1937
260 *Abu Hassan*, music by Weber, text by Hiemer. Performed Arts Theatre, Cambridge, 22 Feb. 1938; rev. 1968, performed State University of New York, Stony Brook, 12 Dec. 1974. Unpublished

LIBRETTOS

261 *Cats and Dogs*, an operetta in three acts. Music by Philip Radcliffe. Banned by the Lord Chamberlain, 1941. Unpublished
262 *Faldon Park*, an opera in two acts. Music by Lennox Berkeley (unfinished)

SELECTED LETTERS TO THE PRESS

263 'Handel and the Victorians', *The Musical Times*, c (1959), 428, 666; ci, 310 (see no. 112)
264 ['Unpublished Letters Concerning Handel'], *Music & Letters*, xl (1959), 406
265 'Handel – More Unpublished Letters', *Music & Letters*, xlii (1961), 395
266 [Oratorio on the Stage], *The Musical Times*, cxix (1978), 653, 1030 (see also 821, 838)
267 'Handel's First Italian Opera', *Music & Letters*, lxiii (1982), 385

OBITUARIES

268 Eric Blom (*The Observer*, 19 April 1959)
269 Dr James Hall (*The Times*, 18 Feb. 1975)

NON-MUSICAL WRITINGS

270 Series, 'Parish Church Architecture', in *The Townswoman* (illustrated with the author's own photographs): I 'Introductory', Jan. 1938, II 'Structure and Development', Feb. 1938, III 'Towers', March 1938, IV 'Windows', May 1938, V 'Doors', June 1938, VI 'Porches', Aug. 1938, VII 'The Nave', Sept. 1938, VIII 'The Chancel', Oct. 1938, IX 'Stone Carving', Dec. 1938, X 'The Font', Feb. 1939, XI 'Tombs and Memorials', Sept. 1939, XII 'Wood Carving' (unpublished)
271 *Hambledon v Feathercombe 1928–1950: the Story of a Village Cricket Match*, privately printed, 1951

Four items have been reprinted in the Garland Library of the History of Western Music, 14 vols., general ed. E. Rosand, New York and London, 1985: no. 20 (with additional note) and no. 104 in vol. xi (*Opera I: up to Mozart*), nos. 119 and 149 in vol. xii (*Opera II: Mozart and after*).